Coaching the 3-3/3-5 Defense: By the Experts

**Edited by
Earl Browning**

ISBN: 978-1-60679-256-8
Library of Congress Control Number: 2013930604
Book layout: Cheery Sugabo
Cover design: Cheery Sugabo
Cover photo: Getty Images

Coaches Choice
P.O. Box 1828
Monterey, CA 93942
www.coacheschoice.com

Contents

1

The 3-3 Defense Blitz Package

Steve Barrows
Indiana State University
2007

There are three main reasons we run the 3-3 defense. The first reason is it makes you play faster. I believe that to be true. We have ten players in our defense that can run. You need a big, heavy noseguard to be a two-gap player in the middle.

The second reason is the defense is unique. It is not as unique as it was two years ago, but not many teams run the defense. Air Force, New Mexico, and West Virginia run the defense as a base defense.

The third reason for running the defense is the recruiting aspect. At the 1-AA level, it is easier to recruit players to play in this defense. You only need one big defender to play inside on the defensive line. I am sold on the defense. I have researched it extensively and I believe in it.

Philosophically, I want to point out a couple of things. We emphasize and preach these points to our players day in and day out. We want players who will run and hit.

There are three building blocks to the defensive foundation. The first is fundamentals. Someone told me a long time ago, if your players were not bored with fundamentals, you are not doing them enough. The linebacker coach does footwork drills every day. The defensive line coach does the get-off drill every single day. The secondary coach does footwork every day. We cannot get enough of fundamentals. The most sophisticated schemes in football will mean nothing unless we are fundamentally strong.

The next building block to our defense is communication. I cannot emphasize that enough. Communication is a key to our success. It is imperative we communicate from player to player, player to coach, and coach to coach.

The final part of the philosophy is discipline. Perhaps of the three, discipline is the most important. We break discipline down into two levels. The first is personal discipline. We want player to do their job and trust their teammates to do theirs. The other area is foolish penalties. You cannot give up yardage because of stupid mistakes. We will be a well-disciplined team.

The last thing on philosophy is our belief in scoop and score. We want to create turnovers, scoop the ball, and score. This mentality begins with an attitude, an aggressive, "can- and will-do" approach to our defense. On every defensive drill, we do some form of a strip or fumble drill. We want an emphasis from the beginning of taking the ball away from the offense.

We used to have a tackle-turnover circuit. This year, we have a tackle-takeaway circuit. Turnover implies the offense is giving up the ball. Take away implies the defense takes the ball from the offense. Every time the ball is on the ground, we want to scoop and score. It is important that when scooping the ball, the players must bend at the knees, not at the waist. Scoop up the bottom half of the football with both hands. Once the player has the football, he should secure it away and score.

The five points to ball security are:
- Peace sign over the tip of the ball
- Ball resting on the forearm
- Back tip of the ball in the bicep
- Side of ball securely against the rib cage
- Off hand and arm covering the ball

The last thing a defense wants to do is turn the ball back to the offense after taking it away.

I am new to Indiana State. In my first meeting with the players, I will assume they know nothing. Our base defense is the 3-3 defense (Diagram 1-1). We align with a noseguard head up the center. The defensive ends align in a 5 technique on the outside shoulder of the tackles. The Lou linebacker is our weakside linebacker and the Rob is the strongside linebacker. The Mike linebacker is in the middle. We play with two safeties. The bandit aligns to the right and the spur to the left. We have two corners and a free safety.

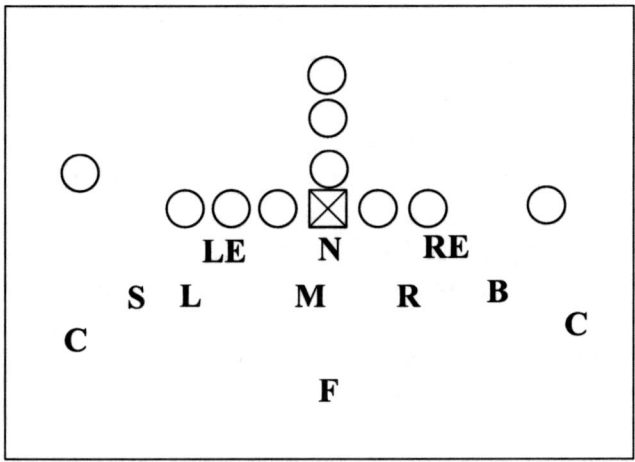

Diagram 1-1. 3-3 base alignment

The Rob linebacker is bigger than the Lou is, and at times we put him down on the line of scrimmage in a 7 or a 5 technique. We bump the front weak when we go to our 4-2 look. The bandit and spur are strong safeties. From a personnel standpoint, the bandit and spur are the two best athletes on the field. In this defense, they have to do everything. They blitz off the edge, blitz in the B gap, as well as play deep thirds. They play in the underneath support as well as deep zone coverage.

In our defensive alignment for our down players, we define our techniques for our linemen and linebackers.

Defensive Line

0	Head up on center
Shade	Helmet on foot of center
2i	Inside shoulder of guard
0	Head up the guard
1	Outside shoulder of guard
4i	Inside shoulder of tackle
4	Head up the tackle
5	Outside shoulder of tackle
6	Head up the tight end
7	Inside shoulder of the tight end
9	Outside shoulder of the tight end
Wide 9	One yard outside tight end

Linebackers

00	Head up the center
10	Align on shoulder of center
20	Inside shoulder of guard
25	Head up on the guard
30	Outside shoulder of guard
40	Inside shoulder of tackle
45	Head up the tackle
50	Outside shoulder of the tackle
70	Inside shoulder of tight end
60	Head up the tight end
90	Outside shoulder of tight end
Wide 90	One yard outside tight end

We teach these basic alignments to our players. We make them aware of the gaps in the offensive line. We make sure they know A, B, C, and D gaps of responsibility. We can never assume that everything is the same from one system to the other.

I want to show you the basic stack front (Diagram 1-2). In our playbook, for each player we have an alignment, assignment, and adjustment section for each defensive front. Our defensive ends align in a 5 technique and have the C gaps on flow toward them. On flow away, he squeezes the C gap and watches for the counter and reverse coming back at him. On pass plays, they have a containment rush. The noseguard aligns in a 0 technique on the center. We say he is a two-gap player, but in actuality, he is responsible for the weakside A gap.

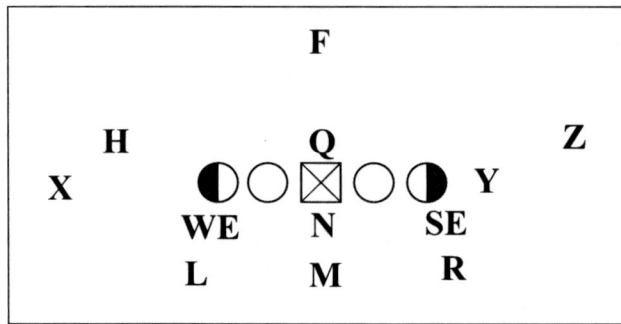

Diagram 1-2. Stack 3-3 defense

The Lou linebacker aligns in a 40 technique on the inside shoulder of the weakside offensive tackle. He aligns with his toes at four-and-a-half yards deep. On flow toward him, he is the B-gap player. On flow away, he is the cutback player or becomes a free runner. For the Rob linebacker, the alignment and assignment is the same as Lou—except he aligns to the strongside. The Mike linebacker aligns in a 00 technique on the center at a depth of four-and-a-half yards. He is responsible for the strongside A gap.

I want the linebackers to move around in their pre-snap alignment. I do not want the offensive linemen to know exactly where they will be when they snap the ball.

The linebackers in our stack defense have to adjust to the sets we face. In any two-by-one set, the linebackers are in gap alignment. That means they align in the gap to the two-receiver side. That means the Mike linebacker moves into 10-technique alignment in the gap to the two-receiver side. The Lou and Rob adjust their alignments to the gap to the side of the two receivers. In the two-by-two set, the linebackers are in base alignment, as shown in the diagram. In a three-by-one set, they align in a pull adjustment. It does not matter what kind of triple set it is; they go to the pull alignment. They move one whole man toward the three-receiver side.

The Rob linebacker in the three-by-one set splits the difference between the third receiver and the offensive tackle. If he sees a tight end to the three-receiver side, he splits the distance between the tight end and number-two receiver. He always splits the difference between the end man on the line of scrimmage and the first receiver in the three-by-one set.

Our secondary coverages are color-coded. The first one is maroon. The maroon coverage is a five-under and three-deep coverage. It is what everyone calls cover 3 (Diagram 1-3). We play the bandit and spur in the hook/flat zones. The Lou and Rob linebackers are hook-to-curl players. The Mike linebacker plays the hook in the middle of the field. The corners and free safety play the deep thirds. Everyone in the defense—with the exception of the down linemen—have to know what the other players are doing. When we start to pressure from the defense, it is important for everyone to know each other's coverage responsibilities.

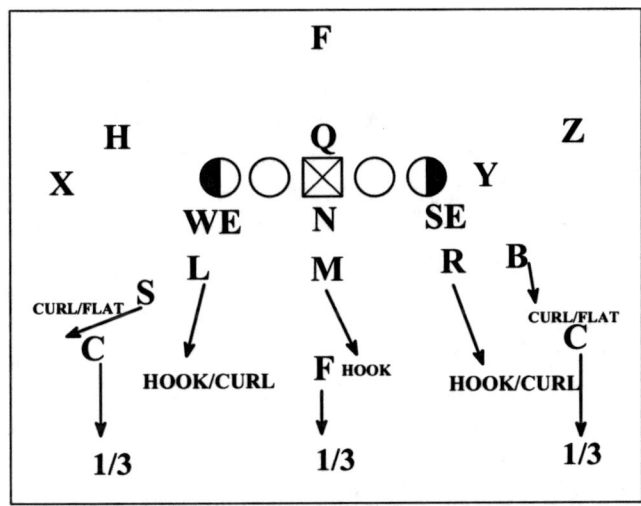

Diagram 1-3. Maroon coverage

The minimum depth of the linebacker's pass drop is 10 to 12 yards. We tell our defenders if the quarterback carries the ball low as he comes away from the center, it is probably not a three-step pass. If he carries it high, they have to play the three-step drop. We ask our backs and linebackers to look at the quarterback's shoulder tilt. If his shoulders are down, it is probably a short throw. If they are up, he is looking long. I tell our linebackers as long as the quarterback has the ball in his hands, continue to get depth. In variably, the linebackers want to jump the route coming under them. When they do that, they open the dig route coming behind them.

It is easier to come up and tackle a receiver in front of the linebackers, than it is to chase one down behind the linebackers. We do not drop to a certain spot. We drop into an area and do pattern reading in our scheme.

I want to talk about the bandit and spur from an alignment standpoint. The bandit and spur are mirror football players. Their alignment is zero-by-three yards on the end man on the line of scrimmage. They are on the line of scrimmage three yards outside the end man.

If there is a stand-up receiver as the number-two receiver, the spur or bandit has what we call an INC alignment. That means he has an inside leverage alignment at five yards over the number-two receiver. We treat the tight end differently than we do a stand-up receiver.

The corners are INC alignment at eight yards on the number-one receiver. The base alignment for the free safety is the middle of the field (MOF) at 12 yards. That is the base alignment, but we preach to our players to move around and disguise the coverage.

The number-one objective of any defense is to stop the run. Here are the run responsibilities for the bandit and spur as force defenders. There is a difference between turning the play in and forcing it to turn back. We want the defender to attack the blocker at less than a 45-degree angle and force the ball to go inside. We want him to close down the D gap and force the ball to run inside as opposed to turning the ball inside and allowing it to get outside again.

In a cover-3 situation, we have an "I'm here" call. When a bandit or spur defender has the flat-to-curl zone, they give an "I'm here" call to the next outside linebacker. If the bandit tells the Rob linebacker, "I'm here," that means the Rob linebacker can pursue the football with reckless abandon. If the ball goes away, he has no cutback lane to cover. He has no real run responsibility and is free to play football. The bandit becomes the hole and cutback player. The "I'm here" call does not affect the passing-game drops of the linebacker or the bandit. In our disguise scheme, we have a term called "performance alignment," which means that the defenders can align anywhere as long as they can get into a position to do their job.

As the linebackers read the ball position in the hands of the quarterback, they drop for width in the three-step passing game instead of depth. When we reroute receivers, we have to emphasize getting physical with them. Simply bumping him is not a reroute. If the receiver is not knocked off his course, that is not a reroute.

If we have a threat of four verticals in a maroon cover-3 coverage, we call a "vert check." That is an alert for the possibility of four verticals. The corners have to apex the number-one and number-two receivers. Apex is a fancy word for split the distance between the first and second receiver. The spur and bandit run with the number-two receivers if they go vertical. This amounts to man-to-man coverage by the spur and bandit and zone coverage for the three deep.

It does not matter that we do not have a curl/flat defender because the only receiver left to run the curl/flat is the tailback. The Rob and Lou linebackers on the "vert check" think width because they play the curl/flat. I am not worried about a curl/flat route, when the offense runs four verticals.

The free safety aligns in the middle of the field at a depth of 10 to 12 yards. We expect the free safety to make a play on the ball from number to number. The vertical pattern will be a deep thrown ball and the free safety has to make the play on anything in the middle of the field from number to number.

The next coverage is "stack black" (Diagram 1-4). To most coaches this alignment is cover-2. Stack black is cover-2 to us, except we have a robber who is a high-hole player in the middle of the field. The six inside defenders remain the same as in maroon coverage. The spur and bandit's initial alignments are two-yards outside and five-yards deep on the end man on the line of scrimmage.

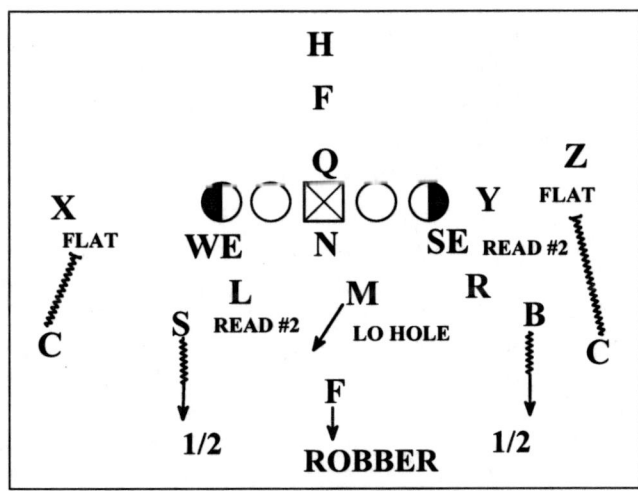

Diagram 1-4. Stack black

They stem 10 to 12 yards deep at the snap of the ball. They are the half players in the coverage. In base alignment, black coverage looks like maroon. The corners align at eight yards and stem down to six yards at the snap of the ball. The free safety aligns at 10 yards, plays the high hole on pass, and is a box player on run. He reads guards and center for his run/pass key. He plays robber on a pass play and is a free player down in the box on a running play.

The Mike linebacker is the low-hole player on a pass play. He covers the low hole up to 10 yards. The free safety sits at 10 yards and makes his reaction from that position. The Lou and Rob linebackers read the number-two receiver to their side. In the diagram, the number-two receiver for the Rob linebacker is the tight end. The number-two receiver for the Lou linebacker is in the backfield.

If the tight end takes an outside release and goes to the outside, the Rob linebacker looks up the number-one receiver on the outside. If the tight end runs the flat pattern, we think the wide receiver will run the curl. The Rob linebacker does not jump the flat route. He squeezes and matches the movement of the wide receiver. He does not sit and let the quarterback throw the ball to the curl behind him at 12 yards. He squeezes the distance and matches the pattern of the outside receiver.

This is not man coverage by the underneath defenders. We spend numerous hours teaching the squeeze-and-match concept to them. If the number-two receiver goes under, the Rob linebacker yells "Under" and looks for a crosser coming the other way. He passes the inside route to the next underneath player.

If the number-two receivers give a vertical release, the Rob and Lou linebackers run with him for 10 to 12 yards. They want to get inside, squeeze the number-two receiver, and trail him to a depth of 10 to 12 yards. When they reach a depth of 10 to 12 yards, they pass them off to the safeties, which in this case are the spur and Bandit.

We want our linebackers to make a man-coverage turn to cover the receiver. The man turn puts the linebacker in a face-to-face position on the receiver. If he makes the zone turn, he is back-to-face in his coverage. The zone turn takes longer to execute and allows more space between the linebacker and Bandit. By alignment, the space between the Rob linebacker and Bandit is seven yards. If he makes the zone turn, the quarterback can drop the ball into the hole much easier. If he makes the man turn into the receiver, the ball must be thrown perfectly.

When we play cover 2, we do not run the Mike linebacker deep with the number-three receiver. The free safety sitting in the deep hole picks up the number-three receiver deep like the Mike linebacker in a Tampa-2 defense. That keeps the Mike linebacker in the box for run support.

We make an adjustment in the black coverage, particularly in the red zone. Because the bandit is vacating the area, he bumps the Rob linebacker out to take care of the five- to eight-yard pop routes the offense may throw. I like this coverage in such a situation because the free safety is a free box player. He can run downhill and create all kinds of problems for the blocking scheme. It gives us seven defenders in the box.

If we call maroon coverage and the offense comes out with a twins alignment, we check to black coverage. We adjust by sending the free safety into the half field and the bandit plays the number-two receiver using the techniques and reads of the Rob linebacker (Diagram 1-5). The bandit reads the number-two receiver and plays him for an outside, inside, or vertical pattern. We roll the bandit down to the passing strength of the formation. The spur is to the run strength of the formation.

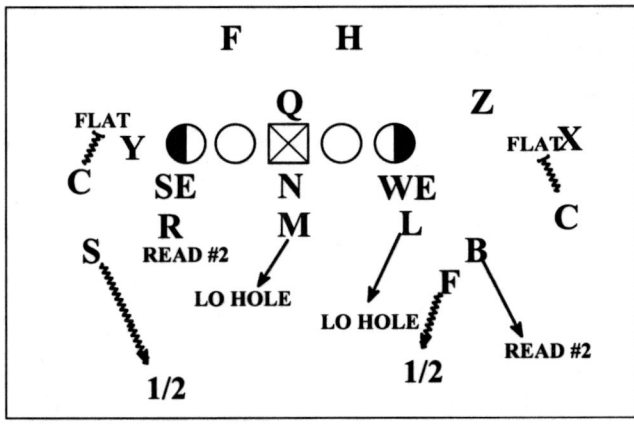

Diagram 1-5. Twins adjustment.

The Rob linebacker moves to the running side of the formation and the Lou linebacker is toward the twins set. The Mike and Lou linebacker play the low holes in the middle underneath coverage. One of them has to run with the number-three receiver if he goes vertical down the middle of the field. If the number-three receiver comes out to the Lou's side, he takes him. If he goes the other way, the Mike linebacker takes him.

The corners in black coverage have to be tough run stoppers. They have to come up and play the hard corners on runs their way. The Rob and spur are both reading the number-two receiver to that side. The Rob linebacker runs with the number-two receiver to a depth of 10 to 12 yards. The spur drops into the deep half field.

Another coverage we like in the two-minute drill is "black jack" (Diagram 1-6). The corners roll up into hard corner positions with three-deep behind them. The bandit and

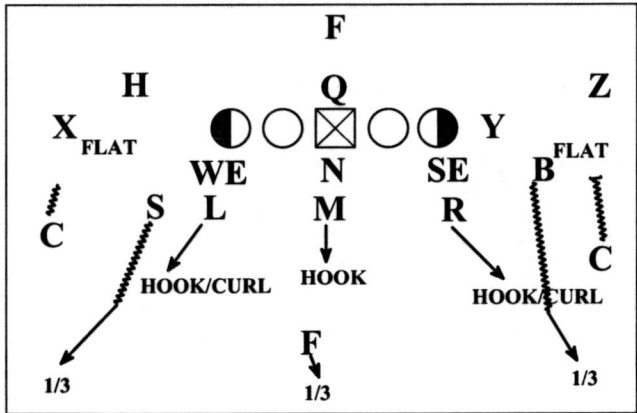

Diagram 1-6. Black jack

spur stem out into the outside thirds of the defense. The free safety plays the middle third. The Rob and Lou linebackers play the hook/curl and the Mike linebacker plays the hook in the middle.

Our Miami coverage is a man-free concept (Diagram 1-7). It is a simple coverage. The corners take the number-one receivers and the spur and bandit take the number-two receivers in a two-by-two set.

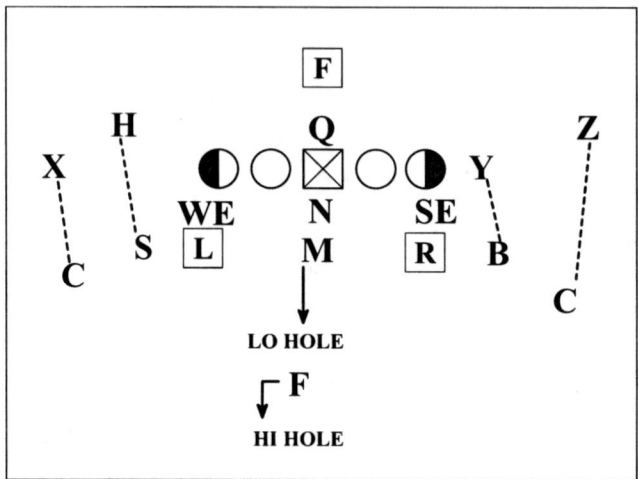

Diagram 1-7. Miami versus 2-by-2

In the three-by-one set with a tight end as the single receiver, the Spur takes the tight end (Diagram 1-8). The bandit and both corners align on the three-receiver side with the corners matched to their normal split receivers. The free safety plays in the middle.

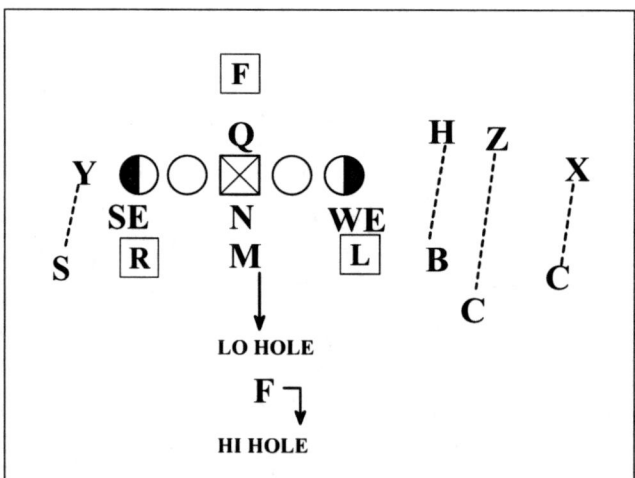

Diagram 1-8. Miami versus 3-by-1

We call our pressure package four different ways. We can run strong and weak, right and left, field and boundary, and tilt and pop, which refers to the one-back sets. Tilt is toward the offset back in the backfield, and pop is away from him.

We call the first pressure scheme "attack" (Diagram 1-9). From the alignment standpoint, everything is the same. They defenders align in a position so they can run the stunt. If they have to cheat their alignment, they do it at the last moment. The "attack" involves three players. They are the Mike and Rob linebackers and the noseguard. This stunt is "attack strong." The noseguard goes away from the strength call. He runs what we call "Olé" to the weakside A gap.

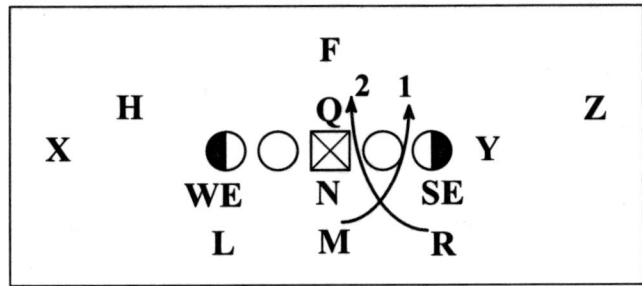

Diagram 1-9. Stack attack

The Mike linebacker blitzes through the callside B gap. The Rob linebacker follows the Mike linebacker and blitzes the callside A gap. The olay call for the noseguard means he tries to get through the gap without making contact with anyone. It is not a swim technique, but he tries to finesse himself through the A gap.

The coaching point for the Mike linebacker is on the alignment of the quarterback. If the quarterback is under center, the linebacker blitzes from depth. I do not want the Mike linebacker at the line of scrimmage with the quarterback's hands under the center. If he gets to the line of scrimmage, the quarterback may include him in the protection scheme as a lineman and change the protection to block him. I want him to hit the gap on the run from depth. If the quarterback is in the shotgun, he can get into the line of scrimmage early.

The Rob linebacker runs a delay blitz from his position. The Mike linebacker goes first and the Rob linebacker delays and goes second. In the secondary, we play garnet, black, or Florida, which is cover zero for us.

When we involve one of the outside linebackers in the blitz, we have to make an adjustment in our black coverage. In black coverage, the Rob and Lou linebackers have the number-two receiver. If one of them blitzes, the free safety voids the middle hole and replaces the blitzing linebacker in his coverage.

We call the next pressure "ram" (Diagram 1-10). We try to keep things similar as we run them. On the ram, the Mike linebacker does the same thing he did on attack.

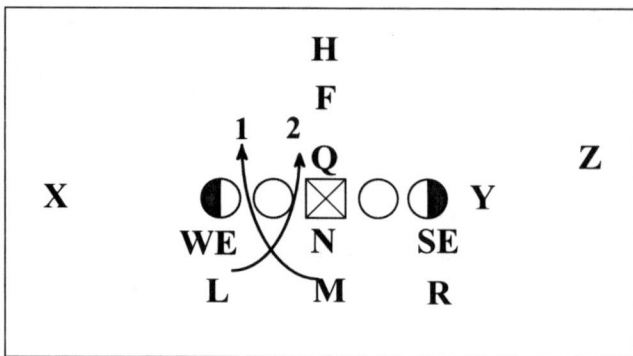

Diagram 1-10. Stack ram

That gives us carryover teaching. The callside defensive ends run what we call the long stick into the A gap. He bypasses the B gap and hits the A gap. The Mike linebacker lets him clear and blitzes the B gap. Since it is a weakside blitz, the Lou linebacker blitzes off the edge. He has to contain the pass toward him.

The stack "thunder" is a good combination stunt for the defensive ends and linebackers (Diagram 1-11). The noseguard uses a wrap technique and loops to the C gap on the side away from the call. The defensive ends run a long stick from the 5 techniques into the A gaps. The Lou linebacker runs through the B gap. The spur aligns at five yards off the line of scrimmage and blitzes from the edge.

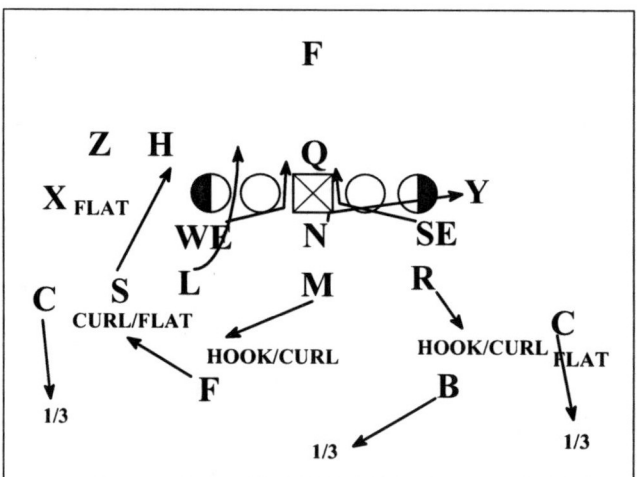

Diagram 1-11. Stack thunder/sky check

In the secondary, we can play a strong sky check from our cover 3. The spur blitzes off the edge and the free safety rolls up to take the curl/flat coverage from the spur. The bandit rotates back and covers the deep middle third while the corners play the outside thirds. The Mike linebacker runs hook/curl to the strongside and the Rob linebacker runs hook/curl/flat to the weakside.

A combination coverage we can use is a cloud adjustment (Diagram 1-12). In that case, the free safety rotates into the third behind the corner and the corner rolls to the flat/curl area.

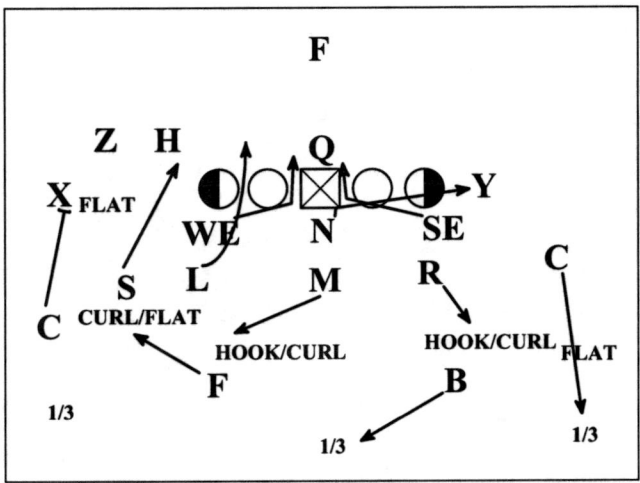

Diagram 1-12. Stack thunder/cloud

I have two more blitzes to show you before I stop. I will cover them quickly. The first one is the stack "double fire" (Diagram 1-13). This brings the Rob or Lou linebackers off the edge along with either the spur or bandit. The defensive ends run a stick into the B gaps. In the diagram, the Rob linebacker and spur blitz from the edges. As they blitz, they have contain responsibility. We play black coverage against a two-by-two set and garnet coverage against three-by-one. The stunt run the other way brings the Lou linebacker and the bandit.

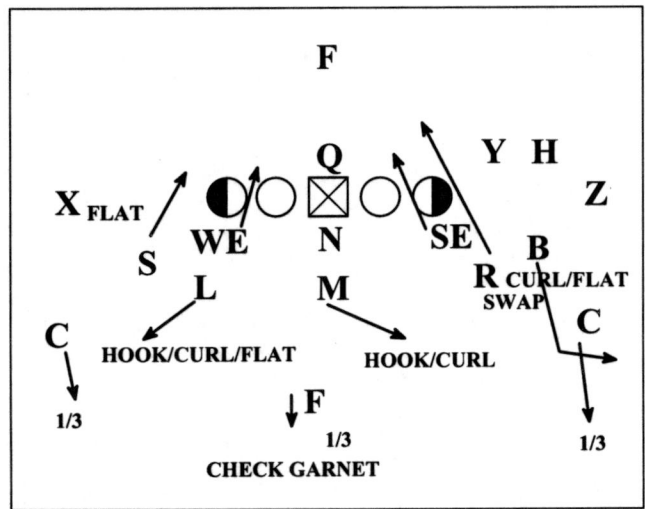

Diagram 1-13. Stack double fire

The last blitz I will show is the "maniac" (Diagram 1-14). If we run the blitz to the strongside, the strongside defensive end draws a block for the offensive tackle. He draws the block and drops into coverage in the hook/curl/flat area. The noseguard runs the olay into the A gap opposite the call. The weakside end squeezes the C gap and watches for a counter or reverse.

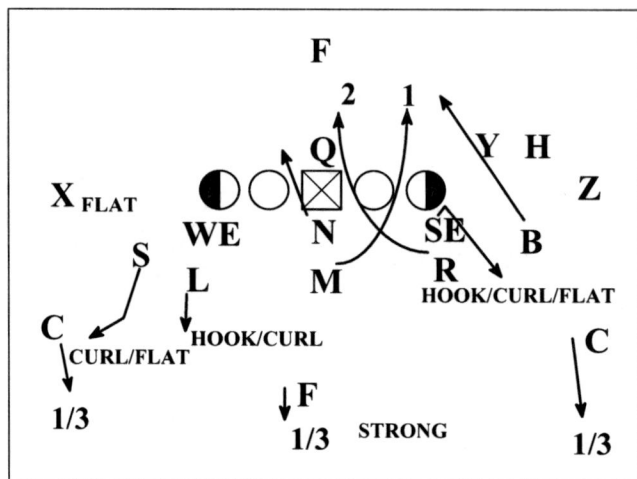

Diagram 1-14. Stack maniac

The Lou linebacker plays for the cutback or becomes a free player with an "I'm here" call. The Mike linebacker runs a B-gap blitz to the callside. The Rob linebacker delays, lets the Mike linebacker clear, and runs through the A gap. The bandit on that side runs a blitz off the edge. We play cover 3 with the spur going to the curl/flat zone, the Lou linebacker into the hook/curl zone, and the strongside defensive end into the hook/curl/flat zone to the side of the blitz.

2

Fundamentals of the
3-3 Stack Defense

Adam Barth
Cathedral High School, Indiana
2011

It is a pleasure to be here today. I want to talk about our 3-3 stack defense. I will be going into my sixth year at Cathedral High School. The first two years, we ran a 4-3 defense. Why did we change to the 3-3 stack from the 4-3? Three years ago, we got to the point where we did not feel we had two safeties that were good downhill cover 4 and cover 2 safeties.

We also felt we did not have enough depth at the defensive line position. Our kids are typically smaller athletic kids. We do not get a lot of Division I kids. We have a lot of good Division II and III kids, which is why we have been successful. This defense gives us a chance to get those kids on the field and get different pressures from a lot of different areas on the field. When we changed to the 3-3 stack, I got my information from Gordon Elliott in Seattle, Washington.

Why 3-3 Stack?

- Lack of defensive linemen and lack of efficient safeties
- Allows us to get more athletes on the field and utilize the speed we have

- Allows us to pressure from multiple places versus multiple formations
- We can involve more players more often, which equals more enthusiasm for the defense

With the 3-3 defense, we use three down linemen and they can be moving all the time. At least 50 percent of the time, we are bringing one linebacker, if not two. That also means 50 percent of the time we are not blitzing. We want the offense to read and think we are blitzing on every down. The defense is high impact, high energy, and our players get into it. Kids like to blitz.

Players today want to see an immediate impact of what they are accomplishing and to see results. We give them goals so they have something to look at and to measure their performance against.

Major Team Defensive Goals

- Create one or more turnovers than touchdowns against in each game.
- Cause and recover two fumbles each game.
- No runs over 15 yards
- Stop 75 percent of all third and fourth downs.
- Score or set up a score.
- Five minus-yards plays per game (three sacks)
- No passes over 20 yards

These goals are self-explanatory. You have probably seen something similar at other clinics. Following are what we use as position names. You may have seen other position names for the same defense. We tried to use old terminology from our previous 4-3 defense.

- Nose
- Anchor end (strongside)
- Blood end (weakside)
- Mike (middle inside linebacker)
- Sam (strongside inside linebacker)
- Will (weakside inside linebacker)
- Snake (strongside outside linebacker)
- Bear (weakside outside linebacker)
- Corners
- Free safety

The following diagram shows how we number our defensive techniques (Diagram 2-1). We teach them to all of our defensive players.

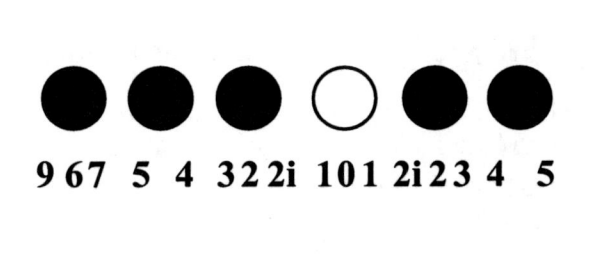

Diagram 2-1. Defensive technique

This is how we break down our alignments, keys, and responsibilities for our base defense. I will start with the nose and work my way down the list.

Nose

Our nose man is in a 0 technique. We are head-up on the center all the time. We have used two types of noseguards. We have had big players that could not be moved on defense. We have had smaller, quicker guys that we could use to slant. Both types of players have been effective for us. You can fit this position to the type of players you have.

Alignment: 0 technique, and a yard to a yard and a half off of the ball.

Key: Ball

Technique: Predetermined slant to A gap given by the Mike or attack the center, read his block, and keep him off the Mike backer.

Ends

Alignment: 5 technique or outside shade of the tackle. We never call for the tackle to line up head-up on the offensive tackle, so we do not have a technique number for that situation. This helps keep the defensive end from being hooked by the offensive tackle.

- Anchor goes to callside, tight or wide.
- Blood goes *away* from callside, open or short.

Key: Ball

Technique (base): He will attack the outside shoulder of the tackle, and then he will read. What the offensive tackle does will determine the gap responsibility of the defensive end. The defensive end and the stack linebacker have gap exchange responsibility for the B and C gaps when we are in base. If we get a down read, the defensive end will close hard and be the B-gap player. We are not running upfield. For any trap or counter, we are wrong-arming everything.

Mike

Alignment: Four and a half yards deep and stacked behind the nose.

Key: Varies based on formation and game plan. It could be the tailback or the fullback. If the offense is in the gun with one tailback, he will key the tailback. If it is a gun formation with two backs, he will key the quarterback to the first back he goes to.

Technique:

- Run—A gap to C gap. Mike has the A gap opposite the A gap of the nose slant. If the ball goes to the nose slant side, he will come over the top from A gap to C gap. If his key goes to that side, he will fill the A gap hard and bend pursuit to the ball. He will check for crossers. If Mike's key goes away from the assigned A gap, he will fill the C gap to flow. Check for crossers. Crossers are guards or tackles coming on traps or counters. We work crosser drills every single day of practice. He has to have a point two yards behind the line of scrimmage to where he looks for any crossers coming. He will then redirect, dip, and rip to come through.
- Pass—His pass drop is to the #3 receiver. If we are blitzing, he will take over for the blitzing linebacker.

Sam/Will

Alignment: 50 Technique on the heels of the defensive end. We want them right on top of the defensive end. This gets them closer to the line of scrimmage, and when they get their read, it looks like a blitz.

Key: Varies based on formation and game plan. If the offense is in an I formation backfield, he will read the tailback most of the time. We read backs most of the time. If it is a shotgun formation, we will cross read.

Technique:

- Run to—Fill assigned gap, B or C, depending on where the defensive end goes. Fill like a blitz. Use clear/cloudy fit off the defensive end. For an iso technique, he will take on blocks with his outside arm and keep his inside arm free. He will spill all plays outside to fit to the free safety or Mike.
- Run away—Shuffle in and check for crossers, pulling offensive linemen, or backs coming back across from the opposite direction.
- Pass—Drop off to the #2 receiver. We will make an outlaw call if the #2 receiver is too wide and detached, or if there is a trips formation. Sam or Will makes an outlaw call that sends the defensive end to Sam or Will's side into the B gap and widens Sam and Will's alignment outside of the stack. He will bump out and split the difference, or at least a third of the way toward the #2 receiver. He will now have C-gap responsibility. This will make it easier for him to get onto the #2 receiver. All gaps are still covered. An outlaw call overrules any call from the sideline.

We do not have a lot of coverages. We use cover 2, cover 4, and Bronco, which is our blitz coverage. These are our three main coverages. We will throw in a man-to-man coverage on occasion if we are blitzing. Our philosophy is the less we have, the better our players can know it.

Bear/Snake

Alignment:

- Cover 4—Creep inside before the snap using the prowl technique to a 4x5 alignment off the offensive tackle. We give this as a landmark, but they should never be standing in one spot at the snap of the ball. We want them moving back and forth to give the quarterback a possible blitz look. We do not want the quarterback to read the outside linebacker and determine what type of coverage we are playing. Once the outside linebacker gets to his alignment, he must get his shoulders square and buzz his feet.
- Cover 2—Align one to two yards outside the #1 wide receiver at a depth of five yards. At the snap, he should not backpedal. He should sit at five yards and wait for the #1 receiver to come to him. He should make sure he gets contact. If the football is not in the air, we are going to hit receivers.

Key: Guard or tackle based on the game plan. The outside linebackers will read linemen every single play.

Technique:

- Run to—If they get a run read and flow is coming toward them, they are the contain player. They are a controlled contain player. Take on kick-out blockers, but never get deeper than two yards past the line of scrimmage. It will create a seam for the running back, if they are too far upfield. They want to force the ball back inside and let our flow come from over the top to make the tackle.

  On the option, they have the pitchman, and they slow play it. They bait the quarterback, so he does not know what we are going to do. He is not just going to attack; he is going to sit at the line of scrimmage. Most high school quarterbacks do not know what to do if a defender is just sitting there. We have 10 other guys that are running over to make the tackle. They cannot come up the field too far. We teach our kids to build a fence. If they come upfield too far, they open the gate.

- Run away—CRCB means the counter/reverse/cutback/boot. That is their main responsibility. They stay home. Take the back out of the backfield in the flat or any shallow receiver in the flat.
- Pass, cover 4—Open to the #1 receiver and get under the #1 receiver. His aiming point is six yards. That usually ends up at four yards when you are talking about a high school player coming at his angle. Our outside linebacker should be able to stop any hitch the quarterback will throw. Continue to sink or trail the #1 receiver until the flat is pressured by the #2 or #3 receiver. He will not come off of the #1 receiver; he

will split the difference until the quarterback totally commits to the out. We want to keep everything in front until we have to rally to get to anything in front of us.

- Pass, cover 2—Typical cover 2 corner technique, which means they will outside trail the #1 receiver with their butts to the sideline as long as the #2 receiver is going vertical or inside. If the #2 or #3 receiver comes outside, the outside linebacker will squat and reroute the #1 inside and level out over the #2 or #3 receiver at 10 to 12 yards. They stay on top of the flat route and break on the ball.

Corners

Alignment: Split the #1 and #2 receivers at a depth of seven yards. It does not matter what coverage we are in, the corners are half-field players. They have to range as deep as the deepest receiver does. To do that from seven yards is tough. If it is a long distance situation, we may let them drop back a little farther.

Key: Quarterback to backfield action.

Technique:

- Run—Initial backpedal and check the #1 receiver for play-action or crackback. His eyes are on the quarterback. If he gets run action his way, he checks #1 to see if a crack is coming. If there is, he will come up and replace right now. On any other play, he is a half-field player.
- Pass, three-step drop—Be ready to break on the ball at the interception point, where the ball will be, not where the man is when the football is thrown.
- Pass, five-step drop—Backpedal until his cushion is threatened, then open and play as deep as the deepest, while ranging.

Free Safety

Our free safety is our best player on the field. He is our Stud. Everything has to go through him. If he cannot make plays, he is a wasted player on the field. Any offense has to change their blocking scheme to account for our free safety. If the offense does not account for him, he will be unblocked and he is our best tackler. Our free safety has been our leading tackler for the past three years. When you line up and pick out the best football player on your team, you want to put him at free safety.

Alignment: He will line up 10 yards deep over the center and guard gap to the #2 or #3 receiver side. His alignment is based on formation. It is not based on the call. Calls do not matter to him.

Key: He will always read linemen. He will read the guard to the #2 or #3 receiver side for run or pass. The guard is uncovered, so it is an easy read for him. He will look for a low hat or high hat from the guard. He does not have a specific gap responsibility.

Technique:

- Run—He goes to the ball. The free safety takes on the block with his outside arm and bounces the play to our Bear or Snake. On the option, the free safety has the quarterback. He does not worry about the handoff, he only worries about the quarterback.
- Pass—Coverage is based on the offensive formation, not on our defensive call.
- Pass, 2 back—He will be in a robber technique off the #2 receiver. If #2 goes six or seven yards vertical behind our linebackers, he locks on man-to-man. If #2 goes out to the flat, the free safety is going to drop and rob underneath #1. If #2 drags across the field, he will stay on top of the drag and look for something to come back at him. He will drop off the drag to take the dig if it shows.
- Pass, trips with 1 back—Robber technique off the #3 receiver.
- Pass, any other 1 back—High hole player under their #2 receivers.
- Pass, empty—High hole player under the #2 and #3 receivers. The corners have over-the-top; the free safety has underneath those receivers. He will play robber off of the #3 receiver. We can change this in our game planning, but he will be ranging on the #3 to the #2 receiver.

We have little variation to different formations we see. Adjustments are minimal. Our players do not have to do a lot of thinking. You will see them aggressively running to the football.

When we look at the overall gap responsibility, the nose and the Mike linebacker are responsible for the two A gaps. The ends and the Sam and Will linebackers are responsible for the B and C gaps.

We are a two-platoon team. Our defensive linemen get a lot of practice versus different types of blocks they will see on any given week. We will work specifically on each type of block based on our scouting report. We have 20 minutes of individual time to work on fundamentals and 20 minutes of group time to work on any specific scheme blocking our opponent will throw at us. Even if they get double-teamed, they have to stay at the line of scrimmage, they cannot get pushed back.

I will close with something we go by at Cathedral High School. We put a lot of emphasis and importance into this.

Cathedral Football Players:
Points to Live By

- We will never compromise our standards. It takes 100 years to grow an oak tree. It takes 10 minutes to chop it down. There are many young men who have worn the gold helmet before you, which is why we are representing the school with the most wins in the state of Indiana.
- Play with tremendous enthusiasm 100 percent of the time. Remember, 100 percent of the body and 100 percent of the mind!
- Remember, character is the ability to stand up for the things that are right and say no to the things that are wrong, even when no one is watching.
- Live in the *past*, you die in the *present*. You have to be able to move on to the next play in practice or in the game.
- Academic integrity, athletic integrity, and character are the key ingredients of a Cathedral football player.

We play good, hard football at Cathedral. We have good kids, we have good parents, we have a good coaching staff, and we have a tremendous tradition at Cathedral High School. We love our football. It has been a pleasure to be invited to speak to you this weekend.

3

The 3-3 Stand-Up Defense

Bobby Bentley
Byrnes High School, South Carolina
2006

Thank you for that introduction. It is a pleasure to be here today. I appreciate you guys being here. I am going to make this very informal. I am going to talk about our defense. I hope you get something out of it. What we do is a little different, but it fits our players and it fits me as a coach. On our defense, all 11 of our players stand up.

That may seem as if we are unsound, but we have won four state championships in a row. I do not want to come off as if I know everything. I do not know anything except what we do at Byrnes High School. I do not know if we can take this defense anywhere else and win. I have no idea. To play this defense, you must be able to run. If you cannot run and all 11 of them are standing up, the offense will run over you. Our defenders will run around blocks to get to the football.

I want to show you the general idea via a PowerPoint presentation, and then I will go into more detail to explain the defense. At the end I will show the defense on film.

Building the Program

- We had 28 players in 1995; now we have over 100.
- In 1995, 10 players ran sub-4.9; now over 45 do.
- We scored 138 points in 1995; we scored 776 points in 2005.

- We allowed 32 points in 1995; we allowed 9.5 points in 2005.
- We threw nine touchdowns in 1995; we threw 73 in 2005.
- Our budget was $20,000 in 1995; it was over $100,000 in 2005.

When I came to Byrnes High School, we started with 28 players on the team. I won one game the first year and two games the second year. Over the last four years, we are 56-1. I do not know what we are doing, but we are doing something that our players believe in. We now have 260 players in the program.

We play Glades Central High School of Florida on ESPN at 12 noon on August 26. They have a well-established program. They have 27 ex-players in the NFL. We had one player make it to the pros and he plays in the NFL in Europe. They are a lot better than we are. We go to Cincinnati to play Moeller High School on TV on September 16.

In 1995, which was my first year, we had 10 players run under 4.9. Right now, we have 25 players who run under 4.9. I cannot take credit for all of that because all of our players run track. In 1995, we scored 138 points on offense. Last year we scored 776 points. In 1995, we allowed 32 points per game. Last year we averaged 9.5 allowed points per game. We threw for nine touchdowns in 1995 and 73 last year. In 1995, when we gave up 36 points per game, we were everyone's homecoming game. Now we cannot get anyone to play us. We have to play Glades Central High School from Florida, and we have to go up to Cincinnati to play Moeller High School to get games. Not many teams in our area want to play us.

In 1995, our football budget was $19,800. In 2005, our football budget was $102,000. Our touchdown club raised over $100,000 last year. I do not say that to be bragging, I say this because we have many loyal people in our program. They are going to install a $350,000 scoreboard next year.

The first year I taught seven out of eight periods in the school day. Next year I will not teach any classes. I am telling you this to let you know you need to be patient in your program.

In our program, we started out by focusing our entire program on offense. When we get to the championship season, we focus on defense. We focus on defensive alignment. Before practice every day, we put our players through R-and-R. They work on reaction and recognition. We want our players to be able to recognize certain formation and certain tendencies.

Just for curiosity's sake, how many of you have an editing system in your school? Can you break down films of the opponents? I know it is a big investment and it costs a lot of money to begin with, but it is worth it. We give our players a DVD of the opponents and their tendencies on Sunday. When they come to practice on Monday, they know what the opponents' best plays are. In high school football, most teams have strong tendencies in certain formations. Our players will know those tendencies and they will know the plays the offense is likely to run. We recognize and react to certain formations.

This next thing I learned from Coach Nick Hyder. He was a coach at Valdosta High School in Georgia. I heard him speak at this clinic many years ago. He talked about being a collision expert. When I was younger, my thoughts were you had to be an X-and-O expert. He changed our entire terminology. To play the game of football, you have to be able to block and tackle. Those are the most fundamental skills, and if you cannot execute those skills, you will not win.

In 1998, we had a state championship team's defensive coordinator come to watch us practice. I could not wait until practice was over to see what he had to say. I said, "Mike, what did you think about our practice?" He told me this. "I saw you run a bunch of plays, and a lot of drills, but I did not any blocking and tackling."

I told him we had done those drills earlier in the week. He told me that to be a good football player, you have to tackle every day. The moral of that story is this: today in our practices, we block and tackle every day. We have board drills for our offensive and defensive linemen every day.

We run our nitro drill every day for ten minutes. We run the old Oklahoma drill every day. We go one-on-one everyday. We have offensive linemen against defensive linemen and a linebacker. We work a tackling circuit every day. We are probably the only team that has a tackling drill on Thursday before our games on Friday. We have become collision experts. Our players have become successful at tackling and they get better every year. In our circuit we head-on-tackle, angle tackle, tackle on the sled, and many other drills.

Be Good at Something

- Focus of all workouts/practices
  - ✓ Speed and agility
  - ✓ Passing game
    - ⇨ Protection
    - ⇨ Quarterback development
    - ⇨ High-percentage passing
  - ✓ Defensive alignments
  - ✓ Collision technique (tackling and blocking)

We want speed and agility at all positions. If you cannot run, you play offensive line for us. It does not matter the size of the player; if he cannot run, he cannot play defense in our scheme. Even in short-yardage situations, we do not believe in putting some big player in the middle of our defense. We do not do it.

Rebel Defense

- Focus on tackling.
- Work the tackle strip circuit.
- Focus on speed and agility at all positions.
- Create an atmosphere of wanting to play for the strike force.
- Stop the run; we gave up four rush touchdowns in 15 games in 2005.

We want to create an atmosphere for our players for the strike force. We do all kinds of things to motivate our players about playing defense. When we started our program, we concentrated on the offense. We had all of our good players on the offensive side of the ball. We had to change our way of thinking.

We give a helmet every Sunday for the Player of the Week. We give a green-beret helmet that we have painted silver and which have the words "strike force" on it. It is a big deal for our kids to get that strike-force helmet. Also, we give them "dog tags" with their names on them if they are selected as a Player of the Week. We give them a chain with a dog tag similar as the dog tags used in the military. We give a dog-tag award every week for the Defensive Player of the Week. Our players love to get those dog tags with their names on them. We try to point out to them, "You win games with offense, but you win championships with defense."

Key Thoughts on Defense

- A defense cannot do everything.
- Attempt to stop or neutralize the greatest offensive threats.
- Move around on defense.
- Attack the quarterback. (The best pass defense is a strong rush.) Try to send five to eight rushers.
- Team quickness and reaction time are critical to our defense.
- Size is not an issue.

On defense, we want to stop the run. We pride ourselves on our ability to stop the run. We want our players to know how many yards they are giving up per rushing down. We play 4A football in South Carolina. We have won four state championships in a row. In 2005, we gave up four rushing touchdowns the entire year. That amounts to 15 games in the season. That is tough to do, especially when we are playing with a three-man front three-quarters of the time.

Building the Defense

- Play linebackers at defensive line.
- Play larger defensive backs at the linebacker positions.
- Play the most agile/hostile athletes at defensive back.

- Practice one position for one hour and 45 minutes.
- We were successful with our offense; we won championships with our defense.

Here is what we do on defense. We play linebackers in our defensive alignment. Not one kid on our defense weighs over 198 pounds. We play larger defensive backs at linebackers. We play the most agile and hostile players as defensive backs. The biggest and meanest hostile defensive backs play at the strong-safety position. We call the safeties "swords." They are savers and they are mean—and hostile. The corners have to be fast because we play a lot of man coverage. However, we can play cover 3 and cover 2.

We practice at one position for one hour and 45 minutes. For a player to become good on defense, you have to put him at one position and coach the fire out of him. He has to understand what other teams are trying to do to him in this defense.

We practice one hour and 45 minutes on defense, and 20 minutes on special teams. We want to be off the field in around two hours, or two hours and five minutes.

We were successful with our offense, but we won championships with our defense. We believe this very strongly. We have a sign in our locker room that has that written on it. Our defensive coordinator works hard and the players have a lot of respect for him. They work hard for him.

The 3-3 Stand-Up Defense

- Defenses should appear to be distortions of reality.
- Schemes do not win games; people do.
- Great defenses have speed and quickness, and play with emotion.
- How we win on defense:
  ✓ Neutralize the offense's best plays.
  ✓ Tackle well.
  ✓ Run to the ball on every play; demand it.

Our defense is a distortion of reality. When we line up on an offensive tackle—and we align head up, that offensive tackle should never know where the defensive man is going. We very seldom line up in a gap. We may end up in the gap, but we are not going to line up in the gap.

The offensive tackle does not know if we are going inside or outside. If we line up in the gap, we do not stay there. If we line up inside the offensive blocker, we probably will go outside of him. However, he will not know that.

Our defensive linemen get down on all fours and scramble around on the line of scrimmage. Before the offense snaps the ball, the defenders stand up. We work hard the week before the game to find out the offense's snap count. We will find a way to figure that out a week before the game.

Schemes do not win games. I had to learn that the hard way. I always thought that meant something about X's and O's and alignments on defense. To play defense, you must have speed and quickness and play with emotion. We harp on running to the football. To play defense, you must run to the ball like your life depended on you getting there.

When we have a seven-on-seven drill, it is for one simple reason. We can coach our players to get to the ball. When we are in a seven-on-seven drill, we can coach them on the line. We do not worry about formations. We are going to get the quarterback. We are not going to sit in coverage.

What We Base Our Defense On

When we come in for our meeting on Sunday, we break down the opponent's film. We want to stop the offense's best plays. We view the opponent's tape and we rank the opponent's best plays. We put them in rank order of their best plays. Usually they have three plays they are good at running. If they are a good team, they may have five top plays. We set our defense to stop those plays. If the tailback is the key to their offense, he is the player we want to stop. It does not matter what defense we are playing.

If we play a wing-T team and the tailback is their best player, everyone is going to be reading on him. If the wingbacks are the best players, we cross key them and take them out of the equation. If the fullback is the man, all three linebackers will be keying him. We are going to take out your best play. We are going to take out your best player. We are going to make sure we can tackle him. We are going to get to the football and make sure we gang tackle. I think the difficulty of open-field tackling is overrated. I played safety in college. I practiced open-field tackling in practice, but in the games, I always found myself turning the runner into the pursuit.

The strong safety wants to build a wall so the back does not cross his face. He knows he has a corner outside and he has nine other players coming from the inside on an angle to make the tackle.

What Is Our Defense?

- *What is it?* An eight-man front defense with most, if not all, defenders standing up and constantly moving. Defensive end is up or down, his option.
- *From where does it come?* It is not new; it began in the late 1960s and early '70s in high school football.
- *Why use it?* It has evolved into an excellent way of attacking a shotgun-snap offense. Players love it! It is a great scheme for little, quick people to showcase their talents.

Our defense is an eight-man front (Diagram 3-1). Most of the time we have all eight of the defenders in a two-point stance. The defenders are standing up and most of the time there is constant movement. The defensive ends are always in a two-point stance. People may refer to our defense as a 3-3-5, or a 3-5-3. The thing we are going to do is have an eight-man umbrella around the football.

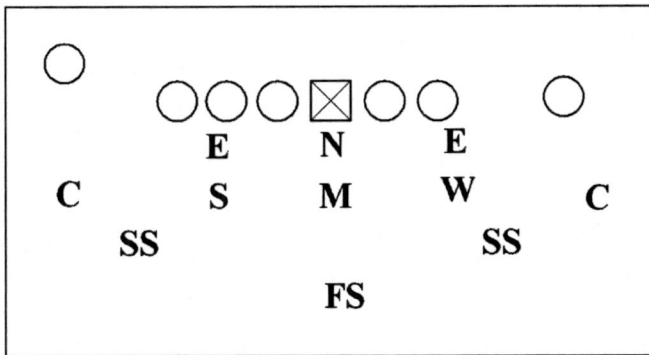

Diagram 3-1. Eight-man front

It is basically a 3-3 alignment, but we do not call it a 3-3 because all the defenders are standing in the umbrella. We can put the Mike linebacker and end up in a 4-2 look, but the entire eight-man front is going to be in the box on most of the defense we play.

Where Did This Defense Come From?

I had a coach that used to coach with me who is now 67 years old. His name is Mike Martin. He saw the defense at Salem College in West Virginia. He showed me a lot of tapes on this defense. Mike gave me a lot of tapes to watch because two or three teams from up in the mountains were running this defense.

They designed the defense to disguise the pass rush. The players on the defense were shifting and jumping around all over the place. They tried to get the offensive line to jump offside and keep them confused. They wanted to mess up their blocking schemes. They would jump all over the line of scrimmage. They would drop down, do a push-up, hop back up, and fake a blitz in one of the gaps.

We started using this defense against shotgun teams. We used the defense on third-and-long situations. We stood everyone up so we could rush the quarterback. We stood them up so they could see the ball.

When you think about the cadence in the shotgun snap, the center is the one calling the snap. The quarterback is raising his leg, but the center is in charge of snapping the ball. We played four teams that used the shotgun offense and we gave those shotgun teams fits with the defense.

It looked so good we thought we should be doing this on every down. We looked at our roster and discovered we had only 12 players over 200 pounds. However, we had a bunch of fast players. We decided to use all of the fast players, put them around the line of scrimmage, and mess with people. We could score a bunch of points on offense and it might be fun.

We gave our little, quick players a chance to be successful. We gave them a chance to play and they were really aggressive. Our nose guard weighed 160 pounds in 2002. He could power-clean 360 pounds. We want to get him playing for us. He ended up as our nose guard. It is amazing how the defense evolved with a bunch of little kids running around and chasing the football. It was great for our high school.

What Are the Strong Points?

This defense gives the offense many different "defensive looks" and does not broadcast the stunts and coverages. You can move the defense on each down because all the players are almost all interchangeable. The movement and stunt disguise any intentions. We can put all eight of the defenders on the line of scrimmage, each one with his outside foot back. That is so they can bail off the line. We do not want the inside back. This drives offensive linemen crazy. The defense operates on speed and quickness, and not size and strength. It allows for easy adjustments.

What Are the Weak Points?

The weakness of the defense is short yardage and goal-line situations. What do you think we practice the most on? Short yardage and goal-line situations. When we get into those situations, we have to get into something to plug more gaps. Playing this defense, we gave up 2.9 yards per rush on this defense last year.

Why Do We Run This Defense?

- We experimented with various forms of the rebel defense in the 2000 football season at Byrnes versus shotgun/one-back offenses. Since that time, it has evolved into our primary defensive package.
- We run a basic eight-man-front scheme with eight defenders on or near the line of scrimmage in constant movement.
- All or most of these defenders are standing up. It allows us to read or penetrate with an attacking style. It is subject to change on a weekly basis to give us the best personnel match-ups and to ensure our ability to defend what the offense does best.
- The rebel defense has helped us produce four straight 4A state championships (with a four-year record in South Carolina of 56-1).

This is our primary defense. We run eight men on or near the line of scrimmage. We have constant movement on the defense. All of our defenders are standing up. This allows us to read and to penetrate the offense. When we say "read" in this defense, it is not like the read in the old 50 scheme. We work on the match-up and defend what the offense does best. We are a big-sweep team so we put the strong safety outside along with the outside linebacker. We slant the nose guard in that direction and blow the Mike linebacker through the B gap. We are coming to get you. We make sure we take away the sweep.

When we line up, we know the defense is not good against the pass. If we are in man free, the defense is not good against the pass. We have to get to the quarterback in order for us to be successful. If you have a great receiver, we put a corner in his face, and we are going to put a safety over the top.

The defense is always on the move, because we want the offense to have to hit a moving target. We are going to attack the quarterback. We make sure the quarterback does not have a lot of time to throw the ball. We want to hit him on every play. By the third quarter, he is not looking to pass; he is looking to pull the ball down and run. We want to get many defenders in his face. We send five to eight rushers in our pass-rush scheme. We are not going to sit back in coverage and try to cover receivers. We are going to go get the quarterback.

Key Thoughts on Defense

- A defense cannot do everything.
- Attempt to stop or neutralize the greatest offensive threats.
- Move around on defense.
- Attack the quarterback. (The best pass defense is a strong rush.) Try to send five to eight rushers.
- Team quickness and reaction time are critical to our defense.
- Size is not an issue.
- Rarely run the same defense two times in a row.
- Script and practice third-down situations every day. Hold opponents below 35 percent of third-down attempts.
- 2005 opponents converted 29 percent of third downs.
- Prepare for and practice against the unseen and the unexpected.
- Keep something in your pocket for the second half.
- Move around four different fronts.

In our defense, size is no issue. We do not care how big the defenders are. Our left defensive end to our left side is 6'0" and 185 pounds. The right defensive end is 6'0", 215 pounds, and runs a 4.5 in the 40. The nose guard is 5'8" and 180 pounds. The three linebackers are clones. The Mike linebacker is 6'2", 190 pounds, and runs 4.6 in the 40. The other two linebackers and 5'9" and 200 pounds, and the other one is 190 pounds, but they both run 4.5 in the 40.

One of the savers, or strong safety, is 5'8", 130 pounds, and runs 4.38 in the 40. He was in Texas over the past week and ran at that time out there. The other saver is 5'7" and 150 pounds. The free safety is a big defensive back. He is 6'3" and 180 pounds. The corners are 5'8" and 150 pounds, but they can run.

The other thing we do to find our defensive players is to do our agilities. If a player can run better than 4.7, and they can cut and change direction, they can play defense for us. We practice the third-down situation every day. Very seldom do we run the same defense. We want to hold our opponents to 35 percent efficiency rate on third down. If you feel like you are not doing a good job on defense, go back and check your third-down plays. If you cannot compete on third down, you will not win many games. This past year we held teams to 29 percent on third down. We have stats people that gives us the percentages in all our defensive categories after the game.

You need to prepare for and practice the unseen and unexpected plays. Make sure you go over trick and gadget plays in practice, especially on Wednesday and Thursday. On Monday and Tuesday, practice the defense that stops what the offense hangs their hat on. On Wednesday and Thursday, throw in the wrinkles. Run the reverses, halfback passes, and anything you think the offense might do. Make sure you try to do something with the unbalanced line.

This scheme is a balanced defense. Put in the unbalanced look to make sure you match up correctly with the formation. Run both unbalanced run formations and pass formations.

Always keep something in your pocket for the second half. If you have done a good job stopping the offense in the first half, keep something new for the second half. The offense will adjust to things that have been successful for you in the first half. If they solve their problems, have something they have not seen for the second half. We want to let our kids know we are saving something for the second half.

Move around in your defensive front. We try to use four different fronts. Those are the types of defense we run.

I have shown you the base 3-5 earlier in the lecture. In the 3-4 defense, we have a Sam linebacker that gets into a tilt 9 technique on the tight end (Diagram 3-2).

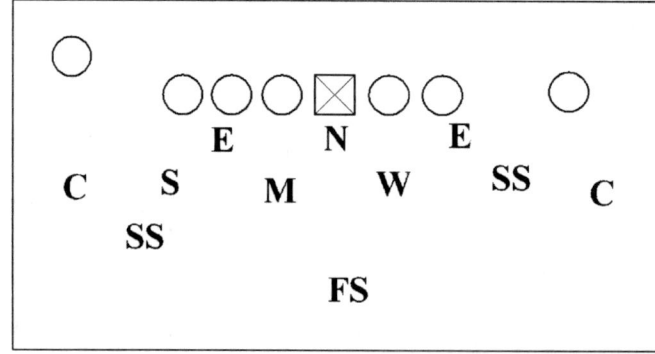

Diagram 3-2. 3-4-4

We align in a regular 3-3, with the strong safeties on the outside helping on the number-one receivers (Diagram 3-3).

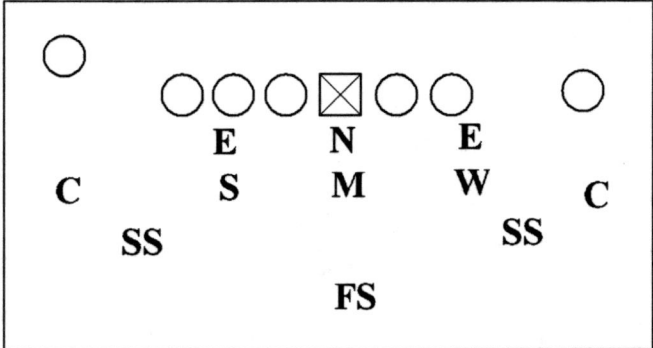

Diagram 3-3. 3-3-5

We align in a regular 3-3, with the strong safeties on the outside helping on the number-one receivers (Diagram 3-4).

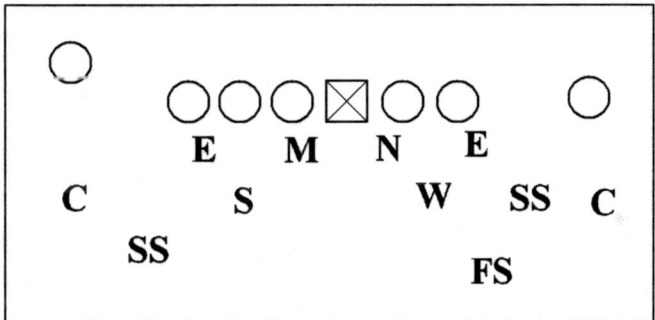

Diagram 3-4. 4-2

We can get into a 4-3 defense. When we go to that defense, we substitute a fourth lineman for a strong safety (Diagram 3-5).

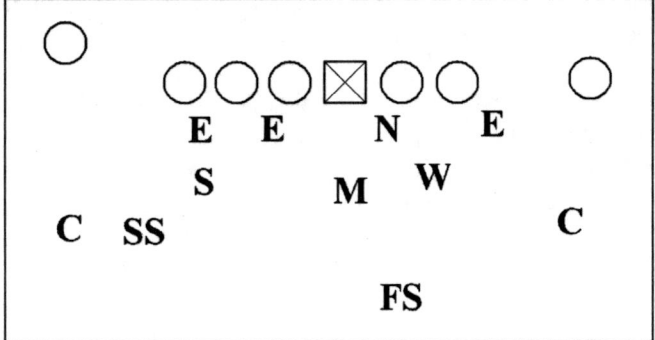

Diagram 3-5. 4-3

In the 4-4 alignment, we put the Mike linebacker down and stack the strong safeties behind the defensive ends aligned on the tight ends (Diagram 3-6).

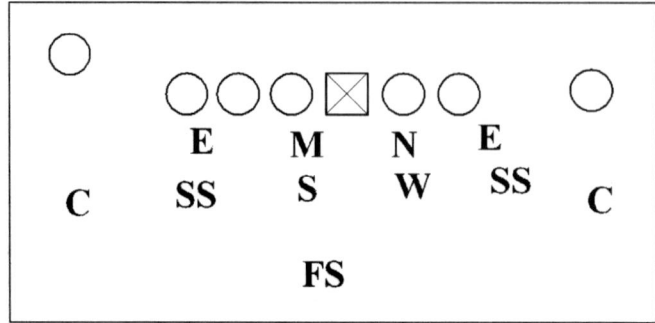

Diagram 3-6. 4-4

The last defense is the bear front, in which we let the linebackers do the adjustments (Diagram 3-7).

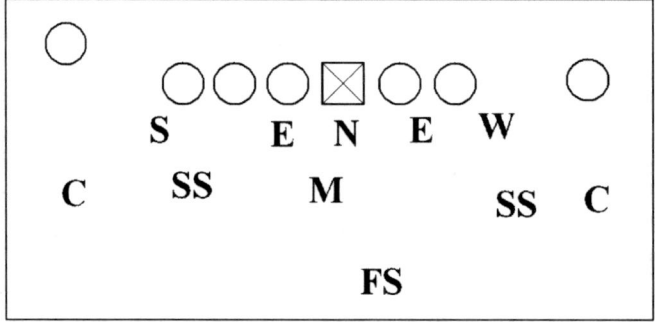

Diagram 3-7. Bear

We go through those schemes every single day because we do not run a base defense. I want to show you how far we have come with our personnel.

This defense has endless possibilities for stunts. You can run any combination of stunts from all of the alignments. You must be able to communicate the stunt. Let me cover a few of our favorite stunts. You can create your own terminology to name the stunts.

In the first stunts, both outside linebackers blitz the B gap with the strong safety coming off the edge (Diagram 3-8).

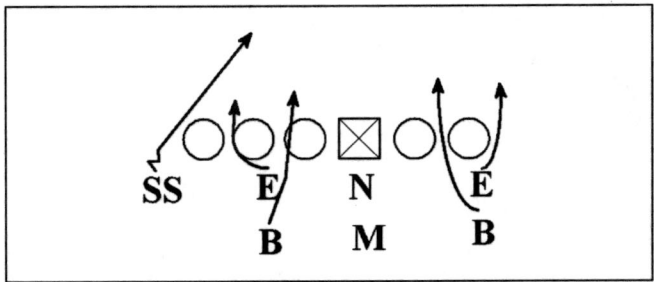

Diagram 3-8. Linebackers and strong safety blitz

The next stunt is similar to the first stunt. We reverse the blitz pattern of the linebackers and the ends (Diagram 3-9).

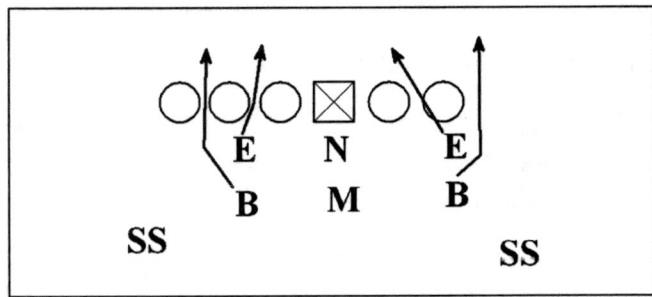

Diagram 3-9. Linebackers sunt to C gap

Here the down line slants to the tight end (Diagram 3-10). Both strong safeties come off the edges, and the strongside linebacker blows the B gap.

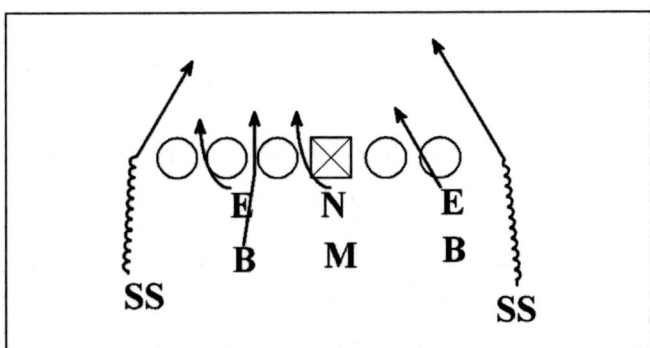

Diagram 3-10. Double bullets blitz

The defensive line slants to the openside of the formation on this next blitz (Diagram 3-11). The weakside linebacker shoots the B gap and the strongside safety comes off the edge.

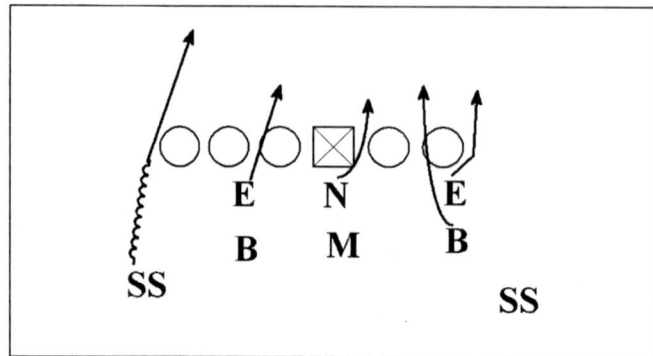

Diagram 3-11. Slant to the weakside

The next stunt is the pinch blitz (Diagram 3-12). The defensive ends pinch inside to the B gap. The weak safety blitzes from the edge, and the strongside linebacker fires the C gap. The noseguard slants to the weakside A gap.

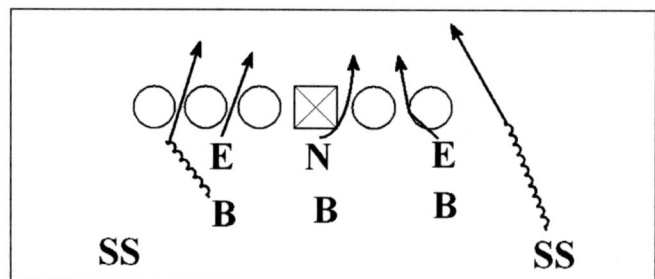

Diagram 3-12. Weakside pinch blitz

This stunt is the opposite of the stunt run to the weakside (Diagram 3-13).

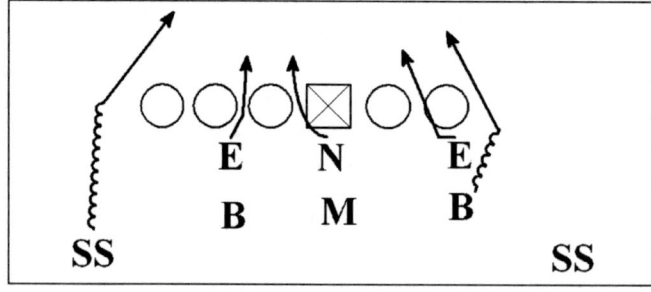

Diagram 3-13. Strongside pinch blitz

We use two primary schemes on this defense to get maximum coverage in the secondary. The first is cover-3 zone utilizing five under defenders (Diagram 3-14).

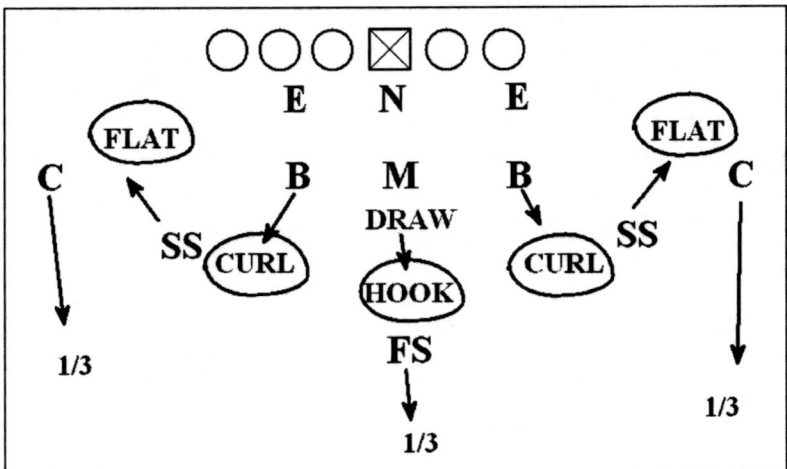

Diagram 3-14. Cover 3—drop eight defenders

You can run the next scheme by bringing the strongside safety or the weakside safety (Diagram 3-15). This gives us a four-man rush and seven defenders in the secondary. We play three-deep, and the linebacker to the side of the blitz covers the flat.

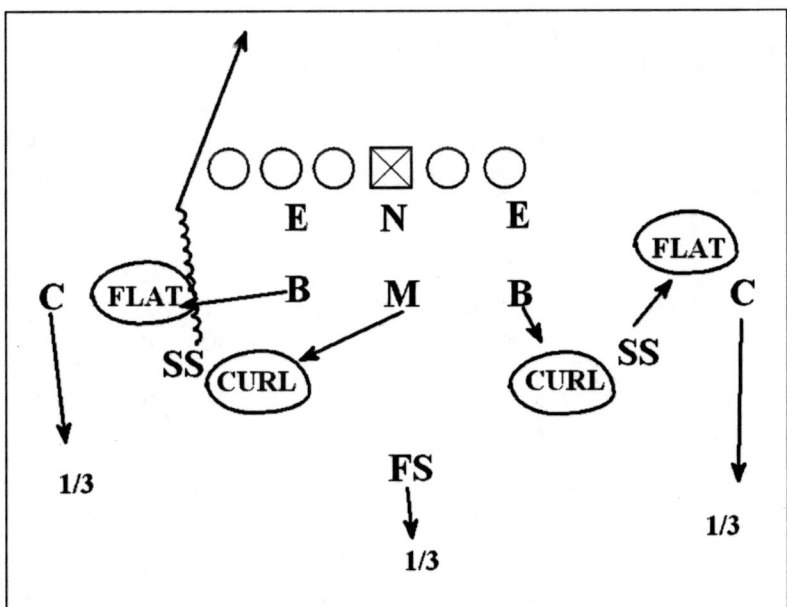

Diagram 3-15. Cover 3—strong safety blitz

In this defense, we try to caxsll them by city names. South Carolina was using this defense when Charlie Strong was coaching there. Also, Mississippi State was using the defense. We went to Memphis State to study Joe Lee Dunn to see what he was doing on defense. We thought we could get something from him.

At first, we thought we could sit our linebackers inside and let them play like they play at South Carolina. We thought we could take the fullback on with the inside shoulder and make the play. We figured out we could not play it that way. We were not good enough to sit in our base defense. We ended up with the Mike linebacker covering the B gap. The Sam and Will linebackers became cover linebackers. The cover linebackers did not have to take on the isolation play. That gap was taken care of. The ball was bounced to the outside. He was able to take on the fullback in a glancing shot instead of straight on.

We figured out that we only had one linebacker in our scheme that had to plug the gap and that was the Mike linebacker. The other defenders just went to the football. We needed our strong safeties to be the run-support players. We found out that was not the way it was, because we played a lot of man-free coverage.

When we played man-free coverage, we decided to put the big, strong safety in the blitz package. He lined up six yards off the ball and one yard outside the tight end. We put our corners that really like to hit, as savers. All of a sudden, the defense started to fall into place. We have a plugger, two strong safeties, and two free safeties that can play man coverage.

What kind of front are we going to use in our defense? We are going to look at the personnel. If we have a running back that "has no hands," we put him at the nose-guard position. He understands what offenses are doing. Here is an example. If the offense runs a sweep, the nose man can make the play a lot of the time. He understands what the offense is trying to do and he can get outside and make the play. Most defensive linemen get tied up inside and chase the play. The nose man can flatten out and get outside coming down the line of scrimmage because he understands the purpose of the play.

The defensive ends are bigger, stronger, linebacker-type players. I hope this helps you. I wish someone had told me about this defense two years ago. It would have saved us a lot of time and perhaps we could have won more games.

I hope you got something out of this lecture. I appreciate your attention. God bless all of you, and good luck next year.

4

Heavy 3-5-3 Defense
With a Shade Front

Neil Blankenship

Swain County High School, North Carolina
2012

Thank you. I want to get right into the defensive lecture as I have a lot of information I want to share. Often, we are asked what makes our defense different from other 3-5 schemes. First, I will give you a brief history and the purpose why we moved to this defensive scheme.

In 2001 at the state championship game, we began a variation of this defense due to the fact our opponents deployed an offense that spread us out across the field. We were playing a 4-2 look, so we took our strongside end and walked him off the line, and backed him off. That was the start of changing our defense.

During the off-season, Coach Rod White began studying the 3-5 defensive systems. He found there were several things about the 3-5 that other teams were doing that we didn't like, such as blitzing, playing head-up, and slanting their linemen. A lot of our kids play both ways, and we didn't think it was possible for them to play that style of defense the whole game.

We chose to take the old shade 52 and combine it with the 3-5 look. Over the past several years, we have integrated other defensive principles to create a custom fit for our style of play and our athletes. Our base is the 3-5 alignment (Diagram 4-1). We like this defense because it gives us so much versatility against the various offenses we face

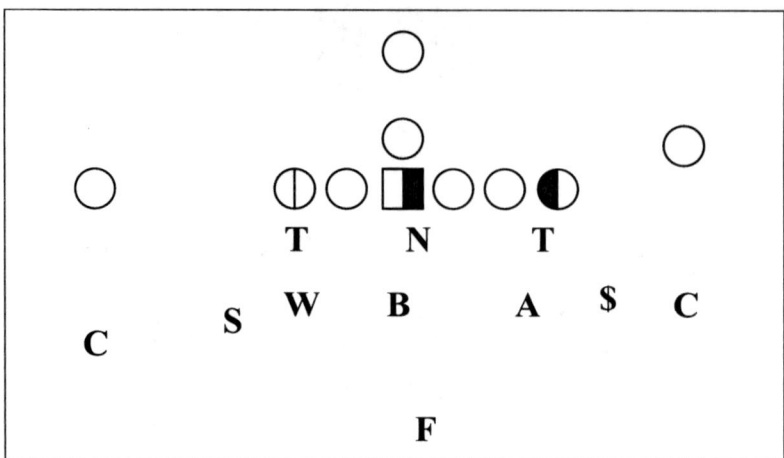

Diagram 4-1. Base 3-5 Wolf heavy

today. The tackle on the tight end plays a 7 technique. The nose is shaded to the tight end. The backside tackle aligns in a 4 technique. This is our base defense, which we call "Wolf heavy."

If we face two split ends, or a 2x2 slot set we play our Wolf alignment (Diagram 4-2). The noseguard is head-up with the center. Both tackles are head-up in 4 techniques. We make the adjustments with our safeties. This is called our Wolf alignment. There is no tight end, so we don't heavy it. Again, the down lineman will be head-up.

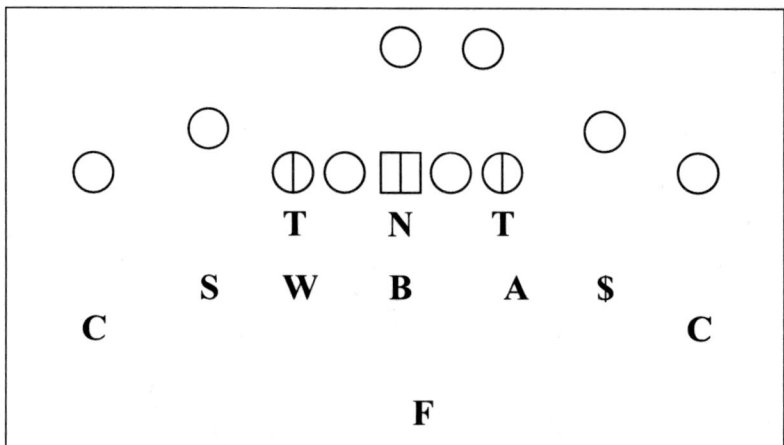

Diagram 4-2. Wolf alignment

This defense allows us to call our strength to the wideside. We have the tight end to our weakside. The nose uses his heavy technique to the tight end side, and the two tackles trade responsibilities (Diagram 4-3). The ace and weak backer trade spots. We do this so the offense can't dictate who they want to run at or throw at.

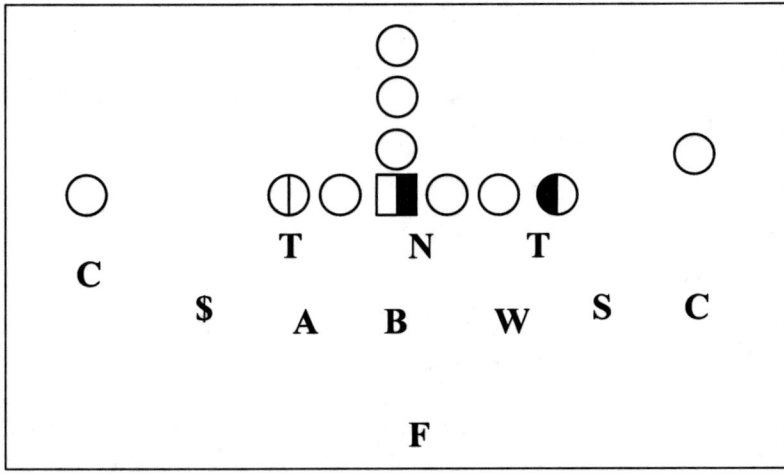

Diagram 4-3. Backers trade alignments

Defensive Line Play

What makes us different from other 3-5 schemes? One of the big things we do differently is that we do not use the number system with our defensive line. The main reason is that most of our kids play both sides of the ball, so we only use numbers on the offensive side. We talk more about head-up, outside eye, and inside eye. We do talk to them about A, B, C, and D gaps.

One of the most important steps in setting up our defensive front is to find players who have the characteristics and skills to be able to play the positions. Our three down lineman (strong tackle, nose, and weak tackle) all have different characteristics.

This alignment is Wolf heavy (Diagram 4-4). This is the down lineman's alignment and who they jam and read.

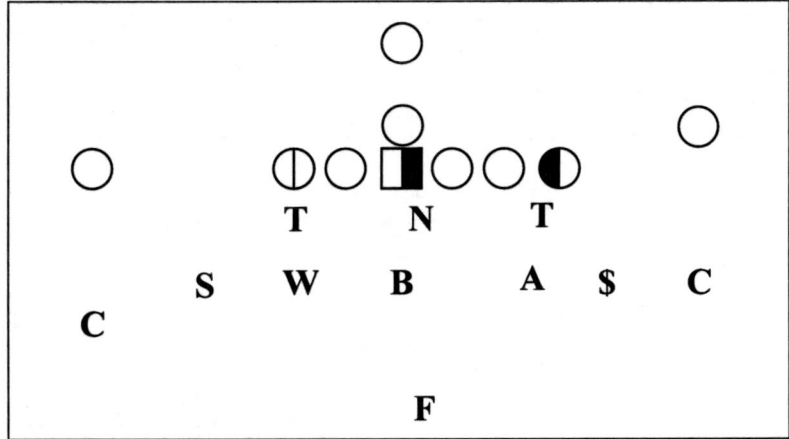

Diagram 4-4. Wolf heavy alignment

- Strong tackle: Lines up on the inside eye of the tight end; jams the tight end, and reads the tackle.
- Nose: Lines up on the strongside eye of the center, jams the center and the guard.
- Weak tackle: Lines up head-up on the tackle and reads the tackle.

This is what we look for at each of those three down line positions. There are certain characteristics that we are looking for in each position.

- Strong tackle: Is our biggest down lineman; we want him to be big and athletic.
- Nose: We have two different types: one who is quick and one who is bigger.
- Weak tackle: He is our quickest down lineman.

Next, I want to talk about jam and read techniques. First is the jam. The most-important priority that our linemen are taught is to be able to jam and control the line of scrimmage. The jam is a fairly simple process of squeezing the line of scrimmage, reacting to movement quickly and explosively. We want them to get both hands into the offensive linemen on the breastplate on their shoulder pads.

We do not want our defensive linemen to use their face mask to create separation. Our defensive linemen are smaller than most offensive linemen, and if they put their face in the shoulder pads they get blocked and they can't see. During the season, they will jam every Monday and Tuesday at practice.

Next is the read. The read is much more difficult for players to grasp, and it takes a tremendous amount of time and repetition. To help us to read, we do a drill called the "three-way read drill." During pre-season, we do the drill every day. During the season, we do it on Monday and Tuesday.

We also teach our down lineman to jam one player and read the block of another player. For example, our strong tackle will jam the tight end and read the tackle.

We want to teach our linemen to take proper pursuit angles and how to move up and down the line of scrimmage. We do not want our defensive linemen to get upfield. They are coached to work up and down the line of scrimmage. If they are getting upfield, then they are not getting a good jam. We have several drills we use to help our kids to jam and work up and down the line of scrimmage.

I want to cover our linebacker play and discuss how we are different than other 3-5 schemes. Our linebacker positions are as follows: strong safety, ace, strong backer, weak backer, and spy.

Blitz

Most teams who play a 3–5 use a lot of blitzes. One of our main reasons we do not blitz a lot is because most of our kids will be playing both ways. Those kids begin to wear down and cannot blitz at that speed or level the whole game.

Following are our alignments for the five linebackers. We play all of these positions four to five yards deep. I want to give you a short comment about each position.

- Strong safety: Strong safety alignment is four yards outside of the tight end and four yards deep (unless they have wideside or twins). This player has to be good at run support and must be able to defeat blocks.
- Spy: Spy is built more like a safety. He lines up four yards outside of their tackle, and four yards deep. This may vary with down-and-distance. They could be lined up tighter and deeper. This will also be different if they come out in a twins set.
- Ace: Ace needs to be able to play up on the line of scrimmage or at the backer position. He is one of our best defensive players. He is also our biggest linebacker. The ace lines up on the inside leg of the strong tackle.
- Strong backer: The strong backer is bigger than our weak backer. The backer lines up head-up with the center.
- Weak backer: The weak backer lines up on the inside leg of the weak tackle, and he needs to be the athletic type.

We play five positions in the secondary. The positions are: field corner, short corner, free safety, strong safety, and the spy. We talked about the strong safety and the spy as linebackers. They are also defensive backs. We use multiple coverages. We like this defense because of the ability to play different coverages in the secondary. The defense allows us to make adjustments with our linebackers and secondary. We can make a lot of different adjustments without a lot of teaching involved.

This is how we line up in the secondary. Linebackers are not included in this alignment.

- Free safety: Free safety lines up 9 to 11 yards deep.
- Field corner: We play a field corner. He is deeper than the other corner, depending on the offensive set.
- Short corner: The short corner plays four to six yards deep.

We play a lot of cover 3. We do not play cover 2 very much. We can play one type of coverage to one side, and a different coverage to the other side of the ball.

I want to show you how we line up against a twins set with a tight end away from the slot (Diagram 4-5). We make the adjustment with our field corner and strong backer.

I want to cover five different adjustments we make with our Wolf heavy 3-5 defense. These are simple adjustments that can be made during the course of the game, depending upon the type of offensive sets we face.

First is the Wolf heavy switch (Diagram 4-6). The first question we must ask is: why? Why do we want to switch? It is important that the tackle not get reached, and it is important that the ace does not get down blocked.

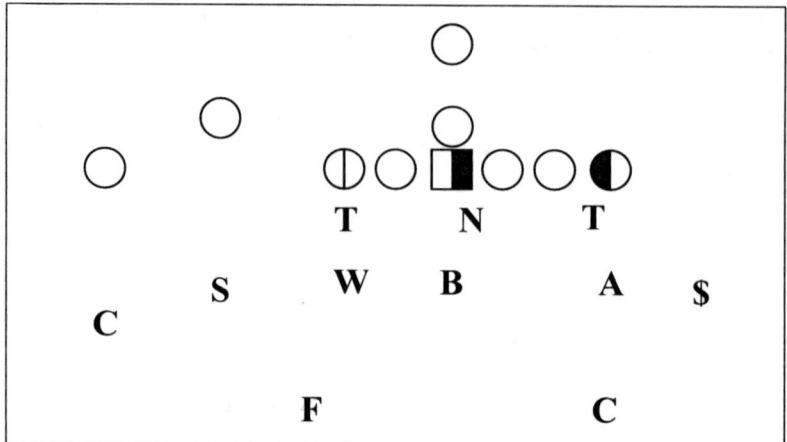

Diagram 4-5. Twins—one tight end

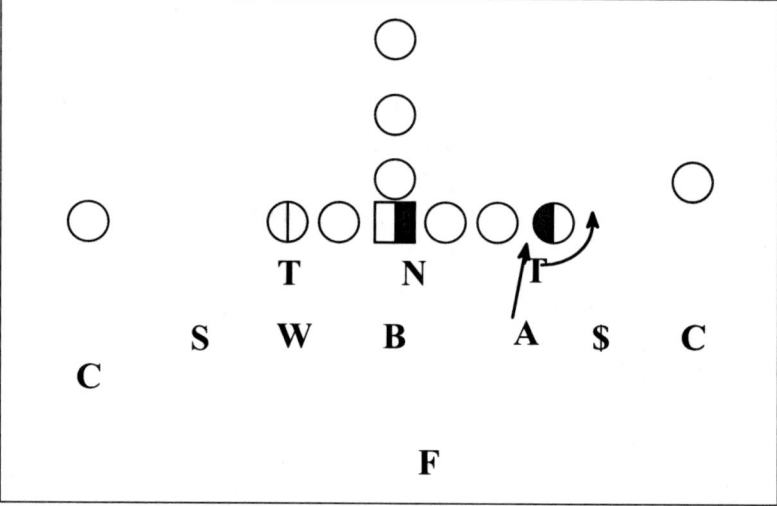

Diagram 4-6. Wolf heavy switch

Why

- Changes who has quarterback and who has dive.
- Changes the cutoff player if the play is going away.
- Changes blocking schemes.
- Can give you a delayed blitz on a pass rush.
- Will use on the strongside most of time; will use it on the weakside some (depends on what type of offense we are playing against).
- Gives players ownership to call it "on" or "off."

Next is our Wolf heavy space adjustment (Diagram 4-7). I plan to cover when we use it and what it offers us. This is great against the spread because it allows us to effectively play the slant from all slant receivers. We can unload the box after the speed teams have counted the box players. This works well against option teams and teams that use rules for blocking defenses.

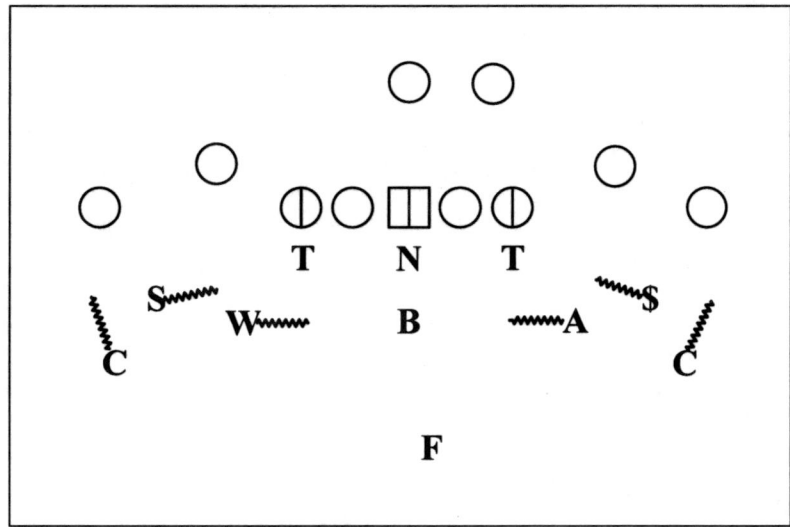

Diagram 4-7. Wolf heavy space

When

- We use this when teams are spreading us out.
- We like to use this when ball is in the middle of field.

What It Offers

- Gives the quarterback a different look.
- Puts us in the curl and flat.
- Can help you contain a team with more speed.
- Changes angle of a blitz, if that's what you like to do.
- Linebackers can slide and adjust easy with different sets.
- If there's motion, it's easy to bump and slide linebackers.

Our next adjustment is our Wolf heavy spy adjust (Diagram 4-8). I want to make one important point: this is not a called defense. The spy learns throughout the week when to adjust. This is determined by offensive formation, field position, and the down-and-distance.

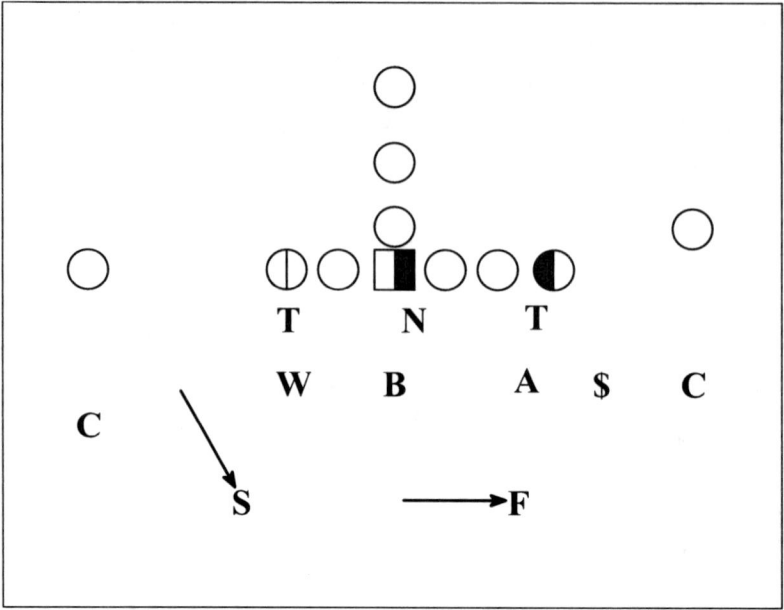

Diagram 4-8. Wolf heavy spy adjust

Spy Alignment Adjustment

Closer to the boundary = closer to formation, plus added depth. He never aligns outside of the #2 receiver, unless the #2 receiver is a tight end.

When

- Use when there is a wideside.
- Can rotate free safety to field.

Why

- Allows us to play different coverages.
- Allows different coverages on each side.
- Allows us to play cover 2, cover 3, and man, with the availability of extra safety help.
- The free safety is able to cheat into the wide/strongside as the spy player gets depth.

Next, we go to our Wolf heavy banjo adjustment (Diagram 4-9). When do we use this adjustment? We use it to cover wide receivers by sliding the defense. We dare the offense to run into the boundary on this adjustment. Following are our options on the adjustment.

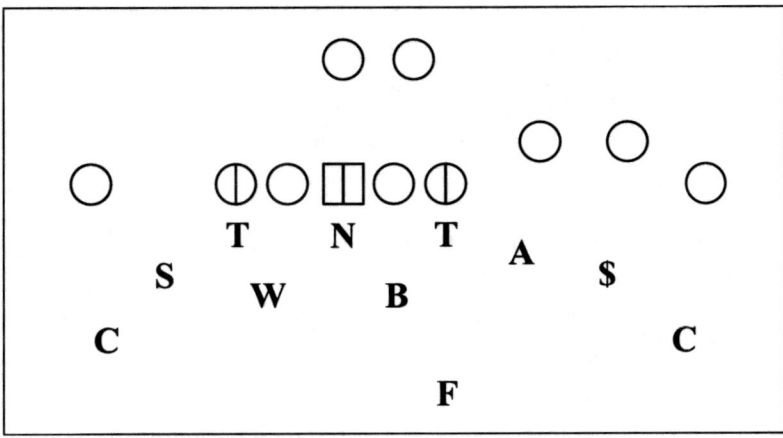

Diagram 4-9. Wolf heavy banjo

Options

- Allows ace to adjust to formations.
- Can bring ace off edge.
- Can drop ace into coverage and bring strong backer for contain.
- Can slide spy back.
- Can play multiple coverages.

Our last adjustment is our Wolf heavy bite (Diagram 4-10). It is our zone blitz. This is how it looks.

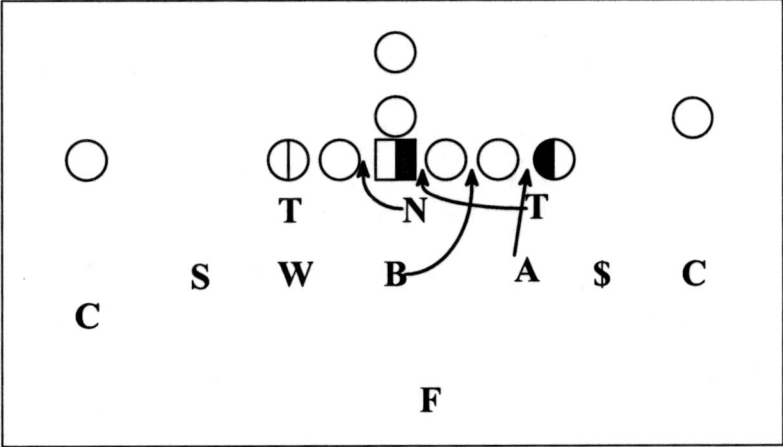

Diagram 4-10. Heavy bite (zone blitz)

- Strong tackle: Run a long stick to the A gap.
- Nose: Crosses the face of the center.
- Weak tackle: Has to have contain out the backside.
- Strong backer: Comes through the B gap.
- Ace: Comes on outside for contain.

I will be around if you have any questions. It has been a big year for us. We have won the state championships eight times. We were fortunate to win it again last year.

If you are interested in anything we do, just contact me. Thank you.

5

The 3-3 Stack Defense

John Bowers
Morgantown High School, West Virginia
2005

I want to talk about our 3-3 stack defense. We started out running this defense against teams that did not have a tight end in their formation. This is our secondary defense. We played it 48 percent of the time last year. We also ran some even-front defenses last year. You will be able to see our defense and how we get into the even front and how we stem and move in and out of the defense.

If you have any questions let me know. I might not know the answer but I will promise you I will give you an ideal of what we do. Together, we might be able to figure out the answer. If you can get one or two ideas from this lecture, it will be worthwhile. We can learn together.

In the last two years, we never ran this defense against two tight ends. We were afraid we could not stop the run. But since the team has had so much success, we started running the defense against teams that employed two tight ends at times and learned to like it.

We like to squeeze the football. We play a very tight force defense. Some defenses like to funnel the defensive end and tackle inside. Our base is a 4-4 defense. We wrong arm and spill everything in our defense. It is almost as if we are two-gapping the defense. If we destroy the tackle, our eyes are inside.

The one linebacker we play around with is our rover. He is the "move" player. He is four-and-one-half yards off the line. He is one of our defensive ends or the rover. Last year, he was a secondary player and it allowed us to shift our defense and change fronts. The offense sees us in an even front one play and in an odd front the next play.

I want to talk about our alignment. Our *Bandit* is a 2-by-2 player from the tight end. We will adjust that distance from time to time, particularly if there is not a tight end on his side. We adjust him depending on down, distance, and the formation.

The heels of the *corner* are at six-and-one-half yards, inside with his back to the sideline, and his eyes on the quarterback through the uncovered linemen. That tells us if we are going to play a lot of zone coverage and what kind of throw we are going to face.

Our *free safety* lines up with his heels at eight yards over the uncovered offensive lineman, so he can read the high hat or low hat on that lineman. This will tell you if it is a run or a pass play. We cheat him to the two-receiver side.

Making the Stack Defense Work

The following things illustrate some of the factors that help make the stack defense work. The first thing I will tell you about the defense is don't try to fool the offense. You only fool yourself. You must have something on which you can hang your hat. If our defensive coordinator did not show up for a game because he was sick, we would still know what we are going to run because all week we have practiced the defense we are going to use.

I call the offensive plays. If I do not show up, the coaches still know what to run in the game. The game plan will be fine. The key point is to get good at what you can do and stay with it.

In our stack defense, we send the Bandit and Sam linebacker to the strongside or the called side. The Will linebacker, the Mike linebacker, and the stack tackle go to the weakside. Our linemen vary their stance, depending on down and distance, ball location on the field, and stunt called.

We do not want to allow the offensive linemen to "find" us on defense. We like to move around to confuse the offense. By moving around, you would be surprised how many times the offense jumps offside.

We want to game-play to defeat what the offense is going to do in the game. We want to defend what the offense runs. When we look at defending the offense, we want to know the team's five best runs. We want to know their five best passes. We want to know their five favorite formations. If we get three scouting reports, we are not going to be able to defend everything they do on offense. We want to defend what the offense does best. That is what we try to do.

Our alignment is going to change, depending on the formation. Our assignments are going to change against different formations. If the offense lines up in trips and uses the bunch formation, what are you going to do? We are going to line up one defender outside of the end man, one man inside, and one player who will take the area down the middle of those two defenders down the field. You can bet the offense is going to run a play toward the bunch. That is why they line up in the bunch. It does not matter how they align in the bunch, we are going to play them the same way. We have a man inside, outside, and in the middle of the bunch.

Coverage Defense

We play sound base defense and coverage defense. This changes when we get into our blitz game. We are playing with three stacks on the line. We are going to play sound coverage. We are going to get to our landmark. We are going to read the elbow of the quarterback in pass coverage. If the quarterback has his passing elbow down, it is going to be a quick drive throw on a hitch or a speed-out route. If the quarterback has his elbow high, it is going to be a pass deep down the field. The secondary will drop a little more on the high elbow.

In the shotgun formation, we read the front shoulder of the quarterback. If the shoulder is down, it is going to be a drive throw. If the shoulder is up, it is going to be a deeper pass. That is how we teach the read on the quarterback.

We ball-react, except when we are blitzing. We do not like to play a lot of man-to-man coverage. We want discipline by tackling the ball to the ground and playing another play. "Get them on the ground and line up and play again." It is hard for a defense to take the ball on their 20-yard line and drive it down the field for a score, unless you make a mistake in coverage. Get them on the ground and play defense again. There is nothing more demoralizing than a big play.

If the opponents have the ball on their 20-yard line, we can play soft defense. When the ball approaches the five-yard line, we are on a tenuous course to lose field position. Even if the defense stops them at the 50-yard line and they punt the football, you have lost field position.

What you have to do is to make a decision if you are going to play sound defense, or if you are going to turn the defense loose and get after the offense and make a stop so you do not lose field position. That has to be part of your team concept. That is what we do on defense.

We try to determine what we are going to do on first down, second down, and third down. We want to know how we are going to defend the offense on each of those situations.

Anytime the inside linebacker does not like the stunt called, he can change it or call "Omaha" which changes the call. He is an extension of our defensive staff on the sideline. When we make an "Omaha" call, it means the stunt is off. We do not want to give the offense a big play. We want to get them on the ground and play defense again.

Defensive Line Play

Let me talk about the defensive line. We play on the line of scrimmage. We do not run up and down the field. We do not want teams to run the trap play against us. We do not want to get the counter play, and we do not want to be hooked on a play. Our defensive ends and tackle only rush one yard over the line of scrimmage on the pass rush. When they get across the line one yard, they look inside to see if there is a pulling guard or a fullback blocking on them. We want them to be aware of what is going inside.

Blitzing

On the blitz, all of the moves change. We are going to be a penetrating team. The offense sees us in a read-and-react defense for two or three plays, and then all of a sudden, we become a penetrating defense.

When we run the blitz to one side of the line, it is imperative for the other defensive end to generalize a little and pull the play up so the stunt can be there. We do not want the quarterback forced outside on the stunt and then get around the end. We want to pull him up with the end. Why would we want to bring heat on the quarterback if you cannot pull him up to keep him from getting outside on the play? This is something we believe in very strongly.

There is nothing worse for a secondary player or a flat defender playing against a "mad dog" passer. We are talking about a quarterback with the football on the perimeter who has the ability to run the football, and a receiver behind the corner, looking for the pass. We do not want to get into that situation.

Another thing we work on is to differentiate the quarterback "on" or "off" the line of scrimmage. This is important to how we react.

Installing the 3-3 Defense

The next point I want to cover is how we install the 3-3 defense. How many of you practice in the middle of the football field? We have found that 85 percent of the plays occur outside the uprights. Don't practice in the middle of the field on offense or defense. We put the ball on the hash marks and we move the ball from position to position on the field. That is what is going to happen in the games.

It is important to know how to use the space on the field to your advantage. It is important to answer the following questions about your opponent:
- What formations are you going to see?
- From those formations, what plays are you going to see?

- What route combinations will you see?
- What routes hurt you last year?
- What type of motion and shifts are you going to see from your opposition?
- What plays gave you trouble last year?
- How many big plays did you give up last year?
- How many stops did you make inside the red zone?
- How many stops did you have when you were facing a first-and goal situation?
- How many times did you make a stop on fourth down?

One of the ways we teach our kids is to put the offense in the most basic formation possible. The kids have to know the defense better than the coaches do, if possible.

We practice against specific formations. For example, we know we are going to see the full-house formation from two of our opponents (Diagram 5-1). That gives us eight gaps to defend. In practice, our offense runs anything they might do against us, including counter plays.

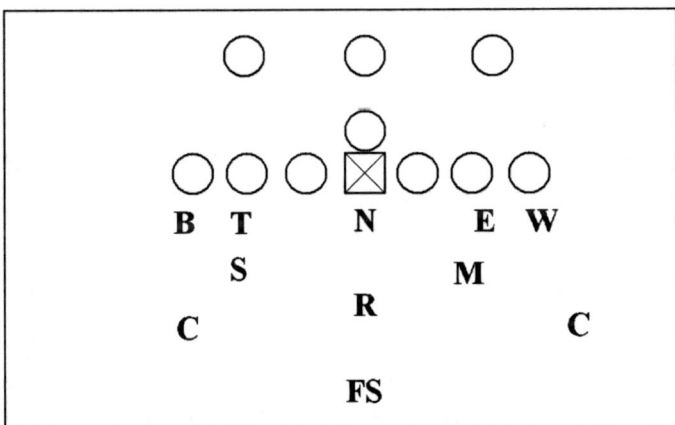

Diagram 5-1. Full house formation

We coach our defensive backs to answer the following questions: How many wide receivers does the offense have? What receiver can threaten them first? The most obvious answer to this query is the tight end.

We ask our outside linebackers to be aware of who can run through the flats first. They do not know this unless you cover it with them. If the near back disappears, they must know the fullback is going to be coming on some type of waggle play.

We require out inside linebackers to be aware of who can block them. It is the same question for the Rover. He must learn to read the triangle. I will cover that later. We want the Sam linebacker to know who can block him. It is the same for the down linemen. Where can the blocks (including double-team blocks) come from? This is what we teach from the first day of camp.

Always remember that you are teaching this to young kids. I think about it as teaching it to sophomores. If I can teach this to the sophomores, the seniors will get it.

The next step is to show the defense another formation. Now, we show them a full-house formation with a split end (Diagram 5-2). You must cover how the defense is going to change. For example, we ask the corner how many receivers he has. Which receiver can attack him first? As a result, he will be aware of the split end, who is his first threat.

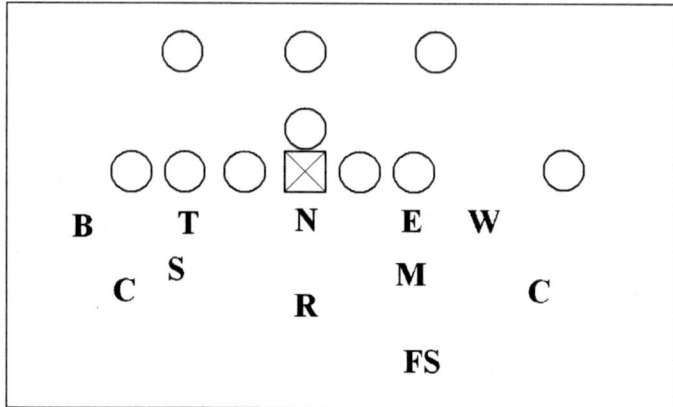

Diagram 5-2. Full-house formation with a split end

We ask our outside linebacker who can attack the flat first. Who is the second man who can attack the flat? This offensive player has a potential crack block against the linebacker. You must coach him to look for that block.

We ask the inside backer the same questions. Who can block him? He must know where everyone is on the field.

We ask the other linebackers if their reads are going to change. All of the positions must know the changes that will have a bearing on how they adjust to a particular formation.

Next, we go against some type of wing set. We go through the same ordeal with the secondary. Who can threaten him? It is the same for the linebackers as well. We want the linebackers to know if their reads are going to change. We ask them what the down blocks mean to them against the wing-T teams. They must know what down blocks mean to them. We teach this in the first week of camp. We do not want to have to teach it in the fourth game of the season when we are facing a wing-T team. We do not want to take a week to teach them what to do against the down blocks. We install it in early season camp.

Next, we look at a split end and a flanker set to one side (Diagram 5-3). Go to the defensive backs and ask them who can threaten them first. Go over all of the questions you need to cover with them. What type of route combinations can we expect from this formation? Then, go over all of the types of blocks the inside linebackers and down linemen can expect from this formation.

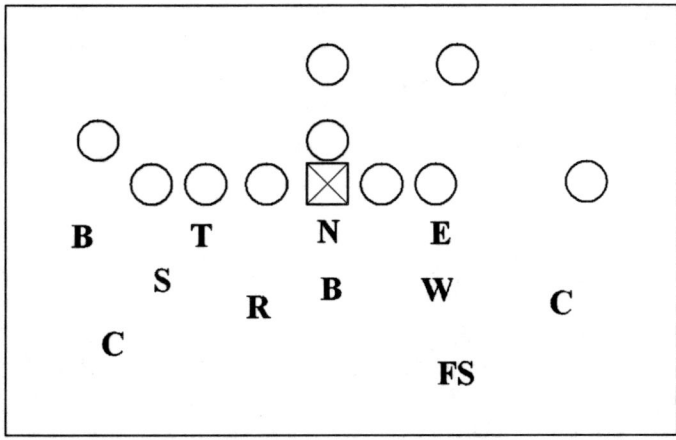

Diagram 5-3. Pro set with split end and slot

We look at all formations that we may see in a game. We may see two split ends or two split receivers to the same side of the field with other alignments. We go over all possible formations. We want them to know what can happen to all of the different positions on defense. Then, when we face a different formation during the season, we have a guideline to use to prepare for those formations. It is not a new formation for them to learn. We think this is very important when you are installing the defenses.

We go over all formations in the first three or four days when we are in shorts to start practice. Then, when we start game planning, the players have seen the formations before and can pick things up quicker.

Against a basic tight end run, how do we fit up against the play? We see some type of tight end run. Our Bandit is going to be the force on the line of scrimmage. He keeps his outside arm and leg free. He has to set the edge. It is important to set a "hard" edge. It creates an alley for the running back when the offense can kick him outside. We like to keep him on the line of scrimmage. If the edge sets too far outside, our linebackers cannot scrape inside and cover the play. We want to reduce the distance on the field we have to defend. The outside linebackers or your flat defenders are the key to this defense.

We have a concept named the "Dome." That term applies to our outside linebackers. The imaginary line extends from the inside foot of the tight end to the inside foot of the ghost end's inside foot and through the heels of our stacked linebacker.

The Will and Bandit do not enter the "Dome" or the area from end to end. If the Bandit gets inside that arc and the ball bounces outside, we are in trouble because we cannot get outside. We do not want the outside Bandit and Will linebackers entering the "Dome." If the ball breaks inside, they can make the tackle inside as the ballcarrier crosses the line of scrimmage. By doing that, we can handle the isolation play and any play that slips through on the inside, and we can handle the bounce.

The eyes of the tackle are inside. We want him to destroy the tackle and take him inside. If he gets an inside release, he can wrong arm the trap and the counter. He is almost a 2-gap player, but his eyes are inside.

Our Rover is not a run-through player. He is a midline and scrape player. We do not want to run him through the gaps.

The backside tackle comes off the butt of the tackle, and he plays chase contain. He has his eyes inside for the cutback. When the ball clears, he is running through the B gap.

We put all of this in the first week of practice. When we work on the pursuit drills, we make sure the tackle on the backside plays the chase-contain technique.

We want to get our linebackers to the playside. We want our Sam and Rover to the strongside. That is the reason we line them up in those positions.

We said the Will never enters the "Dome." He is the last man to chase on the pursuit drill. He aims for the far number of the man he is chasing. We do not want him to overrun the play. We teach the Will to run toward the ballcarrier's back number, so if the he cuts back, he will run into the Will linebacker. We teach him to chase the back number at a proper angle. He is also our BCR man (i.e., the bootleg, counter, and reverse defender).

In the secondary, our corners are always filling from the outside to the inside. The free safety runs in the alley inside-out. The backside corner is also in the proper pursuit angle.

Is what we do right? I do not know for sure. Is what we do wrong? We do not think so because we have had some success with our 3-3 defensive alignment.

On the split-end side of the defense, the Will linebacker is the force man. We want him to force the ball to the inside. We do not want him to let the play get around him. He must squeeze the hole as the ball comes toward him. He must give the Mike and Rover a chance to make the plays. If he opens up the hole eight yards wide, they cannot make the play.

On the backside, the Bandit becomes the pursuit man. We fill in the play—the same as we did on the strongside. The corner plays from the outside to the inside. The free safety plays inside to the outside.

The following illustrates the order of plays in which we install the defense. First, we go against the veer option. This play forces us to read and to react to how we are going to play it.

This play teaches the Bandit how to set the edge. He plays with his outside arm and leg free. He keeps the option man to his inside ear. He keeps his hand inside on the quarterback. We want to feather the quarterback. We do not want to run downhill on the quarterback. We do not want to chase the pitch upfield and give the offense a seam. We want to keep the ball on the line of scrimmage. We want the Bandit to put his hand out toward the quarterback because it gives the quarterback the illusion that the Bandit is closer to him than he actually is.

The eyes of our tackle are inside. He is on the line of scrimmage. He is on the dive. The nose man is helping on the dive play. He controls the center. He reads the triangle. We want him to get to the frontside. Our end is chase-and-contain.

When we defend the play, Sam is on the quarterback. We have the ability to keep him on the quarterback. The Rover is reading the quarterback on the pitch. He is going to scrape from the B gap to the C gap to the ball. The Mike linebacker is a middle scrape player. He is not running through the gaps. He is reading the play as he comes down the line of scrimmage. He is a slow-read player on the play away. He is the cutback man on the play toward him.

The defender who is not accounted for a great deal of the time is the free safety. We run him through the quarterback pitch. His path is inside to the outside.

We play the option to the split end the same way. Again, we are going to "feather" the play. The Will keeps everything on the line of scrimmage. It is the same technique as we played on the tight end side for the rest of the players.

On Cover 3 against a straight dropback pass in the middle of the field, we want the Sam and Mike to be curl-to-flat players. We spend a lot of time with them to make sure they do not cover "grass." We tell them to go where the "fish are biting." We work with them a great deal of the time on landmarks. As the season progresses, we get into the tendencies of the opponents. We ball-react to the quarterback's arm, shoulder, and elbow as I talked about earlier. This is against the pro set and a dropback pass play. We are going to play one thirds in the secondary.

The Bandit and Will try to get under the first outside receiver. The Sam and Mike linebackers play curl to flat on the number-2 receiver. We do not want them going outside just to cover grass.

The release of the number-2 receiver tells us the route. If the number-2 receiver goes inside, there is a high probability the outside man is going to come inside. It may be a shallow route, or it may be an outside route for the receiver. He may run a trailing route. If the number-2 man runs a vertical route, the Sam or Mike stays outside. If he runs a vertical route, the linebackers stay vertical. If the number-2 receiver goes outside, you can bet the number-1 receiver is coming inside. We coach the kids on this theory.

Then, we get into the combo routes. We want the Bandit and Will to disrupt the route of the receiver. Within the rules, we want to disrupt the receiver's route. We do not get up in his face.

When the ball is on the hash mark, the Bandit can push off the sideline. It is tough for a high school quarterback to throw the ball across the field in that area. We played

14 games this year, and we only faced three quarterbacks that could make the throw across the field when the ball is on the hash mark. They were good quarterbacks. If they cannot throw the ball across the field, the Bandit can play off the sideline more. We hang on the inside route as much as we can. It is much easier for the quarterback to throw the curl, than it is to throw outside to the flat.

On the backside, the defense can do several things to cause problems for the offense. You can bring the Will outside and have him eye the wide receiver. That allows the corner to drop off and play one third of the deep field. We can blitz the Will on the backside. We can run several different stunts to the backside.

When the ball is on the opposite hash mark and we get a straight dropback by the quarterback, the release by the number-2 receiver, again, tells us the route. If the number-2 receiver is going outside, the number-1 man is going inside.

Four verticals do not scare us as much as it did two years ago. If our linebackers are very good athletes, they will not allow four receivers to get vertical against us. They are going to disrupt the routes. We do not think we will have to cover four verticals across the field. To the best of their ability and within the rules, the linebackers are not going to allow the four receivers to get vertical on us. If the number-1 receiver stays outside, the number-2 receiver stays inside. The offense is not going to run two men in the same spot. We are not going to allow the offense to run four vertical receivers against us.

The defense must be aware how of the width of the field can affect the game. What kind of throw does it take to get the ball from one hash mark to the outside of the other hash mark? We do not see that type of passer very often. We are going to defend where the receivers are. We are going where the "fish are biting."

We consider it a vertical route when a receiver is five yards deep. We used to get on the receiver's hip and chase him when he got seven yards deep. But now, we use five to seven yards as a vertical route.

Base Reads

Let me talk about our base read against the run. We start with our nose man. If he gets a reach block, he tries to get to the playside. Our nose man is a good player, and we want to get him to the ball. Against the double-team block, we want him to keep them on the line of scrimmage, and we do not want the blockers to get to our linebackers. He wants to get down the line to the frontside A gap.

Against the pass, we are going to bull rush the nose man. Against the straight drop, we want him to collapse the pocket. Against a rollout play, he is through the A gap and becomes a force player.

The difference between the tackle and the end is that there is a tight end on the tackle side. That tight end can down block on the tackle. We really have to work against the down block. He does not want the tackle to reach block against him. He wants to stay even with his eyes inside. He is looking inside to cover the B gap. We do not want him reached, but he is not going to give up the B gap. We are talking out of both sides of our mouth with him. We coach him to get his eyes inside toward the center.

Against the double-team block, we want to keep the stack on the line of scrimmage. We do not want the offense to force him off the line of scrimmage. He is a B-gap player.

Against an outside fold block, our eyes are still inside. If the back cuts it back, we are in good shape, because we have the linebacker there. We must remember we are an inside release defense first.

Against an outside release, we want to spill everything and wrong shoulder the blocker. Against a pass or a dart set, our eyes are always inside. If the offensive tackle pulls away from the tackle, he becomes the chase-and-contain man. It is the same as if it is a pulling guard. It does not change that much for the end.

The only difference for the end is the fact that he does not have a tight end on his side. We do not want him to be reach blocked. His eyes are inside all of the time. Against the dart and the inside fold, he does the same thing. He is a B-gap player. He does not rip inside. He keeps his eyes inside. On the inside release, he wrong arms and spills the play.

Our linebackers read the offensive guards when we are in our 4-4 defense. The guards will take us to the ball. We used to play the 4-3 defense, but this became easier for us to play.

If Sam gets a pull toward him, he becomes an "over-the-top" fill player. He can do that because he knows the Rover is covering his back.

If the Sam gets a pull-away, he becomes a midline-to-scrape player. He plays one-half a hole behind the play. If they reach block him, it is tough. The tight end has a chance at reaching the Sam. Against the pass, he gets into his drop. Against any fold block, he wants to get on the outside of the tackle.

The Rover is the player with whom you have to do a lot of coaching and with whom you must spend a lot of time working. For us, the Rover is a defensive end or a secondary player. The reason you have to spend so much time with him is that he is not used to playing this position. He gets better as the year progresses. He reads the triangle in front. He is reading from the B gap to the C gap. Against the trap, he is a B-gap and a C-gap player. Remember, we have a cutback player taking care of the A gap. The hard play to read is when the offense runs a base block. He does not get a read on the base block.

We coach our linebackers not to play flat-footed. On the snap of the ball, we do a bounce on the balls of our feet. We bounce on our heels. On the snap of the ball, they bounce on the balls of their feet. That gets the feet moving a little better. The Mike linebacker plays the same as the Sam linebacker.

We want to use the sideline to our advantage. There is more space on the wide side than there is on the hash mark to cover. We will move a full man on the hash mark. The reads change when we move the defense. The kids should not have any problem with this because we installed it in August.

We can do several things with the defense that are different. We can bring the Will back and let him play deep. If we do bring the Will back deep, we can play quarter coverage. We can play soft-man coverage if we want.

We do run a couple of stunts from this defense. We run a S-l-a-M stunt (Diagram 5-4). The "S" is for Sam and the "M" is for Mike. We keep it simple and call it Slam. We move the Rover up on the guard and make sure he occupies that guard. We want to make sure we get a free run for the Sam. We can molly him to the weakside so the guard cannot get outside and block the Mike.

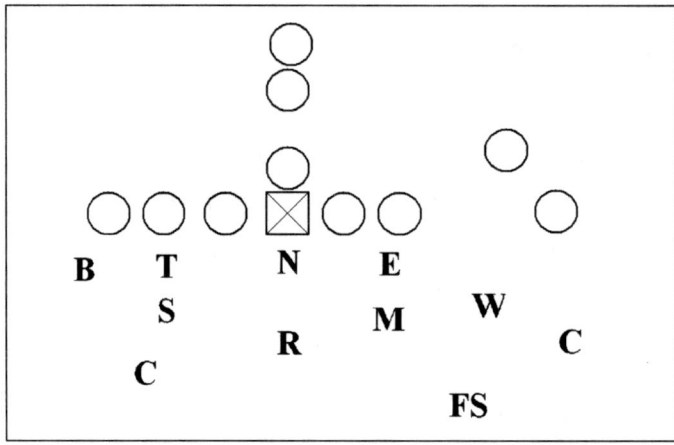

Diagram 5-4. S-l-a-M stunt

On the Fire stunt, we have a two-man blitz to the same side. We cheat Sam over a little on the snap of the ball. He is going through the B gap and the tackle is going through the C gap. We can run the Rover up through the A gap on our Razor stunt. The nose man goes opposite the call on Razor and bull rushes. He wants to make the center turn his shoulder on the bull rush.

When we send a linebacker on an inside blitz, we coach him to be an athlete, lower his shoulder, and rip trough the blocker. You must coach the players how to run the blitz. We are sending them on the blitz to get through the line. We do not want them running into the guard. We teach them that the offensive players are going to block them on the blitz. It is either going to be the center or the guard who blocks them. Let them know from whom to expect the block to come. Teach them to be an athlete—dip, and rip, and get through the gap.

6

The 3-3-5 Stack Defensive System

Randy Coddington
Concord High School, California
2011

Before I get started, I want to give you an overview of Concord football. In 2004, when we arrived at Concord, it was a tough situation. What made it tougher was two-and-a-half miles down the road was De La Salle High School, which is the most prominent program in the state. We looked at that as a negative because they were a national power and were recruiting our players. In 2006, we turned the program around by sheer will. The campus turned into a positive environment. Also in 2006 as a staff, we made a philosophy change.

We made a decision to become a spread no-huddle offense. On defense, we went to a 3-3-5 so we could get more speed on the field. We decide not to punt the ball as much and go for two on extra points every time. It was fun to go and win it all this year with that crazy mentality because we did it our way.

We simply thought since we were right down the street from De La Salle, if we win or lose by 70 points, who would care. They will get all the headlines in the local papers anyway. We were willing to lose by 70 to win by one. Making aggressive decisions during the games have paid off as well. The players bought into it. During the game, we began to impose our will on the opponent and their coaching staff. I could see it happening from the booth. In 2006, that is the reason we went to the 3-3 stack. Since then, we have had nothing but success.

Why Run It?

- Fewer defensive linemen
- More linebacker and safety-type players
- Speed on the field
- Attacking style
- Easy linebacker reads
- Create turnovers

I want to talk a little about our position groups. The defensive line is an important grouping in this defense. We refer to the nose tackle as the Stud. We named him that because he has to play that way. He is important because he must demand a double-team from the offense. If they do not double-team him, he will wreak havoc in their backfield. We call the defensive ends Eagle and Rover. The Eagle aligns to the left, and the Rover to the right.

The Rover end had 130 tackles this year. He is small, but extremely quick. He gets off the ball as fast as anyone I have seen. It is funny because my Stud and Rover were my two best linemen, and the Eagle ended up with a scholarship from San Diego State University. The three down linemen slant to the right, left, in, out, and pinch. It is very simple.

When we run an in or out movement by the defensive ends, the nose tackle goes into the left A gap (Diagram 6-1). On the in movement, the defensive end is a B-gap player, and on the out movement, he is a C-gap player. On the pinch call, they both are B-gap players. On the pinch movement, the Stud goes to the right A gap.

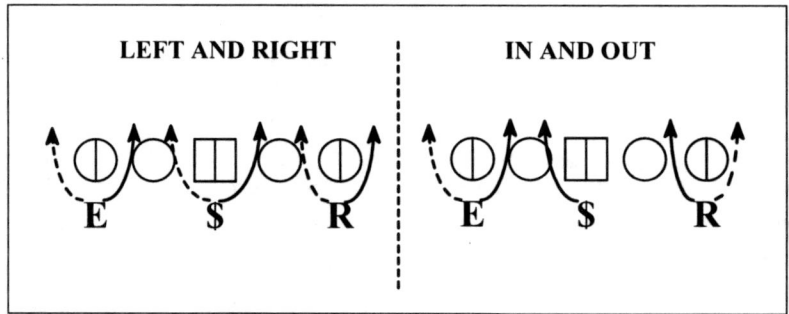

Diagram 6-1. Defensive line movement

It is very simple for the linemen. All they have to do is focus on their slant technique. We align all the linemen in a head-up position on the offensive center and tackles. Initially, when we teach their stance, we teach them with their right hand down and left foot back. The offensive lineman began to read the stances of the defensive ends. We now put them in both right- and left-handed stances to confuse the reads of the offensive linemen.

We use a sprinter stance with the feet beneath the hips with the butt high. We want them to get off the line and create havoc in the backfield. The defensive ends are spill players. If the offensive scheme does not block them at the line of scrimmage, they look inside and wrong-arm all blocks.

The linebackers are the next grouping of players. We give catchy names to all our players. We gave them patriotic names, and since they play like missiles, we named them Tomahawk and Patriot. The field linebacker is the Tomahawk, and the boundary linebacker is the Patriot. On the inside, we call them the conventional names of Sam, Mike, and Whip.

The inside linebackers align in a stack position behind the nose and defensive ends (Diagram 6-2). They align at a depth of three to four yards from the line of scrimmage. The Mike linebacker stacks behind the Stud. The Sam linebacker stacks behind the Eagle end, and the Whip linebacker stacks behind the Rover end. We align the Tomahawk and Patriot four yards wide by four yards deep off the end man on the line of scrimmage. At times, we have the linebackers moving, and sometimes they are stationary.

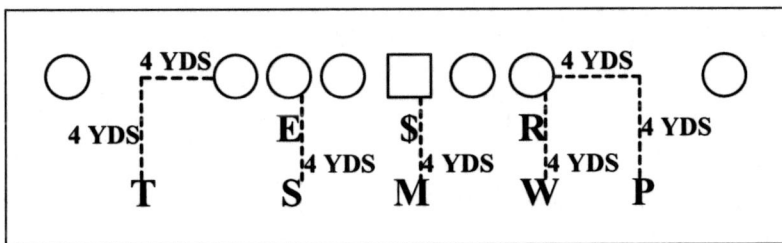

Diagram 6-2. Linebacker alignment

The Tomahawk and Patriot have freedom to move in, out, up, and back from the line of scrimmage. They may align on the line of scrimmage, on a receiver slot receiver, or in the base alignment, depending on game planning. We use their alignment positions as disguise for their actual assignments.

The Sam and Whip linebackers are outside linebacker types. They can play the run effectively, but can also cover in tight areas. The Mike linebacker is a plugger type of linebacker and suited to stopping the run.

We are not concerned with the size of the defensive players we put on the field. We want speed instead of size. When we play bigger offensive linemen, we are very effective in our movement at getting by their blocks. The Rover end this year weighed 185 pounds and made a tremendous amount of tackles.

The big asset to our team was the ability to tackle in space. We work tackling in practice every day. We tackle on Thursday before we play on Friday. If you cannot tackle, you cannot play defense. Our personnel assignment puts wide receiver types at the Tomahawk and Patriot positions. The slower people on our defense are actually our corners.

The thing I like about this scheme is the advantage we gain on the outside. Sixteen-year-olds playing on offense have trouble deciphering the end defender on the line of scrimmage. We constantly change the defender as the end man on the line of scrimmage.

The first year we installed the defense, the offensive line coach talked about how he blocked the front. He said the offensive guard and tackle were responsible for the stack over the tackle. He did not mention the outside linebacker because they are coverage players. It made sense to me to send the outside linebacker to rush the quarterback instead of a bigger slower lineman. I love blitzing the outside linebacker because the offenses turn that responsibility over to a running back or a quarterback's hot read.

I generally send the outside linebacker early in the game to see how the offense is trying to account for them. Most of the players we have in these positions are 4.6 or better. They can get to the quarterback in a hurry.

Our blitz system is simple. When I began to learn this defense from research and other coaches, I had to learn the terminology that went with the blitz schemes. They all had names, and I knew the players would have trouble with remembering the different stunts. We play with many resource players in our defense. They are special-needs students in school. They need special attention in the classroom.

I knew I had to come up with a simple way to call our blitzing game to keep the players from getting confused. In this defense, you must bring pressure from a blitzing scheme. It is not a straight-up defense. You must move and confuse blocking assignments, or you will not survive in this front. I wanted to run many blitzes and keep it simple for them.

The way I did it was to number the linebackers (Diagram 6-3). We numbered the linebackers from left to right. The only people who had to think at all were the outside linebackers because they flipped from side to side. If the Tomahawk was on the left side of the defense, he was #1. If he was on the right side of the defense, he was #5.

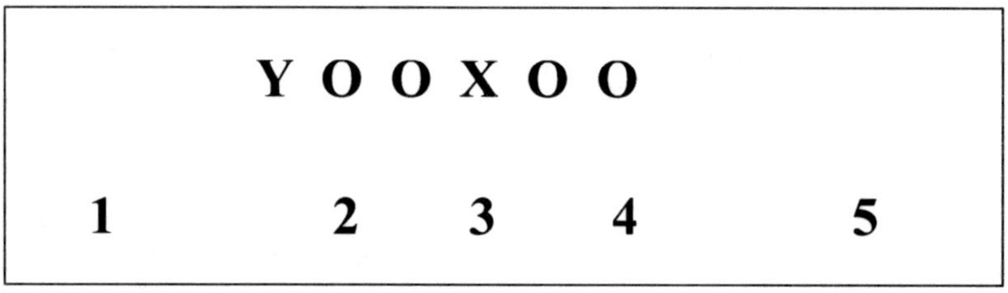

Y O O X O O

1　　　　　**2**　**3**　**4**　　　　**5**

Diagram 6-3. Linebacker numbering

The inside linebacker are #2, #3, and #4. If we call "24," the Sam and Whip linebacker blitz straight ahead. They blitz the opposite gap of the down linemen movement. If the blitz call is "left 24," the defensive line slants to the left, and the Sam linebacker blitzes his B gap (Diagram 6-4). The Whip linebacker knows the Rover goes inside and he blitzes the C gap.

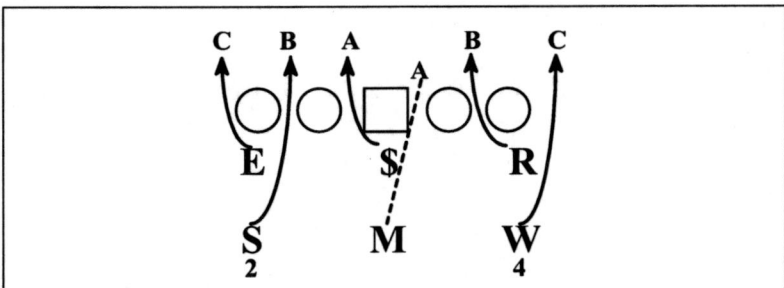

Diagram 6-4. Left 24

This allows us to call a limitless amount of stunts and not confuse our linebackers. We can call double numbers or triple numbers. We can call hundreds of blitz and stunt combinations. If we call "pinch 15," the defensive ends slant to the inside gaps, and the Stud slants into the right A gap. The "15" call gives us a double outside linebacker blitz off the edge. The defensive ends play the B gaps, and the outside linebackers are C-gap players.

An example of a three-digit call is "out 234" (Diagram 6-5). On this blitz, the defensive ends slant outside, and the Stud slants to the left A gap. The "234" call sends all three inside linebackers. The Sam and Whip linebacker blitz the B gap to their side and the Mike linebacker blitzes the right A gap.

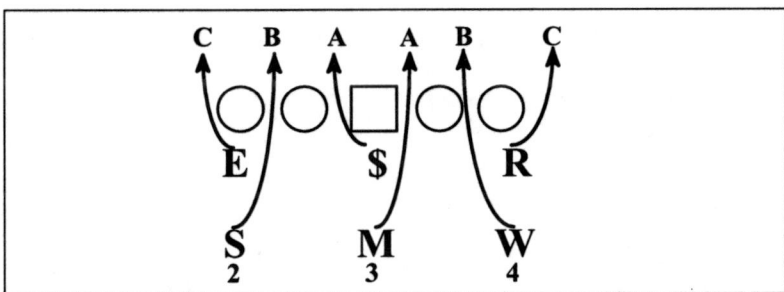

Diagram 6-5. Out 234

The players are playing at full speed and not trying to think where they are supposed to go. In the defense, you either blitz or drop into your coverage responsibility. We created many turnovers with the pressure we bring.

In our game planning each week, we may assign a mark to an offensive player. If the offense has a running back that we mark, that means to hit him on every blitz involving him. We run past all other defenders. We do not want to contact a blocker unless absolutely necessary.

We had two teams on our schedule that ran a double wing formation with two tight ends. In the last three years, I have not substituted linemen for my players. I want the speed on the field. If you do not see double wing in this area, you will soon. It is like a disease. It travels.

When we play these teams, we keep all the base players in the game. We have a smallish lineup, but we depend on speed to be the equalizer. The Tomahawk and Patriot linebackers walk up tight to the line of scrimmage on the outsides of the wing players (Diagram 6-6). They come off the edge, looking for the fullback on the power play. They want to wrong-arm him. If they cannot wrong-arm, they fall down and create a pile. If they want to play in a Neanderthal style of play, we do it.

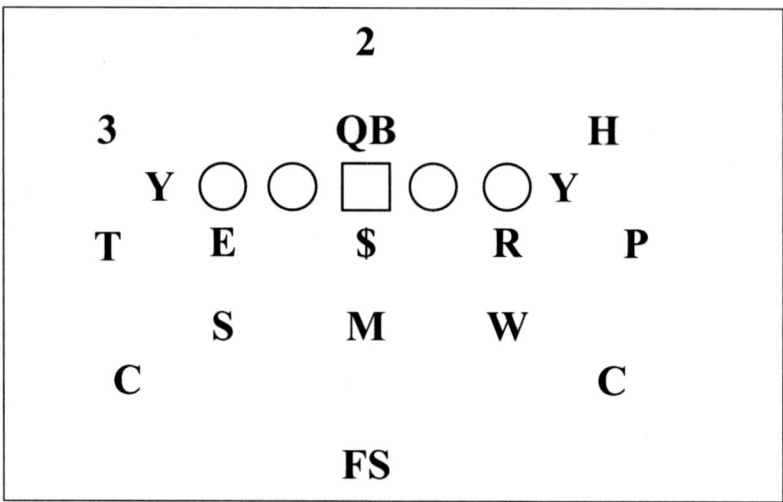

Diagram 6-6. Double-wing adjustment

Everyone else aligns in their normal position and runs the stunts and blitzes as normal. We run our stunts and blitzes off the alignment on the field or by their motion scheme. That is a game planning decision that we can automatic. The Mike linebacker makes the call, when he sees the motion.

When we played Northgate High School, they were 8-0 at the time. They ran the double wing formation. Our offense did not touch the ball until two minutes to go in the first quarter. We kicked off, and they hit us with a big play-action pass on the first play of the game. They onside kicked the kickoff and recovered. They hit a long play-action pass, but only got a field goal out of that possession. They onside kicked and recovered again. They got another field goal, and we were down 12-0 and had not run an offensive play. We made some adjustments on defense and won the game 78-12.

Since we play with smaller players, our tackles are gang tackles. We get people to the football. We pursue and swarm the ball. If the wing goes in motion, our corners are cross-keying the other side of the formation.

In practice, we coach the Tomahawk and Patriot on two different kinds of blocks. If they run the sweep, the guard pulls and tries to loop around the linebacker. On the power, the fullback comes at the linebacker and tries to kick him to the outside. The angle on the two blocks is different. With the looping guard, the linebacker attacks his outside shoulder. The fullback tries to kick him out, and he attacks the inside shoulder of the fullback. If the wing goes in motion, he looks for the counter coming away from the motion.

If the formation is a triple set, we like to run cover 3 or cover 1 (Diagram 6-7). The Tomahawk walks out and aligns on the #2 receiver. If we play cover 3, the Tomahawk is a flat/curl dropper. He drops to the short zone to that side. If we play cover 1, he has the #2 receiver in man coverage. To the inside, we want to keep the integrity of the box.

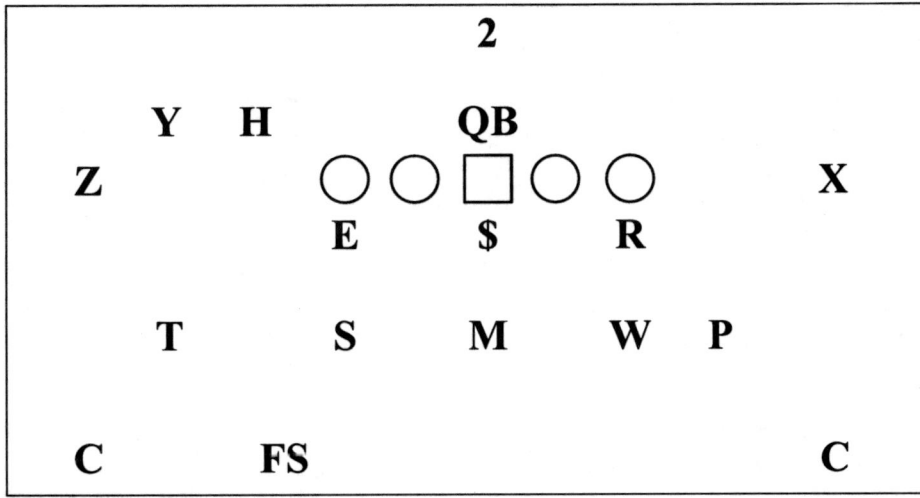

Diagram 6-7. Trips formation

If we played a 4-2 defense, the linebacker would be over the guards. This alignment is like the 4-2, even though we stay in the stack position. We rush the three down linemen, and one of the linebackers will come on the blitz to give us four-man pressure. We end up in a 4-2 after they snap the ball.

If the offense empties the backfield, we like to keep two linebackers in the box (Diagram 6-8). We want to have five defenders in the box. That keeps two linebackers

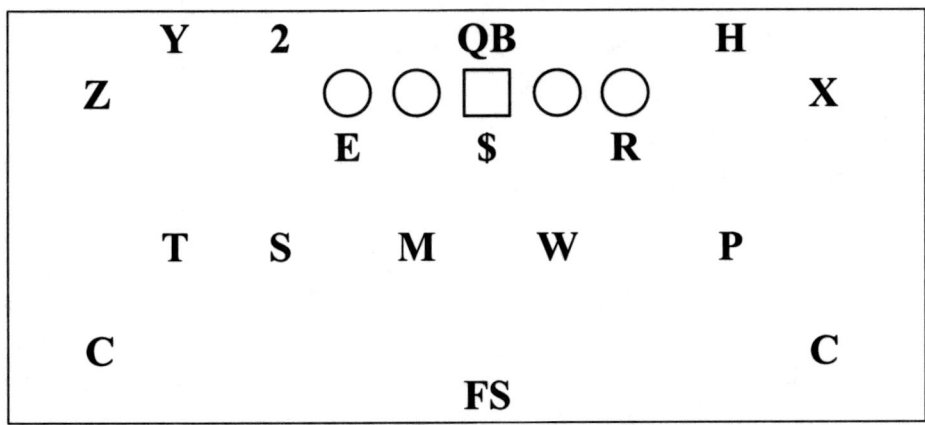

Diagram 6-8. Empty

in the box to defend the quarterback run. With the 3x2 formation, we adjust to the three-receiver side, as we did in the trips set. To the two-receiver side, we walk the Patriot out to cover the second receiver to the weakside. We can play cover-3 zone or go to a cover-1 man-free scheme.

The other alternative we had to the weakside was to expand the Patriot over the slot receiver to that side and play cover 4 or quarter coverage. The Patriot and corner play a cover-4 zone on the slot and wide receivers. They key the slot receiver and play according to what he does.

This year, our Sam linebacker was capable of moving back to the hash. He could play that seam better than the Patriot could. If we pulled the Sam linebacker back to the hash, the free safety moved over into the other half field and the Patriot moved into the Sam position. Next year, we may have to do something different, but we will figure it out.

If we get hurt with the running quarterback in the empty set, we bring the third linebacker back into the box and play the quarterback for the run. When we do that, we give up the bubble screen and the hitch patterns, but we will run those plays down with our speed.

The offense will try to overload the three-man front and outflank the linebacker (Diagram 6-9). The offense can put an offensive lineman over in the formation or move a tight end or blocking back into a wing set outside the tight end. If the offense unbalances the blocking side, we can do two different things. The first thing we can do is overshift the front, and everyone moves over one man in his defensive alignment.

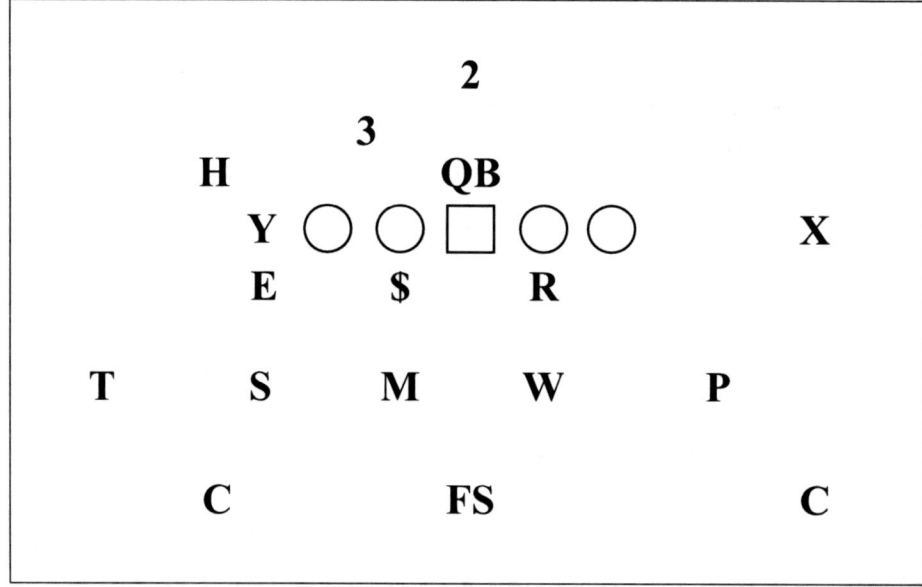

Diagram 6-9. Overload shift (base)

If we overshift the defensive line, we play our base defense, and nothing changes with the stunts, line movements, or blitzes. We do the same thing, except we do it from one gap beyond the center.

The second way we play the overload is to blitz into the overload. We call the blitz "thunder and lightning." Lightning is a left direction for the blitzing linebackers (Diagram 6-10). Thunder is a right blitz. However, we did not run the gap exchange blitz. The linebackers blitzed over one gap. The Sam linebacker and the Eagle end in a gap exchange blitz, switch gaps. On an out movement by the end and a blitz by the Sam linebacker, the Sam linebacker blitzed B gap and the end slants into the C gap.

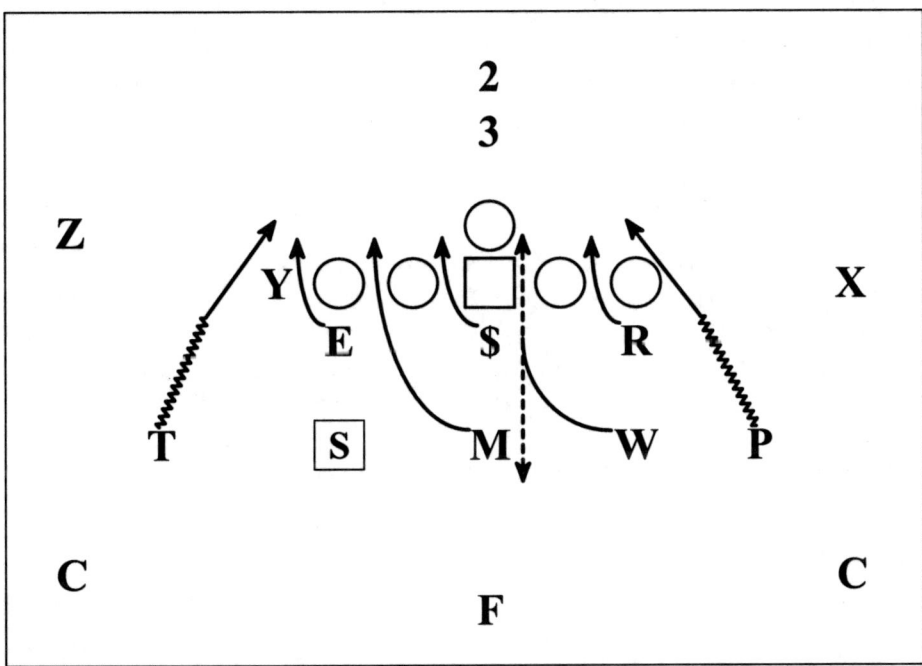

Diagram 6-10. Lightning

In a lightning blitz, the Eagle slants into the C gap, but the Mike linebacker blitzing over one gap fills the B gap. The Stud nose slants into the left A gap. The Whip linebacker blitzes into the backside A gap, and the Rover end slants into the backside B gap. The Tomahawk on flow to him is the D-gap player. The Sam linebacker has no gap and is a free-hitter.

The Sam linebacker is a freelance defender. If the ball runs in his direction, he can fill inside or outside, depending on how the Tomahawk plays. If the Tomahawk were to spill the play to the outside, the Sam linebacker is in position to make that play. If the play is a play-action pass, he locks on the tight end or #2 receiver to that side. The thunder stunt is the same thing going to the right. In that case, the Whip linebacker is the free-hitter.

The Sam and Whip linebackers know when they are free. On the snap of the ball, they may want to shuffle back to stay out of the traffic. It also gives him a good look at the #2 receiver.

This stunt brings the down linemen and the linebacker in the same direction. We like to run the thunder and lightning against a bunched set or a tight wing set. If the offense aligns with 21 personnel, we can run the lightning stunt to the tight end. If that is the tendency of the offense, we can run the thunder and lightning as a regular stunt. It does not have to be an overload.

This year, I did less coaching than I ever have. In 2004, when we took over here, I coached my butt off, and we went 1-9. This year, I coached considerably less than I did in 2004, and we went 13-1 and won the state championship. When you have better players who have experience, you do not need to work as hard. At least you can put your efforts into improving other parts of the scheme.

When you have better players, you coach them less so you do not mess them up. I let them play and make plays. The group we had this year were instinctive players.

We have teams that use a super-overload. They have a tight end set with two wings outside the tight end. We call the "Lion" stunt (Diagram 6-11). The adjustment to this set is a combination of the overshift and lightning stunt. We move the down linemen over one full man and run a lightning stunt into the overload. The offense has created so many gaps to one side that we have to overshift the front and slant into the overload.

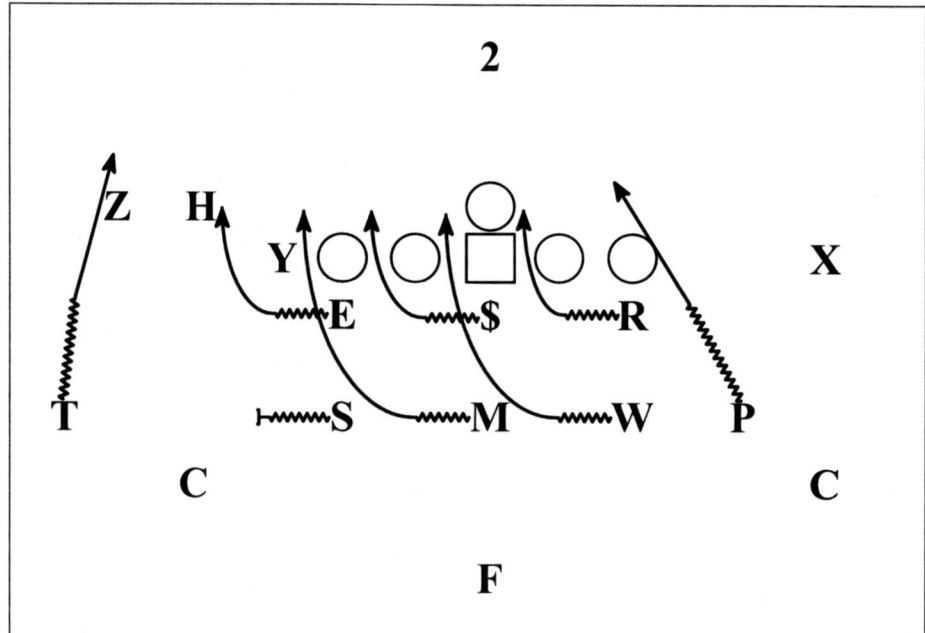

Diagram 6-11. Lion

If we need to call the front to the other side, we call "Tiger." We have a tight end and two leverage blockers to the outside. We have to get the bodies in that direction. I start teaching my Mike linebackers at the beginning of the year to recognize this set. If they do not adjust to it the first time the offense runs it, we may have to call a time-out to get them on the right page.

When you play thunder and lightning, you have to be sound to the backside if the offense runs the counter play (Diagram #12). When we run thunder or lightning, the linebackers involved with the stunt have a key as they start the stunt. Whatever the opponent does in their counter play, we give our linebackers a blocker to key. It could be the frontside tackle or guard. If we run the lightning stunt, the Whip and Mike linebackers are running the over blitzes. They read the frontside guard and tackle as they start the blitz path. On the third step, they will know where to go.

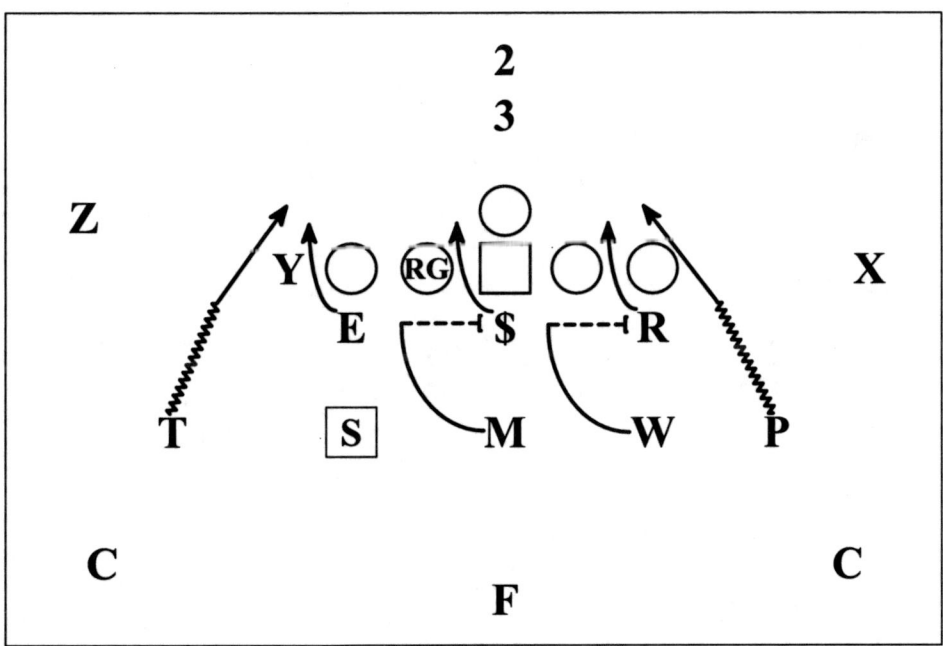

Diagram 6-12. Lightning counter

If the guard or tackle pulls toward them, they redirect their charges on the third step. The Whip linebacker redirects back into the C gap to his side, and the Mike linebacker redirects into the backside A gap. The Rover end slants into the B gap and plays football. We have the Mike in the A gap, Rover in the B gap, Whip linebacker in the C gap, and the Patriot comes up on the outside in the D gap. The Sam linebacker is to the side of the stunt. When the action counters to the backside, he plays the frontside B gap for the cutback and pursues.

We drill this redirection every day in practice, and they have gotten good at the technique. We can be ultra-aggressive to the frontside and prepared to play the counter if it occurs. We were not very good at the redirect when we started doing it. When we worked on it and were persistent in the training, we became very good at that action. Some of our linebackers are so good at reading the counter, they see it on the first step of the guard. It does not look like a lightning stunt because they read it so quickly.

We see the triple option from the opponents we play (Diagram 6-13). I like to bring the Tomahawk up on the line of scrimmage and let him take the dive back in the outside veer. The Sam linebacker to that side has the quarterback, which is hard for him. The dive back comes right up in his face. If he takes the dive, the quarterback pulls the ball, and we are in trouble.

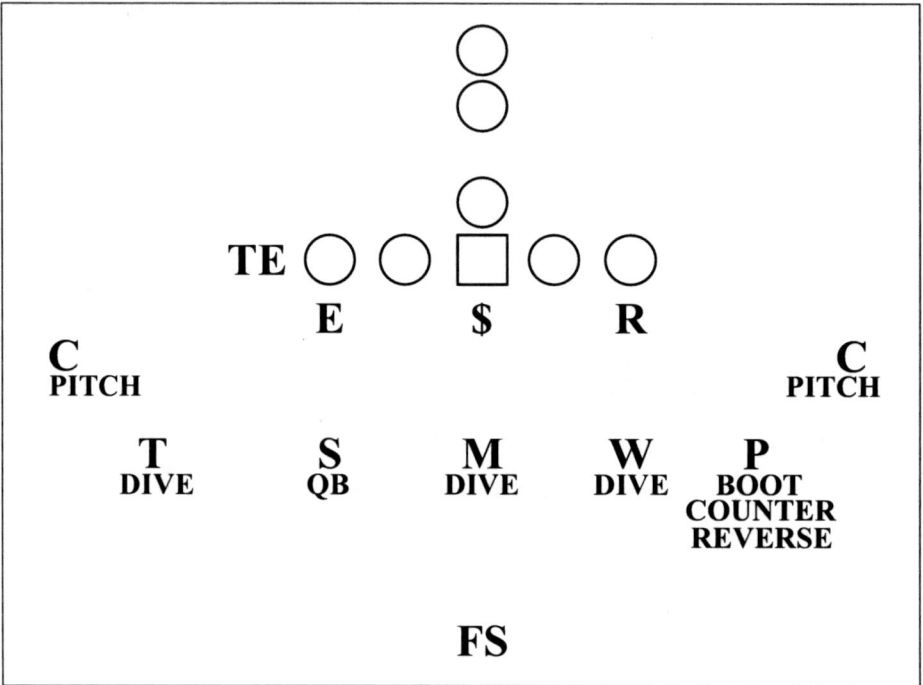

Diagram 6-13. Triple option

You have to drill that into the Sam and Whip linebackers. The corner to that side has the pitchback. If they run the ball on an inside veer play, the Mike linebacker and backside linebacker play the dive. The Patriot to the backside plays the bootleg, counter, and reverse.

The secret to playing a triple option team is not to wait to the week you play them to work on the triple option. You must prepare all during the season if you have an option team on your schedule. We run triple option drill weekly. Preparation is the key for playing an option team. The defense must play assignment football.

In the championship game, I coached against a coach who has run the triple option longer than I have been alive. Someone told me he would figure out what we do by game time. He was right. He scored on his first two drives. In the game, there were seven lead changes. We ended up winning the game in a two-minute drill at the end of the game. We won 40-37.

We have a hammer call we use in a passing situation or if we want to lock up a star receiver. The hammer call is a man-under press technique by the Tomahawk and Sam linebacker. We press the wide receiver and slot with the Tomahawk and Sam linebacker and play a cover-3 corner behind them. We can play double hammer or use the hammer call for one receiver. If we call "hammer 85," we play press-man coverage on #85 and play a deep zone behind it.

The hammer call makes the quarterback hold the ball. When he holds the ball, our rush can get to him. We ran it twice in the championship and got two sacks. If I want to pressure on third down or double-team a receiver, I call the defense.

When we blitz, there are holes all over the coverage. However, we blitz fast people, and the quarterback does not have time to find those holes. They get into the quarterback's face quickly.

In practice, when our players get lazy and show their blitzes, I stop that immediately. If they show their blitzes, the offense blocks them. Blitzing from depth is good, but may not be good enough to get home. We bluff the blitz. When we show blitz, we always want to fake where we are not going. If they come up to the right side of a blocker, they will blitz to the left side. We must practice all those bluffs. When they tip or start early, I stop them and tell them, "Show me later." They understand what I want.

If we play cover 3, the corners come up into a press alignment. When the quarterback gets under the center or starts to call for the ball in the shotgun, the corners bail out into their third. We try to keep the offense honest with our disguises. Disguise is like a skill, and you must work on it in practice.

We are like any other high school program. If we have athletes who can play man coverage, we play it. This year, we played about 80 percent zone coverage. We had good corners, but they doubled at wide receiver and were more interested in catching the ball than playing defense.

7

Odd Stack 3-5-3 Defensive Package

Maurice Dixon
North Gwinnett High School, Georgia
2010

I have been lucky to be on the speaking circuit lately. It is an honor to be here. I am a blunt, straight-up person. What I want to do is to help you find something that you can take back and use with your team. I like these clinics because you get to meet so many people and talk a lot of football. We had a big game this year. We opened up with Prattville, Alabama. They ranked in the top five or six in the nation. Prattville played in the Classic in Cincinnati a couple of years ago. I have been in the Cincinnati area and I have talked to the coaches at Colerain High School and St. Xavier High School. What we talked about with them came in handy when we played Prattville.

People come to clinics for different reasons. I sat up in the room last night with a bunch of local coaches and we talked a lot of football. That is what the clinics are all about. I want to stay on task and shoot through some things I think will help you. When I sit down to talk football with coaches, I am not necessarily interested in the defense you run. I want to know what you run, where it came from, and why you run it.

When I started out in coaching, we ran a 50 defense. At the next job I had, we ran a 4-2 type of defense. When I went to Knott County Central in Kentucky, we ran a 50 slant defense. We played with 145-pound tackles and a noseguard, and we slanted them strong and weak. That scheme came back into play when we put the defense in that we run now. I went to Lexington Catholic to coach, and we installed the 4-3 defense and ran it for 14 years. We played cover 3 and cover 2 and stunted occasionally. When I went to Hazard High School, we had some good-looking athletes. We had good safeties when I was there. At Hazard, we played a lot of 4-3 with quarters coverage. I like the quarters coverage, but we were not a big pressure type of team. I had good athletes, and I did not want to get in their way. However, I did not trust them enough to play straight man-to-man.

Next, I went to North Broward Prep in Florida. We ran a 4-3 defense with the under front. We took our Sam linebacker, angled him, and played quarter coverage over the top of that alignment. When we started doing that, we brought more pressure into our scheme.

When I went to North Gwinnett High School, Bob Sphire was the head coach. He was a spread offensive coach that wanted the tempo of the game run as fast as possible. He liked the 3-5 because of the fit, the tempo, and the way it helped us in practice. This defense fits his offensive ideas. He told us the opponent will bust a long touchdown on you sometimes, but the turnovers we will produce will outweigh the risks.

The thing I liked about the 4-3 defense was the shade techniques we played and our ability to force the double-teams. However, I wanted to slant and go at the offense in two or three different ways. This is what we came up with and we play it well.

North Gwinnett High School

I want to show you some things about our school:

- Located in Suwannee, GA
- 3,400 students
- Gwinnett county public schools
  - ✓ 126 schools in county
  - ✓ 18 5A schools in our county
  - ✓ 4 5A schools in our town
- GHSAA, Region 7, Class 5A
- We were the fourth staff in four seasons when hired
- Prior to our arrival, playoffs three times in 52-year history
- Outstanding administration

Before we got there, North Gwinnett had been knocked around a lot. We put together a great staff. I was a head coach for 12 years, and I know you must have a good staff to win. You have to find people that fit what you are planning. If you are a young coach and working with a head coach or an older coach, you will learn something every day. No matter what you do, it always comes down to being in a great situation, being around good people, and having an opportunity to be successful. I do not care where you go or how many different jobs you have, that is what you are looking for. If you find that, get the best out of it and whatever happens will happen.

We have had a lot of success, but we have not won the state championship yet. We have to compete with 18 other 5A programs in our county, and we had to do something different to build our image and increase our attractiveness to potential athletes. We started to play nationally ranked teams like Prattville. That stirred the interest in our school.

Quickly, I want to show you our defensive philosophy.

Program Philosophy

- Lexington Catholic offensive and defensive philosophies matched, ending in 2005 state championship
- Help establish tempo; can control it on both sides of the ball
- Exciting style of play
- Play in the extremes
- Bob Sphire philosophy: Throw it all at them at once, and then go back and reteach; no spoon feeding

Fifteen minutes into our spring training, you will see the offense and defense going at each other 90 miles an hour. It is blood and guts in a blitz period. We have a five-minute blitz period where someone is going to win and someone is going to lose. You have six coaches and 50 players on each side of the ball going at it. We must have that part of our package in the first day of spring practice.

Package Philosophy

We have a package philosophy. This is not clinic talk. This is what we do:
- Be multiple but simple
- More than one way to defend a scheme; never be locked into a front/coverage; never be dictated to…
- Sound against the option
- The ability to attack and overload any blocking scheme
- Ability to play a shade technique, a slant technique, and a read technique
- Zone and man coverage with ironclad adjustments
- Our scheme forces our opponent to adjust, not vice versa

Never be dictated to is a mind-set. If you do not watch yourself, particularly on defense, you will worry about what the offense is doing. You need to run the defense and let the offense worry about how to handle your defense. You have to work harder than the offensive coaches to cover all the things they run. If you are not careful, you will end up with too much defense. You can play this defense against teams that are bigger, faster, and better and hold your own. Our scheme is going to force the opponent to adjust. The offensive tackle will not see one technique from the defender all night long.

We are going to disguise what we do. There is movement before the snap and movement after the snap. We are going to disguise the coverage and stem the line. We will walk the linebacker and safety men up, back, and do many different things.

We want to present as many looks as possible to force our opponent to spend practice time preparing for us. We want to create a major burden for them. We want them to spend more time on us than on anyone else that they play. Strategically and tactically, we want to be more creative and more intelligent than anyone we face. We want to play in the extremes.

We want to force our opponent to make decisions before and after the snap. Never allow them to just line up and tee off on you. Line up one way, and attack out of another look. After watching us on film, we want two individuals to be concerned. We want the quarterback to be concerned and the head coach to be concerned about the quarterback. We want him to worry about protecting the quarterback. The opponent has to find ways to protect their quarterback. When they see the quarterback getting killed on film, they will adjust their practice schedule.

You do not have to hit the quarterback every time, but you have to be around him. That makes him uncomfortable in the pocket.

The 3 5 3 defense provides the best chance to adapt to all styles of play. Every year we play the defense it has changed. One year, we played with a stunting front and cover 1 and zero in the secondary. Now, we play a lot of match-up zone coverage. We are getting the same results as we did in man coverage, but it allows us to play the run better. In this coverage, we can play the four vertical patterns. We have to tweak the defense and improve the package because of the teams we are starting to schedule.

We are an attack, gap-control defense. All defensive linemen are responsible for one gap that is pre-determined by the huddle call. We will line up pre-snap and play great technique by attacking the offensive linemen or the tight end, or we will slant to our gap responsibility using our quickness to offset our opponent. All linebackers are two-gap players depending on flow. The outside Buck and Will linebackers play either B gap or C gap. On flow to them, they play C gap. On flow away, they play B gap.

Our goal is always to outplay the other team's defense. Stats give you an indication of how your defense is playing. However, there are only three stats we are concerned with. They are *points allowed, turnover ratio,* and *quarterback touches.*

It is imperative that the defense gives the ball to the offense on turnovers as much as possible. On average, each team will have 12 offensive possessions per game. If we can take the ball away on three of those possessions, we have eliminated their scoring opportunities by 25 percent. You do not always have to have highly talented athletes to play defense. The one thing that you must possess is a great desire to get to the ball. This is something that we stress and practice daily.

We are complicated, and we have a lot of personnel packages. We had a number of injuries last year. Teams try to formation us to dictate our fronts and coverages. If you do only one thing in your adjustment, the offense is dictating to you how to play. We set our defense to what the offense does best and make our adjustments to what they do. We are going to force the offense to do other things. In the league we play in, you must stop the run. I know they throw the ball more in Kentucky than we do in our league. However, if the ball is in front of your defensive backs and it is not going over your heads, you have a chance.

From 2006 to 2009, we have added to and adapted our package. The first year, we played more base than anything. In the following years, we added coverage packages and blitz packages to fit our personnel. However, we continued to play top programs from across the nation.

We divide our defense into three component parts. The front is made of the down linemen and three linebackers. They play in three tandems. The Mike linebacker and nose tackle are one of the tandem parts. The Buck and Will linebackers and the defensive ends are the other two parts.

Scheme Is Divided Into Three Parts

- Front six defenders play in three tandems
  - ✓ DL must play shade technique, master slant technique
  - ✓ LB flow read and adjustments, primary run defenders
- Adjusters: Rover, dog, and free
  - ✓ Rover is LB/DB, dog FB/LB
  - ✓ Free can be dog type player (big on run support)
- Corners
  - ✓ Must be able to play 1/4, 1/3, zone coverage, and man (no primary run support)

In our base alignment, we play with two defensive ends aligned in a 4 technique head-up the offensive tackles (Diagram 7-1). We have a nose tackle in a 0 technique head-up the center. We play with three linebackers in a stack position behind the down linemen. They are five yards off the ball. The Buck linebacker aligns to the tight end side. The Mike linebacker aligns in the middle, and the Will linebacker aligns away from the tight end. The Rover is a strong-safety type that goes to the tight end side. The dog is the fullback/linebacker type and plays opposite the Rover. In the base alignment, the corners are one yard inside and seven yards deep on the wide receivers. That alignment will change with our coverages. The free safety is 11 yards deep in the middle of the defense.

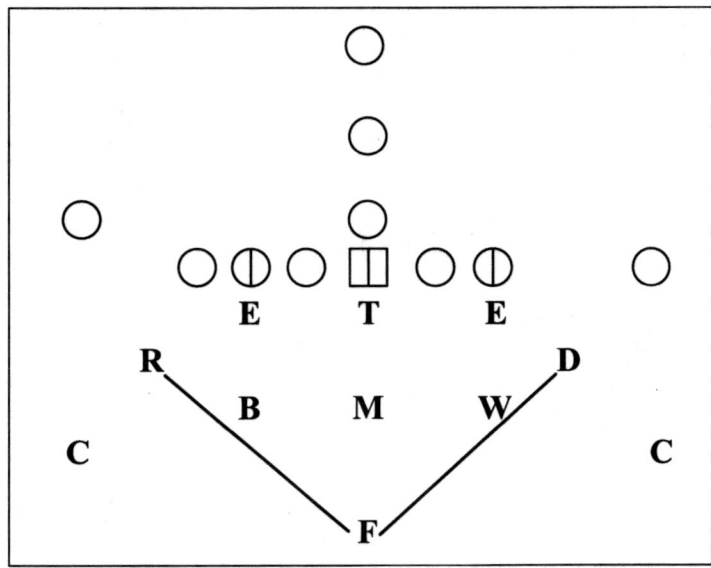

Diagram 7-1. Base 3-5-3, cover 3

When we slant, we have to utilize our speed. We use what we call a *veer slant*. We do the exact same thing an offensive tackle does on a veer block. When we slant, we are going inside, keeping the shoulders parallel to the line of scrimmage. We rip with the outside arm and get skinny coming inside. If we meet a trap blocker, we use a wrong-arm technique. We played small players at this position last year. People could not block us, and we were getting in the backfield.

Our linebackers are no different from anyone else playing this defense. The Mike and Buck linebackers read the fullback, and the Will linebacker reads the tailback in a two-back set. They play flow. If there is a one-back set, they all read the single back on their first step.

The corners must be able to play quarters, thirds, and man coverage. We do not teach press man coverage. We play five yards off the receivers. If we have corners that can cover, we play straight. However, we switch most in-and-out routes and banjo the coverage. The corner plays the hips of the receiver and keys where he is going. The *banjo technique* is all about the eyes. The corner aligns on the outside hip, and if it goes to the inside, there will be some type of out pattern coming to him. This has worked very well for us. When our personnel get better and are ready, I will let them press, but that all happens in practice.

We played five different option schemes this year. The free safety is the extra man in the option scheme. He has to be big in run support. In the four years I have been at North Gwinnett, we have had two free safeties. Both of them were average football players with below-average speed, but you could not block them.

I want to get into the nuts and bolts of what we do. These are our main elements of our defense.

Main Elements

- 30 stack technique fronts (Strong, 55, 55 strong, stack)
- Change-up fronts (Bear, Okie, angle)
- Aggressive slant package, which enables us to use speed over size
- Relentless pressure package where we can bring four, five, six, and possibly seven defenders
- Three zone coverages and three man coverages with adjustments that are sound in all situations

In the strong front, we shade the ends and nose to the strongside of the set. The tackle shades the center to the strongside. The ends play a 5 technique to strength and a 4i technique to the weakside. The Buck linebacker is at five yards in a 4i technique. The Mike linebacker aligns at five yards in a weakside shade on the center. The Will linebacker is at five yards in a 5 technique. The dog and Rover backs are 3x3 yards outside the tight end. The corners are 7x1 yards off the wide receivers, and the free safety is 11 yards deep over the center.

In the *55 front*, the defensive ends move into a 5 technique on the outside shoulder of the offensive tackles. The Buck and Will linebackers move up to three-and-a-half yards, and the Mike linebacker moves back to six yards. The perimeter players have the same alignment as the strong front.

The *55 strong* is a combination of the two fronts (Diagram 7-2). The ends align in 5 techniques, and the nose aligns in a strong shade as he did in the strong front. The linebacker depth is five yards on this front, and the perimeter players are the same.

The *stack front* moves the defensive end into a 4 technique head-up the offensive tackles. Everyone else in this front is the same as the base front.

We can change up the fronts with Bear, Okie, and angle fronts. In the Bear front, the defensive end moves into a 3-technique alignment, and the Buck and Will linebackers move to the outside in a 6 technique on the tight end or a 5 technique on the tackle. We like to stunt from the Bear front (Diagram 7-3). The *Okie front* is a straight 5-2 defensive alignment. Because we play so many run teams, we had to get defenders closer to the line of scrimmage. We walk the Rover up on the tight end, and he plays hip to hip on the line of scrimmage and does not come off for pass coverage.

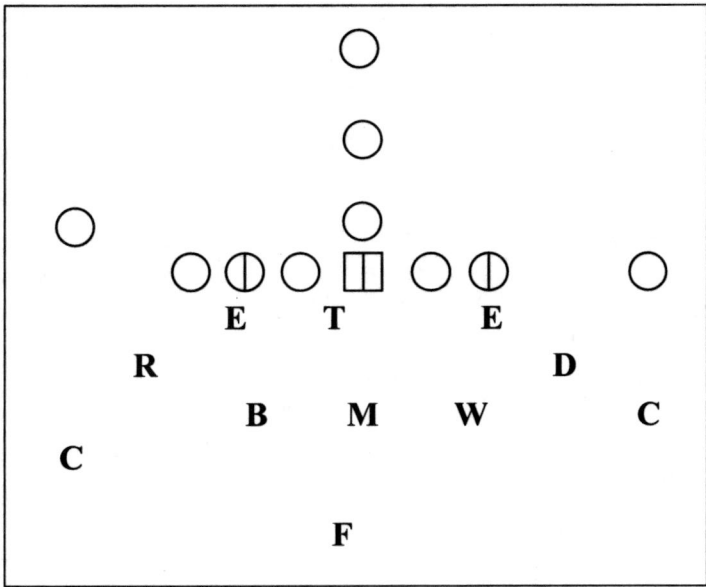

Diagram 7-2. 55 strong

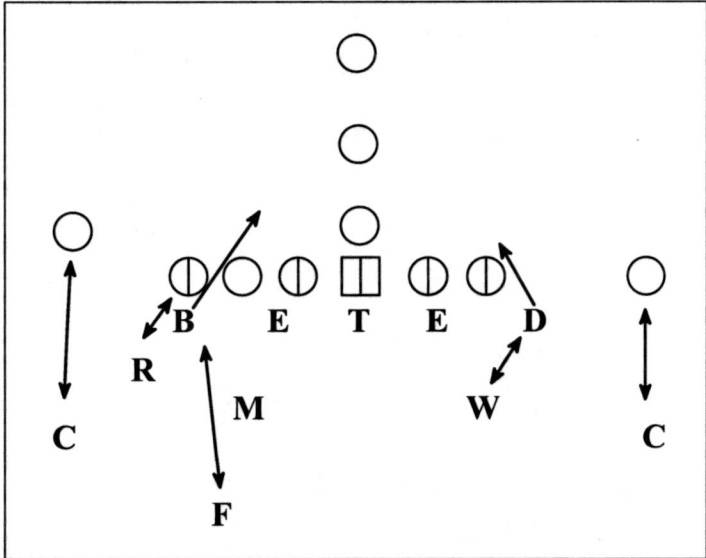

Diagram 7-3. Bear front

The *angle front* is our 4-2 look (Diagram 7-4). We shift the down linemen to the weakside and walk the Buck linebacker down into a 6-technique position on the tight end. The strongside defensive end aligns in a 3 technique, and the end to the weakside aligns in a 5 technique. The nose tackle moves to a 1 technique to the weakside. The Mike and Will linebackers align in stack positions behind the 3- and 1-technique linemen.

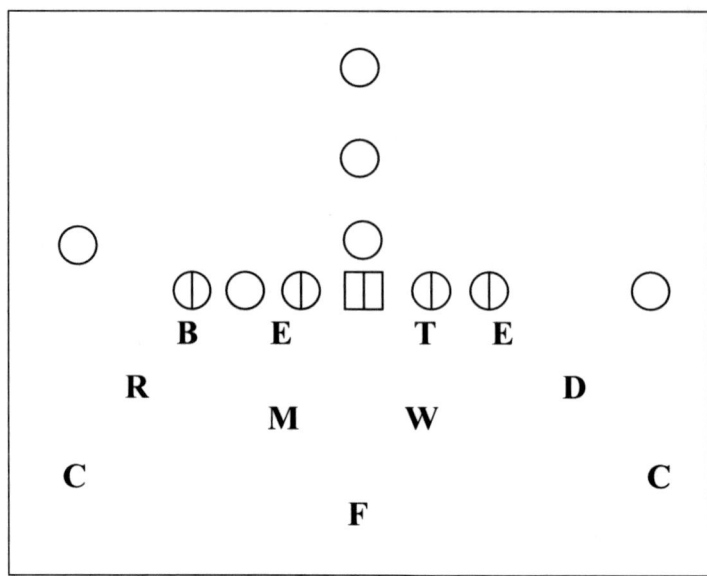

Diagram 7-4. Angle front

We can move the three-man front as a unit with *slash, whiz, pinch*, and *out calls*. The slash and whiz calls are slant calls to the strongside and weakside (Diagram 7-5). The nose tackle slants to the strong A gap and uses an evasive technique. He rips to the offensive lineman's heels with his eyes inside. The defensive ends do the same thing, and the linebacker steps opposite the defensive line move. The whiz move is the same movement weak. The pinch movement is an inside movement by the ends. The out movement is the opposite movement by the defensive ends.

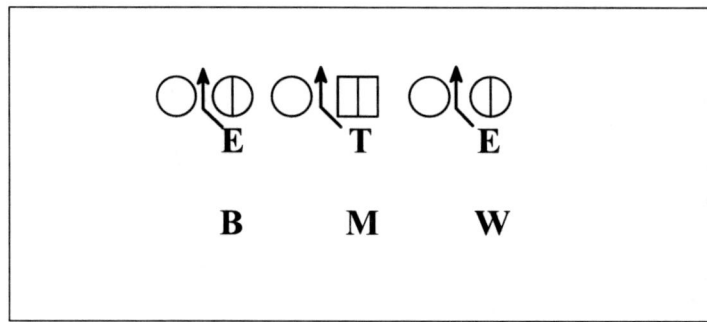

Diagram 7-5. Slash

We will set our defensive strength to the tight end 80 percent of the time. We can set the strength to the field or boundary (if we have scouted tendencies). We have the ability to set the strength to the strong receiver side. We also have the ability to use a "check with me" system, which determines our front, based upon our opponent's offensive formation.

If the offensive set is balanced in the middle of the field, we will always declare the strongside to our left because most teams are right-handed. Our Mike will give a *lucky* or *ringo call*, which is left and right for the front. If the tight end lines up on the left, Mike will yell, "Lucky, lucky." Our safeties will give *lightning* and *rocket calls*, which is the passing strength of the formation.

When we make our defensive calls, the first thing we call is personnel. We call the front, stunt, second stunt, and the coverage.

Defensive Calls

- Personnel
- Front (with tag)
- Stunt (with tag)
- Second stunt (with tag)
- Coverage (with tag)

Example: Strong Green

In this defense, the front is a strong front and green coverage, which is cover 3. There is nothing tagged which means we are playing base defense and cover 3.

Example: 55 Blood Cross Green Disguise

In this defense, we align in a 55 front with a blood-cross stunt by the linebackers. Blood is a strongside, two-linebacker stunt. The coverage is cover 3, but we are going to align in another shell and move to cover 3. We align in disguise coverage and roll to a cover 3 in the secondary. We either use wristbands with the defensive call, we signal the defense, or I yell what I want.

The linebackers have four flow reads. They read fast, hard, split, and counter flows. The fast-flow read for the linebackers is a wide play to the outside (sweep). The hard reads are both backs in the same hole with the ball inside (isolation). Split flow is one back inside and one outside (option). Counter flow starts one way and goes the other (misdirection).

The overhang linebackers are the cutback players. We use *pull calls* to get them into different alignments. We can pull them to the line of scrimmage if we like. We have gotten into zone blitzes and used the pull call to get the linebacker into a position to blitz. We can pull the linebackers into double coverage on a receiver.

In the *55 front*, the linebackers align in a 4i technique at three-and-a-half yards deep. They read the near back through the guard. If we align a defensive end in the 4i technique, his read is the same as the linebackers.

Coverage

We play six primary coverages:
- Green = Three-deep
- Blue = Two-deep
- Orange = Four-deep
- White = Four-match
- Purple = Five-match
- Black = Man-free

I do not have time to get into the coverages, but we can change the force players by adding words or running blitzes or stunts. We can force with the corner, Rover, dog, linebacker, defensive end, or free safety. An example of the coverage is *strong white* (Diagram 7-6). This coverage is set against a trips set. The Will linebacker makes a pull call and shifts the backers to the openside to cover the gaps. The Rover is a flat player to the trips side. The corners align at 7x1 and play a quarter of the field. The free safety aligns 10 yards deep, splitting the #1 and #2 receivers, and plays a quarter of the field. However, he is keying the #3 receiver strong.

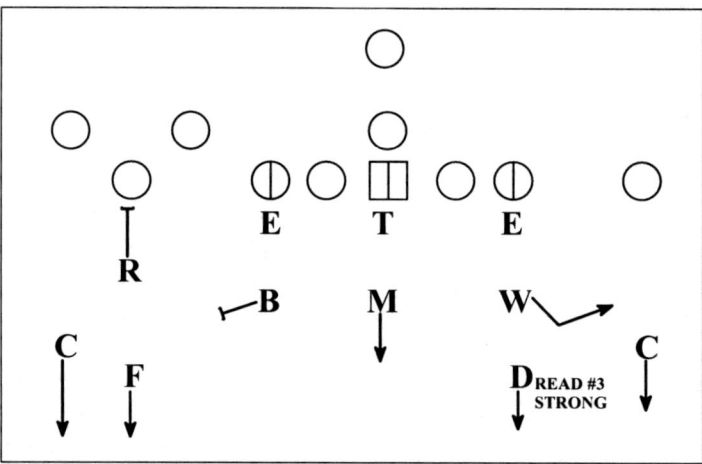

Diagram 7-6. Strong white (four-match)

This is a quarter-coverage defense. In our coverages, we number the receivers moving from the sideline to the inside (Diagram 7-7). The widest receiver is the #1 receiver. The next widest receiver is the #2 receiver. The third receiver in the trips set or the running back in the backfield is the #3 receiver. We number the receivers from the sideline to both sides. In a quarters coverage, the #2 receiver will tell everyone how to play the coverage.

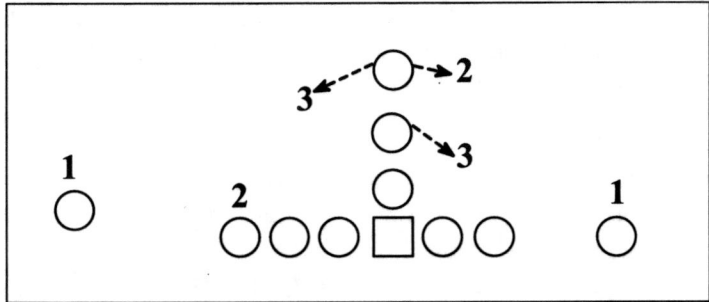

Diagram 7-7. Numbering of receivers

We move our defense at all levels. In the defensive line, we run line games between the defensive ends and the nose tackle. The line game I am going to show you is a *loop weak* (Diagram 7-8). I will show this from the Bear front. The 0 technique twists to the weakside B gap. He comes off the butt of the defensive end. He is doing the loop technique. The weakside defensive end crashes the A gap and becomes the penetrator. The defensive end goes first and wants to occupy the guard and hold the center from getting outside. The strongside defensive end is B-gap player. The Buck linebacker is aligned in a 6 technique and slants into the C gap. The Mike linebacker is aligned at five yards and is head-up the center, and the Will linebacker plays a 5 technique.

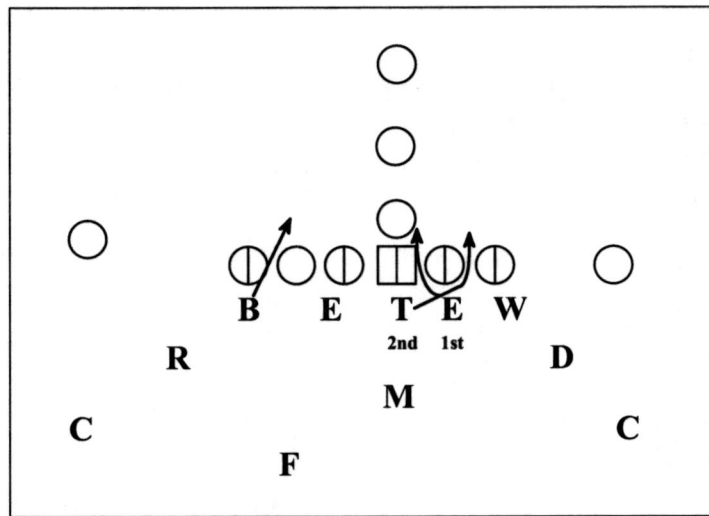

Diagram 7-8. Loop weak

At the second level, we can run one-, two-, and three-man stunts involving the Buck, Mike, Will, Rover, or dog. This gives a four-, five- or six-man pressure scheme. If we want to send one blitz runner, we simply call the position we want to blitz. If we call *55 Buck*, the Buck linebacker shoots the B gap. That is his gap of responsibility and he blows it. If we call *55 Rover*, the Rover blitzes off the edge of the defense. We can also add the word *twist* to the call and the down lineman and the linebacker run an in-and-out movement from their position. A *Buck twist* call sends the defensive end into the B gap and the Buck linebacker blitzes the C gap.

If we want to bring five-man pressure, we add another linebacker into the stunt. We have a war-and-blood package. That package brings two linebackers from the same side. The *war stunt* for us is the Mike and Will linebackers running through their gaps to the weakside of the defense (Diagram 7-9). The Mike linebacker blitzes the A gap, and the Will linebacker blitzes the B gap. The nose tackle slants into the strongside A gap. The defensive ends on these packages are C-gap players. If we run a *blood stunt*, the Mike and Buck linebackers run through their gaps on the strongside. It is the opposite stunt to the other side.

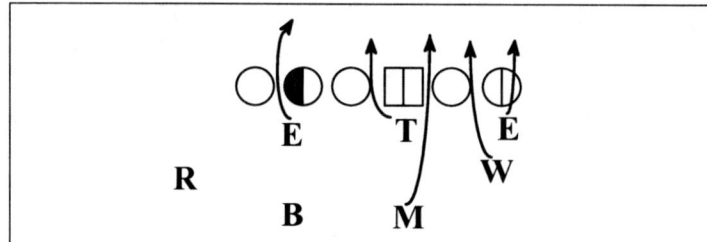

Diagram 7-9. War weak

If we want to add a sixth man to the scheme, we tag another linebacker stunt. We just showed you the war stunt. This time, we will tag that stunt with a different look, plus we add a Buck twist to the strongside. We add X to the war stunt and switch the gaps for the Mike and Will linebackers. The stunt is *55 war X switch Buck twist* (Diagram 7-10). Since we are sending all the underneath coverage, we play a purple coverage in the secondary.

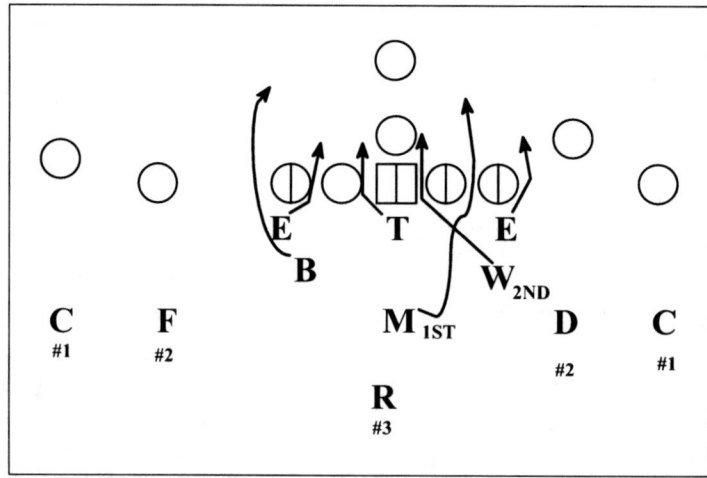

Diagram 7-10. War X switch Buck twist

Purple coverage is a man scheme. In purple coverage, the Rover and dog stay over the top of the #2 receivers to their side. They jump all out routes by the #2 receivers. The corners stay over the top of the #1 receiver to their side. The free safety has the #3 receiver. The corners, the Rover, and the dog play banjo coverage and switch crossing patterns between the #1 and #2 receivers. They must play with their eyes and communicate.

We can also run blitzes with our third-level defenders. The corners and free safety can get involved with this game.

I will be around, and I am ready to talk some football. Thank you for your attention.

8

The 3-3 Pressure Defense

Joe Lee Dunn
University of Memphis
2006

Thank you. It is a pleasure to be here representing the University of Memphis. Coach West would rather be here than where he is today. He sends his best to all of you.

Today, I am going to talk about the 3-3 defense and some of the conditioning we do in our program. When we come into fall camp before the opening of the season, we do two things that really help us prepare for the season. We have one workout in the morning practice and one in the evening that is devoted to conditioning.

In the morning practices, we do what I refer to as Packer Day. I have done this since I was at Chattanooga back in the early 70s. It comes from the Green Bay Packers under Vince Lombardi. We take the last 15 minutes of practice and do the Packer Day workout. The first day we do two-and-a-half minutes of up-downs, followed by two-and-a-half minutes of 40s or three sets.

The second day, we increase the time on the up-downs and follow with 40s for the remaining five minutes. We do three sets of those on the second day. We increase the time on the up-downs each day until they reach graduation day, which includes 15 minutes of up-downs. Coach West and all the coaches I have worked for know the last three periods of defensive practice in the morning is Packer Day.

In the afternoon practice we do a conditioning period called Fourth Quarter. That drill takes 20 minutes, or the last four periods of defensive practice. We do our conditioning program and that is part of the understanding I have with the head coach. Those conditioning drills are talked about before I take the job. I feel the conditioning program is vitally important to the success of our defense.

This conditioning program is what allows us to run to the football in the fourth quarter as hard as we do in the first quarter. In the Fourth Quarter Drill, we have four stations. At one station, we run 40-yard sprints. We have a bag station, which acts as a conditioning drill. We run over and in and out of the bags using agility-type drills. We have a push-up and sit-up station. The final station is a cone-run station. This requires changes of direction and shuttle runs in and out of the cones.

We do these workouts during two-a-day practices. Once we finish with early practice, we are finished with Packer Day and Fourth Quarter. During the season, we run 20 40s as our conditioning, plus one 40 for each point we give up in the game.

We practice on Sundays, and Monday is their off day. Our conference has a bunch of teams that score a bunch of points. We have been in some wild games involving lots of scoring. We have run as many as 90 40s on Sunday. You have to be motivated to complete the workout. It takes some time to run 90 40s. We allow them to run in groups of 10, so we can finish before dark. We hope we do not have to run that many too often, but scoring points is the big thing in football these days.

On Tuesday, we run 15 40s. On Wednesday, we run five 40s. We do not run on Thursday or Friday. We do the same thing in our conditioning each week. They know it and I do not have to tell them.

We do run- and pass-pursuit drills during practice. These are two other drills we do only during two-a-day practices. I will show you the drills if I can. The Run Pursuit Drill is somewhat weird (Diagram 8-1). We align the defense and run a dive-option play to the defensive left. We place two cones 40 yards from the line of scrimmage, with a coach behind each one.

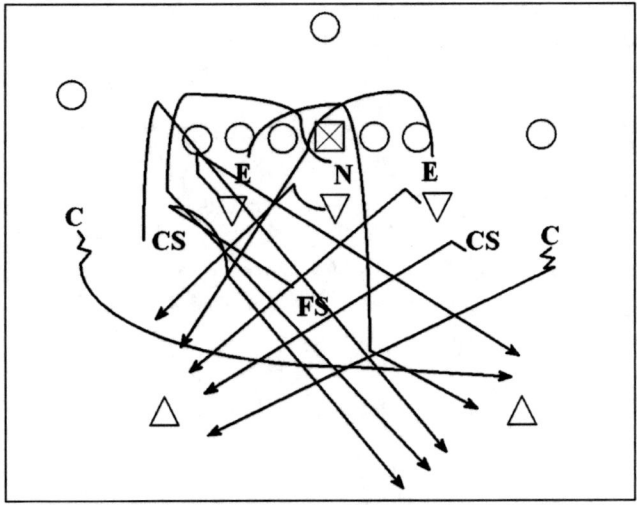

Diagram 8-1. Run pursuit drill

We have one cone on the right hash mark and one on the left hash mark. Defenders on the right side of the defense pursue the football and sprint to the cone on the left. Defenders on the left of the defense pursue the ball and sprint to the right cone. We play a 3-3 defense, with two cat safeties, two corners, and a free safety.

The left defensive end comes off the ball, goes to his responsibility, comes flat behind the line of scrimmage, and turns up between the backside center and guard. From there, he sprints to the cone on the right. The right end does the same thing and sprints to the cone on the left. The noseguard stays flat to the line and sprints to the left cone.

Everyone on the defense goes through his responsibility and pursues the ball. Everyone goes at once and sprints to the opposite cone from their alignment.

I have the whistle and any time within the drill, I can blow the whistle. When that occurs, everyone on the defense stops and does an up-down. I may blow the whistle five or six times during the drill. On each occasion, the defense has to hit the ground and get up. There is no live tackling or blocking in this drill. Everyone goes through their pursuit angles and sprints 40 yards to the opposite cone.

When all the defenders get to the cone, they circle around the coach, chopping their feet. I blow the whistle one more time. They hit the ground, get up, and sprint off the field. They jog back to the position of the ball and prepare to go again. We have three teams run this drill. We can use all our calls and stunts during this drill. If you are interested in seeing this drill, send me a blank tape and I will make you a copy of the drill.

We run the pursuit against the option, but we do not see the option as a full-time offense anymore. The game has changed for the defense. The rules have legalized holding by the offense. With that change, the offenses are throwing the ball all the time.

College football has turned into a pass-first, run-second scheme. The pass now sets up the run. It used to be that all you had to do was stop the run to win the game. Now, you had better have something in your scheme to stop the pass.

The Pass Pursuit Drill (Diagram 8-2) is similar to the Run Pursuit Drill. We line up in the defense and snap the ball. The quarterback throws the ball to the left and everyone goes through his pass-coverage and rush responsibilities, then sprints to the ball. When they arrive, they chop their feet around the ball. I blow the whistle, they hit the ground and get up, and they sprint off the field. We throw the ball to the left, right, and down the middle deep. In each rep, they go through the defense and pursue the thrown ball. They go three times before they get off the field.

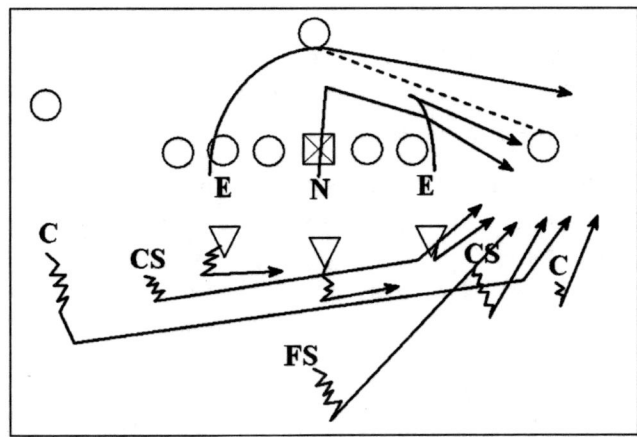
Diagram 8-2. Pass pursuit drilll

That is how we run our conditioning drills. The next part of the lecture concerns the defensive scheme and the way we present it to our players. We call the defense "33." This defense evolved from the old 5-3 defense. The 5-3 defense was hard to run against and was very sound. In the old defense, we used the strong safety as one of the linebackers. That way, we did not have to substitute. I still do not like to substitute to run any phases of the defense.

The first time I coached at Memphis, in 1990, we developed this defense. We had to open in the Coliseum against Southern Cal the next season. They sent me to watch their spring game in the Coliseum. That was before the NCAA made scouting in the spring illegal.

I was standing outside the stadium as Southern Cal unloaded the bus to go on the field. They were huge and had some big players. I looked at them and thought to myself, "I don't know what we are going to do." I went into the Coliseum to watch the game and was surprised to see very few people there to watch the game. If there were 1000 people in the stands it would have been a surprise.

I decided I would not watch much of the game. At halftime, I went to the Santa Anita racetrack to watch the horse races. There were 53,000 people at the racetrack betting on the ponies. You could tell where those people's priorities were.

The next year we played Southern Cal with our defensive ends in the alignment played by our cat safeties. We did not let them play man coverage, but they did play the zone coverage. We ended up beating Southern Cal in this defense. They were a hell of a lot better than we were, but we won the game.

It was so effective that I began to run it as a full-time defense. Steve Spurrier changed the face of defensive football in the SEC. He instituted the empty set as part of his offense. He spread five receivers with only the quarterback in the backfield. People did not think he could run that against them.

They made the mistake of not covering all the receivers. Florida quarterbacks got good at hitting the receivers that the defense did not cover. He made the defenses in the SEC change because he did not run the ball—he threw it. Offensive linemen today are so much bigger than they used to be.

I want to keep my players as far from the offensive linemen as I can get them. We have a better chance of dodging those huge offensive linemen after they come off the ball. If we get up on the line of scrimmage, they grab and hold. I guarantee you the offensive linemen will hold you. We played three games last year against teams that threw the ball over 50 times. In those games, the offense did not have one single holding call.

There is no team in America that good. It is unbelievable. We try to keep them away from us unless we can match up with another big player.

The defense is the old 5-3 defense with the end pulled off the line of scrimmage. We added defensive backs into the scheme because of the passing threat.

The makeup of the defense is three down linemen, three linebackers, two cat safeties, two corners, and a free safety (Diagram 8-3). The down linemen are in head-up positions on the center and two tackles. The linebackers stack behind the down linemen. The cat safeties are three yards outside the tight ends and seven yards deep. The corners are press corners and play within four yards of the line of scrimmage. The free safety aligns somewhere within the middle of the field.

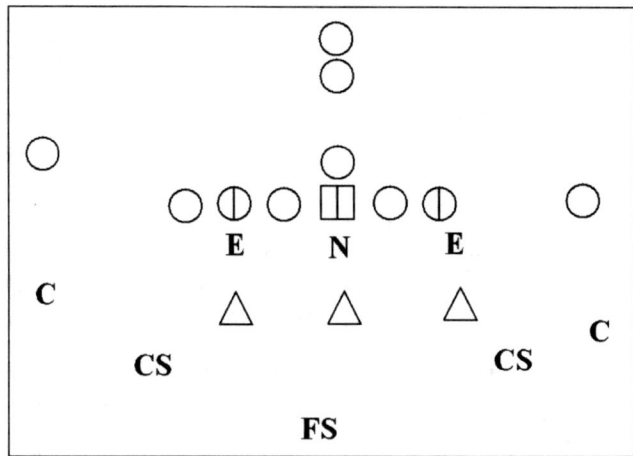

Diagram 8-3. 33 defense

The design of the defense is to defeat the offense with movement, stunts, and numbers. It is not the design of the defense to play a base look and take on offensive blockers. We are a gap-control defense with all the defenders assigned a gap to defend. We defend those gaps on the move.

We do not play anyone straight in this defense. We move the down linemen and linebacker on every play. We have three movements for the down linemen. We can move in a left-and-right direction (Diagram 8-4). We can move the down linemen to the tight end or to the openside of the formation. We can also pinch the defensive line. Our middle linebacker calls all the directions for the down linemen.

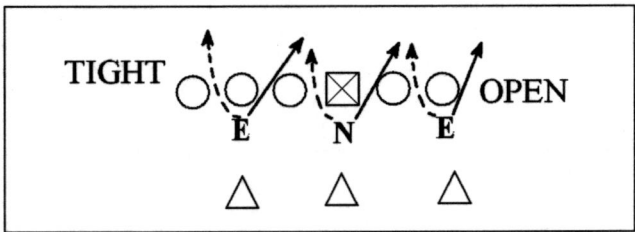

Diagram 8-4. Tight/open

He calls the direction of the tight end. The down linemen have to know if they are going toward or away from the tight end. If there are two tight ends in the game, the linebacker makes the call and the linemen apply the defense.

When we run the pinch (Diagram 8-5), the defensive ends slant inside into the B gaps. The nosetackle uses a stuff technique on the center. On the stuff technique, the nose almost tackles the center to ensure that he does not get off the line of scrimmage.

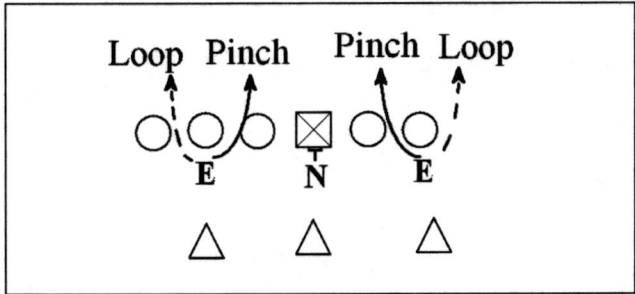

Diagram 8-5. Pinch/stuff

If we want to send the defensive end in the opposite direction, we loop him to the outside. On the loop call, the nose stuffs the center as he did on the pinch. We use the loop call in passing situations.

The next part of the defense uses one linebacker blitzing along with front movement. We have a left and right linebacker and a middle linebacker in our scheme. The ram and lion stunt sends the outside linebackers on blitzes. The ram is the right linebacker and the lion is the left linebacker.

On the ram stunt (Diagram 8-6), the right linebacker runs through the B gap to his side. The defensive ends loop to the outside and the nose slants into the A gap toward the linebacker stunt. If you want to add another wrinkle to the stunt, we can move the nose into a G position on the guard and slant him inside into the A gap.

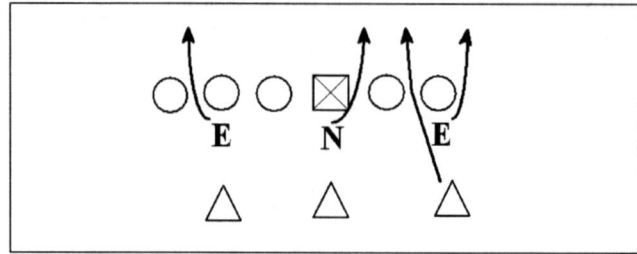

Diagram 8-6. Ram

The same stunt going the other way is lion (Diagram 8-7).

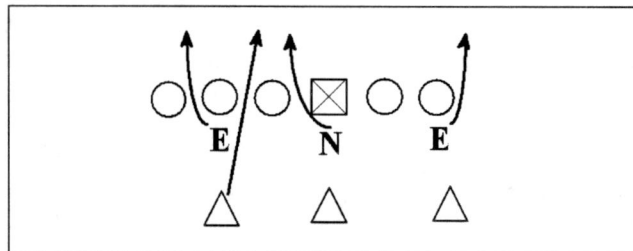

Diagram 8-7. Lion

The middle-linebacker blitz is "X" (Diagram 8-8). The direction of the linebacker varies with game planning. However, he runs through one of the A gaps and the nose goes the opposite way. We like to combine the X stunt with a line movement. We run X-pinch or X-loop to get movement in all the down linemen.

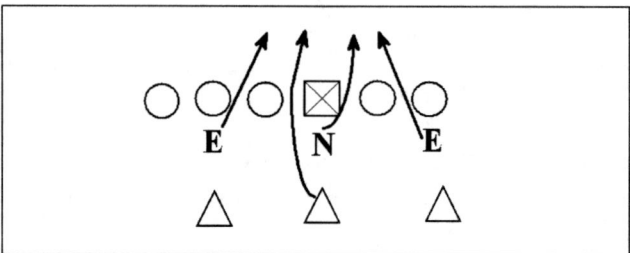

Diagram 8-8. X-pinch

To bring the outside linebackers off the edge, we call thunder (Diagram 8-9) and lightning. Thunder comes from the tight-end side and lightning from the split-end side. The outside linebackers come out of their stack alignment and cheat up to the line of scrimmage at the last minute. They run the bullets charge from the outside coming off the edge. The line movement is away from the tight end.

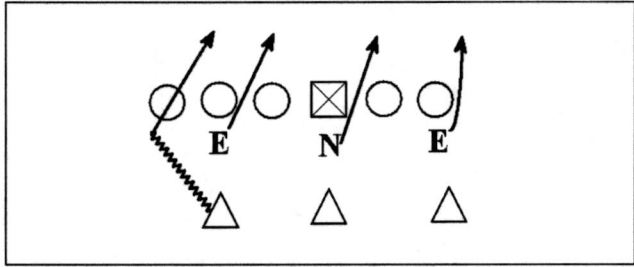

Diagram 8-9. Thunder

Coming from the openside of the formation is the lightning call (Diagram 8-10). On this stunt, the defensive-line movement is away from the openside with the linebacker coming off the edge.

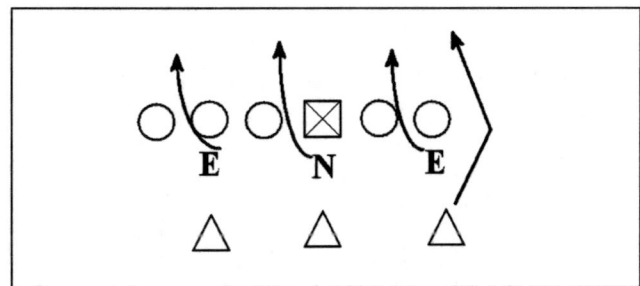

Diagram 8-10. Lightning

When we teach this in the spring, we go through the progression, from the one-linebacker blitzes to the two-linebacker blitzes. The two-linebacker stunts are go and away. In the go stunt (Diagram 8-11), the linebackers go toward the tight end. The Mike linebacker runs through the A gap to that side and the left linebacker runs through the B gap. The defensive ends loop outside and the nose slants into the weakside A gap.

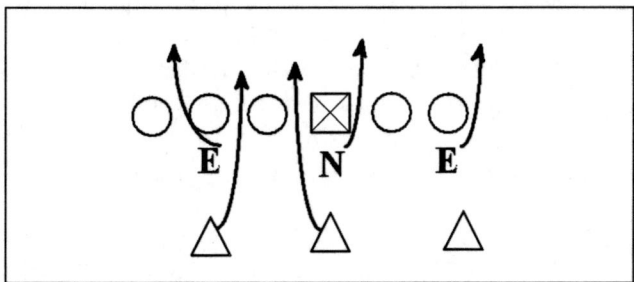

Diagram 8-11. Go

If we want the linebacker going the other way on the stunt, we call go-switch. That sends the linemen and linebacker into the opposite gaps. The away stunt (Diagram 8-12) is the same blitz going away from the tight end.

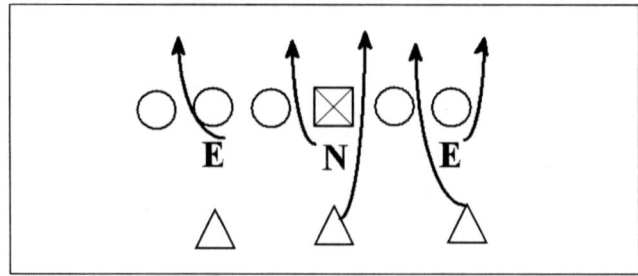

Diagram 8-12. Away

The backside defensive end on these stunts loops to the outside. We do not have a bunch of big players at Memphis. That is why we move them on every play. If I had a bunch of players that could whip the crap out of the offensive linemen, I would play more base.

The next two-linebacker stunt is spike (Diagram 8-13). That involves the outside linebackers. We send both of them into the B gaps and loop the defensive ends outside. It is a good stunt, if you have good blitzing linebackers.

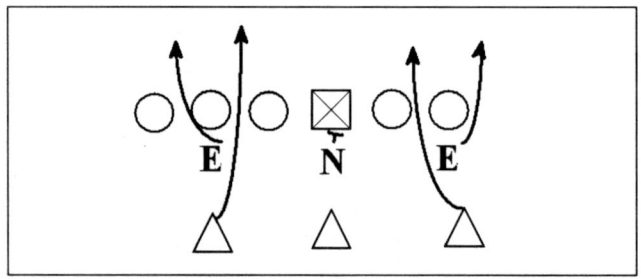

Diagram 8-13. Spike

In 1992, I was at Ole Miss. We did not move the defensive line as we do now. We had two defensive ends named Norman Hands and Tim Bowens. They both became franchise players in the NFL. This is a little story about Tim Bowens. He did not get eligible and did not practice with our team until the Thursday before we opened with Auburn at Auburn, Alabama. That was the first time he dressed out in football equipment. We started him in that game and told him to tackle anybody that came through his gap. He made more tackles than anyone did in the game.

He was a player extraordinaire. You do not coach players of that caliber. Tim Bowens was as mean as a snake. He would whip your butt in a heartbeat. Norman Hands was entirely different. Norman did not get mean until he got to the pros. You could slap Norman and get away with it. If you did that to Tim, he would kill you. Players like those two will make you a good coach.

The next stunt involving two linebackers is bullets (Diagram 8-14). This stunt is the thunder and lightning run at the same time. They both cheat outside and come off the edge.

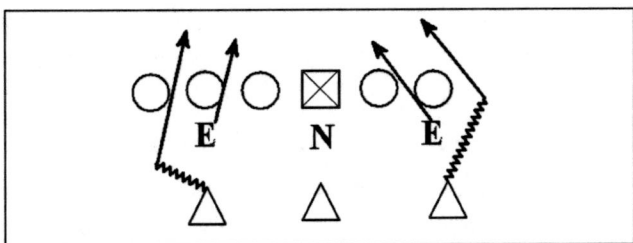

Diagram 8-14. Bullets

The secondary coverages behind all of these movements can be the same. We can run man-to-man, man/free, or zone.

The progression continues with the three-linebacker blitz. The three-linebacker game is trips (Diagram 8-15). When we run this scheme, we have to play man coverage. We rush six defenders and the offense has five eligible receivers. We have to cover them all with the five remaining defenders.

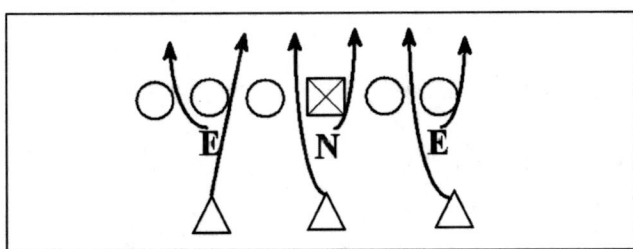

Diagram 8-15. Trips

When we run the trips, the outside linebackers run through the B gaps and the Mike linebacker runs through the strong A gap. We can combine the line movement with the trips call. We can run trips right or left, which sends the linemen in a direction and the linebacker blitzing the opposite gaps. We can do the same thing with the tight and open calls. The third thing we can do is trips pinch. The middle stack runs their trips stunt and the outside stacks send the ends inside and the linebackers outside.

The last thing we do from the trips package is bullets X (Diagram 8-16). That puts the outside linebackers on the line of scrimmage coming off the edges with the Mike linebacker running the X stunt inside.

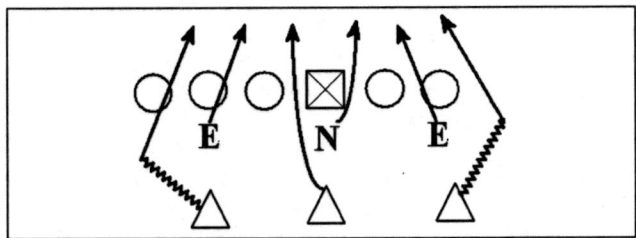

Diagram 8-16. Bullets X

When we run a six-man blitz, we need to have some peel adjustments. That means that one of the outside blitzers may have to come off his blitz to cover a back coming out of the backfield.

We teach the defense the hawk look (Diagram 8-17). The hawk look is on the tight-end side of the formation. We move the defensive end from the 4 technique head up on the tackle to a 3 technique on the outside shoulder of the guard. To the split-end side, we can do the same thing. We call that adjustment eagle. If we want both sides to move we call double eagle.

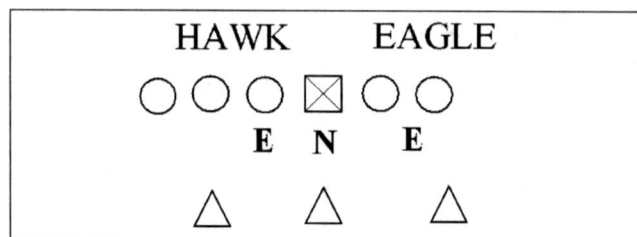

Diagram 8-17. Hawk/eagle/double eagle

We like this adjustment because it lets you get a defender into the B gap before they snap the ball. If we have a defensive end that does not pinch very well, we line him up there. Hawk is the adjustment to the tight-end side only. Eagle is to the split-end side and double eagle is the adjustment to both sides.

Of course, you can move the end into a hawk position and move back out on the snap of the ball. We have no problem with line movement, as long as the linebackers know where the linemen are going. You cannot do everything the same way week after week. If you show an adjustment, you can play it one way one week and a totally different way the following week. When you become predictable, it destroys the defense.

The next progression adds a secondary blitz with a one-linebacker stunt. The first stunt is mad thunder (Diagram 8-18). The stunt comes from the tight-end side of the formation. We run the Thunder stunt with the linebacker coming off the edge. The cat safety to that side cheats up in his alignment. At the last minute, he comes outside of the linebacker off the edge.

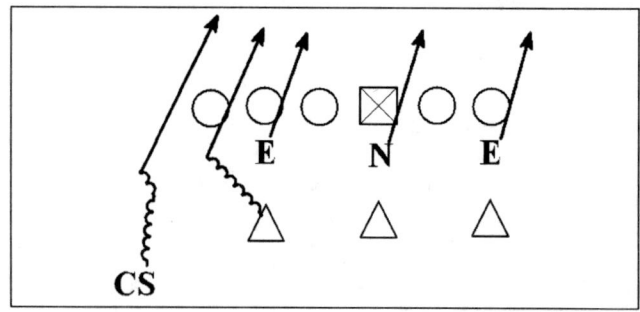

Diagram 8-18. Mad thunder

The opposite of that stunt is bad lightning. Bad is to the open or boundary side of the formation.

The hardest thing we find in running this stunt with secondary players is the path they take. Instead of running straight lines to the quarterback, they want to bend their paths. They cannot understand that a straight line is the shortest distance between two points. If they run straight lines, it hits quicker.

The next scheme involves two linebackers and one defensive back. We run mad-thunder-X (Diagram 8-19). That is a combination stunt that brings the linebacker and cat safety from the tight-end side, with the Mike linebacker coming through the strong A gap. It is the same stunt, adding the middle linebacker to the stunt.

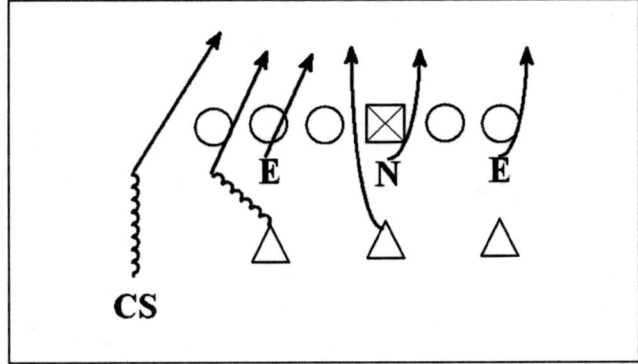

Diagram 8-19. Mad thunder X

If we blitz the other outside linebacker, we call mad-thunder-fire (Diagram 8-20). Instead of an X stunt in the middle, we get a ram stunt to the right side of the defense.

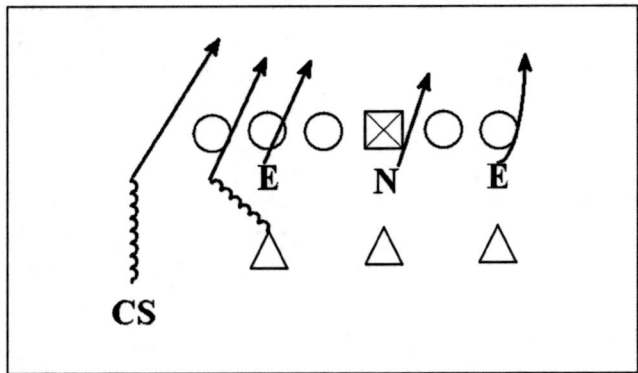

Diagram 8-20. Mad thunder fire

A change-up we added this year that helped us was mad-thunder-bullets (Diagram 8-21). We brought the backside linebacker from the edge and it helped us tremendously. The defensive end slanted into the B gap and the linebacker came off the edge.

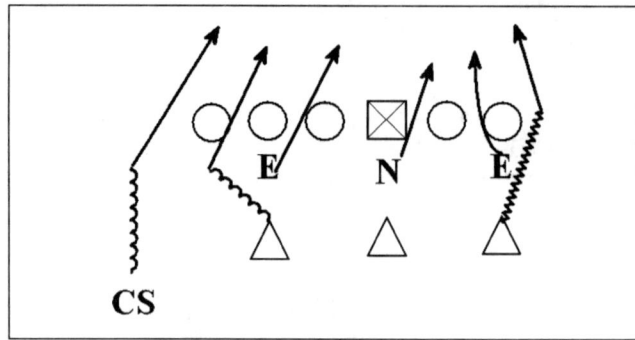

Diagram 8-21. Mad thunder bullets

We can run exactly the same stunt from the openside of the formation with the Lightning package. We can run bad-lightning with the X, fire, and bullets combination coming from the split-end side.

If we want to bring seven defenders with the scheme, we call combo. That call brings the thunder, X, and fire stunts all in the same stunt. The problem with that is the number of secondary defenders. When you bring seven, someone in the blitz is responsible for a back in pass coverage.

However, sometimes it does not matter how much you cover and practice a particular point. In the heat of the game, someone misses their assignment and fails to execute. It happened to us in the bowl game this year. We came with an eight-man blitz. We covered the exact play in practice a number of times. We were in dead man coverage. The corners and free safety locked on the three wide receivers. The right linebacker had the tight end.

To the twin-receiver side, the cat safety and left linebacker had coverage on the remaining back. They were both senior players and the coverage went to the player the back tried to block. As it worked, the linebacker charged outside and the safety went inside. Neither of them covered the back and he went straight down the field, wide open for the touchdown. Every time in practice, the defender took the back, but he missed him in the game.

When you involve secondary players in line stunts, the secondary has to move to compensate for the back leaving. We squirm the free safety toward the side of the stunt. The cat safety away from the stunt balances back to the inside of the formation. This is also a time when we can use the hawk call as a change-up alignment. If you continue to tweak the alignments of the defensive linemen, it makes it hard on the offensive blockers.

One of the strong points of this defense is the ability to confuse the offensive blockers. You need to move the defensive linemen into as many places as you can.

The key is to get them to their responsibilities. The hard part with all the freedom is not being in the right place when the offense snaps the ball.

At the end of the season, we found ourselves without many defensive linemen. Let me tell you a little about our season. In the first game, our starting quarterback broke his right leg on the third play of the game. In the third football game, our second quarterback broke his left leg. Our third quarterback was a true freshman that joined the program in January. He became the starting quarterback for a while.

I believe things happen in cycles. We got so many injuries from that point on that it was downright discouraging. It occurred on both sides of the ball. We lost our best defensive lineman in the first game for the year. Our best linebacker played three games and missed the rest of the season. The good news is that both return next year.

These things went on and on during the course of the season. We even had a coach get his knee torn up in practice before the seventh game. He spent the rest of the season in the press box. The following week, the team doctor went down on the sidelines and tore his knee up. The week after that a cheerleader got hurt. They threw her in the air and dropped her.

If that was not enough, one of our best receivers burnt his hands in an apartment fire and was lost for the rest of the year. Of course, after the season, Coach West had triple bypass surgery. I hope that is the end to all the maladies.

We feel that this defense allows you to play with lesser players. You can hide the linebackers in stacks behind a defender. You can get by with a lesser player as a down lineman if you move him.

If we play a team that empties the backfield, we bring a six-man blitz. If they empty and have a tight end as one of their receivers, we bring the defender covering him on the blitz. That assures us that the tight end does not block anyone but the back assigned to him. We do not let the offense use the tight end as their sixth blocker in their scheme.

If you stay in this business long enough, you will see everything. I believe if a team did not have spring training one year and won 10 games the following year, there would be a bunch of people who would cut out spring training. That is how trendy some people are in this game. People follow programs that win. It is the nature of the beast.

I got off track. Let me show you a defense that was good for us. We call this double eagle special (Diagram 8-22). This is the number-one defense that has been successful since I have been coaching. We go to the double eagle alignment by sliding the defensive ends into 3-technique alignments. The outside linebackers and cat safeties move up to the outside and come off the edges with their mad and bad schemes.

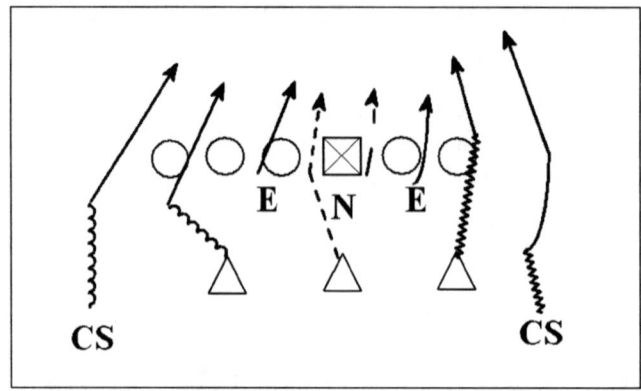

Diagram 8-22. Double eagle special

If you want to bring eight on the rush, we call double eagle special X. That stunt puts the Mike linebacker into the A gap to the strongside and the nose into the A gap to the weakside.

I like to play this defense in short yardage or when we have the offensive backed up in their own territory. You take a chance because you are dead man in the secondary and peeling on back receivers as you go.

We can get into the split (Diagram 8-23) look from the 3-3 defense. We take the linebacker that can play on the line of scrimmage and align him over the tight end. We overshift the three down linemen to the weakside of the defense. The left defensive end goes to a strong 2-technique alignment and the nose goes to the weak 2-technique alignment on the guards. The right defensive end slides into a wide 5 technique on the offensive tackle.

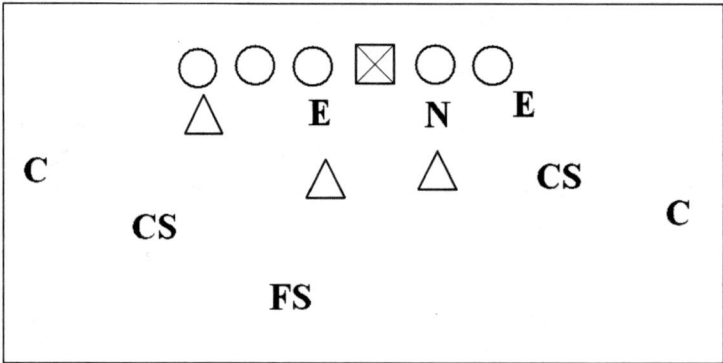

Diagram 8-23. Split

The remaining linebackers stack behind the 2 techniques. If we do not have a linebacker that can play over a tight end, we slide the line to the tight end. We play the linebacker to the openside of the formation and a defensive end over the tight end.

We can play a split-1 right (Diagram 8-24). In this diagram, I will show the line overshifted to the tight end and the linebacker to the openside of the set. We align in the split front and slant the down linemen to the right. The left linebacker comes out of the 3 stack and moves to the edge outside the tight end. He comes off the edge and gives the offense an overload to handle from the strongside. The Mike linebacker moves over the center and gives us a one-linebacker look.

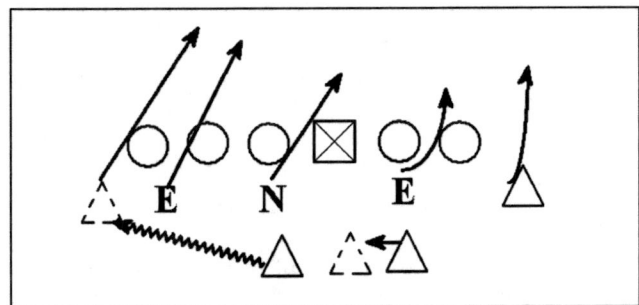

Diagram 8-24. Split-1 right

If we call split-1 left, we slant the line to the left. Last year, we substituted a defensive back for one of the blitzing linebackers. We played this defense at Mississippi State a bunch. The defense fit our personnel there.

We have many stunts we can run from the split-1, but the mad and bad stunts are the same stunts from the 3-3 as well as the split-1. One thing we have done is blitz two defenders outside the tight end (Diagram 8-25). We bring a safety up and blitz him outside the linebacker.

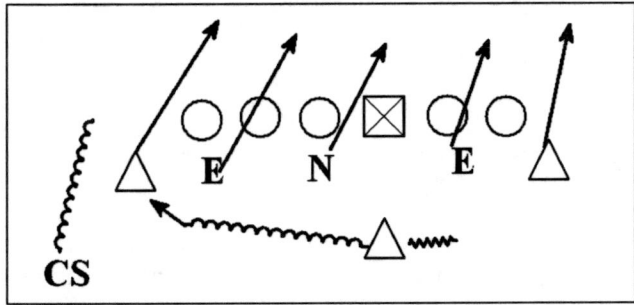

Diagram 8-25. Split-1 safety blitz

This year, because of our injury problems, we ended up playing two down linemen and four linebackers (Diagram 8-26). They were in 2-technique alignments on the offensive guards. The four linebackers are at linebacker depth in 20-stack. They are aligned in a 60 technique to the tight end and a 50 technique to the split end.

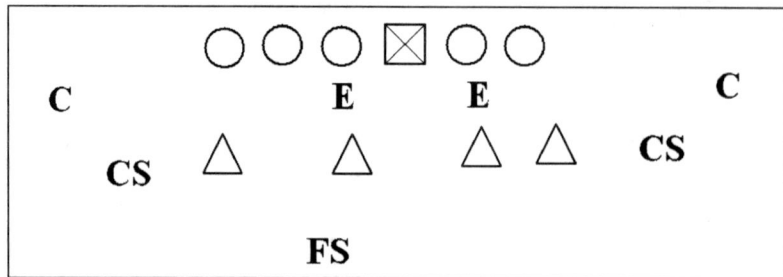

Diagram 8-26. Two down inside

The linebackers started out at linebacker depth, but as the quarterback began to snap the ball, they were on the move to their responsibilities. We really moved from this alignment.

Our wild look is similar to that set. We align in the 3-3 defense, pull the nose off the line of scrimmage, and play him in the middle of the defense. Nothing changes in his stunt package except his position. At the snap of the ball, he is moving down to the line of scrimmage instead of aligning on it.

It is another confusing defense for the offensive linemen. It gives them another chance to block the wrong man and let someone come unblocked. From this alignment, the stunt we like to run is wild go (Diagram 8-27).

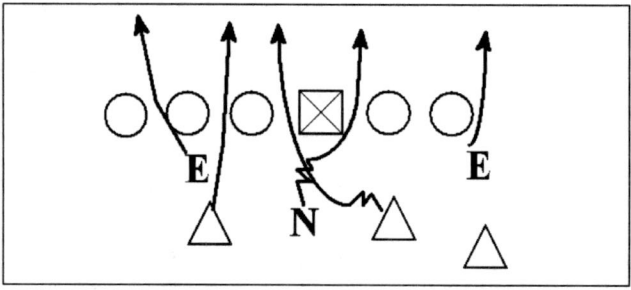

Diagram 8-27. Wild go

We played that at New Mexico because of the personnel we had. What this all boils down to is, you do what you have to do. When you get hurt, you cannot cancel the schedule. We played hard all year long with the people we had available. This defense has a lot of flexibility to it. You really have to depend on your secondary to keep you from being blown out. When you blitz for a living, you have to get there. It is too much pressure on the defensive backs to cover good wide receivers when the quarterback has time to get the ball off.

9

The 3-3-5 Stack Defense

Tony Gibson
West Virginia University
2004

I am going to give you an overview of some of the things we do on defense. However, the main thing I am going to do is to talk about our 3-3-5 off stack defense. I am not going to talk a lot about philosophy. That is one of the reasons coaches do not like to come to clinics today. You get so much philosophy and very little that you can use in your program. I will talk about our base alignment and our coverage rules, our techniques, and the fundamentals of our defense. I will go over our defensive philosophy, our defensive goals, and our grade sheets.

Our defensive system is an odd stack package of multiple fronts and coverage that is simple, flexible, and capable of attacking any offensive system that we may encounter. We use a multiple system that is based upon the learning and perfecting of a limited number of fundamentals and techniques through repetitions. Our approach presents problems for opponents by forcing them to prepare for the multitude of looks that they may see from our defense.

Our defense is not just a stack package. Two years ago, when we started at WVU, we were 103 out of 117 on defense in the nation against the run. After the season was over, Coach Rodriquez came in our defensive meeting and said "I want to run the type of defense Joe Lee Dunn uses." Our staff were all 4-3 guys, so we had a lot to learn. In the first year we used the defense, we went 9-3. Over the last few years, we have finished in the top 30 in rush defense in a predominately run conference. We do play some good teams in our conference.

Our defense is built around players who possess four primary attributes:
- Mental toughness
- Outstanding work ethic
- Physical conditioning
- Coachability

We believe these are characteristics that every player can develop and improve upon, regardless of the individual's talent level. These attributes are the foundation for our style of play. Our team will be recognized and known for the following characteristics:
- Disciplined alignment
- Excellent technique and fundamentals
- Relentless attacking and pursuit of the football
- Physical and punishing tackling
- Outstanding physical conditioning

Our practice and preparation each day reflects and reinforces the commitment to our approach on defense. It will take a great effort each and every day from everyone involved in our program to distinguish us as the best defense in the country.

I want to go over our defensive priorities. I will put them up so you can see what we are trying to accomplish:
- Stop the run. No one will run the ball successfully against our defense. We will commit as many people to the line of scrimmage as necessary to stop the run. No one will run the football against us.
- Control the pass. We are primarily a zone coverage team. We will take away the long ball and force our opponents to throw into our underneath coverage. By becoming proficient in disguising our intentions and being sound in our drop keys and responsibilities, we will break on the ball and create collisions, turnovers, and incomplete passes.
- Tackling. We will be the best tackling team in America. By doing reps on the fundamentals every day in practice, we will punish ballcarriers and develop the attitude necessary of a physical defensive football team.
- Pursuit. We will get 11 people to the football on every play. It does not take a great athlete to run with the red line effort to the football. It takes a football player with a great attitude. We want as many of our helmets on the ballcarrier as possible, and we want to wear down the opponent in the fourth quarter.
- Turnovers. We will create a minimum of three turnovers per game with our attacking and aggressive style of play. We will work fundamentals every day that force turnovers and create a short field for our defense.
- Eliminate the big play. We will force the offense to travel the length of the field by not allowing a run over 10 yards or a completion over 18 yards.

- Eliminate mental mistakes. Most defensive breakdowns that allow big plays are the result of a mental mistake. By practicing with total concentration and learning our assignments, we will eliminate mental errors.
- Sudden change. We must accept the challenge of stopping our opponent after we have turned the ball over. We will go into a sudden change series with the attitude of getting the ball back and regaining the psychological advantage.
- Discipline. We will be recognized as a disciplined defense. We will do what we are coached to do on each and every play. Discipline in practice will enable us to develop good habits.
- Have fun. We are fortunate to be involved in the greatest game in the world. Enjoy the game and everything that goes into winning a championship.

Our defensive goals are no different than most of your defensive goals:
- Win!
- Team hustle: +90 percent team grade
- 3.5 yards or less per carry
- 17 points or less per game
- Force 3 or more takeaways.
- Score or set up two scoring opportunities for our offense.
- No big plays. No runs over 15 yards. No pass plays over 25 yards.
- No TDs after sudden change.
- 4 or more 3 and outs per game.
- Win third down 70 percent of the time.
- 100 percent efficiency on fourth down.
- Less than 290 yards total offense.

Of course, the number-one goal is to win the game. If we win by a score of 62 to 61, we have met our number-one defensive goal. It does not matter what the score is as long as we win.

We want to force three or more takeaways. We do not want to call them turnovers because that is like the offense is giving us something. We want to be creative and take the ball away from the offense.

We have all of our defensive goals on a board in every defensive meeting room. The players get to see them every day. When the players come into our team room, the first thing they look at is the defensive goal board. If we meet our goal during a game, we put a star or a WVU Mountaineer logo for each of the goals we meet for that week. We may gain the first goal and not do very well on the other eleven goals, but we tell our players that it is all right because our number-one goal is to win the game.

I want to show you our team grade sheet. We put up a productive board with the kids' names on the board. We upgrade the board every week. After we grade our players, we put the results on the board to show how productive we were for that last game. We keep the board running and total the points for the year. I want you to understand this is not the grade that we are showing. We are showing how productive we are in games. This tells us who is making the plays.

PLAYER PRODUCTION BOARD

	Total Plays	Assists	Tackles	Tackle for Loss	QB Harass	Sack	Big Hit	Exceptional Play	X Mile	Caused Fumble	Recovered Fumble	Pass Break Up	Caused INT	INT	Score on Defense	Missed Tackle	Lost	Missed Assignment	Penalty	Play Grade	Total Points	Contact with Ball
POINT VALUE		1	2	3	3	5	3	3	2	5	5	4	5	7	8	-2	-1	-1	-2			
NAME																						

We put the play grade in separately. Then we calculate the total points scored for each player. The last point is contact with the ball. That included the number of times you are involved in a play. If you played 60 plays and were involved in 10 plays, that would mean you were involved in one out of every six plays. We want our players involved in one out of every four or five plays if they are a lineman or a linebacker. If they are a defensive back, we want them to be involved in one out of every seven plays. All of our defensive coaches use this form. This is what we take into our meetings with the head coach on Sunday morning. After we talk about the scores in the meeting, we post everything up in the team room. Our kids have a lot of fun with the grading system. They look forward to seeing the grades each week.

The next thing I am going to cover is our player alignment in our stack defense. We play a 3-3-5 stack defense. We have three down linemen, three linebackers, and five defensive backs. I will go over each position and tell you how we align.

Coach Bill Kirelawich coaches the three down linemen. Coach Jeff Casteel coaches the three linebackers. Coach Bruce Tall works with our spur and our bandit. I have the three deep men, which include the two corners and the free safety.

We play with a head-up nose man. He is our 0 technique. Our two ends play 5 techniques. Our linebackers are our Lou, Mike, and Rob. We are in a true stack with the Mike stacked on the nose (see Diagram 9-1). Our Lou linebacker is in a 50 alignment. If the man lines up in a 5 technique and is off the line of scrimmage, we add a zero to the number, so we say he is in a 50 alignment. The Rob linebacker is also in a 50 alignment. They line up four yards off the heels of the down linemen so they are about 5 yards off the ball. We do not flip our linebackers. They play on the same side all of the time.

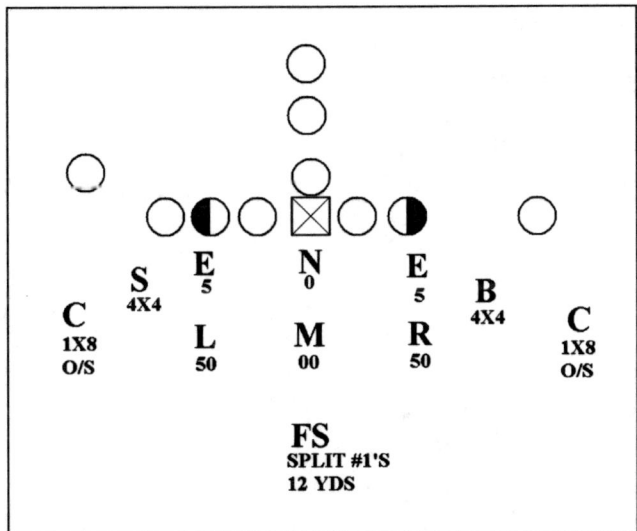

Diagram 9-1. Player alignment

Our outside spur and bandit have to think a little more. The spur is on the strongside of the formation. He is in a 4 X 4 split off the heels of our defensive end. We do not line up off the offensive end. We line up off our defensive end. Our bandit goes to the weakside and he is a 4 X 4 player off our defensive end.

We have a field corner. If the ball is on the hash mark, he goes to the wide side of the field. He is 1 X 8 outside. His alignment changes when the wideout lines up outside the numbers. Then he automatically goes inside with the wideout. The bandit is our boundary corner. This is the man we usually give the inside alignment. We tell our free safety to split number one. If the ball is on the hash mark, we move him over the tackle. He is 12 yards deep.

I will go over what we look for in a player for each position. Our bandit is the next best defensive man besides the two corners and free safety. He would be a safety in the 4-3 alignment. He is an athletic type that can cover and can play man coverage. The spur could be an outside linebacker. Our spur defender is larger than the bandit. He must be able to play on the tight end side and take on the blocker. He must be a physical athlete. We never pull the spur off the line of scrimmage. He is always in the 4 X 4 alignment. Our corners must be able to cover in man coverage. The boundary corner must be more physical than the field corner. Our free safety is the corner type player that we have moved back to that position. We recruit quarterbacks and tailbacks to play this defensive position.

Let me cover the gap responsibilities out of the stack alignment (see Diagram 9-2). We start with the nose man. The nose is an A gap player. He is the frontside A gap man. The Mike is the backside A gap player. The ends are C gap players. The spur and bandit are D gap players. The Lou and Rob linebackers are B gap players.

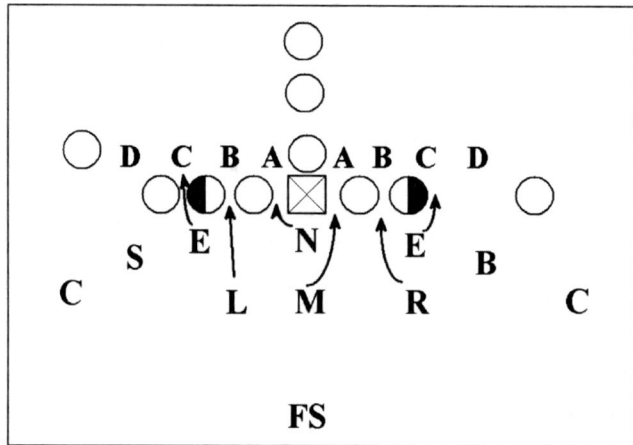

Diagram 9-2. Gap responsibilities

Our free safety is an alley player. The bandit and spur force the play, and the free safety fills on the play. The corners secure any play action pass or deep pass.

We always have a force man, a secure man, an alley man, and a cutoff man (see Diagram 9-3). What we call the cutoff man is the corner away from the action. If the

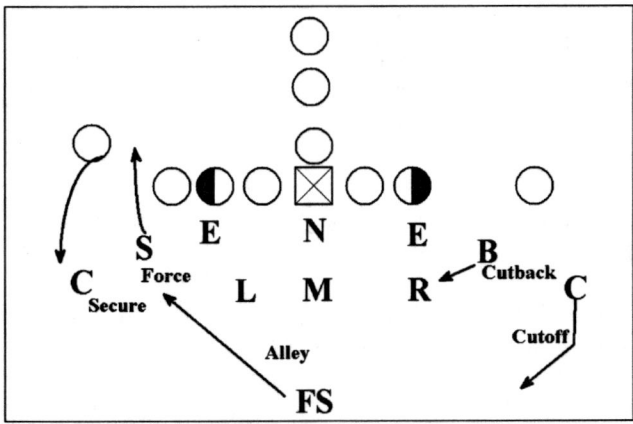

Diagram 9-3. Force, secure, alley and cutoff

play is a toss sweep to the tight end side, the corner on the backside is the cutoff man. He wants to get 10 yards depth and check for the reverse or throwback. He pursues the play gaining depth. He is the deep man on the pursuit. He can save the touchdown if he pursues the play properly. We make the backside corner tell us his responsibility when we are running the film and the play goes away from them. "What do you have on the backside corner?" We expect them to reply, "Cutoff man."

Let me go over the toss sweep using this concept. As the spur sees the quarterback toss the ball to the tailback, he becomes the force player. He wants to get up the field to restrict the back from getting outside. We want him on the outside path of their fullback. He wants to make the tailback cut back inside. He does not want the play to get outside. This should be the easiest play in football to read. As he sees the quarterback turn and pitch. he wants to get downhill and get in the face of the fullback (see Diagram 9-4).

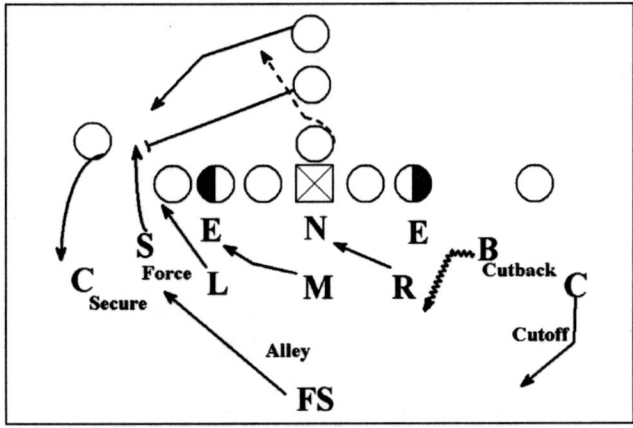

Diagram 9-4. As he sees the quarterback turn, the force player wants to get in the face of the fullback.

Once the spur sets the corner for us and there is nowhere for the ballcarrier to go but inside, he is going to get hit by the Lou, Mike, or Rob linebackers. We bring out linebackers over the top of everything.

Our free safety is flat foot reading, and his eyes are on the triangle. As soon as he reads the quarterback make the toss, he is up in the alley. That is the reason the corners are our secure players. The onside corner secures the play, and the backside corner is the cutback player.

The Lou linebacker is over the top of the tight end, the Mike linebacker is over the top of the guard, and the Rob linebacker is over the center. We use the bandit as the cutback player.

If the offense sends the outside man in motion to the other side, we kick the free safety over to the motion side and the corner comes back to replace the free safety (see Diagram 9-5). We move the shell. We do not move the spur on the tight end side.

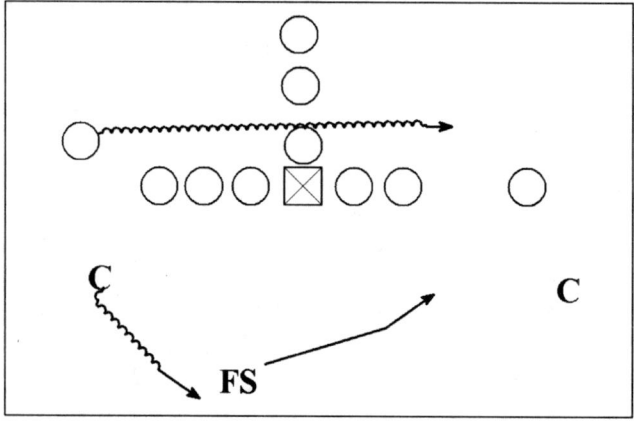

Diagram 9-5

This is basically our stack against the 2 X 1 set (see Diagram 9-6). Nothing changes for the linemen. It is the same as we have covered in the alignments.

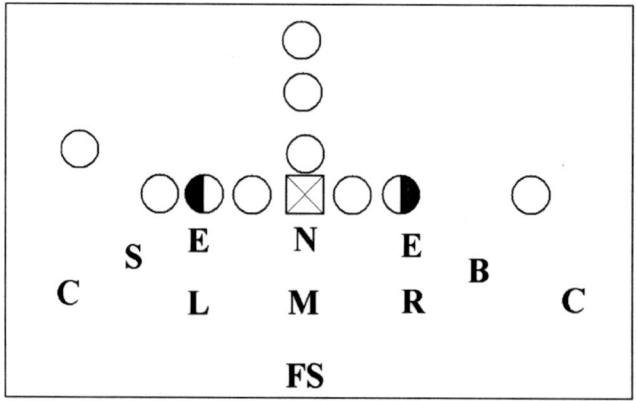

Diagram 9-6. Stack vs. 2 X 1 set

Next I want to talk about the stack vs. 2 X 2 set. This is the reason we started running the stack defense: because teams were using the spread offense. When you get into this alignment, the match-ups are good (see Diagram 9-7).

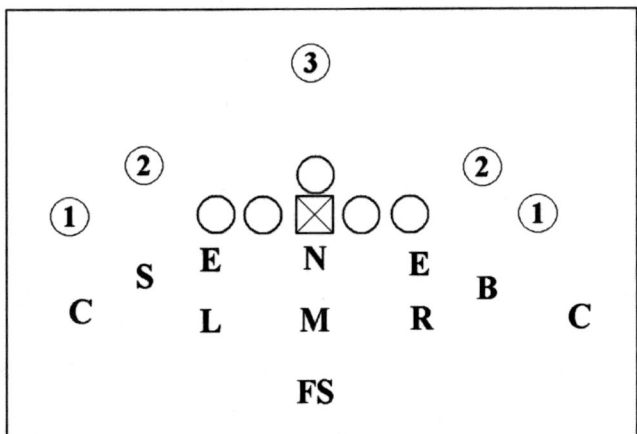

Diagram 9-7. Stack vs. 2 X 2 set

The bandit and spur have inside leverage on the number two receiver. We count from the outside to the inside. So the bandit and spur have the two receivers in the slot. The corners still are outside. Nothing has changed for them. The free safety still splits the number one receivers.

We play mostly cover 3 with this defense. The reason we like it is because it allows those linebackers to play. We think that is the key. Line them up, teach them how to play technique out of stack cover 3, go against different combinations in practice, and see what you are going to get. Then after you see the problems, you can work on adjusting the defense. This is a lot better than trying to teach cover 2, cover 3, and cover 4. If you teach a lot of different coverages it leads to mistakes. I like to stick with the coverage and adjust the players. If the offense sees the stack alignment, there is only one way they can block it. You will not see a lot of different blocking schemes up front.

We tilt our corners inside so they can read the quarterback. He is eight years off the line. He wants to be able to see the number one receiver, but he is reading the quarterback. The quarterback is going to tell the corner what is happening. The wideout will not tell the corner what is going on when the ball is snapped. We turn them inside and use a shuffle step and slide as the ball is snapped.

Next in our progression is the 3 X 1 set. That is a trey set for us. We adjust no different but we pull the defense. We pull the three linebackers one full man over to the trips side (see Diagram 9-8).

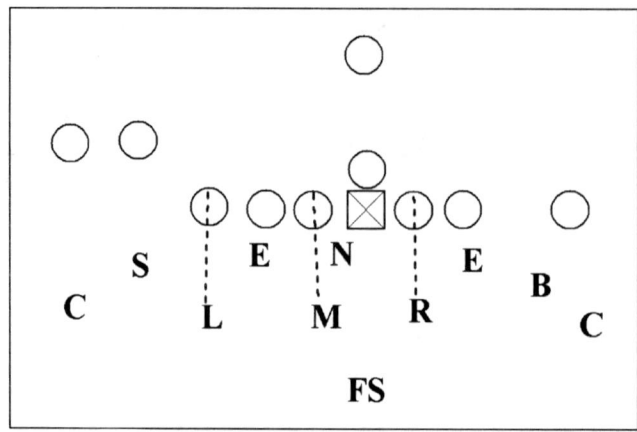
Diagram 9-8. Stack vs. 3 X 1 set

If one of the two wide receivers motion back to the split end side, we move the linebackers back to their original positions in the box. This is one of the things we like about this defense. We can move the cover players without making a lot of adjustments. The responsibilities of the cover players do not change against the 1 by 1, 2 by 2, or 3 by 1 set. When we spot drop it in a zone, it does not change anything. As I said, we play cover 3 a lot.

The corner is a deep one-third player. He has outside leverage. He will play up tight against the quick passing game. The free safety is a middle one-third player. His alignment is splitting the number one receivers. He is a middle one-third player. The other corner is a one-third player.

The bandit and spur are flat players. Their landmark is to the numbers on the field. They want to get to a depth of 10 to 12 yards deep. They play everything from the top downhill. They must get depth and width on his drop. That is the hard thing for them to do. They want to stay skinny and not get deep enough and not wide enough. We tell them to get to the numbers, and we will coach them from there. If the quarterback pulls up on his drop, they must back up and get depth.

Out of the spread sets, we see the bubble screen play with our soft corner. That is why we have to move our corners up and down on the receivers. We have the corners come up like they are going to press to play man coverage, and then we retreat into one-third coverage. We mix it up by playing man cover as well. We do different things with the corners. We do not sit them in a 1 by 8 alignment all of the time.

The spur and bandit align with their inside foot up. They look inside to the quarterback. As soon as they get the read and they know it is a pass play, they come outside, keeping their eyes on the quarterback. They want to get depth and width.

The Lou and Rob linebackers are hook-curl players. They work 10 to 12 yards deep. The Mike linebacker is a hole player, and he is 10 to 12 yards deep.

What we are talking about here is basically a five under with three deep. We play against some great quarterbacks. In cover 3, if we hit the right landmarks, we should have the players covering the flat, hook-curl, hole, hook-curl, flat, one-third, one-third, and one-third (see Diagram 9-9).

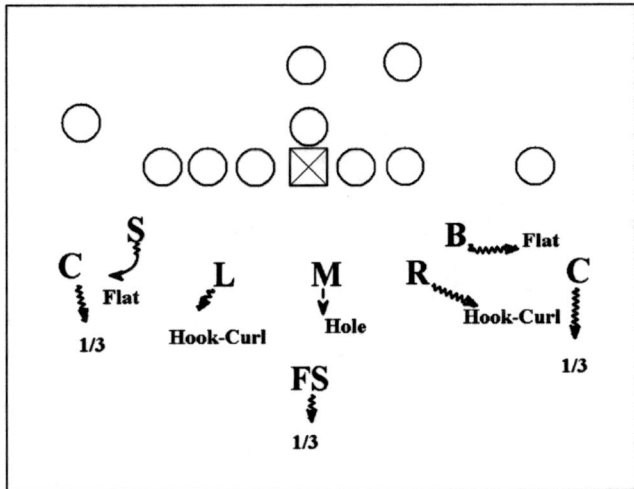

Diagram 9-9. In cover 3, if we hit the right landmarks, we should have the players covering the flat, hook-curl, hole, hook-curl, flat, one-third, one-third, and one-third.

If we want to blitz one of the linebackers, we end up with a four- under-three-deep coverage. We move the linebackers in and out of the gaps to mess with them. We can show the blitz and drop off, and we can walk them up and blitz. The same is true with the corners. We move them up and fake man coverage. We move them up and play man coverage. We mix it up with the coverage.

The key is that we want our linebackers aggressive. Against play action, we want them to play aggressive. Our linebacker coach tells them, "Stick your face in the fan." Remember, our number one priority is what? Stop the run! Right! If the offense runs play-action plays, we are telling our linebackers to stop the run. We tell the other backs they must play man-to-man when they read play action pass.

I want to talk about cover 1 for a few minutes. Everything is from a loose alignment. With our corners, we have inside leverage, and we line up at seven yards deep. We stagger the stance. We do not care which foot is back. We used to coach it one way, but it really does not matter. We want to get all the weight off the back foot. If the weight is on the front foot, the corner can go in any direction. If he is going back, he must push off the front foot. If he needs to get downhill, he can push off the front foot and get moving forward. He wants all his weight on the front foot.

Against the trip set we roll our free safety and bandit if they line up on one side and motion back to the other side. We do not move across the formation (see Diagram 9-10).

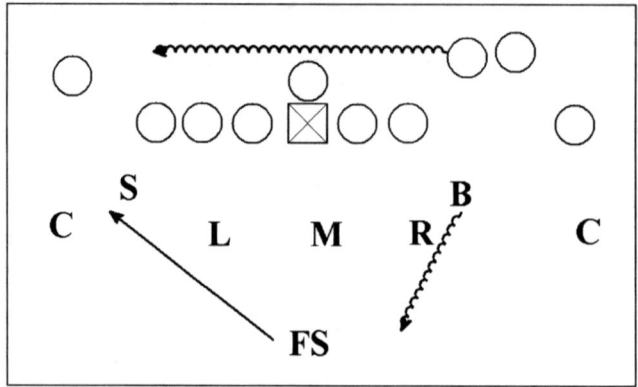

Diagram 9-10. Invert coverage vs. motion

In talking about our drills for the secondary, we do stance, start, and back peddle every day. The key is to relax the arms. We tell players to play the piano with their fingers. When we back peddle we want them on their toes. We stress keeping the elbows in tight.

I do want to show the film on our drills for our defensive backs. We have a net that we use in our defensive drills. In all of our drills, we have the defensive backs slap the ground before they start the drill. That is a just a reminder for them to stay low. We make the players get in their stance, slap the ground, and then go. If you want to get more on our drills, drop me a note. We use a lot of different techniques. I like man-to-man techniques the best.

That is a little about our defense. If you want to visit us you are welcome. If we can do anything for you, let us know. Thank you.

10

The 3-3 Stack
Fire Zone Blitz Package

Jeff Giesting
Anderson High School, Ohio
2009

It is a great honor to be here. This is a great clinic. I want to thank the Nike Coach of the Year Clinic for having me. At one time, I coached at Franklin, Indiana, and we came to this clinic several times. This clinic has always been a place where you could learn football.

Last year, I spoke on offense at another clinic. This year, I am speaking on defense. I will never speak on special teams because I do not know enough about that part of the game. I realize that special teams is an important phase of the game, but I have some good assistants who help with that phase of our game.

Our defense has evolved over the last several years. When I came to Anderson in 1988, we were in a 50 defense. Five years later, we switched to the 4-3 defense. We were a 4-3 team for about 10 or 11 years, and we had a lot of success with that defense.

Five years ago we were 5-5 and we struggled on defense. The reason we struggled was because we did not have enough defensive linemen. We switched to the 3-3 and one of the reasons was the fact that we did not need to have as many defensive linemen.

The thing about changing is the fact you should always evaluate what you are doing on offense and defense. You need to look at the things you have been doing and see if you can change a few things to make you a better football team. You must be willing to change what you are doing if there is something you can do to make your team a better team. You do not have to make drastic changes, but you can get an idea or two, and it helps. I have taken other ideas from many coaches.

I think it is important to note: the longer you coach, the more you realize the game is more about player development and their attitudes than it is about X's and O's. To learn the X's and O's is not that tough to do, but coaching kids' attitudes and getting them to play as they can is much more important.

In my bio, it was mentioned that we were state champions in my first year as a head coach. That was a great accomplishment, but we had 15 seniors on the team. We had lost 38 seniors the year before, and we were just hoping to survive that next year. Our players stepped up for us, and we got some breaks along the way. This year, we went down to the last 32 seconds before we lost in the state finals. We have been successful in this game in the last two years.

The thing I have been able to look at in the last two years is the fact that it is not just the end results that matter. The result is not always going to be the most important thing in the game. Working with the players every day and developing a relationship with them and the other coaches is a big part of the game.

I think it is important for coaches to find out what works best for them in football. Not all of the things we do are going to fit in for you, and that is fine. You must make an evaluation of your kids is selecting an offense or a defense.

If you are looking for defensive players, you do not want those who cannot make plays. You must find players on defense who will make plays. You must make an honest evaluation of the knowledge of the defense you are switching to run. You have to ask the question of how much you know about the defense. You need to know the weakness of the defense.

It is important to study your opponents and know whom you have to beat on your schedule. Can you beat them with the defense you are selecting? You must select a defense that will give you a chance to get into the playoffs. Once you get into the playoffs, then you have a chance.

In Ohio, we are a large Division II school. We were in Division I for a long time. We were in a district with Moeller, Colerain, Elder, and St. Xavier. These schools are great teams. We could never get out of the first round of the playoffs. Now that our enrollment has dropped, we are in Division II. Now, we are a large Division II team in Ohio. There is a big difference in playing those teams in Division I and the teams in Division II.

You must have assistant coaches to go along with the other things needed to be successful. I am fortunate in that I have 9 out of 10 coaches who are in the building with me. I know that is not the case in most schools, but that is a big plus for us. Two of our three freshman coaches are in the building.

I want you to know that I am not bragging when I tell you about our program. I am just telling you some of the things that have worked for us over the years.

You must have a philosophy to start out with on offense or defense. Here are our objectives on defense:

- Prevent our opponent from scoring.
- Get the ball back.
- Score, or set up scores.
- Execute all defenses perfectly.
- Everyone is on the same page.

We need objectives when we put the defense into place. We want to prevent teams from scoring. We do not shut teams out from scoring. Now, we are giving up more points than we did before, but we are winning more games. The most important stat on defense is the number of points scored against you. It is not first downs or yards given up. It is the points scored against you.

We would like to get three-and-out every time if possible. We know that is important to the offense as well as the defense. We know third down is the money down, and we must get off the field on third downs.

We must be able to communicate to the players. Players have to communicate with each other and to their coaches. When our players come off the field, they go to their position coaches to let them know what is going on in the game. There is a lot of communication between the press box and the field. The style of play for us is as follows:

- Physical
- Relentless
- Attacking
- Recognition
- Communication

We want to be physical. This can be developed in the off-season. We lift weights four days a week. Our staff does a great job in the weight room. We develop leadership by physically attacking each other. The players go through a series of exercises that are tougher than anything they do in two-a-days. They keep coming back for more. They build confidence in these drills. You can see as they go through the program.

The players develop camaraderie as they are going through some difficult workouts together. They help each other through some difficult times. They learn to care about their teammates, and they care about their teammates' success. This is very important in developing teamwork.

They have to learn to be relentless. They just cannot quit. They must be willing to work through problems. Gaining confidence in what they are doing helps a great deal here.

Recognition is important. It is important to match up with personnel. Communication is important in dealing with all phases of the game.

Good defenses are always going to align correctly. This is what we base our defense on, and this is what we want on every play:

- Align correctly.
- Diagnose plays and schemes.
- Separate from blocks.
- Run to the ball.
- Tackle.
- Great attitude ("The most important choice ever made" –Hal Urban).
- Great habits that show up in stressful situations.

The good defensive players line up correctly. They know their responsibility, and they know their gap. They know the depth they need to be off the ball. They know their shade techniques.

They must be able to diagnose plays and schemes. It is important for the players to come off to the sideline to tell the coaches what they are doing. It is important for players to be able to communicate with the coaches when they are out of the game.

We want to find players who can separate and get off blocks. It does not have to be technical and playbook style, but players must get off blocks. Find players, for some reason, get to the football. Find players who can find the football, and who do not let other players get in their way.

We want players who can tackle the football. Tackling is getting tougher to teach more and more. You see a lot of articles that state tackling is getting worse over the years. I am not sure if it is or not. It may be the offensive-skilled players are becoming more athletic. Tackling is something you must work on all of the time.

It is important to have a good attitude. Hal Urban wrote a book about attitudes: *Choices That Change Lives*. I read his book, and I got a lot out of it on attitude. He said, "The most important choice you will ever make is your attitude."

Coaches can tell the kids who are going to step up and be leaders. Those players have a great attitude. Bad things can happen sometimes when you are playing defense. How does the player react to a bad situation? Does he have his head down for the next four plays? If he does that, he is not the kid you want as your leader. Most of the time, when the offense sees that player with his head down, that is the person they are going to run at for the next two or three plays. Eventually, he figures he better get his head up and play tough. This is especially true with secondary players.

Great habits show up in stressful situations. In the long run, to be coached on what players need to do will pay off when the players get in a stressful situation.

Why play the 3-3 stacked defense? We have had three Division I players in the last 15 years who have gone on to college to play defense. We have not had many good defensive linemen. This is one reason we like the 3-3 alignment. Here are some reasons we play the 3-3:

- Only three defensive linemen are needed
- Six in the box to stop the run
- Five defensive backs
- Variety of fronts and looks
- Bluffing and deception
- Adjustments and flexibility
- Aggressive downhill defense
- Creates turnovers

We would like to have six defensive linemen to rotate into those three down positions. Those three positions are very demanding positions.

We like the idea of always having at least six men in the box to stop the run. We are very hesitant to break our stack. We want to leave the six defenders in the box. If the offense starts to outflank us, we will move some defenders outside.

We like the idea that we have five defensive backs. That puts more speed on the field. It allows us to give the offense a variety of fronts and looks. It is difficult for the opponents to learn a lot of different looks each week. We disguise the defense as much as we can. Walking up into a seven-man front is easy to do in this defense.

This defense allows us to mess up the offensive scheme by moving around. We have the ability to adjust the defense. It is very flexible in that we can change the defense without disrupting the rest of the defense. The adjustments are very easy, and we have a wide variety of defensive looks we can line up in.

You do need to have some ideas on how you are going to play against certain formations. One of the first things you need to decide on is how you are going to play against a double-tight-end set. Teams will line up in two tight ends and try to run the ball right at you. You need to decide how you are going to handle a wing-T set. How are you going to play on the wing? Are you going to walk the linebacker, or dog as we call them, down to the line and play on his outside shoulder? There are a lot of ways to play that set, but you need to decide how you are going to play it before you get in to the game.

You have to look at your personnel in making these decisions. You may have to make a personnel change against certain offenses. You need to have a certain amount of adjustments in your package that will help against certain offensive looks.

Our defense is an aggressive downhill defense. Those inside linebackers are running to the football. We like the defense because it helps create turnovers. This past year, we had 18 interceptions and recovered 9 fumbles. I think one reason we get the turnovers is because of the hesitancy of the offense by our crashing defense. The offense is looking for the blitz, and they make mistakes.

The keys to our success are as follows:
- Execution
- Play recognition
- Communication
- Fun

We feel you must make football fun for the players. You cannot just scream and yell at them all of the time. It can be tough on the players after they have been in school all day. They come to practice, and they have problems on their mind. It may be a problem at home, a problem with a girlfriend, or something that is keeping them from performing at a high level. It is up to the coaches to get them going. In the time that you have with the players, it is your job to make it fun for them. You want them to enjoy practice and want to come to practice every day.

In our base alignment, we line up head-up with the nose man (Diagram 10-1). We line up in heavy 5 techniques with our tackles. We are close to being head-up on the tackles. Our Mike backer may shade just a little to the strong A gap. The backers will shade one way or the other, depending on the boundary and the field. They still are stacked behind the tackles. We try to play the five backs across the back line. We do not line up in 4x4 alignments. We can move them around and drop them back between seven and eight yards deep. They can still cover anything in front of them.

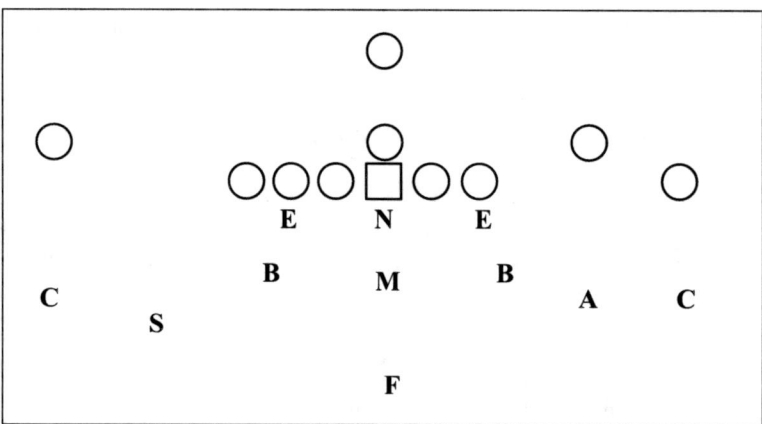

Diagram 10-1. Base alignment

It is easy to disguise who the robber is going to be, and to disguise the coverages, or to determine who is going to be the run support at times. We can play a variety of three-deep out of this defense. All of our linebackers have their heels at five yards deep as their starting point. It depends on how good you are up front. You may have to move the linebackers up some if the front three are not that fast.

St. Xavier High School does a great job with this defense. They play their linebackers up tighter at three-and-a-half yards deep. The front three are very physical, and they all tackle well. They do a lot of different things from this look.

We have visited a lot of places to talk about this defense. We went to West Virginia. We talked with Steve Specht of St. Xavier about the defense. When Todd Graham was at West Virginia, we talked with him about the defense. Todd Graham is at Tulsa now. We do not do a lot out of this defense, as other teams do. You have to find what works best for you.

We like teaching from this alignment from day one. Two years ago, we started out by teaching from the 4x4 alignment. Then, we worked on backing a man off the line of scrimmage. However, the last couple of years, we have started with the 3x3 from day one. I think this approach has helped, especially with the young kids.

I want to give you the things we expect from our personnel. Our nose is going to be an A-gap player.

Nose

- Can be big or small and quick
- Must be tough, physical, and relentless
- Has to handle double-teams
- Unselfish

Our ends are more athletic than the nose man is. Our ends are not very big. Next year, one end will weigh 205 pounds, and the other end will weigh 195 pounds. They are not big, but they are tall and rangy.

Ends

- Taller and more athletic than nose
- Able to handle double-teams
- Able to close on down blocks
- Able to run

Our Mike backer is an A-gap player. He plays off the nose man. He must be smart enough to read the triangle to know what is going on. He cannot be wrong in his movements.

Mike Linebacker

- Physical
- Smart, can read triangle
- Able to get over the top of blocks

Our outside backers are B-gap players. They play behind the ends.

Outside Linebackers

- Able to run
- Good blitzers
- Disciplined for cutback
- Able to defend inside zones and reroute receivers

You cannot just go out and tell a player to blitz the gap. You must teach him the techniques to get through that gap. They must help on disguising their moves. They must play the cutbacks and not just go flying around. They must be able to protect the inside zones and reroute receivers. The play is similar to an outside linebacker on the 4-3 defense. They can be as light as 160 pounds to 200 pounds, depending on their speed.

The Dogs are B-gap players. They play pass and run. They must be a good athlete to play this position.

Dogs (Apache and Sam)

- Strong safety types
- Good tacklers
- Good blitzers
- Able to defeat blocks in space

We do prefer someone who is a little taller than the other defenders. We want them to be able to get into the passing lanes. The big point is that they must be good tacklers and they must be able to blitz efficiently. We want to let the offense know that we can come off the edge on a blitz. This will keep them honest.

Our free safety must be a smart player. In most cases, we want our best athlete in this position. This year, we played free safety with a 150-pound kid, but he was tough.

Free Safety

- Smart
- Ideally, the best athlete
- Good tackler
- Good ball skills

Our corner must have good ball skills. He must have good hands, and he must be able to catch the football. If he gets his hands on a pass and does not catch it, he should be upset. When we look back on the games, you have questions about those plays. They are on an island by themselves. They must be ready to play every play.

Corners

- Good ball skills
- Able to play man and zone

We line up in our defense, and we call "front" (Diagram 10-2). We are going to stack the backers behind the line and play with five secondary players.

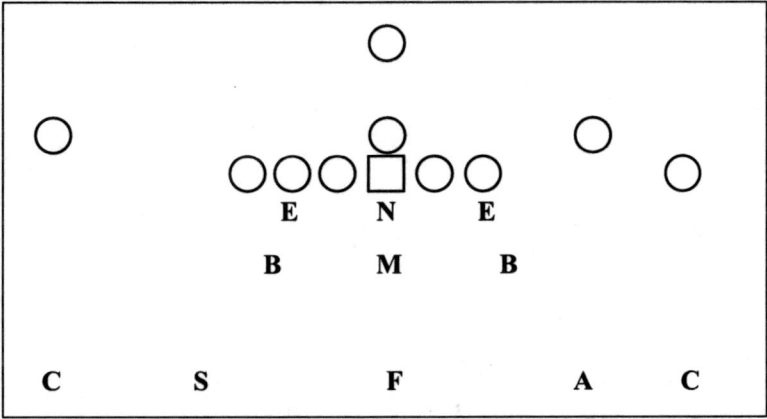

Diagram 10-2. Front stack

If we call "down," we are going to bring the Dogs down. We have them labeled with S and A (Diagram 10-3). That puts us in a 5-3 look. This gives us a chance to blitz and to bring a defender from the edge. It is hard to ask a back to play one-third deep middle when they are up on the line of scrimmage. However, when they are eight yards deep, they can play a deep-third, or a deep-half in the secondary.

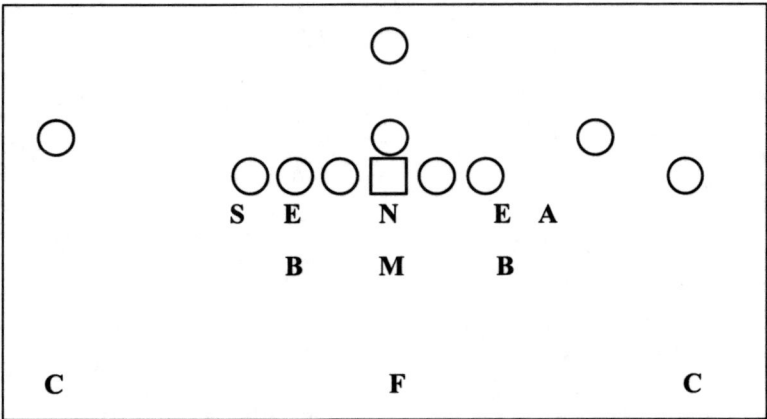

Diagram 10-3. Down

We run our spread look, which is our 5-1 look (Diagram 10-4). We walk the dogs up on the edge. When teams see us in this defense, they want to attack us on the inside. We still have the A gap covered with the Mike backer and the nose. You can mix things up and take care of the B gap. If the ball comes free in the middle of the defense, the deep-middle defenders must come down inside and converge on the play. We like to line up showing a blitz from one area and bringing the blitz from another area.

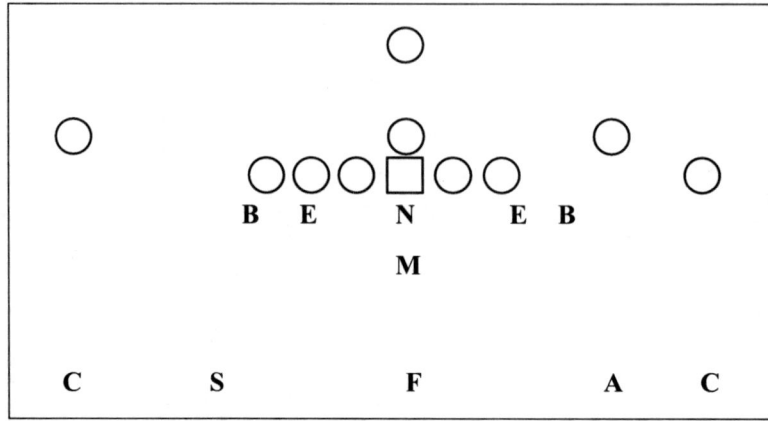

Diagram 10-4. Spread

We use the nickel call on long yardage (Diagram 10-5). This is our 3-2 look. We have six deep defenders. We can take a lineman or a linebacker out of the lineup and replace him with a defensive back.

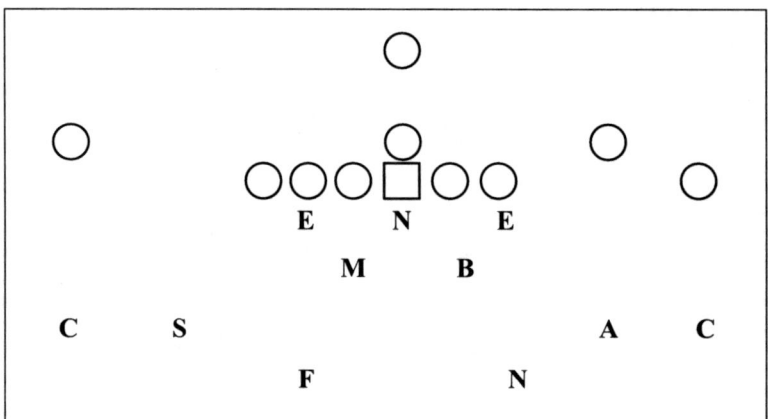

Diagram 10-5. Nickel

If you have a kid who is smart enough to play outside linebacker, you could bump the linebackers over and put him outside, or drop him back in the middle. When the offense sees us in this defense, they want to run the ball because they only see five men in the box. We did well in this defense against the run by having two men, including the nickel, who could come down to support on the run. If you have five in the box and they cannot run the football, you should win the game.

I want to move on to our coverages. Primarily we are a three-deep cover team. Our corners play the deep outside (Diagram 10-6). The free safety is in the deep middle. The Dogs play the flats, and the three backers drop in the middle.

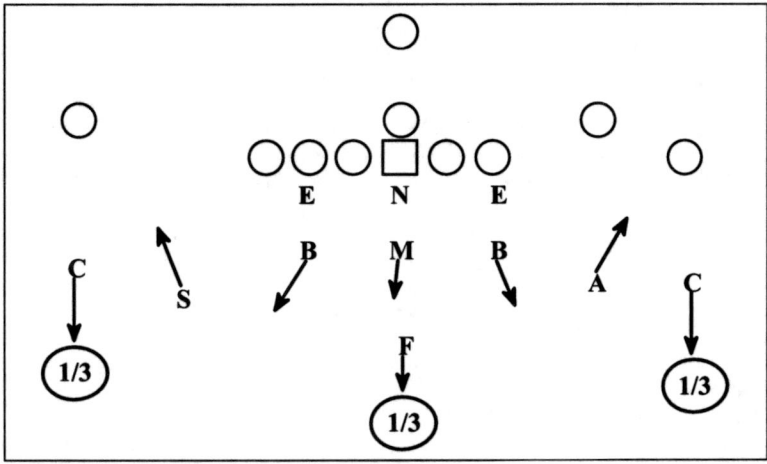

Diagram 10-6. Three deep coverage

We are only rushing three men from this front. Sometimes, we will bring four on the rush. We can move the linebackers up closer to the ball, which will allow you to do different things out of that look. We are unlimited on the different combinations that we can run form this defense.

We play a lot of robber coverage (Diagram 10-7). Against the one-back-set, you can bring the dogs to the flat, and drop the backers. You do not have to send the Mike backer every time you run this look. We do not run this look very much against the one-back-set, but we can. We think this defense is good against the two-backs set.

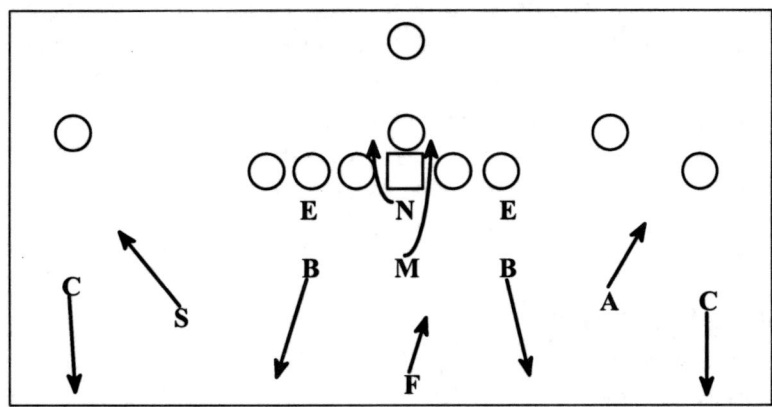

Diagram 10-7. Robber

On our man free, the deep free safety is deep in the middle (Diagram 10-8). He is free on the call. Again, this is against the one-back set. Here, the Mike backer is also free. You must know your rules as far as the man-to-man matchups. It all depends on who is blitzing on the plays as far as pass coverage. That is why it is so important to communicate on defense.

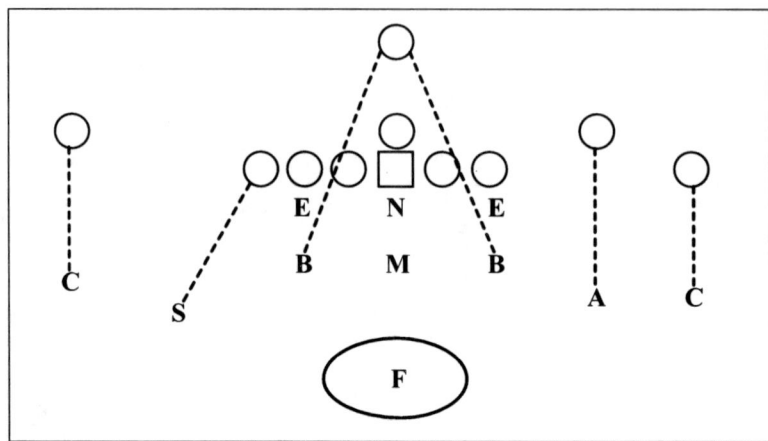

Diagram 10-8. Man free

I want to talk about our fire zones for a few minutes. Here are the advantages of running the fire zone-blitz package:
- Defense can always see the ball.
- Good for run support.
- Hole player can be used to spy the quarterback.
- Fewer one-on-one tackles in space.
- Average athletes can make plays.
- Defend crossing routes, and picks better than in man.
- Only limited by your imagination.

I want to talk about the rules for us on the three-deep fire zone defense. It is very simple. I heard this explanation of the defense at a clinic from Kevin Coyle when he was at Fresno State. It has held up all of this time since I first heard him talk about the defense. The thing you must do, and to stress when you look at film, is to decide who the hot-route receivers are. If you can do that, you have a good chance of shutting them down. This is what you must have on this defense.

Three-Deep Fire Zone

- Two seam-curl-flat defenders
- One or two hole defenders
- Three deep defenders

We call the hole defenders the "skip" players. They defend the seam, the curl, and then the flat. We work inside-out to take away everything to the inside and work to the outside. We defend one or two holes, depending on the blitz.

I want to show you the first fire zone blitz to the split end side. We are bringing the nose, end, Dog on the backside, and Mike (Diagram 10-9). We want the rush end to read the backside guard. If the guard steps outside, the end goes inside of the guard. If the guard comes down inside, the end comes off the butt of the guard. We are not just running that end into the B gap. We want to know where the gap is after that backside guard moves.

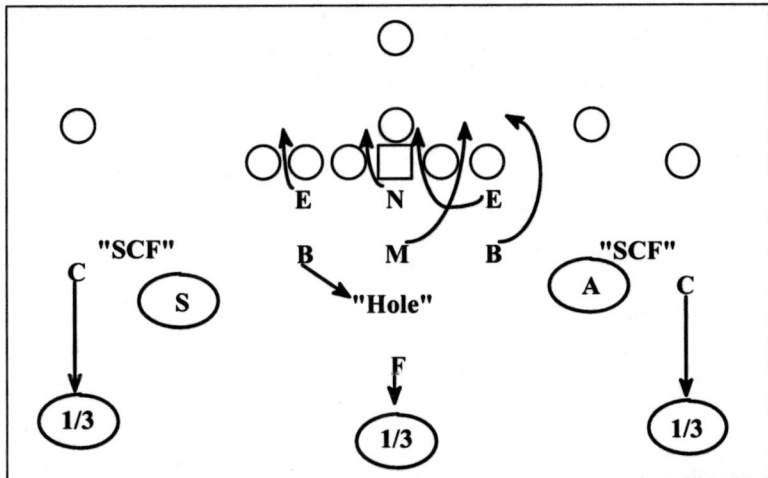

Diagram 10-9. Three-deep, split-end side

We run the blitz to the tight-end side or strongside as well (Diagram 10-10). This is easier to play for us. If the tight end releases inside and tries to go vertical, the outside Dog walls him off and forces him to the outside.

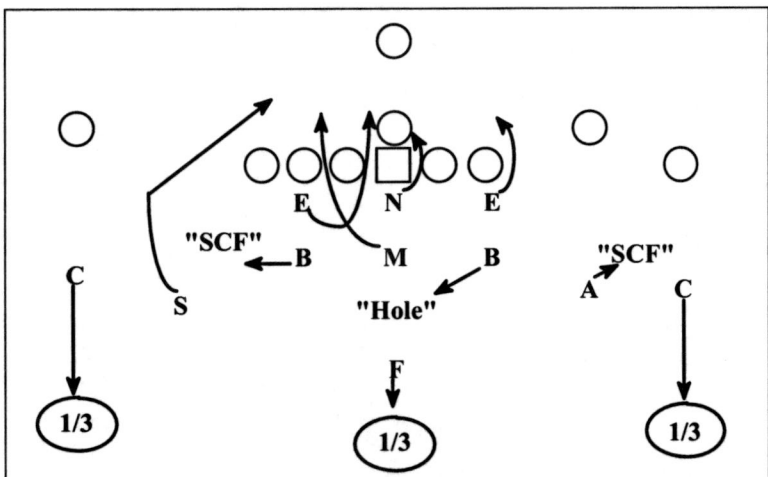

Diagram 10-10. Three-deep, tight-end side

We also run the fire zone blitz with a two-deep zone coverage. If the offense starts throwing to the flat because we are not defending that area that well, you must have a defense to come back to stop the pass to the flat. We are bringing the Sam and Apache backs deep and have each of them play the deep half. You can run the play with the cornerbacks playing one half (Diagram 10-11). This is what we need to play the defense.

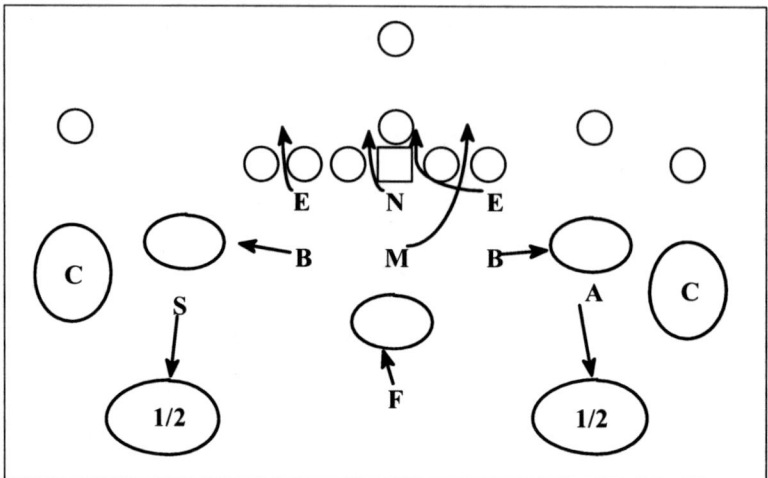

Diagram 10-11. Two-deep, split-end side

Two-Deep Fire Zone

- Two flat defenders
- Two curl defenders
- One hole defender
- Two deep defenders

You must coach the kids and make sure they understand where they can get hurt. The down linemen are not doing anything any different from what they did before.

On the strongside, it is the same as before with the two-deep. Because the corner is covered, he cannot play the flat. He is going to cover deep (Diagram 10-12). Sam and the free safety will each play one half deep. Again, the down linemen are doing the same as before.

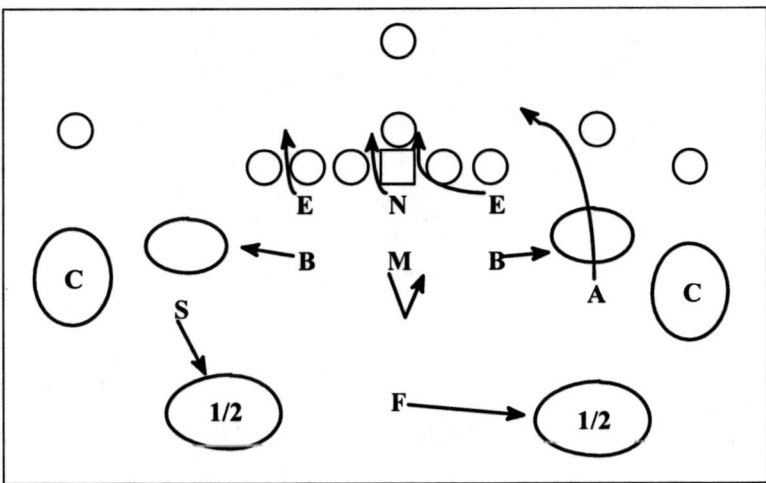

Diagram 10-12. Two-deep, tight-end side

I do have a film that will show the defense much better than I can describe it. Again, you can contact me if you have questions on the defense. I think one of the most important things about football coaches is the amount of information that is shared at various activities. I want to thank you for your attention.

11

The 3-5-3 Defensive Fronts and Stunts

Smitty Grider
Beauregard High School, Alabama
2010

First, I want to give you a little bit about my background. I coached junior high football for 10 years in Montgomery. I figured that was probably all I would do as a football coach. Then, a friend of mine got a coaching job at Opelika High School and it just hit me—I wanted to be a high school football coach. I called him and said, "I am calling you to ask that if you let me come up there and be a volunteer coach for one year, I will quit my job, and you do not even have to pay me. If I do a good job, I want you to hire me full time."

I told him that is what I wanted to do. I know he thought I was crazy, and my whole family thought I was crazy. He said, "Okay, come on up here. I will take you." I coached the defensive line for a year and he hired me. Two years later, he gave me the coordinator's job. I was the defensive coordinator for five years. We were a shade 50 team and played a cover-2 secondary, and we played seven men in the box. We had seven studs and we would beat your butt with seven people—it did not matter what you did. I learned a lot about coaching and coaching techniques from him.

Let me give you some advice. Do not always take the first opportunity to be a head coach. I took a job at a small country high school in Alabama that did not have much money and they had not had much success. I wanted to be a head coach, so I figured it was time to do it. In a lot of ways, it was a great experience. I learned a great deal. I learned it is tough to coach at a school that does not have much football experience.

I went from Opelika High School, with great facilities and a lot of great support, to a school that had to pay for coaching supplements out of the gate receipts. We had no money. We went 5-5 that first year, but we did a good coaching job.

Next, the opening at Beauregard came up, which is closer to where I am from. It was a similar situation in that they were a down program and never had a tradition of winning. The resources were a lot better there, and it was a better situation in the community.

I have been at Beauregard High School now for four years, and we have evolved into the 3-3 defense. I have taken the shade 50 defense with me everywhere I have been. We still use it some each year. However, we play the 3-3 defense most of the time, and that is what I want to talk to you about today.

In Alabama, we get 10 days of spring practice. Two years ago, I was in my office looking at spring practice tape of our 50 shade defense, and I realized we were not very good. Our defensive linemen were small, and we did not do a very good job of reading on defense. I called in my defensive coordinator. He was teaching P.E. and I told him, "We are going to go to the 3-3 defense today." He said, "Let's wait until after we get through spring practice, then we can put it in over the summer." We had a scrimmage scheduled the next week. I said, "No, we are going to do it now."

We had some DVDs on the 3-3 defense from Georgia Military College. We do the same thing that the Georgia Military does and we use the same terminology. The defensive coordinator and I sat in my office, and he let his P.E. class run wild while we figured out the base stuff. At 4 p.m., we put the whole team in the weight room with the offensive coaches while I met with the defensive coaches. In about 45 minutes, we put a practice plan together for that day. We went out and installed the 3-3 defense, and we completed it in four days of practice. We played the scrimmage and we actually played pretty well.

What that is telling you is that this defense is simple. It is not that complicated. If your kids are not real smart on the defensive line, it is a good defense for them. The defensive line only has to remember about four things. It is a little more difficult for the linebackers and defensive secondary because they have to know what the defensive line is doing. The defensive linemen have to know four defensive stunts. They have to know open, closed, pinch, and jacks—that is it. If they can learn those four things, they can play the defensive line.

I will start with our position names and fronts. Our mascot is the Hornets, so we call our outside linebackers Hornets.

Position Names

E = End (4 technique)
N = Nose
H = Hornet (outside backers)
B = Bat (stack backers)
M = Mike (middle backer)

Defensive Fronts

- Base
- Solid
- Tough
- Under
- G

We do not rush only three or four defenders very often. We like to put pressure on the opponents with five or more rushers. My defensive coordinator is also a baseball coach. You probably know that baseball coaches like to call a lot of hand signals. He likes to signal in a lot of moves, so we run stunts all of the time.

The first year we did not make the playoffs because we were a small 4A squad that had moved up to 5A. We played in a tough league and went 6-4 and 4-3 in the region. However, we did not get into the playoffs.

We had 106 tackles for loss in 10 games, plus 21 sacks. We were averaging at least 12 negative plays per game. Our turnovers were not as good as we wanted them to be, so we worked hard on that in the off-season. We got those turnovers a little better this year. In addition, our sack totals went up. We get a lot of negative plays from this defense.

We are in our *base front* most of the time (Diagram 11-1). We also run a solid front, which is our four-man front. Our under front is also a four-man front. When we run our under front, we usually change personnel at the Hornet position. It will be more like a shade 50.

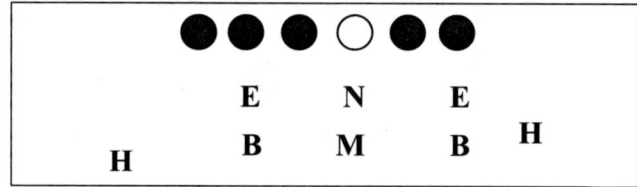

Diagram 11-1. Base

If we are in cover 3, our Hornets are going to be at three yards and three yards off the edge. They are outside three yards and back off the line three yards. We want them showing blitz and making it look as if they are coming on a blitz every time. Sometimes we will jockey those guys back and forth to make the offense think we are coming. We are always coming with someone. However, we are trying to confuse the offense on *who* is coming. That is our base alignment.

In our solid, we will move some players (Diagram 11-2). We do not make a strong right or a strong left call to the strength of the offense. Our linebackers make a closed or open call, depending on the formation and the position of the tight end. In this situation, the Mike linebacker will call, "Closed left, closed left." We are going to move to this front. We will be in our base defense with our stack.

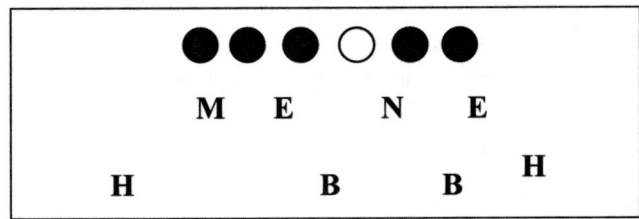

Diagram 11-2. Solid

We move our defense after the quarterback puts his hands under the center, or we move when the quarterback gives his leg kick when he is in the shotgun. We are going to move away from the strength. The nose will go from a 0 technique to a 1 technique on the weakside. The left end then will drop down to a 3 technique, and the Mike comes up to play a 7 technique. If there's not a tight end, then he is in a 5 technique.

I am not going to talk about our stunt package out of every front. Once you see our stunt package, you can match the same stunt out of any of the fronts. It all works together, and that is why it is so simple.

In our under front, we are going to move to the strength (Diagram 11-3). Mike is still going to make a closed left call. The nose is going to move to a shade on the strongside. Our 4-technique end will move to a 5 technique, and our backside 4 technique would drop down to a 3 technique. We don't flip-flop anybody. If you play on that side, then that is your side. We want to be able to line up and play. We do not want to have to worry about where to line up.

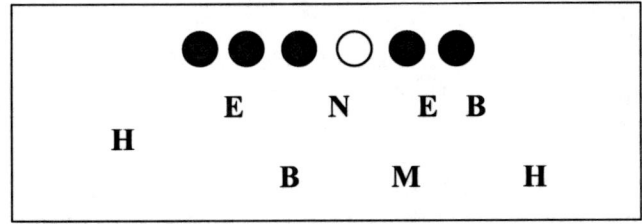

Diagram 11-3. Under

Here is the difference between G and under (Diagram 11-4). In the under look, the nose is in a 1 technique. In the G look, he is in a 3 technique to the strongside.

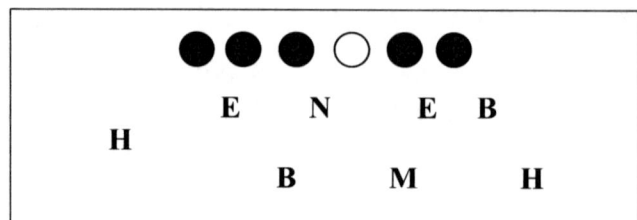

Diagram 11-4. G look

In this defense, you have to have a noseguard that demands a double-team because he is going to be double-teamed every snap. He has to be able to handle the double-team. If the offense knows the noseguard is going to slant every time, one way or another, they are going to double-team him every play.

Our ends were too small to play 5A football in Alabama, but they could run and that is what we were looking for. Our linebackers are not big, but all of our linebackers can run and they are intelligent kids. We want to put as much speed on the field as we can. That is another reason why we went to this defense.

We play five defensive backs. Our Hornets are hard-nosed defensive backs. They may not be able to cover your best receiver in space as a corner, but they are defensive backs. The free safety needs to be the smartest kid on the field. He has to make the checks, give our coverages, and set everything up. He has to be a physical guy that will run and make a lot of tackles for you.

Defensive Line

Stance: Three-point stance (balanced, comfortable); must be able to move either direction.

Aiming Point: Near hip of the offensive lineman he is moving toward.

Assignments: Control the gap you are moving toward and run to the ball.

We want our defensive lineman in a three-point stance—no more than a heel-toe alignment because they are stepping in one direction or the other 90 percent of the time. The aiming point is going to be the hip of the lineman that they are slanting toward, and they have to read that guy. We have to work hard when we are slanting. We do not want forced out of position on the blocks because we are going to get a lot of down blocks and a lot of back blocks.

They have to realize that when they feel that pressure and they are slanting in one direction, they cannot keep going in that direction and let that offensive guy wash him out. If you do not coach that up, he will be knocked out of the gap. On the other hand, they will be so concerned about it that they will not get across the face of the offensive lineman and they will not be in the gap you need. There is a fine line those guys have to play.

We do a lot of drills with them stepping just a half a step with the correct foot. They need to step at a 45-degree angle with that near foot. A lot of kids will have one direction that they are not good at. It is real important that you work hard on those steps with the defensive line. We do not want them upfield once they get in that gap. We want them flat down the line of scrimmage, chasing.

These are the calls the defensive linemen have to know. They need to know the open, closed, pinch, and jack calls.

The defensive linemen only have to listen to the first word of the call. If we call *open*, it means the linemen are slanting away from the strength, or away from the call (Diagram 11-5).

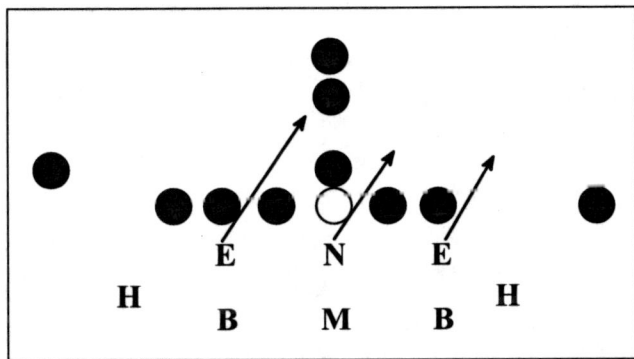

Diagram 11-5. Open

If we call *closed*, they are slanting to the strength, to the call, or toward the tight end (Diagram 11-6). We call strength to the tight end side, then to the side with the most receivers, then to the side of the back. If everything is balanced, we will call strength to the field.

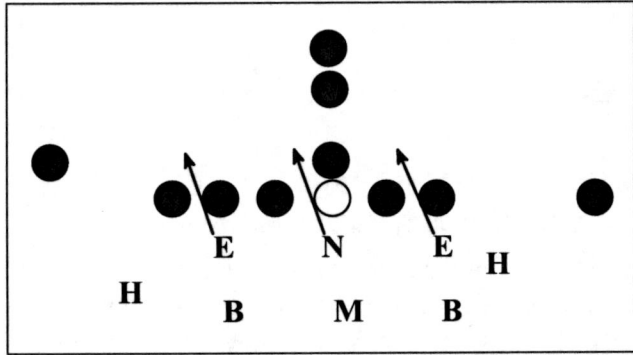

Diagram 11-6. Closed

If we call *pinch*, our 4-technique ends are slanting to the inside and going to the hip of the guard (Diagram 11-7). Our noseguard could go either way and we give him a choice. It really does not matter to us but the Mike has to know, so they work together. We give our kids a lot of freedom, which gives them ownership in the defense.

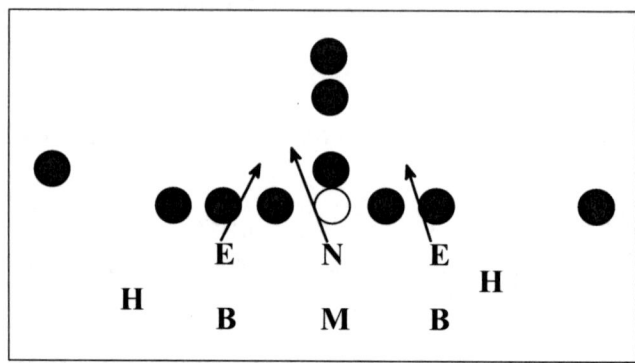

Diagram 11-7. Pinch

If we call *jacks*, our ends must control the C gaps (Diagram 11-8). Our nose controls the strongside A gap.

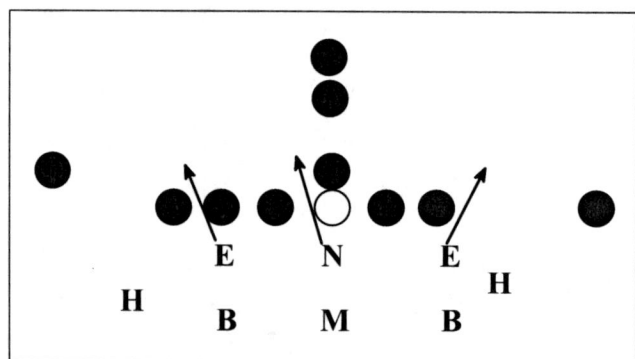

Diagram 11-8. Jacks

Linebackers

Stance: Shoulder over your knees, knees over your toes, weight on the inside balls of your feet.

Keys: Near running back to pulling lineman.

Drills: Key drill, blitzing, get off blocks, pass drops.

The linebackers' stance is the same stance that everybody else has with their heels at five yards. The linebackers are going to key through the line to the near running back. If we are in man coverage, they really want to key the running back to get an idea of where the play is going. We coach just as everyone else does on getting off blocks. We are going to use our hands. We are going to lock out the same as what everybody does.

We expect our linebackers to be our best players. They have got to run and make plays for you. You want to put your smartest guy at Mike, and you want to put your most athletic guys at the Bats. It is very important that they understand their fit. Because this defense is so simple, you can get by with playing some guys that are not seasoned. The Mike linebacker is the key to the whole thing. He has to understand his fit, especially because of all the stunting we do. If we get two in the same gap, we are going to have an issue.

There are four frontside keys for our Bats. We base our keys off of cover 3. If they are in cover 3, they can really see through the linemen better.

If the onside guard blocks down, the Bat fills the B gap. If the onside guard and tackle both block down, he fills outside the tackle in the C gap. If the onside guard pulls, the Bat comes outside the C gap and plays the pulling guard. If the onside guard and tackle reach block, the Bat fills outside of the tackle in the C gap.

There are two backside keys for the Bats. If the guard pulls, the Bat goes with the pulling guard. If the guard and tackle scoop block, the Bat plays through the block of the guard over the center.

If we are playing a veer team, we will not stunt as much. We will play a little bit more read so we can squeeze. I do not recommend that you stunt very much out of this defense if you play against an option team.

Hornets

Stance: Shoulders over your knees. If on the right side, the left foot is up and the right foot is back. If on the left side, the right foot is up and the left foot is back.

Keys: Read the V between the quarterback and deepest back and the end man on the line of scrimmage.

Drills: Key drill, blitzing, man-to-man, pass drops.

If the tackle blocks down and the near back kicks out, the Hornet comes up and takes on the near back. If the tackle reach blocks and the near back shows fast flow outside, the Hornet comes outside and covers the near back on the fast flow. If the tackle reach blocks and the near back shows inside flow, the Hornet reads the back. He can stay inside, or he can cover outside. If the tackle shows pass, the Hornet drops outside to his pass responsibility.

We expect the Hornets to be our hardest players to block, and they have to work their tails off to get to the ball because we stunt them a lot. We would like to have guys that can play good man coverage on a good slot receiver. Our defensive backs these past couple of years have been the shortest in the history of football. I do not think we had a defensive back over 5'7", other than our free safety.

Here is our philosophy. The ball has to come out in 2.5 seconds. If we can do that, then we can survive with those guys. They have to play hard against those receivers and we want hard-nosed kids at those positions. They are going to have to give up their bodies a lot, and they are going to have to be able to make some tackles. They are midget linebackers. They have their inside foot up and their weight on their front foot so we give them a look that they are coming every time. We expect them to be willing to go up and take out a fullback—that is what we expect.

Coverages

Cover 1: We bring four- or five-man pressure in man coverage (Diagram 11-9). Either one or two inside linebackers blitz. The free safety is free, our corners have the #1 receiver, and the Hornets have the #2 receivers. The remaining inside linebacker either has #3 or is a low-hole player.

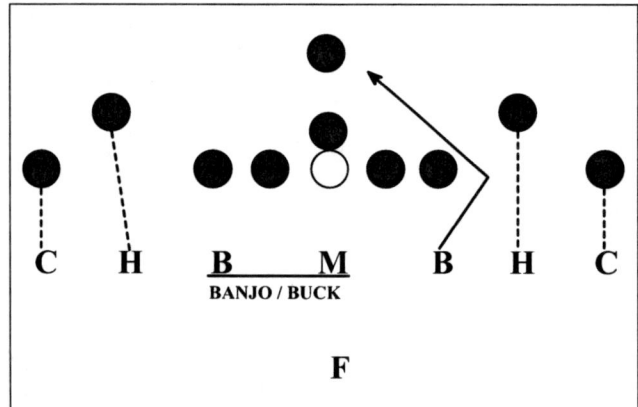

Diagram 11-9. Cover 1

If we are running cover 1, that means we are stunting and bringing four or five people and it is an inside linebacker stunt. Depending on what the offense is showing us, we can check into cover 1 depending on the formation.

Cover Black: We bring four- or five-man pressure in man coverage—either one Hornet or both a Hornet and a Bat blitz (Diagram 11-10). The free safety has #2 to the blitzside. The Hornet away from the blitz has #2. The corners have #1, and the remaining inside linebacker either has #3 or is a low-hole player.

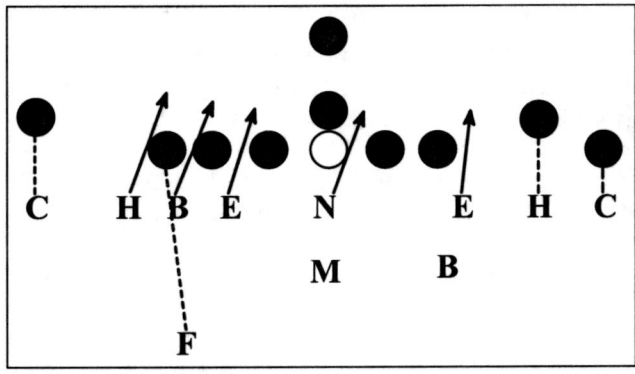

Diagram 11-10. Cover black

Our black coverage means we are bringing one of the Hornets. When we play black coverage, the free safety is going to have #2 to the flipside in man coverage, and we are in cover zero. We do not ever ask our stack backers to cover a wide receiver. They are always going to be on a running back. That way, we don't have a bad match-up with a real good wide receiver. Everyone else is man-up. The way we work our inside linebackers is that the backers that are not stunting have the running backs in the backfield. If there is one running back, then we banjo. In other words, if he comes to me, I have him. The other backer away from the flow of the running back is the low-hole player to watch for crossing routes.

Cover White: We bring five-man pressure in man coverage—both Hornets blitz (Diagram 11-11). The free safety has #2 to the side that he calls (he calls out, "I am left" or "I am right"). The corners have #1, and the inside backers banjo the #3 receiver away from the free safety. The remaining inside linebacker is a low-hole player.

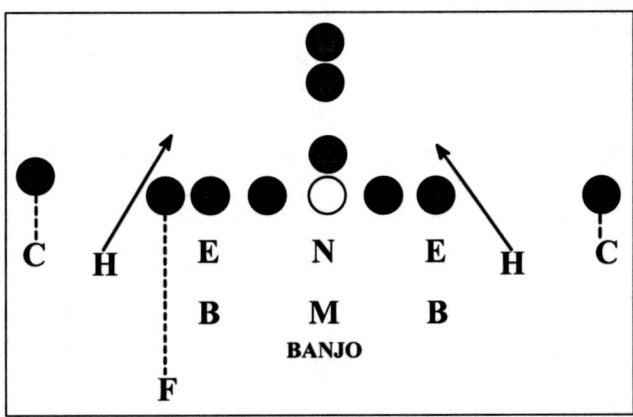

Diagram 11-11. Cover white

We run white coverage when we are blitzing both outside guys. The free safety is going to take #2 on one side or the other. The Hornets are listening for an "I am left," or "I am right," call from the safety, so he can still stunt. If he does not get the call from the safety, he cannot blitz.

Cover Blue: We bring six-man pressure—all three inside linebackers blitz (Diagram 11-12). The corners have #1, the Hornets have #2, and the free safety has #3.

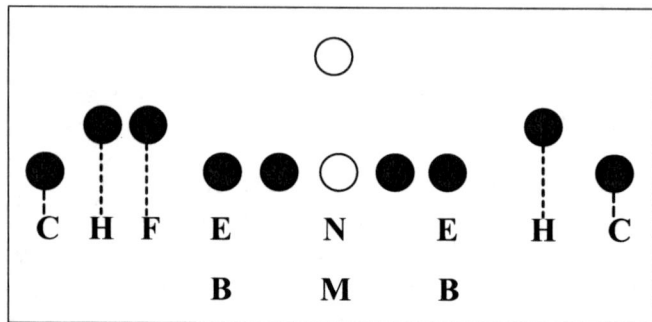

Diagram 11-12. Cover blue

Three Deep: We bring five-man pressure in the fire-zone concept. The two inside backers blitz, and the remaining inside backer has the middle-hook zone. Both Hornets have the curl/flat area. Corners are deep outside one-third, and the free safety has the middle third.

If we get an empty look in the backfield, our check is *zoo blue*. That means we are bringing all six and we are in cover zero.

We run our cover 3 and cover 1 against trips. The corners have the #1 receiver counting from the outside to the inside. The Hornet has the #2 to the #3 wide receiver side. The backside Hornet always gets a spin call and replaces the free safety. The Bats banjo the running back. If the back comes to his side, he takes him. If the back goes away from him, he low holes the play.

On cover 3 against double slots, the corners have the outside one-thirds. The Hornets play curl/flat. The Bats play hook/curl to their side. The free safety has the deep middle one-third.

Pressure Packages—Four-Man Rush

- Bat open/closed right/left 1/3
- Mike strong/weak 1/3
- Bob open/closed right/left 1/3
- Bam open/closed right/left 1/3
- Buc open/closed right/left 1/3
- Hornet open/closed right/left black

The linebackers and secondary must know where the down linemen are going on the pressure packages. They must know which gap they are responsible for when they are stunting. The linemen only need to know closed/left or open/right.

We never huddle. Everyone looks to the sideline to get the defensive signal. On our Bat open right, we send the strongside Bat in the A gap (Diagram 11-13). The secondary plays cover 1 or cover 3.

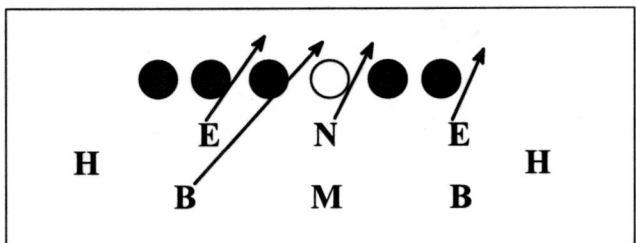

Diagram 11-13. Bat open right 1/3

The opposite of that call is our Bat closed left (Diagram 11-14). We send the linemen toward the tight end and the backside Bat stunts through the A gap on the weakside.

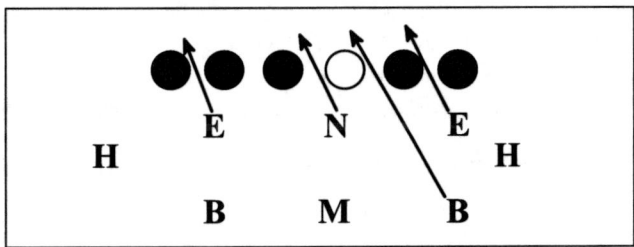

Diagram 11-14. Bat closed left 1/3

Pressure Packages—Five-Man Rush

- Zoo strong/weak 1/3
- Mash strong/weak 1/3
- Double Buc pinch 1/3
- Double Hornet pinch white
- Jacks blast 1/3
- Open/closed boom—Right/left black
- Mob open/closed 1/3
- Lightning weak black

On zoo strong, we are sending five rushers. The ends have the C gap, and the noseman has the A gap strong. The strongside Bat has the B gap, and the Mike has the strongside B gap. We play cover 1 or cover 3.

On zoo weak, we are sending five rushers. The ends have the C gap, and the noseman has the A gap weak. The backside Bat has the weakside B gap, and the Mike has the weakside B gap. We play cover 1 or cover 3.

Pressure Packages—Six-Man Rush

- Zoo blue
- Pinch special white
- Bat open Bob Hornet black
- Bat open Bam Hornet black

On a zoo blue call, we send six men on the blitz. The ends have the C gaps. The nose has the backside A gap. The Bats have the B gaps on each side. The Mike has the strongside A gap.

Pressure Packages—Seven-Man Rush—Pinch Mike Double Hornet White

If white is the call, if a Hornet has two receivers to his side and the free safety is gone, he must check to Buc. We are sending the ends in the B gaps. The nose and Mike play games in the two A gaps. One goes to one side, and the other man goes opposite.

You can see all of the different combinations you can come up with in this defense. You can name the stunts the way your players will remember them. The big thing is that it does not take long to add a stunt once you have the basic system installed.

I know I have given you a lot and I have gone fast. If you want our entire package, drop me a note. Thank you for your time.

12

The Complete
3-3-5 Defensive Package

Les Hamilton
Alta High School, Utah
2010

It is a pleasure to be here. I am the head football coach at Alta High School in Sandy, Utah. I am fortunate to be the head coach of one of the best high schools in the country. It is a phenomenal school. We have 2,600 kids in the upper three grades. We are in south Salt Lake. We are a big school. We have over 1,000 Little League kids that feed into our school. We have seven teams for the 9th grade teams that feed into our one sophomore team. We are very blessed in our program. We have great players, great athletes, and we turn out a lot of kids that go on to Division I colleges.

We could probably line up in any defense and do well with it. We do feel that the 3-3 defense is a big part of our success, and it has enabled us to win championships. We have played some good teams in Utah and outside of the state. We have played some good teams out of the state the last few years—Clovis East High School out of Fresno, Grant High School out of Sacramento, and Rainier Beach High School out of Seattle. We look forward to playing other good teams in the future.

We are not trying to reinvent the wheel. I am from Petaluma High School in northern California. My high school coach just retired after 28 years at Petaluma High School. He taught me one thing when I became a head coach. That point has stayed with me over the years. He said, "Don't get caught up in the X's and O's of football. It is about being able to tackle and being fundamentally sound in blocking."

When I took this job five years ago, I sat down with my defensive coordinator and talked about what we wanted to do on defense. We decided we would run the 3-3-5 defense. We felt this defense was going to give us some advantages because of the personnel that we had coming up. Here are other factors we considered in picking the 3-3-5 defense.

Why Run the 3-3-5 Defense?

- Best fits our personnel
- Minimal adjustments from double wing to empty
- Allows us to platoon
- Attacking, disrupting, pressure defense
- Our players love to play it; our coaches love to coach it

If you can pick up a point or two here today from what we do, I hope it will help you with your defense. I will cover what we look for at positions later.

The type of personnel we get at Alta High School is the long and lengthy type of athlete. Our big competition in Utah is Bingham High School. They have a lot of Samoan kids. They get a lot of linemen that, at times, will weigh over 280 pounds. They have some Division I caliber linemen. They always have a 220-pound fullback, and a tight end that is 6'4" and 240 pounds. They have some good wide receivers that are 6'4" and can run. We felt, that to match up with Bingham High School athletes, we needed to play a defense that best fit our personnel.

In Utah high school football, we see all types of teams. We may see a double-wing team one week, and the next week we may face a team that plays with five wide receivers. Jordan High School in Utah is in our league. Their quarterback led the nation in passing last year. He threw for almost 5,000 yards. We see the spread offense, and we see the wishbone attack, and we see all of the different offensive schemes. We felt the 3-3-5 defense would allow us to adjust week by week with a minimal amount of adjustments.

We are a big high school in Utah. We start at the sophomore level of two platooning our kids. They play either offense or defense. I have coaches in the small schools. If I am in a small school, I am going to at least platoon my linemen. This gives us a chance to use a different type of athlete on the offensive and defensive linemen.

When we look for a defensive end, we want long and lanky, basketball type of players. They look like tight ends. We are going to play those types of kids at our defensive end positions. We may use an undersized noseguard just to create penetration. This allows us to keep our big linemen on the offensive side of the ball. For us, being able to platoon is a huge advantage, especially in the fourth quarter.

In 2008, when we won the 5A state championship, we outscored our opponents in the third and fourth quarter by 100 points. If you can just give the big guys a breather and keep them fresh, it will help in the fourth quarter. This system enables you to use different types of athletes on your offense and defense.

This defense is designed as an attacking, pressure, and disruptive defense. If you want to sit in one defensive look, and challenge the defense to drive the ball the distance without making a mistake, that is up to you. I know it is tough for the offense to drive the ball without a mistake. That does not fit the mentality of our program. We are going to get after it and make things happen. You must decide what you want to do on defense. You must answer some important questions if you want to run this defense:

- Is the 3-3-5 right for your program?
- Will you make your defense your number one priority?
- Will your defensive staff put in the preparation time?
- Will you schedule the needed practice time?
- Will you provide the defense with the best athletes in the program?
- Are you willing to develop defensive backs that can play man coverage?
- Are you willing to play cover zero when you are up 21-17 with two minutes to go in the championship game?

Our colors are the Oakland Raiders' colors. When our kids come out on the field, they think they are the bad guys in the state of Utah. We are going to pressure, and we are going to attack the offense. This is our defensive philosophy.

Defensive Philosophy

- We will outhit our opponent.
- We will be relentless to the ball.
- We will pursue to the ball and take good angles. Do not follow the same jersey.
- We will hit the ballcarrier and blockers violently.
- Every position will dominate their opponent.
- Visualize yourself forcing your facemask into the ball while driving your cleats into the grass, squeezing cloth and skin, knocking him backward with a violent strike.
- No YAC (yardage after contact).
- Be the one that makes the big play.
- Don't wait for someone to make a big play—you make the big play.
- Be stingy—no first downs, no scores. (Our defense is ticked off when they give up a first down.)
- Inside the red zone—bleed to keep our opponent from scoring.
- Know your steps every down—excuses.

There is a lot of reading involved in this defense. We spend a lot of time with linebackers and defensive backs running read drills. We read offensive linemen. We have a pass read, pull read, and down read. We work a lot on footwork.

- Know the down-and-distance.
- Pre-read your key.
- Eyes on your key.
- Take your read steps.
- React on run or pass with no hesitation.
- Pursue to the ball or drop into your coverage and never lose your footing. (We only played two games on real grass last year.)
- Tackle violently; make the big play; no YAC. (We want to intimidate the teams we play.)
- Always think three-and-out.
- Win.

We want to be able to determine what the play is after one-half of a second after the ball is snapped. Our free safety defensive ends will be our best pass rushers. We want to determine in a split second if the play is a run or a pass. We expect our safety to make plays at three yards. We line him up at eight yards, and we do not want him backing up on a run after the ball is snapped.

Defense Wins Championships

Our defense is the number one priority in our program. We run the option read offense, but defense is where our priorities are. Other than the quarterback and center, the defense gets first choice of all the other players. If we did not platoon, we would make sure our best athletes were spending most of their time on the defensive side of the ball.

Our defense comes on the field and they are coming after the offense. They do not care who you are, they are going to come after you. They love to practice defense, and our coaches love the defense—it is exciting football. We call it *organized chaos* because we still must be fundamentally sound. We cannot give up the gaps. We are fundamentally sound—it just looks like a mess. Our players buy into the defense every day.

We do not feel you can sit back in a 3-3 defense and play cover 2 and win. You must blitz and move people around. You must apply pressure on the offense. You must put in time in the film room. Your defensive staff must spend the time to make sure you are going to cover everything that can come up in a game. I do not think you can sit in the base 3-3 defense and be successful. A great deal of this defense depends on movement and moving linebackers. You must spend the time to know what you need to know on defense in each game.

These are our defensive goals. I am not going to spend a lot of time on them, but this is what our defense is trying to accomplish.

Defensive Goals

- Win
- 13 points or less
- No big plays
  - ✓ No run plays over 20 yards
  - ✓ No pass plays over 25 yards
- Hold opponent to less than 220 yards of total offense
- Three takeaways
- One defensive score
- Three sacks
- Eight series' of three-and-outs
- No fourth-down conversions
- Less than four yards gained on sudden change
- Three knocked-down or tipped balls
- Set up one score
- 11 Hawks to the ball every play (three-yard area) before the whistle blows
- Three momentum changes; big hit; goal line or fourth-down stand; interceptions, etc.
- Defense wins championships

This past year we gave up an average of just under 17 points per game. We lost in the state semi-finals. For us at Alta High School, if we do not win the state championship, it is not a successful season. That is okay. That is a good standard to have. To us, 17 points per game on defense is unacceptable. To win a championship, I think you must give up under 13 points per game.

Main Teaching Points

We start with the *stance*. You need to make sure your position coaches teach the proper stance. That will most benefit the player to get to his read steps and get off on movement. We stress balance, quickness, and force.

The *alignment* for our defense is very important. Each position has a gap responsibility. On the varsity level we will stem (move) around, but we will get back to our gap responsibility with proper alignment. We utilize the same terminology on alignment.

The *key* is the opposing player that each defender reads to see if the play is going to be a run or pass. The defender reads the player on his read steps. Then, he reacts to the run if the lineman (key) shows run block. He reacts to pass when he sees his lineman (key) pass set.

The defensive line keys the offensive lineman they line up on and by pressure. The Hawks are our alley players, and they key the first down offensive lineman for pass or run. The Stud and Will key the guard. The Mike keys through the quarterback to the near running back. The corners key the tackles. The free safety keys the guard.

You take your read off your key. You do this during your first two read steps. If you read run, you react to the ball, making sure that you first take care of your gap then pursue to the ballcarrier using proper pursuit angles.

Angles of pursuit need to be practiced. You need to know where the sidelines are. The sideline is the twelfth man. If the ballcarrier crosses the line of scrimmage, we need to take a good angle down the field to where the ballcarrier will be. Make sure to never follow the same colored jersey and never give up. When the ballcarrier has to change direction or slow down, you will be there for the tackle.

Points We Stress on Defense

Force: Everyone must know where the force is coming from on each play. This is a gap-control defense, and everyone has a responsibility.

Tackling: This is about attitude. We teach our defensive backs how to tackle low. I do not want my 150-pound defensive back trying to take on a 220-pound tailback on a head-on tackle. He will get his butt run over. We teach our defensive backs how to tackle low. We teach them how to take ballcarriers down. We have some great open field tacklers. We make sure we have tackling practice for them where they tackle below the thigh pads. We want them to wrap up and to get the runners on the ground. We have been very good with our defensive backs coming up and tackling runners below the waist.

Footwork: We practice our footwork and we perfect it. During the off-season, we have players that jump rope and go to the gym and work on their footwork. They want to be ready when we start up in the spring.

Get off Blocks: We teach them how to get off blocks. We have been blessed with Division I linebackers in our program. However, it is a catch-22. We teach our linebackers how to get off blocks. We teach them hand drills to help them get off blocks and to pursue to the ball.

Keep Your Feet: We never want to be on the ground. You cannot play if you are lying down on the ground.

Run Responsibilities

I am not going to spend a lot of time on this because I want to get to the meat of the defense.

DE: On jacks and slant away from the center you have the C gap, and you have the quarterback on option. When slanting to the center, you have the B gap and dive.

N: A gap. Feel pressure. When slanting, you have the A gap. You are slanting, feeling the center's pressure. Try to get to the guard's hip when he pulls.

S/W: You need to know what gap the defensive linemen are slanting to. If your defensive end slants to the B gap, you have the C gap to the quarterback on option. If he slants to the C gap, you have the B gap to dive, but only after you read your guard.

M: You need to know what way the nose is slanting when you have the other A gap. Read through the center to the near back.

Hawks: On option, you have the pitch. On flow away, look for the boot, cutback, or reverse. Help on powers to the C gap, and if the running back bounces, you will be there for a great hit.

C: Help on run support only after you are sure it is a run.

F: You are the last level of defense—no one gets by you.

Pass Responsibilities

DE: Contain quarterback and pass rush when on jacks or slanting to the C gap. Be relentless. If the running back crosses your face, follow for the screen. When slanting to the B gap and you read pass, stay in your lane and get to the quarterback. Get your hands up. Feel pressure or lack thereof, and read the screen or draw.

N: On a pass rush, stay in your lane and feel for the screen or draw.

S/W: On a blitz, stay in lanes and get to the quarterback. You also need to read for the screen or draw. If not on a blitz, drop into your coverage and redirect receivers.

M: You are a run stopper. If you read pass, get to the middle of the field and knock out anyone running crossing routes.

Hawks: On a blitz, contain the quarterback; in man, contain the #2 receivers.

C: #1 on man coverage.

F: Deeper than the deepest, read the quarterback's eyes.

Our Personnel

We have five defensive backs:
- *Corners:* Confidant; technically sound; quick cover guy. On an island most of the time. Does not have to run a 4.5. Our best ever was a 6'0", 155-pound, 4.9.

- *Hawk:* Aggressive; good open field tackler; good cover guy.
- *Safeties:* Center fielder; great open field tackler. Can read the offense. Has led our team in tackles every year.

We have three linebackers:
- *Mike:* Quarterback of the defense. Understands scheme, offensive formations, autos, and alignments.
- *Will:* Quick and aggressive. Can be undersized but must be a solid open field tackler and good at avoiding blockers.
- *Stud:* Generally, our strongest and most athletic linebacker.

We have three down linemen (two ends and a nose man):
- *Defensive ends:* Long, aggressive, basketball player or tight end type of kids. Good lateral movement; good hands.
- *Nose man:* The most explosive lineman or quick penetrator. He is a linebacker type. You are in business if you have a two-gap player.

I want to talk about defensive line stunts. This is what we call *jacks* (Diagram 12-1). This simply means the defensive ends are going to penetrate to the outside shoulder of the tackle. We line up every time in a 4 technique head-up with the tackle. We have one variation, and I will cover that later. The nose is in a 0 technique on the center. These are our line stunts. If the defensive line does not receive a special call, they are in jacks. That is our base defense.

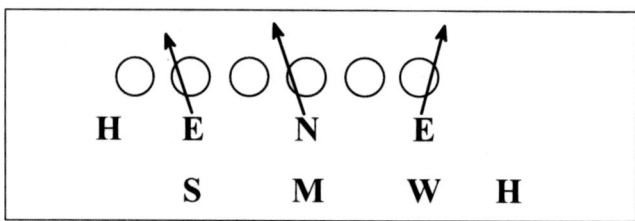

Diagram 12-1. Jacks

We want them to penetrate one yard into the backfield. Now, they must be able to read the offense. If they are not blocked by this time, they must know there is a pulling lineman coming out after them. If the quarterback goes away, they have the bootleg play and the reverse back to their side. You must go over those plays with the ends. We do not want our defensive ends four yards up the field.

We use jacks the most, and then we use pinch next. I only tell coaches at clinics about the diagram on the *pinch* (Diagram 12-2). We show them in a 4 technique pinching inside. The diagram shows we are going through the inside of the offensive tackle. That is not the true angle. We are pinching on the outside hip of the guard. We pinch hard to the hip of the guard and one-yard penetration. We want him to find the ball or to find out why he is not being blocked.

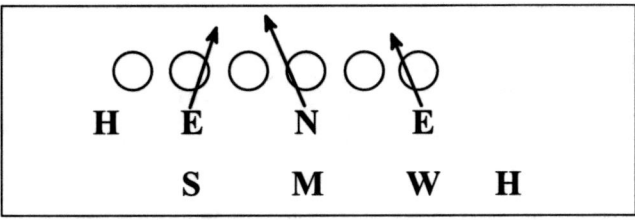

Diagram 12-2. Pinch

On *open*, we are slanting toward the weakside (Diagram 12-3).

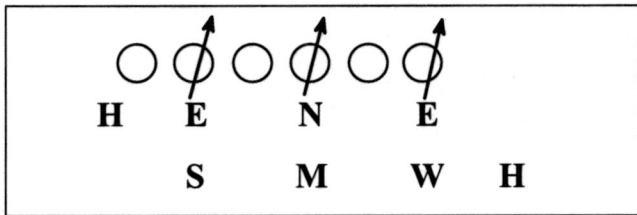

Diagram 12-3. Open

On *close*, we are slanting to the strongside (Diagram 12-4).

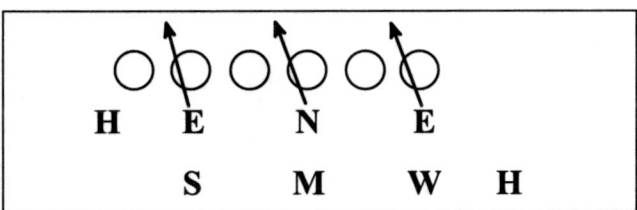

Diagram 12-4. Close

Those are our four basic alignments and stunts for the three down linemen. The only variation is the *force* (Diagram 12-5). It is similar to pinch, but we are bringing the ends down into the 2 techniques. That is all we do as far as the defensive line goes.

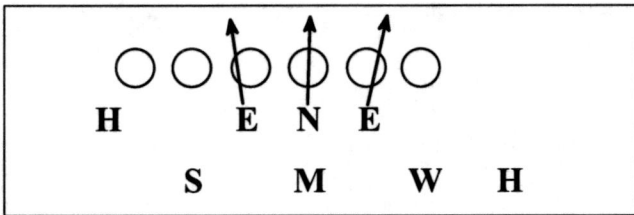

Diagram 12-5. Force

Linebacker stunts include the following. Here are some of our one-man blitzes. We rarely blitz our Mike backer. He is our least blitzing linebacker. He is our best reader, so we rarely blitz him. If we want Mike to go to the tight end, we call *Mike strong* (Diagram 12-6).

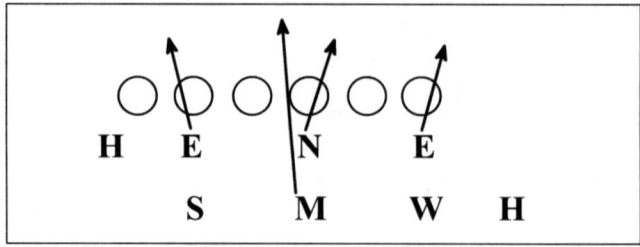

Diagram 12-6. Mike strong

If we want him to blitz to the backside, we call *Mike weak* (Diagram 12-7).

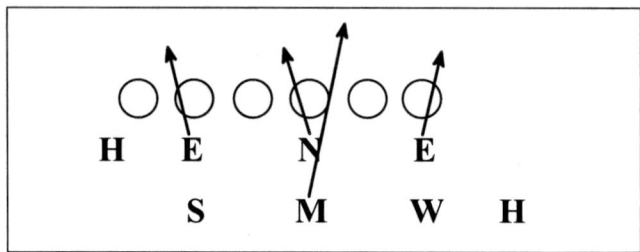

Diagram 12-7. Mike weak

These are our most common blitzes. In *open Will*, we slant the line to the weakside and blitz Will in the B gap (Diagram 12-8).

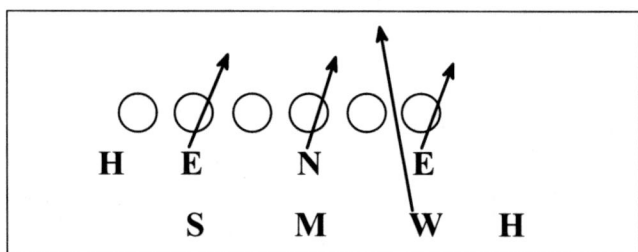

Diagram 12-8. Open Will

If we want to slant to the strongside, Will is going to blitz the backside A gap (Diagram 12-9).

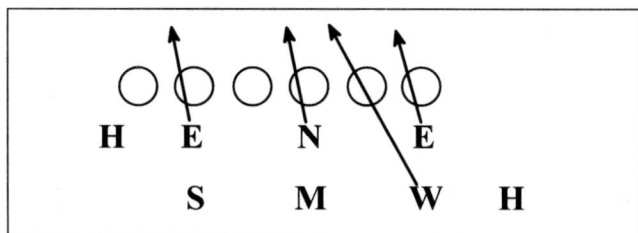

Diagram 12-9. Close Will

Next, we use the same concept but we are slanting away from the tight end and bringing our Stud linebacker (Diagram 12-10). The Stud has the onside A gap.

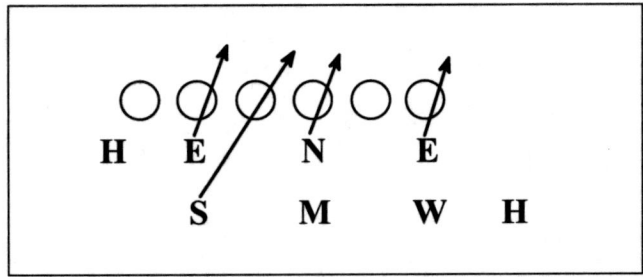

Diagram 12-10. Open Stud

If we slant to the tight end, the Stud has the onside B gap (Diagram 12-11).

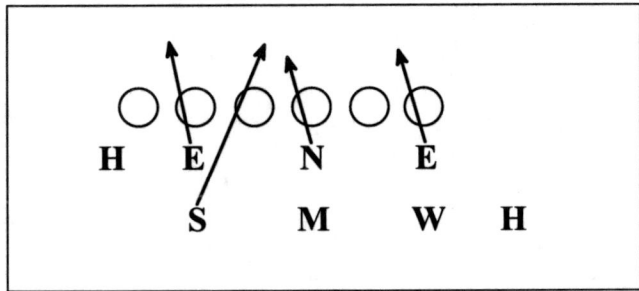

Diagram 12-11. Close Stud

We must spend the time to make sure the players know they must get to the gaps they are assigned. If they do not get to their gaps, we have a breakdown in the defense.

If we are playing an option team, we like to run the *open stick stunt* (Diagram 12-12). The end has the dive, and the Stud has the quarterback on the option. They must understand who has the dive, who has the quarterback, and who has the pitch.

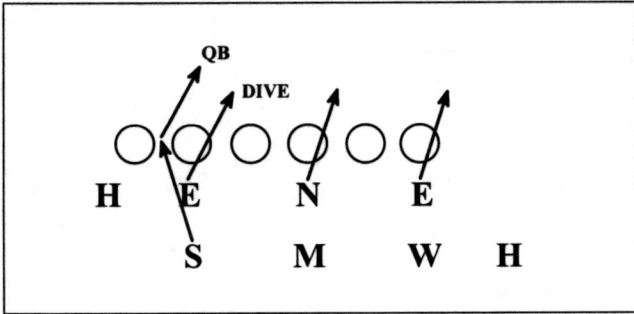

Diagram 12-12. Open stick

Closed whack is the same stunt to the backside against the option (Diagram 12-13). The end has the dive and the Will has the quarterback.

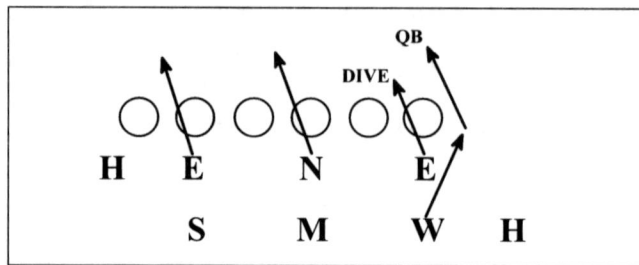

Diagram 12-13. Closed whack

If we want to run the stunt to both sides, we call our *pinch stick whack* (Diagram 12-14). The nose slants to the tight end A gap.

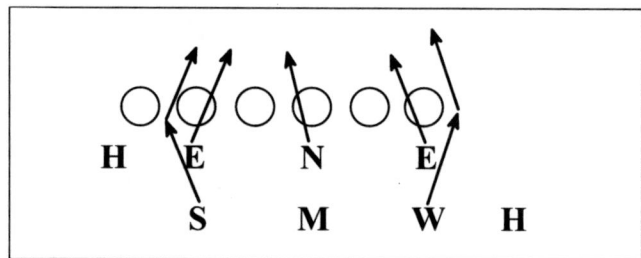

Diagram 12-14. Pinch stick whack

Blast is one of our most often-used stunts (Diagram 12-15). These stunts are not rocket science. The ends go outside and the Will and Stud go inside. The nose slants to the tight end A gap.

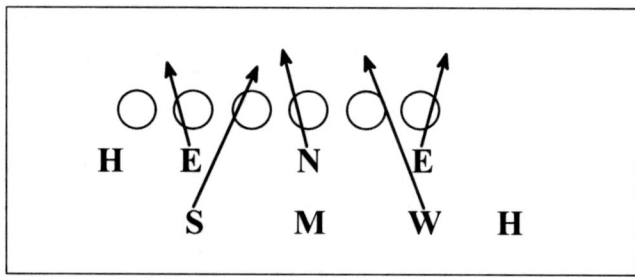

Diagram 12-15. Blast

Our next most often-used stunt is the *mash*. In mash strong (Diagram 12-16), the ends slant outside and the nose slants to the tight end A gap. The Mike and Stud linebackers cross. The Mike blitzes in the B gap to the strongside, and the Stud comes through the strong guard.

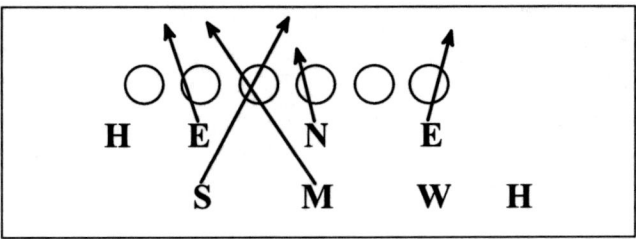

Diagram 12-16. Mash strong

The *mash weak* is to the split end side (Diagram 12-17). Mike goes in the B gap, and the Will backer comes through the backside guard.

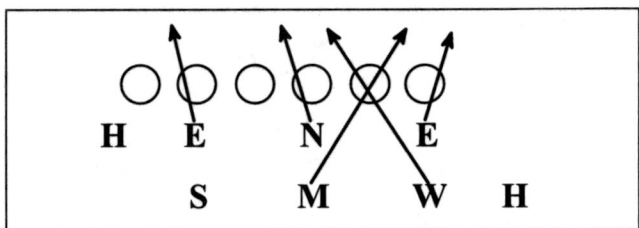

Diagram 12-17. Mash weak

If we want to send all three linebackers, we call *zoo strong* (Diagram 12-18). Now, all three linebackers blitz to the tight end side or the strongside of the formation.

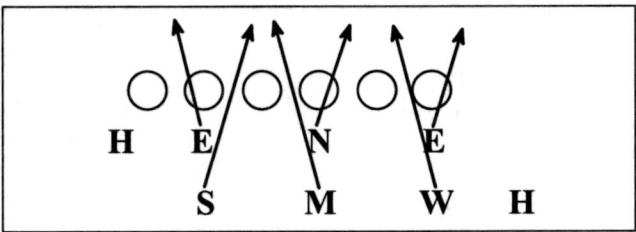

Diagram 12-18. Zoo strong

If we want to send the linebackers to the split end side or the weakside, we call *zoo weak* (Diagram 12-19). All three linebackers blitz toward the split end side.

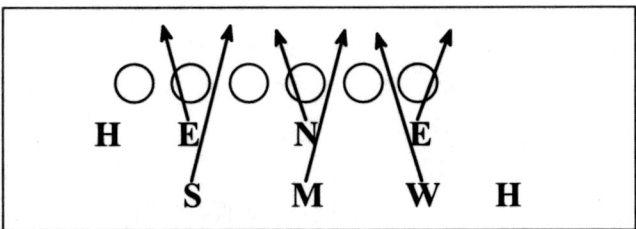

Diagram 12-19. Zoo weak

Now, we want to get our defensive backs involved in the blitz game. We run linebacker and defensive backs combination stunts. We have open Hawk, closed Hawk, pinch double Hawk, open boom strong, close boom weak, open boom strong, and closed boom weak. Now, we start to bring combinations of alley players and linebackers on the stunts. We bring the alley players off the edge. Our linebacker/defensive backs combo stunts include the following.

If we call *open Hawk*, the Hawk on the tight end side comes up and blitzes over the tight end (Diagram 12-20). He comes over the 9 technique. The line is slanting away from the tight end.

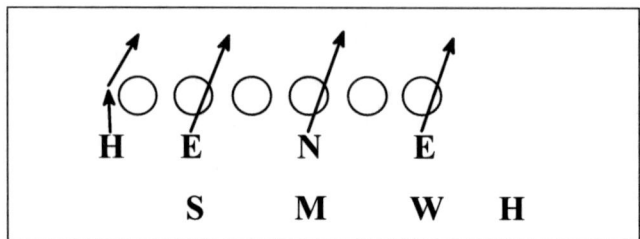

Diagram 12-20. Open Hawk

By now, you can see how we are calling our stunts. When we call the *close Hawk*, we bring the Hawk up on the split end side and send him on the blitz (Diagram 12-21). Again, the line is slanting away from the Hawk toward the tight end.

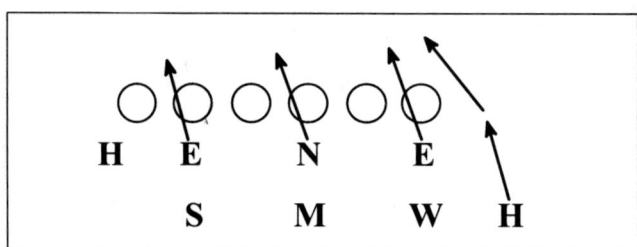

Diagram 12-21. Close Hawk

If we call pinch double Hawk, we are sending both Hawks (Diagram 12-22). The ends slant inside, and the nose slants toward the tight end in the A gap.

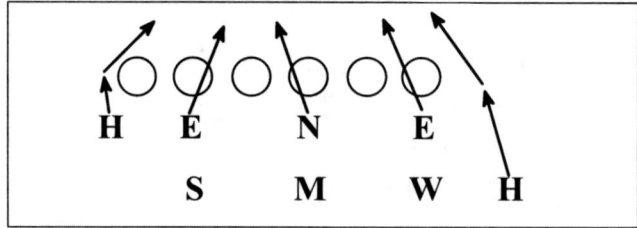

Diagram 12-22. Pinch double Hawk

We add the Hawks to the stunt to get our *open boom strong*. The line and Stud run their open stunt (Diagram 12-23), and the Hawk on the tight end side runs his stunt over the tight end.

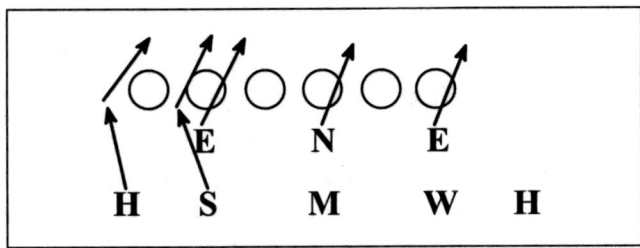

Diagram 12-23. Open boom strong

To run the same stunt to the backside, we call our *close boom weak* (Diagram 12-24). The Will and the defensive line run the open stunt, and the Hawk to the split end runs his stunt. The Will comes inside off the tackle, and the Hawk comes outside, where the end would be up in a tight end set. The Will is coming hard over the tackle, and the Hawk is outside.

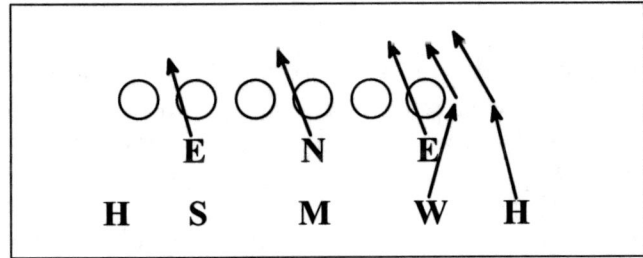

Diagram 12-24. Close boom weak

On the *bang stunt*, we bring one of the ends from the 4 technique down inside to the A gap. On open bang strong, the strongside defensive end slants from the tackle down inside to the A gap (Diagram 12-25). The nose and weakside end slant toward the split end. The Stud and Hawk on the tight end side run their stunt and blitz the C gap and outside the tight end.

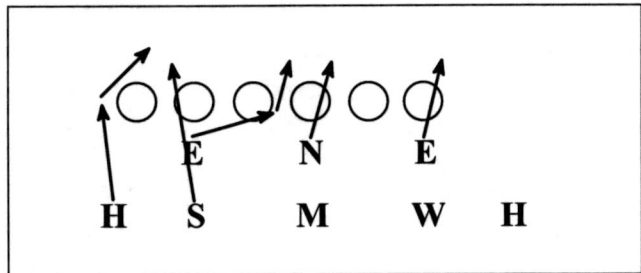

Diagram 12-25. Open bang strong

On *close bang weak*, we are running the same stunt to the weakside or to the split end side (Diagram 12-26). The end on the split end side slants from the head-up position on the tackle down inside to the A gap.

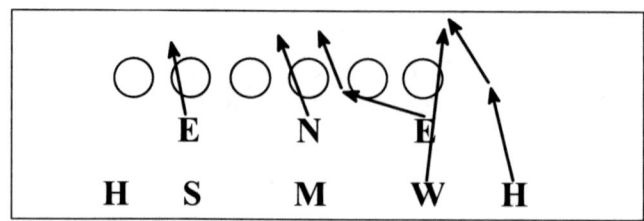

Diagram 12-26. Close bang weak

In wrapping this up, you must decide as a staff to be dedicated to put your best players on defense. You have to put the time and effort into the defense. You must develop confidence in the secondary players that they can play man coverage. I am not telling you that you have to run as much man coverage as we do, but they need to be confident that they can cover man to man. This will allow you to overload the box to stop the run. We do not mind if teams throw the fade route on us—we love it. We know they will be lucky to hit 1 out of 10 of those passes. Our success has been better than 1 out of 10 plays against the fade route.

Make sure your kids are good open field tacklers. Teach the backs to tackle low. Don't try to be a hero. Make sure the defenders never follow a player of the same colored jersey. Then, you need to cultivate the attitude where your defense is ticked off when the opponents get a first down.

Again, this is not rocket science, and we are not reinventing the wheel. We feel this defense gives us an opportunity to defeat some of the teams that we do not match up against talentwise. It gives us a chance to do what we do week after week without a lot of changes. I hope you can find a few points that may help you with your defense. I will be around if you want to talk about the things we do in our program.

Coaches ask me what my number one job is at Alta High School. I tell our assistants this, and I tell those that ask me that question—My number one job is to *develop young men*. As a byproduct of what we are trying to do, we are teaching our young men to make good decisions.

We have been fortunate to win some games, and we have had some great athletes. The number one responsibility we have as coaches is to develop young men in our culture. I think this is something that is going by the wayside. We need to teach young men how to make good decisions on and off the field. We need to teach them to have integrity and discipline and how to become good citizens. We hope they will make good fathers someday. This is our number one responsibility.

It has been my pleasure to spend time with you today. If you have questions, I will be here until noon tomorrow. Feel free to visit with me. Thank you.

13

The 3-3-5 Multiple Front Defense

Rocky Long
San Diego State University
2012

I appreciate you coaches being here. I go to many clinics, and I like to listen to other coaches talk. I go to listen to assistant coaches on offense and defense, and I learn something every time I go. There is a completely different attitude between offensive coaches and defensive coaches. The offensive coaches come up with a nice little PowerPoint presentation. One coach said it does not matter where the receivers align because the first receiver runs a 7 route, the second receiver runs a 4 route, the third receiver runs a 5 route, and the backside receiver runs a complementary pattern. He said it was simple, and I got confused after the first pattern.

They are extremely organized, but he said something in there that got to me as a defensive coach. I wrote it down so I would not forget it. He was talking about throwing a bubble screen. They have two players in the bubble screen. One of them catches it and the other blocks the defender. Offensive coaches are a hell of lot smarter than defensive coaches are. All you have to do is ask them something. He said the offensive player blocks the meat eater and not the lettuce eater. According to his diagram, the safety was the meat eater and the corner was the lettuce eater. Anybody in here that ever played corner should take personal offense to that.

After hearing the offensive coach, I went in and listened to the defensive coach talk. He was showing them how to blitz, run through gaps, and all that stuff. A coach asked him how he covered a particular adjustment. He told him they did not do that.

I catch myself doing this all the time. You come up with a great idea and you start to install it. One of the coaches working with you asks what we do if they do this. The next question is what if they do that. The first thing you know, you cannot do anything with your great idea. The biggest mistake defensive coaches make is they react to the offense. If the offense goes to a particular formation, the defense checks the coverage. That is what most defensive coaches do. Several defensive coaches say, "The hell with that!"

They want the offense to react to what they do. Make the offensive coaches in their room make adjustments in their scheme because of what we do. Make the quarterback read what you do. Make them react to what you do.

If you make them react to what you do, they end up with one or two protection schemes, and by halftime, you know what those schemes are. If you have a multiple scheme that allows you to do things, at halftime, you can come up with something that will kill their butts.

Every offensive coach alive knows how to block a shade defender and a 3 technique defender. If they know how to block it, do not line up in it. Get into something the offense does not know is a shade defender and a 3 technique defender. You can still play the defense; just do not align in something they recognize. We do not get any traps anymore, unless you count the long trap or the counter play. We see two blocking schemes today. We see the zone scheme and the gap scheme. We get no isolation plays anymore. If you can make the offense react to what you do, you can make it a simple game for your defense.

We give the offense multiple looks. I want to show you our base front. We have a base front called a 30 stack (Diagram 13-1). I will talk about all the fronts later. The coverages can make these fronts 4-3, 4-2, over, under, 5-2, or anything else. You can become a 4-3 defense by coverages or stunts. We have three defensive linemen in this defense. We use movement to change their alignment and the front.

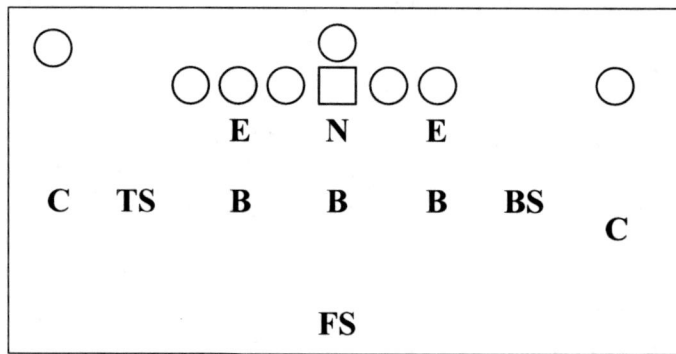

Diagram 13-1. 30 stack

We can adjust to other fronts from this base look. If we want to get into what we call a solid look (Diagram 13-2). If there is one tight end, we can break the stack to that side and step the linebacker down to the line of scrimmage. If there are two tight ends, we step both outside linebackers into shade on the tight end. With one tight end, we are in a 4-2 look with the tight end stack on the line of scrimmage. If we want to create an over look from this alignment, we can move the defensive end into a 3 technique and nose the nose into a 1 technique. The other defensive end moves into a 5 technique to that side and we have an over look.

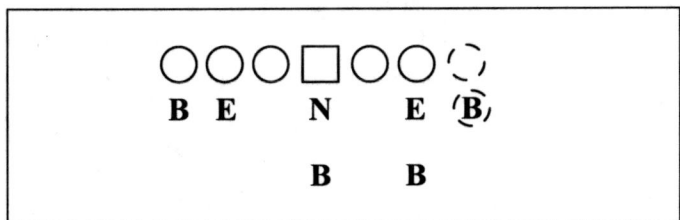

Diagram 13-2. Solid front

We can also get into an eagle look (Diagram 13-3). To get into the eagle front, the defensive ends move into 3 techniques on each side. We can move the outside linebackers to the line of scrimmage or play them in some combinations of alignment based on the offensive alignments.

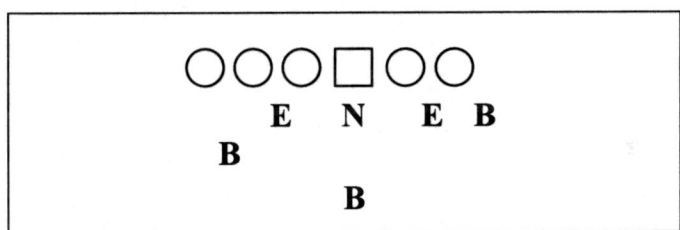

Diagram 13-3. Eagle

There are two reasons for having multiple fronts. Every year, we get different players. The coach from Florida State University talked yesterday about rushing the passer. It has such a recruiting base it can recruit to a scheme. The University of Alabama can stay in a 3-4 every year because it recruits players that can play that defense. If the players they recruit were in California, they would be 6-6 and 225 pounds playing basketball. In Alabama, they are 6-6 and 290 pounds and play football. Most of the colleges in America today are just like high schools. You recruit the best players you can find and they will not necessarily fit into your scheme.

Last year, our noseguard was 6-2 and 285 pounds. We started a defensive end that was 5-11 and 234 pounds. The other defensive end was 6-3 and 240 pounds. That is not what Alabama or the University of Southern California's defensive line looks like. The assumption that everybody recruits and they all have great players is wrong. In high school, it seems to go in cycles. In some years, you have good players, and some years, you do not. In some years, you have little players, and in some years, you have big players.

We develop our defense based on who our best players are. If our best players are little defensive linemen, we stunt. We slant, twist, and turn them in all different directions. The linebackers do not align in a shade technique; they blitz into a shade technique. If we have big, athletic linemen, you would see more of the solid, over, and under fronts with the linebackers roaming.

There was a time when the hybrid players playing down safeties were strong safety types. Now they are nickel backs because of the spread teams we are seeing. That means they are big corners. There was a time coaches looked down on and frowned on this defense. In the NFL today, when they go to their nickel and dime schemes, they align in this defense.

Ninety percent of the high school teams are in the spread offense. About 50 percent of the teams we play are in the spread, and 90 percent of them have a spread package. We see the spread more than any other offense. I have changed my mind on who the best players on the defense must be. The best players in this scheme have to be the two nickel backs, the two outside linebackers, and the safety. That is because of all the bubble screens and having to rush the quarterback.

They are the ones who have to play the backs coming out of the backfield and the bubble screens. The defenders in the middle of the defense are old 50 defense type football players. They have to plug the A gaps and stop the run. The middle linebacker and noseguard take up blocks when they play. Everyone else around them has to be great athletes.

Forty years ago, an old coach told me a fundamental of defensive football. He told me the number one fundamental of defensive football is balance. If you draw a line down the middle of the offense and they have five and a half players on each side of that line, the defense had better have five and a half defenders on each side of that line. There is one way to do that and always be right. You must play man coverage.

I see some coaches already shaking their heads because they cannot play man coverage. That has nothing to do with it. Any coach in here can play man coverage if you can get enough pressure on the quarterback. If you are scared, play stack defense and let them run up and down the field. The score will be 67-56, and I hope you have the 67 points. That was Baylor University and the University of Washington in the Alamo Bowl. Have you ever seen a game like that?

In the past when we played a triple option team, that was real football. You have to be a tough sucker to play against the wishbone. You do not have to be tough to play against the spread. Teams that run the spread offense have trouble with their defense when they play running teams. When that defense practices against the spread all the time, it has trouble against someone that runs the ball at it.

When we call our defense, the first thing the middle linebacker calls is tight end position. If there is one tight end, the linebacker calls the direction to the tight end. If there are two tight ends, he calls the directions to the strength of the formation. If it is a balanced formation, he calls to the field. If the ball is in middle of the field, he calls it to the quarterback's arm.

When we call the stunts, we run them toward or away from the call. We call our stunts with a tight or open call. The same thing holds true with the secondary. You will have to make an adjustment as to who your best players are. That could determine what coverage you play. If you have a real dumb team, which we do at times, the thing your defense will never mess up is a field call. If we have a dumb team, we tell the linebacker to call the tight side to the field. It does not matter whether they align the tight end to the field. That makes all the stunts field stunts or boundary stunts. We base everything we do on a tight or field call.

The three down linemen move as a group on some stunt calls. We call this movement slant, angle, loop, pinch, or go. The linebackers have games. When we run the games and the stunts together, that is a combo.

We run our stunt off the direction calls from the linebackers. If we want to slant the ends and nose to the tight end, we call tight. If we want to run the slant away from the tight end, we call open. If we call tight, open, field, or boundary, the defensive line slants those calls. The pinch and loop calls are for the defensive ends (Diagram 13-4). On the pinch, the defensive ends run their slant techniques to the inside. They become B gap defenders. When they loop, they go to the outside from the 5 technique into the C gap. On the pinch and loop, the nose plays football and the middle linebackers play their normal defense.

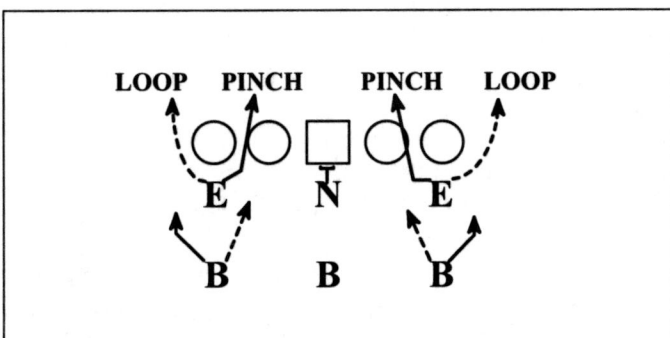

Diagram 13-4. Pinch/loop

We can run stunts involving two defensive linemen. When you run the tac with the end coming down to the inside, he can start from anywhere (Diagram 13-5). We can run the tac stunt from a 9, 8, 5, or 3 technique. That stunt is the end closing into an inside A gap and the nose going around to the outside. We run the stunt the other way, with the nose going out and the tackle coming behind, and we call that a toe. However, the defensive end cannot come from the 9 technique on a toe stunt. Some of these stunts are for pass rushing and some are for zone read teams.

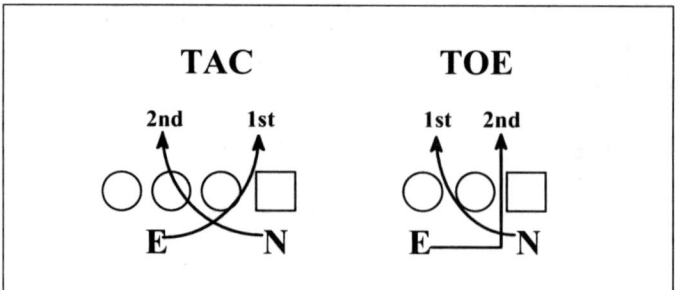

Diagram 13-5. Tac and toe

From this defense, the games the linebackers can run are numerous. It is what the coaching staff wants to do with them. They must know their gap responsibilities on the stunts run by the defensive line, and their fits come off the movement of the line. You can blitz the linebackers in any combination and number of linebackers that you choose. You can blitz one at a time, two at a time, or all three if you chose.

When we slant and stunt, we give the defensive players aiming points as to where we want them to go. We give them aiming points by down and distance. We give them aiming point by formations. We give them aiming points by where the offense's best players are. Sometimes, the aiming points are the face of the guards. Sometimes, it is the inside shoulder of the tackle. To say that a player blitzes through the B gap is too simple an explanation. By game planning, our defenders have aiming points.

If I want to play an under front, I can do it with a single linebacker blitz. If the direction call is tight right and if the boundary linebacker blitzes the B gap, it causes the defensive end to loop to the outside. The nose goes away, which puts him into the tight A gap. The tight defensive end loops into the C gap, and the linebacker steps to the outside. Using the movement of one defender, we end up aligned as if we were in an under front defense.

We can get into these movements and drop the free safety down to seven yards and we have a 4-3 alignment. We did that with Brain Urlacher at New Mexico University. We played the same adjustment out of our two-deep secondary. We rolled him down to seven yards and played him inside outside on the ball. He made about 170 tackles in 11 games. You can get into any defensive front you want by moving your linemen with stunts and getting in to gaps. If your good players are the linebackers, you hit those gaps with the linebackers.

People want to know why we play with 195-pound linebackers. I want to talk about the linebackers we played this year. One of them will be in the NFL. He was 6-2 and 240 pounds and played the right linebacker. The middle linebacker was 5-10 and 195 pounds. The left linebacker was 6-3 and 195 pounds.

The best 3 technique we have on our team is 5-10 and weighs 195 pounds. The best 3 technique on our team is the middle linebacker. He went to the right aiming point, and he was too short for the big offensive linemen to block. He played with leverage and they did not knock him back. He was always in the backfield making something good happen.

I love to watch the linebackers playing downhill at a power play. I never know what coverage it is, but they are aggressive and playing with a lot of toughness. They are hitting the gaps and recovering nicely if the play turns into a counter. It does not matter what the coverage is because it is a power play and we are playing the run.

Everyone we play wants to slide or half-slide pass protect against us. We can get to the quarterback if we put two defenders through the same gap. If you put two defenders through the same gap, that is not fundamentally sound. However, if one defender can pick the offensive blocker, the second defender coming through that gap is a free rusher. We do that with our edge blitzes.

You must play man coverage. If you play a soft zone, the quarterback will complete the ball. If you play the soft zone, the offense will dink and dunk you down the field and score. If you get after their butts, you will stop them and your offense will get back on the field. We are going to play that way. We are not going to take the offense picking and choosing where they want to throw.

The offense always wants the ball back. They hate playing against a wishbone team because wishbone teams run the ball and control the time of possession. They hold the ball for 14 out of the 15 minutes. The offense has to sit on the sideline, it plays crappy when it gets back into the game, and it blames the defense because it is cold. You have to get after the offensive players and make them turn the ball back to your offense.

In the secondary, we play cover 3 and cover 2. When we play cover 2, it is Tampa 2. We put the free safety at the middle linebacker position. The middle linebacker has a hard time running with the seam pattern down the middle of the field. Middle linebackers have a certain mentality that safeties do not. The middle linebackers overreact to the run. Safeties do not. The free safety has to be a good tackler, but his nose will not be up the noseguard's butt.

The middle linebacker stands next to the noseguard. If the offense runs a play-action pass, with the #3 receiver running down the middle, the middle linebacker will never cover him. The free safety will be nowhere near the line of scrimmage until he is sure it is a run. If you want to play Tampa 2, do not do it with the free safety at the middle linebacker.

One of our man-free coverages is gold. If you cannot play man coverage, you must get to the quarterback. I have shown you some five-man pressures. In a five-man pressure, someone on the offensive line is blocking one-on-one. Let me regress here a minute. The offenses are progressing faster than the defense. What they are doing on offense now is unbelievable. They are doing things today I never expected them to do.

If you cannot play man coverage, do not give up on that scheme. Figure out more ways to tackle the quarterback for losses. The smart coaches on offense will keep extra blockers in to block. Most of the teams we play in the spread offense have three wide receivers in a slot formation. They have two players in the backfield with the quarterback. One of the backs in the backfield is another wide receiver. He keys to see if the blitz is coming. If there is no blitz, he releases and runs a pattern. He runs his normal patterns as if he aligned in the slot.

When you blitz and take on the wide receiver that is not used to blocking linebackers or a big defender, your scheme can affect what they do. What they do is replace the wide receiver with a tight end or fullback. The tight end is coming back into the spread set. The spread teams are never under the center because if you go under the center, you are not a smart coach.

Offensive coaches know the defense keys the positioning of the running back as to the slide of the offensive line. The smart coaches set the running back to one side of the quarterback and blocked him on the other side to screw up the blitz scheme of the defense. If you watch enough film, you can get a feel for the slide by watching the offensive linemen. One of the offensive linemen will tip the slide every time by his stance, weight on his hand, or shoulder lean.

The smart linebacker that sets your defense can spot that from the offensive line. When he sees the slide direction of the offensive line, he calls the pressure from the opposite side. To counter that move, the offensive puts in a tight end and keeps him in to block. They put the tight end on one side and the running back to the other side. That gives them seven-man protection. The defense has to have a way to outnumber the offensive blockers to a side.

That is where the combo coverages come into play. Gold coverage is our man-free scheme. In the gold coverage, we can get into a multiple blitz scheme (Diagram 13-6).

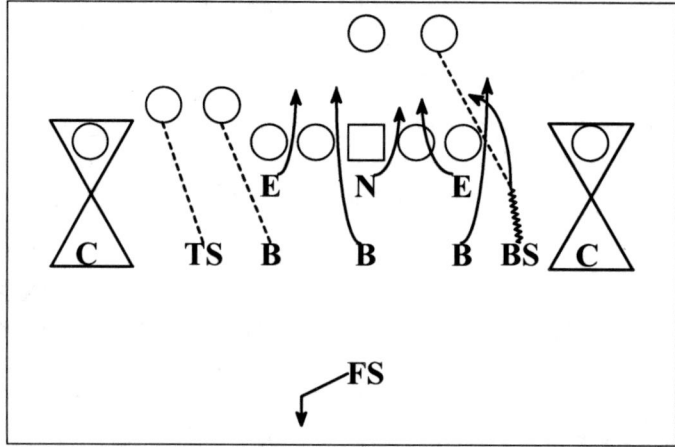

Diagram 13-6. Combo blitz gold coverage

This can give you six or seven blitzers. We cover the back coming out of the backfield with a back at the line of scrimmage. If the offensive tackles are not exceptional, the defenders coming off the edge will get to the quarterback. We bring two rushers off the edge and challenge the athletic ability of the offensive tackle. You have to bring more defenders than the offense can block.

The boundary safety on his play is in the blitz pattern if the running back blocks. If he swings on a hot route, the boundary safety has coverage on him. He cannot try to sack the quarterback and let the back release.

If you do that, you cannot be scared of what happens in the secondary because it is one-on-one coverage back there. The defensive backs fall down sometimes, and other times, they get beat. Nevertheless, you are dictating to the offense what type of pass route it can run. It can only throw two passes. It can throw the slant and the fade. It can throw a hot to the back who swings out of the backfield. However, there is coverage from the boundary safety on the swing hot route.

The biggest problem we have with this scheme is the wide receiver screen. The tunnel or alley screen is the thing that gives us the most trouble. The reason we have trouble is we are going to the quarterback and all the action of the pass goes the other way. If we are not good at turning and retracing our steps, we get hurt.

Another problem we have is a team that identifies our overload blitz. If they know which side it comes from, they run the speed option away from it. If they do that, we are screwed. That is the only place we have had trouble, although sometimes we play teams with better talent. When we played Michigan, we should have sacked the quarterback six times. We did not lay a hand on him on five of those occasions and he scored two touchdowns. We had two defenders come free on the blitz six times and only sacked him once.

You cannot play for them, but you have to give them a chance to win. If you put a player in a 3 technique or a two-gap noseguard, he may be a tough player, but he will get the snot beat out of him. The linebackers face the same thing if the lineman cannot keep the blockers off the linebackers. That happens because you are not aggressive.

We believe in this defense. If we had the best players in the country, we would play this defense. If we had good players, we would play with Alabama. The two best teams we played last year were Boise State University and Texas Christian University. We would never tell our players this, but they were so much better than we were physically. They were bigger, stronger, and faster.

Against Boise State, we fumbled the opening kickoff and the next two punts. We were down 21-0 with less than four minutes gone in the game. The score was 35-28 going into the fourth quarter. Against TCU, the score was 27-21 going into the fourth quarter. What we have are tough players who like to play football. We are a talented team.

I thought Boise State was the best team we played last year, and we played 0 coverage 43 percent of the time. You can align exactly right every time in man coverage if you do it by the numbers. When we play teams that play with 12 personnel, one of the tight ends is a blocker and the other is a pass receiver. One of them is less a threat to block someone. We know that, and we slant off that fact. We do not worry about him blocking, so we slant to him.

When you play man-to-man coverage, you never worry about being outflanked by the offense. If they try to change the strength of the formation with motion, we balance with a defender coming with the motion. We will always have the same number of defenders as the offense has blockers. The defensive back will make the adjustments.

We do not have a 190-pound defensive back in our secondary. Their play is all about attitude. I was upset about the coach who talked about lettuce eaters at the corner. I think Kellen Moore is the best quarterback in college football. We pressured him and gave him fits throwing the football. He missed receiver after receiver because of the pressure we put on him.

This defense keeps the offensive blocker off balance; they are never sure whom to block. It makes them slow down. It makes them uncomfortable with who they are supposed to block.

I want to give a brief explanation about one of our zone coverages. If we run a thunder blitz, we bring five defenders on the rush (Diagram 13-7). With five blitzers, we have six defenders in the secondary. The defensive line slants to the right side of the offense. The left outside linebacker cheats to the line and blitzes through the inside shoulder of the tight end. The tight safety comes off the edge. If we ran the blitz to the boundary, we call it lightning. It is the opposite stunt bringing the boundary safety.

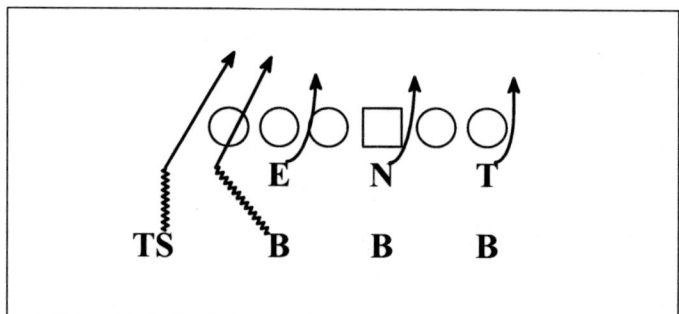

Diagram 13-7. Thunder blitz

If the offensive formation is a 2x2 formation, we play three under and three deep (Diagram 13-8). We call that coverage 33. The corners fake a press coverage and bail out into the deep thirds. The free safety plays the middle third. The middle linebacker plays the curl/flat to the strongside, and the right linebacker plays the middle hook area. The boundary safety plays the backside curl/flat area.

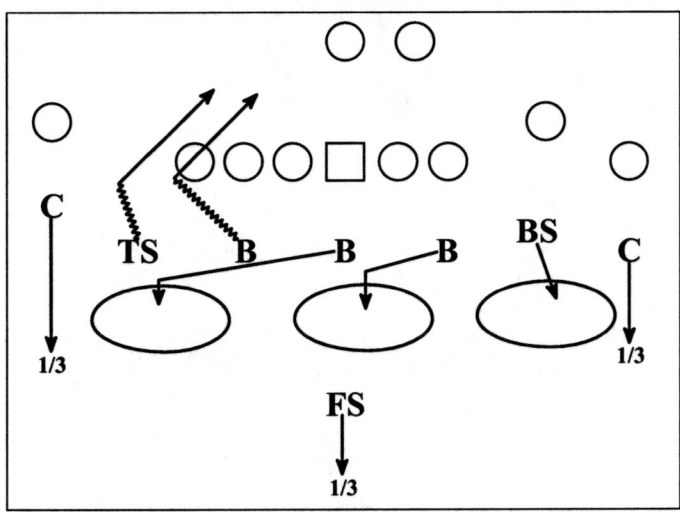

Diagram 13-8. 2x2 three deep (33)

In a 3x1 or 2x1, we play four under and two deep (Diagram 13-9). Twenty-two is four under and two deep. In this coverage, we roll the corners down into the flat area. The middle linebacker is the hook-to-curl player. The right linebacker plays the hook to the curl area to the backside. The backside corner rolls down and plays the backside flat area. The boundary safety drops up the seam and plays half-field coverage. The free safety rolls to the strongside and plays half coverage to that side.

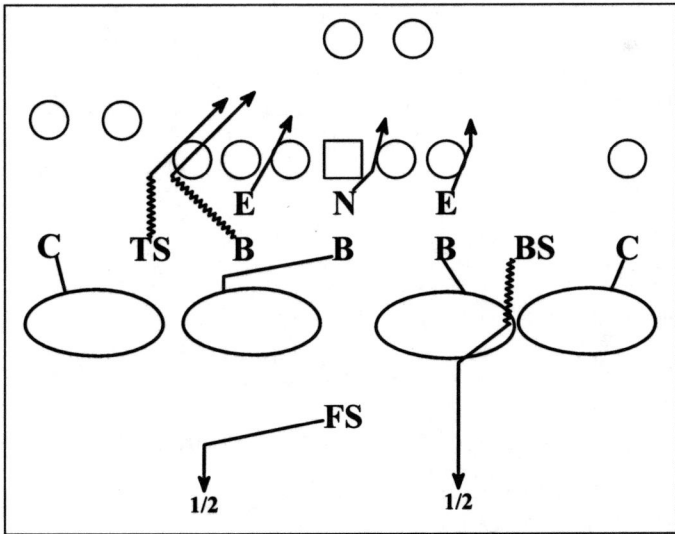

Diagram 13-9. 3x1 or 2x1 two deep

In the secondary, we try to make everything look like man coverage. I am out of time. I am sorry about all the technical difficulty. I hope you got something from this. I appreciate your being here and your attention.

14

The 3-3-5 Stack and Swarm Defense

Bill Powers
Jupiter Christian High School, Florida
2008

Today, I would like to discuss some of the basic reasons why we run the 3-3-5 stack and swarm defense. With regard to the advantages of the defense, we identified seven key points.

Why the 3-3-5 defense?

- Very easy to learn
- Teams have to game plan for it
- Allows smaller, faster athletes to be successful
- Fun for players
- Enables the maximum number of players to be in the box
- Exerts maximum pressure against the pass
- Aggressive, attacking style of play

Our defense had an exceptional season last year. For example, as the statistics indicate, we had a large number of tackles for a loss that came as a result of our stunting, swarming style of play on defense.

2007 Defensive Statistics

- Sacks = 37
- Tackles for loss = 106
- Forced fumbles = 9
- Interceptions = 13

We use a few different key words in our terminology for the different defensive positions. Our secondary consists of two corners and one safety. We call our outside linebackers, Eagles. The down linemen are our e's and nose man. We use a small e to indicate the ends when we diagram the defense. The Eagles are outside-linebacker types. The e's are defensive tackle-type players. We have a strong e and a weak e. Accordingly, one end is the SE, and one is the WE. The inside linebackers are called bullets, while the middle linebacker is the missile backer.

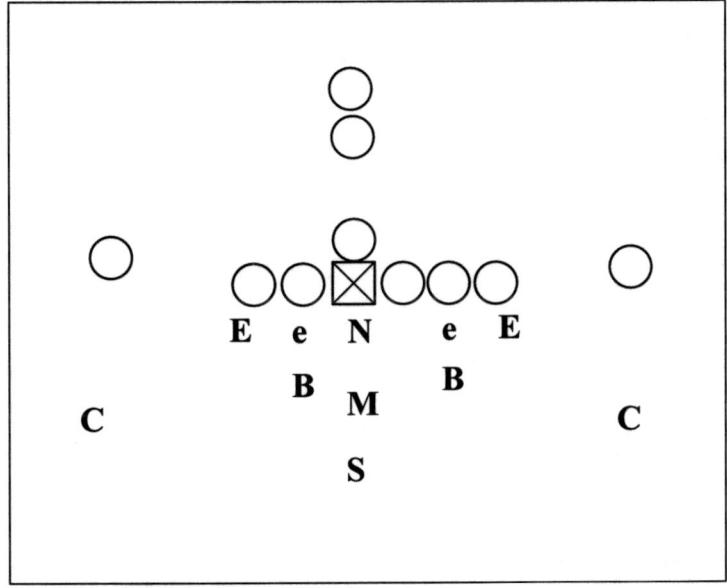

Diagram 14-1. Personnel

Defensive Linemen/Linebackers

❑ Noseguard—Must force double-teams and cause havoc in the backfield.
❑ Ends—Should be agile and fast; can substitute size for quickness.
❑ Missile linebacker—The quarterback of the defense; must control A-gaps.
❑ Bullet linebackers—Typically, the best linebackers; must read nearside the guard to the nearside back.
❑ Eagles—Are a combination OLB/DB.

Stimulus	Response
Down block	Eyes up to the near back.
Out block (pull to)	Scrape tight.
Pull (pull away)	Shuffle, shuffle, fit.
Scoop	Same
Reach	B-gap; if contact, keep the outside shoulder free.
High hat	Cover the first back to his side, or get to the quarterback

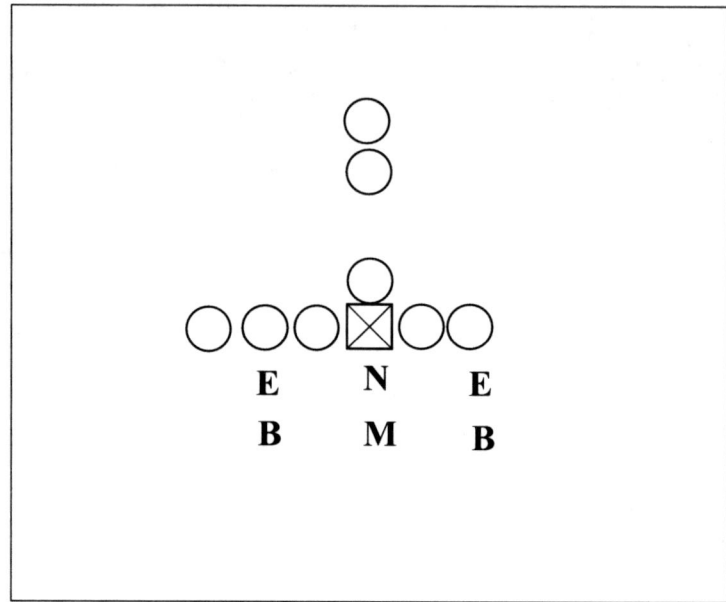

Diagram 14-2. Defensive line and linebackers base cover 3 and cover 2

❑ Strong End:
- Alignment—Head-up the offensive tackle
- Key—Offensive tackle
- Run to/away—C-gap/ trail/ reverse
- Pass responsibility—TE/OT rush lane

❑ Noseguard:
- Alignment—Head-up the center
- Key—Ball
- Run to/away—C-gap; trail/reverse
- Pass responsibility—Inside rush lane

- ❏ Weak End:
  - Alignment: Head-up the offensive tackle
  - Key—Offensive tackle
  - Run to/away—C-gap; backside A
  - Pass responsibility—Outside rush lane
- ❏ Bullets:
  - Alignment—Stack DE's
  - Key—Offensive guard/near running back
  - Run to/away—Fit
  - Pass responsibility—Hash drop
- ❏ Missile:
  - Alignment—Stack noseguard
  - Key—Fullback/offensive guard
  - Run to/away—Fit
  - Pass responsibility— Hole drop

Position Play

- ❏ Noseguard Play:
  - Alignment—Nose-to-nose on the center; play as tight as possible and still be able to key and react.
  - Key—Movement on the center's hand
  - Responsibility—Attack the center and stuff him into the backfield and find the football; wreak havoc.
  - Coaching Points:
    - ✓ On a running play, get one-yard deep in the backfield and redirect to the football; hold ground on a double team.
    - ✓ On pass plays, execute a bull rush, rip, or swim move; look for a draw. Get to the quarterback if there's no draw.
- ❏ Defensive End Play:
  - Alignment—Head-up on the offensive tackle; align tight to the line of scrimmage.
  - Key—Movement of the offensive tackle's helmet.
  - Responsibility—C-gap; make power call; contain the pass rush.
  - Coaching Points:
    - ✓ Step flat with the outside foot.
    - ✓ Keep shoulders square.
    - ✓ Attack the outside number of the offensive tackle.
    - ✓ Punch with hands and react to the offensive tackle's first step.

✓ On running plays, get one yard deep, go flat to the ball.

✓ On pass plays, contain and get to the quarterback.

❑ Bullet Linebackers' Play:

• Play downhill; get to the football.

Stimulus	Response
Down block	Eyes up to the near back.
Out block (pull to)	Scrape tight.
Pull (pull away)	Shuffle, shuffle, fit.
Scoop	Same
Reach	B-gap; if contact, keep the outside shoulder free.
High hat	Cover the first back to his side, or get to the quarterback

• Alignment/depth—Five yards; make shotgun call

❑ Missile Linebacker Play:

• Play downhill; get to the football.

• Depth—Five yards

• Alignment—Stack behind the noseguard; make the formation call.

• Key—The track of the fullback to the offensive guard.

• Coaching Points:

✓ Go through the blocker.

✓ Look for screens and draws.

✓ Cover the second back out of the backfield.

✓ Continue to the quarterback on pass plays if the back is blocking.

Diagram 14-3 illustrates our Eagle alignments. First, we go against the pro set-I, with a split end on one side, and a tight end and wide receiver on the same side.

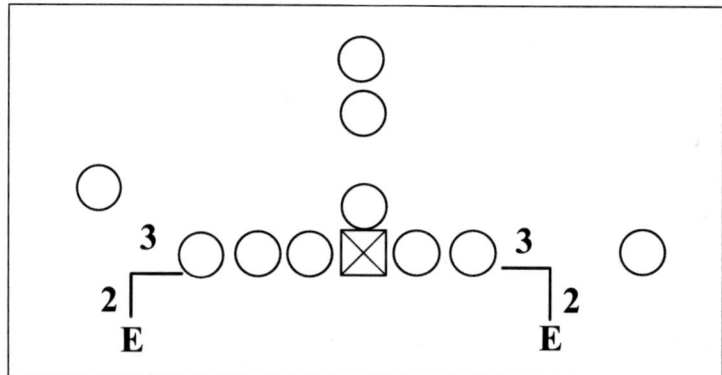

Diagram 14-3. Eagle vs. pro I-set

Diagram 14-4 shows how we line up against the split end and the slot man to the same side. The tight end is on the opposite side. This is how we line up on the slot and the backside. The following list details the responsibilities of the eagles and defensive backs in this alignment:

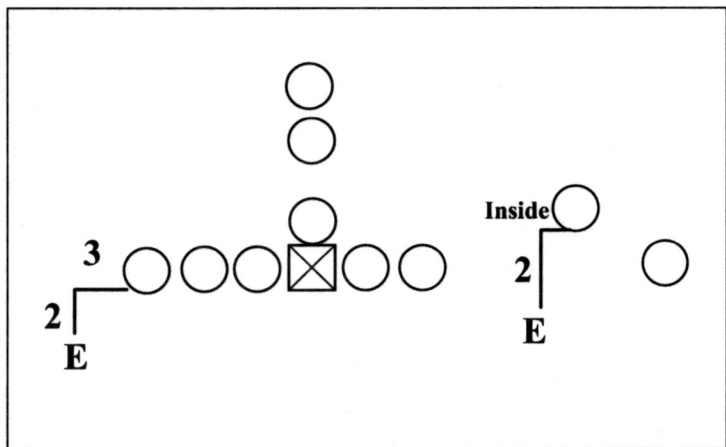

Diagram 14-4. Eagle vs. pro I-set slot

❑ Eagles' Responsibilities:
- On the one-receiver side, play downhill; read the last player on the line of scrimmage to the deepest back.

Stimulus	Response
Inside run to	Stay flat to the line of scrimmage; take away the bounce play.
Inside run away	Watch for bootleg; take away the cutback.
Outside run to	Make play; string out to the sideline.
Outside run away	Watch for a reverse, pursue from the backside.
Pass	Contain, get to the quarterback.

- If more than one receiver is on his side, cover the number 2 receiver man-to-man; take away the inside route, or play zone coverages (flats).
❑ Cornerback's Responsibilities:
- Man-to-man coverage on the number 1 receiver to each side.
- Take away the inside route.
- Disrupt the quarterback/receiver timing.
- Mask the coverage from time to time.
- Cover 2 or cover 3 zone
- Attack the run from an outside-in zone.

❑ Saftey's Responsibilities:
- Man defense—tight end
- Man free—center field; no one gets behind him.
- Call out motion.
- Cover 2, cover 3 zone
- Run support, inside-out

Next, I would like to cover our 3-3 stack blitzes. First, I would like to review our stunts. Most of the stunts are self-explanatory. The following list details the different stunts and indicates how we determine how we move on the stunts:

- Missile—Weak/strong, right/left
- Bullet—Double, weak/strong, right/left
- Eagle—Double, weak/strong, right/left
- Beast—Double, weak/strong, right/left
- Bam—Double, weak/strong, right/left
- Mean—Double, weak, strong, right/left
- Thunder—Send five linebackers; the three linemen stay at the line of scrimmage.
- Storm—Everyone blitzes, including the three down linemen and the five linebackers.
- Corner or safety—Weak/strong, right/left

Diagram 14-5 illustrates our missile stunt. The noseguard goes one way, and the missile goes the opposite way.

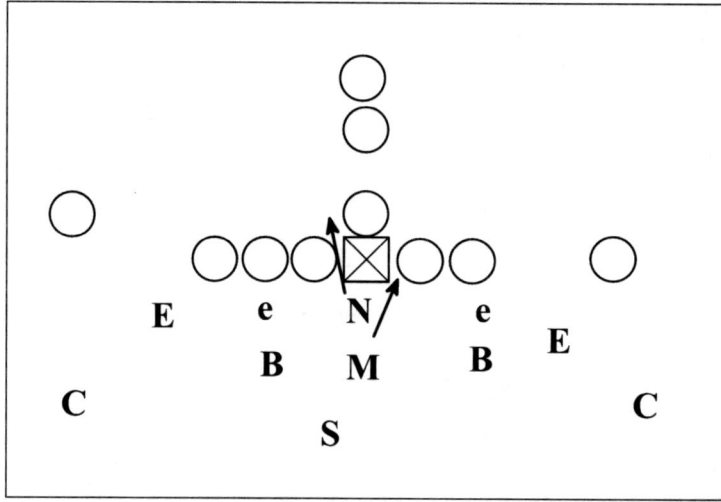

Diagram 14-5. Missile

On the bullet stunt, we involve four inside players (Diagram 14-6). The bullet has the C-gap and the missile has the A-gap.

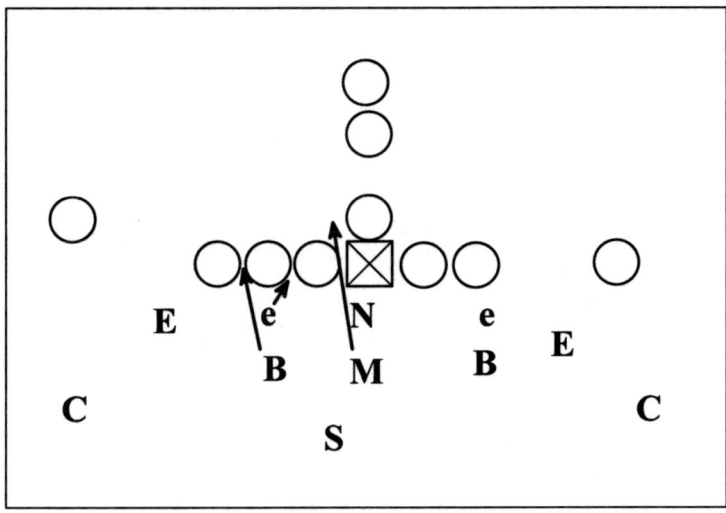

Diagram 14-6. Bullet

On the eagle stunt, we stunt on the backside (Diagram 14-7). The eagle on the backside closes in the C-gap. The missile has the strongside A-gap, and the nose has the backside A-gap.

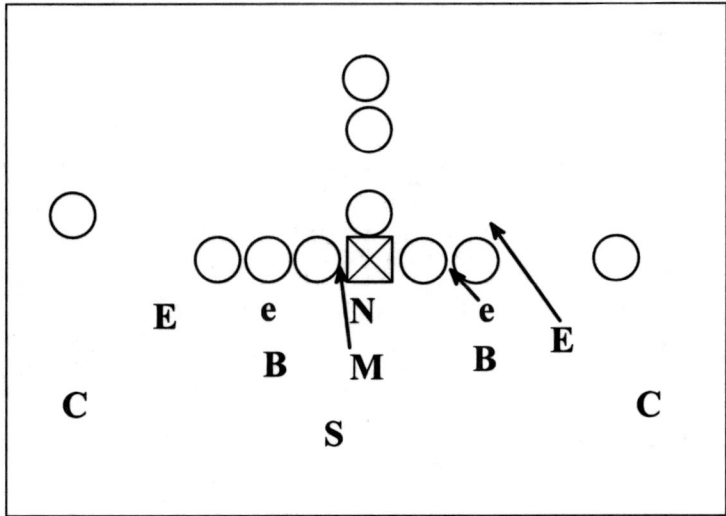

Diagram 14-7. Eagle

The beast stunt is a backside stunt, with the three outside defenders (Diagram 14-8). In this stunt, the backer and the end blitz.

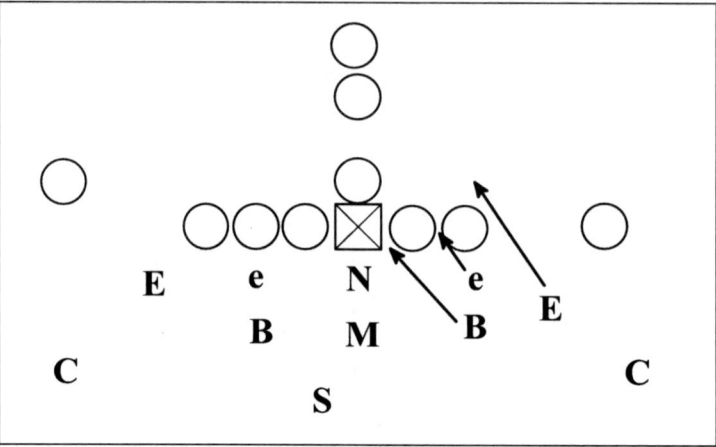

Diagram 14-8. Beast

When we take the eagle stunt and use it with the missile stunt, we refer to this stunt as the mean stunt (Diagram 14-9). The difference is the missile has the option to cover either A-gap. The nose man slants left on the mean stunt. The missile reads both A-gaps and fills if the ballcarrier comes to him.

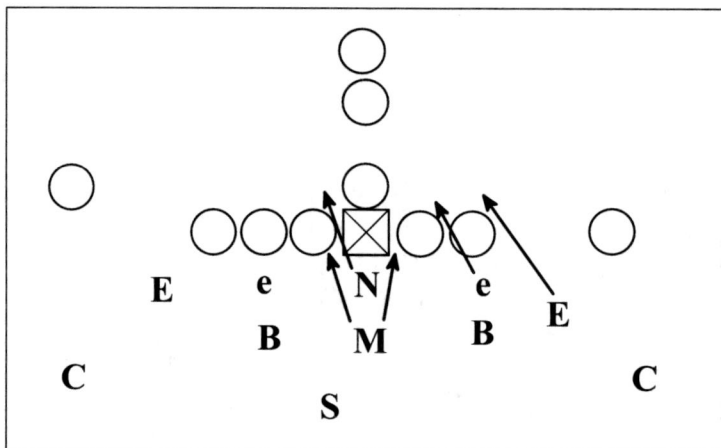

Diagram 14-9. Mean

On the thunder stunt, we involve eight players on the call. The ends are coming hard, and the three linebackers blitz (Diagram 14-10). The down linemen cover for the blitzing linebackers.

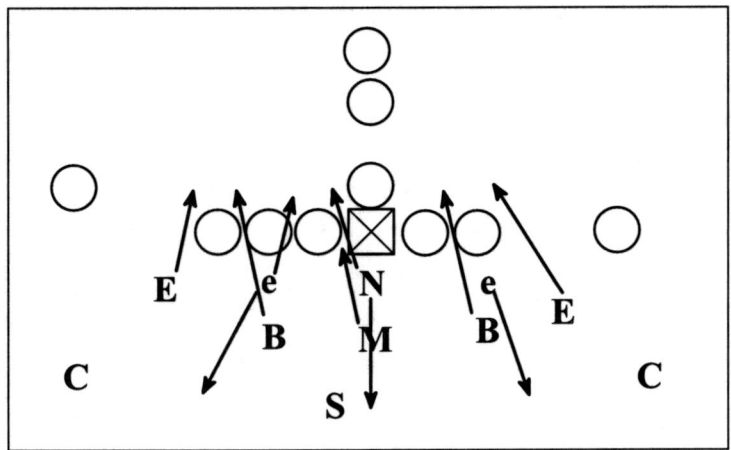

Diagram 14-10. Thunder

On the storm stunt, we send all eight men in the box (Diagram 14-11). It is an all-out blitz, with the two corners and safety playing the pass.

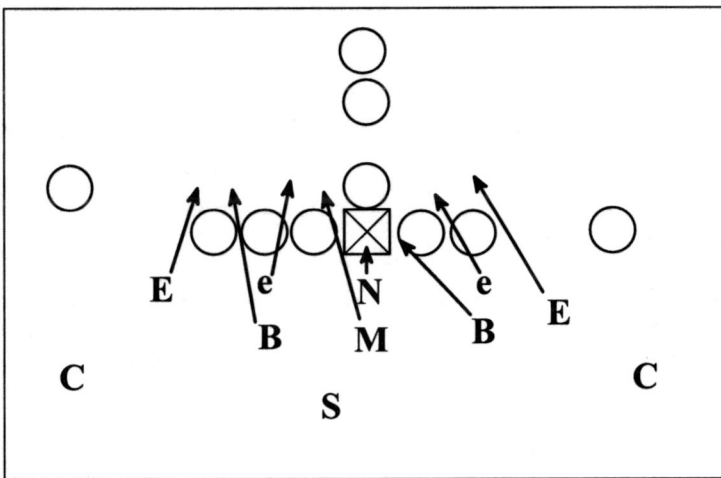

Diagram14-11. Storm

Next, I would like to cover five different formations and show you how we line up against each of them. I would also like to review the key coaching points for each position in each formation.

The first formation is the I-formation. Diagram 14-12 illustrates a standard pro right I-set alignment.

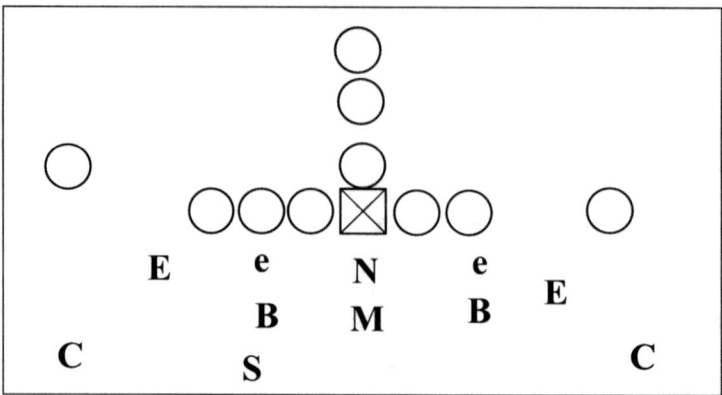

Diagram 14-12. I-formation

❑ Coaching Points:
  • Cornerbacks—Man-to-man pass coverage on the #1 receiver to each side of the line of scrimmage
  • Safety—Man-to-man coverage on the tight end
  • Eagles—Contain on runs; get to the quarterback on a pass.
  • Bullet linebackers—Play downhill; cover the first back out to his side to the quarterback.
  • Missile linebacker—Play downhill; cover the second back out to either side to the quarterback.
  • Defensive line—Get one-yard deep in the backfield; redirect to the ball on runs; get to the quarterback on a pass.

The next formation I'd like to discuss is the double twins formation. The offense is in a slot on both sides of the formation (Diagram 14-13). The eagles have to cover the slots man-to-man.

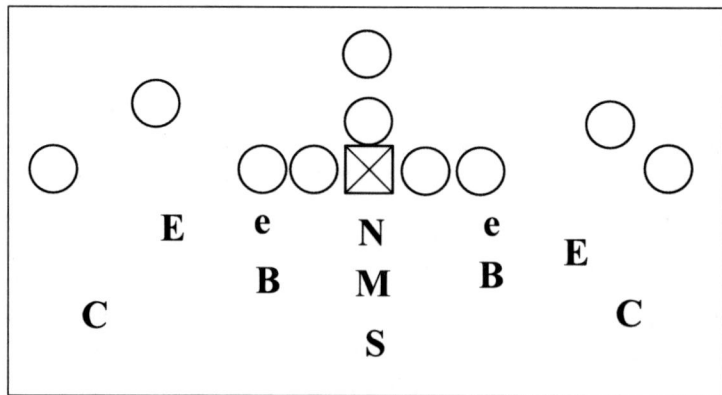

Diagram 14-13. Double twins formation

❑ Coaching Points:
- Cornerbacks—Man-to-manpass coverage on the #1 receiver to each side of the line of scrimmage; take away the slant pass.
- Safety—Man-to-man to run support
- Bullet linebackers—Play downhill; cover the back if he comes out to his side to the quarterback.
- Missile linebacker—Play downhill and read the quarterback.
- Defensive line—Get one-yard deep in the backfield; redirect to the ball on runs, and get to the quarterback on a pass. The ends take an outside rush.

The third formation is the trips formation. Against trips formation, we adjust with our eagles and bring the safety over to the formation to cover the #3 receiver (Diagram 14-14). The corners are man-to-man on the outside receivers.

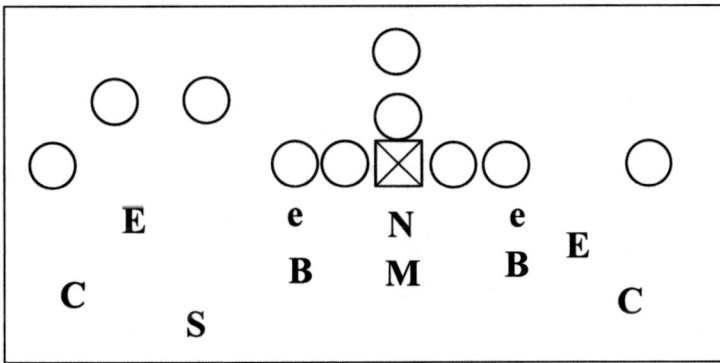

Diagram 14-14. Trips formation

❑ Coaching Points:
- Cornerbacks—Man-to-man pass coverage on the #1 receiver to each side of the line of scrimmage
- Safety—Man-to-man pass coverage on the #3 receiver
- Eagles—Man-to-man pass coverage on the #2 receiver; come hard at the quarterback; watch for the handoff.
- Bullet linebackers—Play downhill; cover the back who comes out to his side to the quarterback.
- Missile linebacker—Play downhill; read the quarterback.
- Defensive line—Get one-yard deep in the backfield; redirect to the ball on runs and get to the quarterback on a pass. The ends take an outside rush.

The fourth formation is an empty formation. Against the empty formation, we cover the three receivers on one side and two receivers on the backside (Diagram 14-15). We keep the inside down linemen and linebackers inside.

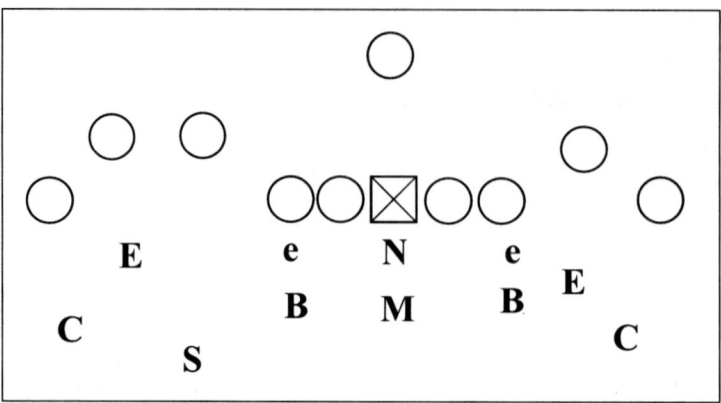

Diagram 14-15. Empty formation

❑ Coaching Points:
- Cornerbacks—Man-to-man pass coverage on the #1 receiver to each side of the line of scrimmage
- Safety—Man-to-man pass coverage on the #3 receiver
- Eagles—Man-to-man pass coverage on the #2 receiver
- Bullet linebackers—Play downhill; cover the back who comes out to his side to the quarterback.
- Missile linebacker—Play downhill; read the quarterback.
- Defensive line—Get one-yard deep in the backfield; redirect to the ball on runs, and get to the quarterback on a pass. The ends take an outside rush.

The fifth (and final) formation involves playing against short-yardage and goal-line situations. As a rule, we encounter the power stack strong set (Diagram 14-16). We adjust by bringing the corners in tighter, and we walk up closer to the line of scrimmage.

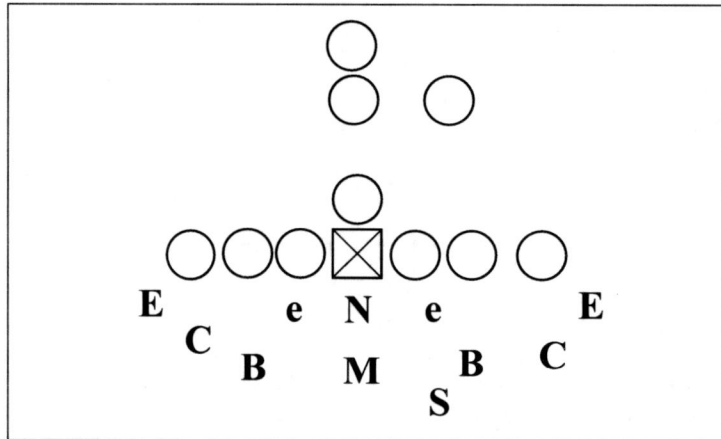

Diagram 14-16. Short yardage/goal line

❑ Coaching Points:
  - Cornerbacks—Man-to-manpass coverage on the #1 receiver to each side of the line of scrimmage
  - Safety—Man-to-man pass coverage on the power back
  - Eagles—Crash hard through the tight end to the quarterback.
  - Bullet linebackers—Play downhill, two-to-three yards deep; cover the back who comes out to his side to the football.
  - Missile linebacker—Play downhill, two-to-three yards deep; look for the quarterback sneak to the football.
  - Defensive ends—Get in a four-point stance; blow in the B-gap.
  - Nose—Push the center back, and look for the quarterback sneak.

My time is up. I want to thank you for your attention.

15

Changing the 5-3 to the 3-3 Defense

Noel Rash
Beechwood High School, Kentucky
2008

Thank you, it is a pleasure to be here. I do not have much time, so I am going to get right into the topic. My topic today is converting from an eight-man front to a six-man front without changing personnel. However, I will be the first person to tell you, we make many personnel changes in obvious passing situations.

The coach at Dixie Heights emailed me after he saw my name on the speaker list. He wondered after I told you that we take our tackles out and put in two defensive backs, what was I going to do for the next 58 minutes.

I am going to show you a couple of ways you can convert the defense without changing personnel. The first thing you have to look at is the type of personnel you want to use in the 5-3 defense. You have to look at the nose first. People like to play against the big heavyset lineman. The small, quick defenders cause them the most problems. There are some coaches here from northern Kentucky who have played against us. They will tell you that we focus on smaller, quicker defensive linemen in our program.

I am going to show you our base stack and shade alignments. When we align in our 5-3 defense, we play a 4-3 defense on the edge. When I talk about the 4-3 edge, I am referring to the three players in the outside triangle: the linebacker, defensive tackle, and defensive end. They play in the B and C gaps. I will show you who they read and where they look. We play our 5-3 defense like a 4-3 defense.

The defensive end in our 5-3 defense is going to squeeze inside like a 4-3 defense. That lends itself to converting to the 3-3 defense. That is one of the key things in converting to the 3-3 defense. The personnel you play at your nose make the conversion easier.

As far as our personnel arrangements, I will show you how we have done it before and other ways to do it. Fort Thomas Highlands runs the 3-3 defense, but they play their tackles in a 5 technique and the linebacker up close to the line of scrimmage. They call their strong safety players dogs. They play their 3-3 differently than we do.

In the introduction, they read my coaching record. That record comes from having a great coaching staff with a lot of experience and tremendous talent on the field. If I can stay out of the way, we will be fine.

At the nose, we want to play a quick player who can back up and play middle linebacker (Diagram 15-1). He has to be the type who will draw a double-team block when he plays down. There are times when we get in trouble with this type of scheme. I will not sit here and tell you we do not. In fact, the tape I am going to show you is from a game we lost. I think that will do more to help you understand the concepts.

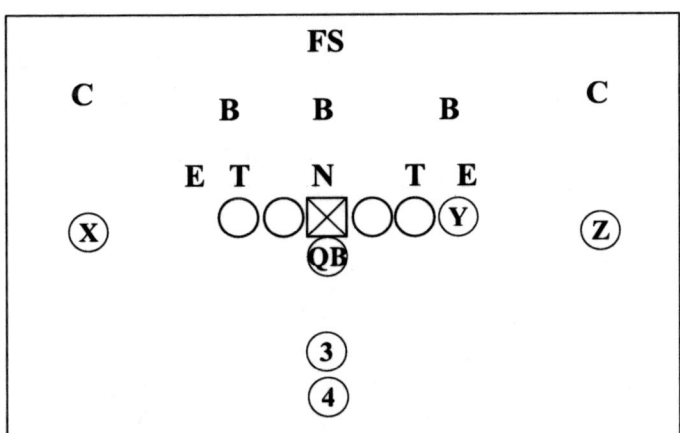

Diagram 15-1. 5-3 defense

The tackles are larger, heavier players in comparison to the nose. I replaced Mike Yeagle at Beechwood. I was fortunate to coach with him for a number of years. The 5-3 defense was Mike's baby. In his 5-3 defense, the tackles were two-gap players. They aligned in a 4 technique and played the B gap and spilled into the C gap late. We made the tackles one-gap players and took the defensive ends and played them like the 4-3 concept. In the 4-3, the great players in that defense are the defensive ends. I made the defensive ends two-gap players. That made the tackles more one-dimensional and made it easier on them.

The defensive ends in this defense are the best leverage players on the field. We want the most athletic players at defensive end. He has to be able to wrong arm a kick-out block, play the skate technique on the option, drop into coverage, and rush the passer. If I need him to play on the hash, he could do it. We do not run a lot of zone blitz, but when we do, this player can cover it.

The middle linebacker is a fill-and-plug player. I told our middle linebacker if he could play from C gap to C gap, we would be a 8-2 or 7-3 team. If he could play from D gap to D gap, we would be state power, and if he could play sideline to sideline, we would have a chance to play in the state championship. He has to be a fill-and-plug player and bounce the ball to the outside linebackers.

The outside linebackers must have good feet and must have great football instincts. They have to play downhill and drop into coverage. They play on the edge and play *outside-in* all the time. The reason we won the championship this year was because I had talented players playing on the outside who understood the game.

I do not separate the free and strong safeties. This is the same position for us. We are a 5-3 team, which means we play one defender in the middle of the field. When we go to a 4-3 defense with a cover-2 look, the free safety is a fill downhill type of player. The corners are players with great feet and vision. They are the type of player you want playing corner in this defense.

When we go to the 3-3 defense, we stack the linebacker, and the end is playing on air. You really must have an athletic player to play on air. That is the position Lawrence Taylor used to play. To play on air and do it well, you have to be a heck of a football player.

I want to show you our base 5-3 defense and some of the concepts that allow us to get into the 3-3 without changing personnel. If the offense gives us two backs in the backfield, we will be in an eight-man front. You have to start with the outside stack in the defense. We call that the *outside triangle.*

To the tight-end side, the defensive end aligns in a 9 technique. If the tight end blocks down, the defensive end closes to the inside (Diagram 15-2). If the fullback or guard tries to kick-out the defensive end, he puts his face mask on the inside V of the neck of the blocker and bounces the ball outside. I do not like to trade one for one in a blocking scheme. The defensive end plays down inside so the tailback bounces outside, but he becomes a D-gap player late. Initially, he is a C-gap player, but he also helps outside.

The tackle fights the double-team in the best way he can. You have to decide how you want him to play. This year, we had one tackle who grabbed grass and stayed low in the hole. The other tackle got skinny and split the double-team. You have to decide what your personnel can do. The outside linebacker reads the down block by the tight end and becomes the D-gap player.

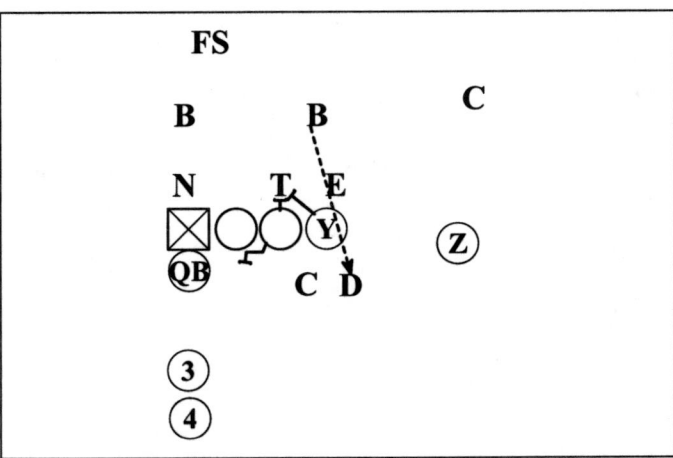

Diagram 15-2. 5-3 vs. down block

We have a simple rule for the defensive end on a base block (Diagram 15-3). We tell the defensive end that if the tight end puts his hand on him, he is a D-gap player. It does not matter what the tight end tries to do. If the tight end tries to arc release, the defensive end fights him outside. If the tight end tries to block the defensive end to the outside, the defensive end is the D-gap player, but he squeezes the tight end back to the inside. He does not run to the outside and open the inside gap. He squeezes and tries to push the tight end back inside.

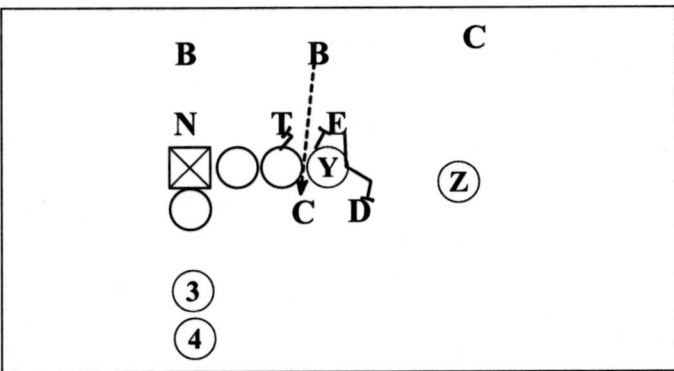

Diagram 15-3. 5-3 vs. base block

When the outside linebacker sees the tight end start to block the defensive end, he becomes the C-gap player. He plays downhill into the C gap as soon as he sees the tight end put his hands on the defensive end. He fills hard the instant he sees it, his eyes go inside, and he plays off what he sees. These techniques lead to the 3-3 defense, which I will get to in a minute.

We have a shade alignment from the 5-3 front (Diagram 15-4). On the shade, the noseguard moves to the shade alignment on the center, toward the tight end. The backside defensive tackle and end reduce their alignments to the outside shoulder techniques on the offensive tackle and guard. Since the backside reduces down, the outside linebacker (instead of stacking) kicks-out to the outside of the defense. The outside linebacker splits the difference between the offensive tackle and the split end. His rule tells him, with two backs in the backfield, he takes one giant step toward the offensive tackle in his alignment. If there is one back in the backfield, he takes one giant step toward the split end. In the one-back set, he aligns wider because there is one less blocker to that side.

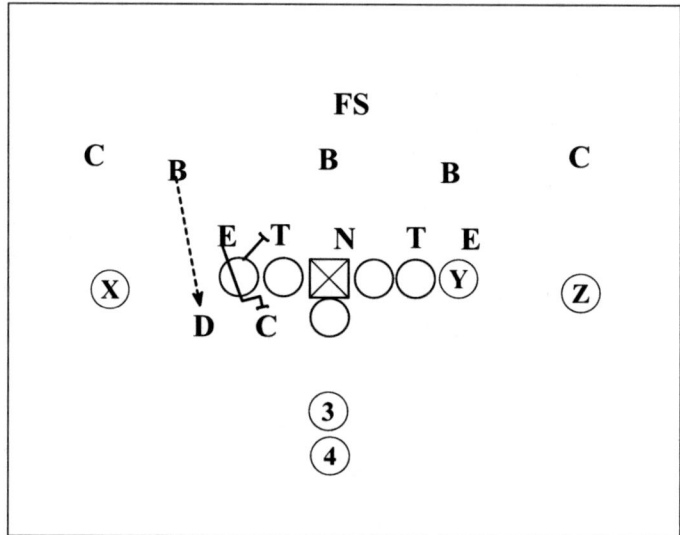

Diagram 15-4. Shade 5-3 vs. down block

On the split-end side, the read for the defense does not change. They have the same read as to the tight-end side. If the offensive tackle blocks down on the defensive tackle, the defensive end is the C-gap player and closes to the inside. As you look at the diagram, I know it is actually the B gap, but we still consider that gap the C gap. The outside linebacker on the down block is the D-gap player. If the offensive tackle base blocks on the defensive end, he becomes a D-gap player and plays with his responsibility to the outside, but squeezing to the inside (Diagram 15-5). The outside linebacker is now the C-gap player and has to get into that gap in a hurry. He is the downhill player looking inside for his next key.

If the offense spreads the outside linebacker with an additional receiver to his side, he gives a *tight, tight* call to the defensive end. That tells the defensive end he cannot fill the C gap on a base block from the tackle. Now, the defensive end has to play the C gap, and the linebacker plays the D gap. Those are the basic reads in this defense, and that is where you have to start. It is a 5-3 defense, but it plays like a 4-3 in the triangles on the outside.

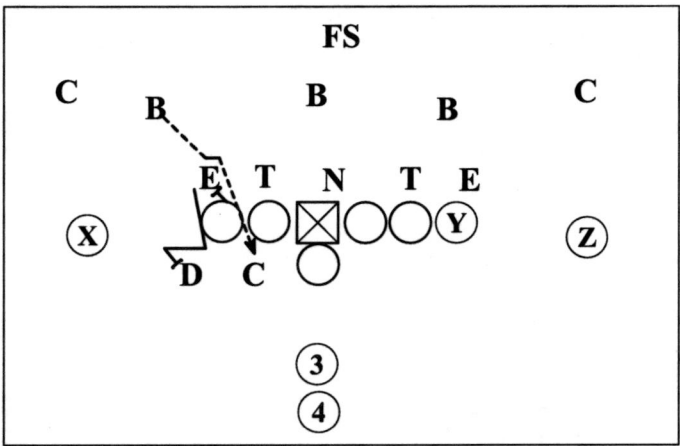

Diagram 15-5. Shade 5-3 vs. base block

When we play the spread offense, the simplest thing to do is leave the tackles in 4 techniques and walk your defensive ends off on the slot receiver (Diagram 15-6). That alignment looks like the 3-3 defense, except for the two-deep secondary. The flaw of that alignment is you need defensive ends who can play in space. Last year, I played with one defensive end who could not play in space. However, I had one defensive end who could. I will always have one defensive end who can play in space. That is the decision I have to make at the beginning of the year. If I want to be a 3-3 team, I definitely must have at least one defensive end who can play in space. It goes back to what I said at the beginning, the defensive ends have to be great players.

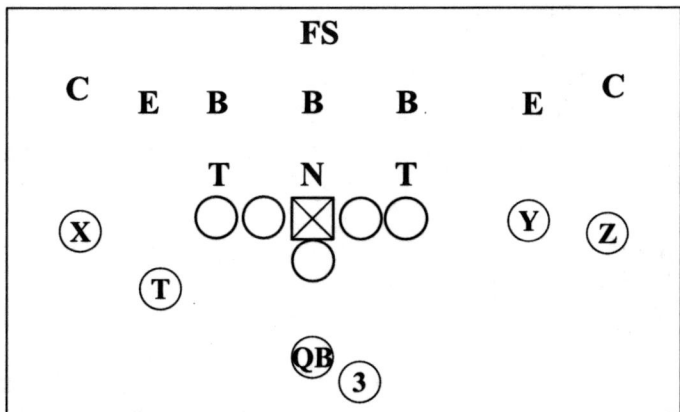

Diagram 15-6. Adjusted 5-3 to spread

From this defensive adjustment, we can play cover 3 with no problem. The ends take the flats, the outside linebackers have hook to curl, and the Mike linebacker has the hook zone in the middle. The safety goes to the middle third, and the two corners play the outside thirds.

We can roll the secondary strong or weak from this alignment (Diagram 15-7). If we roll to the defensive left, the corner and defensive end collide on the outside receiver and slot to prevent them from going deep. The safety plays the deep half behind the left corner, and the right corner plays the weak-half coverage. That leaves us six underneath defenders in five short zones. However, the linebackers will more than likely be in some kind of blitz game.

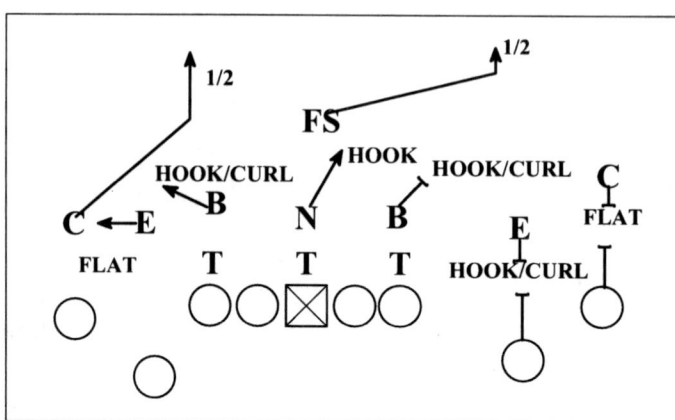

Diagram 15-7. Cover 2 left

If the offense is hurting the defense with an option or some kind of wide play, we roll the corner up to get the hard corner. However, we never drop the defensive end into the deep third behind the corner. We have to get from the clinic to the practice field. You cannot give the defensive ends too much to do. You cannot change their reads so that you are coaching them in an entirely new scheme.

The outside linebacker's read in the 3-3 alignment does not change. However, it is opposite. If he gets a down block by the tackle, he fills the C gap. If he gets a base block, he scrapes. He still reads the same way, except now he has flat coverage or hook-to-curl coverage.

One way to get from the 5-3 to the 3-3 is very simple (Diagram 15-8). You can do all the adjustments from one side of the defense. This makes it simple so you do not have players running all over the field to get into position. You do all the movement from one side. The nose tackle backs off the line of scrimmage and becomes the middle linebacker. The right defensive tackle bumps into the nose-tackle position. The right defensive end becomes the down 4-technique tackle, and the inside and outside linebackers become the outside linebacker and dog player or inside safety. You have to decide which of the linebackers plays better in space and which one is the better run stopper. If your Mike linebacker plays better in space, he could become the outside dog-type player. You have to decide that according to your personnel.

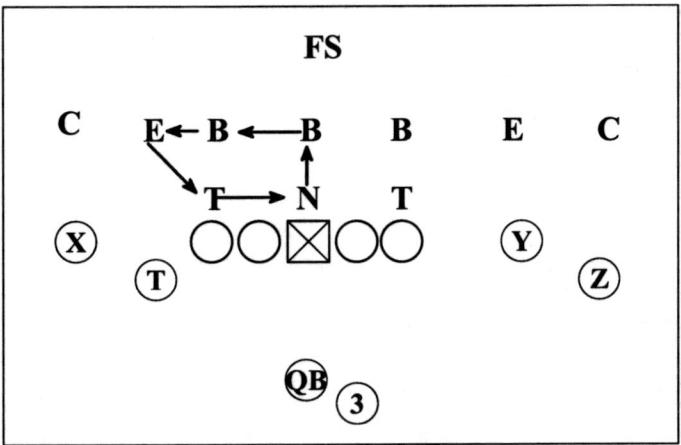

Diagram 15-8. 5-3 defense to 3-3 alignment

In the defense, one end can play in space and the other is a run stopper kind of player. That is the same concept of the anchor end and the drop end. We have six players in the box who can do all kinds of things. However, we have seven cover players in this defense. The next thing you have to decide is how to play your second-level defenders. You actually have six defenders in the underneath second level, because one of the corners will drop into deep coverage every time.

We have different ways to align the six underneath defenders. We can align all the second-level players at five yards deep, or they can align in a press-coverage look (Diagram 15-9). When we align in a press alignment, we bring the outside corners and inside dogs to the line of scrimmage.

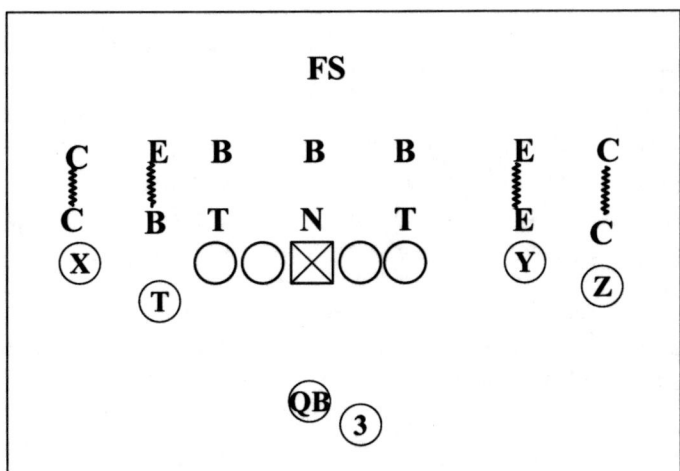

Diagram 15-9. Press

In our 3-3 alignment, the six inside defenders will never come out of the box. The three down linemen and the three stacked linebackers will always be in the box. What that means is the offensive formation will never cause the inside six players to make an adjustment outside the box. The offense tries to get the defense to move with their formations. I looked at the Nike notebook they give us each year and it is obsolete. On the pre-drawn formations on the pad, the quarterback is under the center. You never see that anymore. I can call a defense that causes our players to leave the box, but the offense cannot do anything that affects the way we align.

The offense has rules they try to exercise in their play calling. If there are five defenders in the box, they run the ball. If there are seven players in the box, they throw the ball. With six players in the box, the rules are cloudy. If you keep six players in the box, there are so many things you can do. That makes the defense very diverse, without changing a thing from your base teaching. The linebackers and ends are still reading the triangle. If you get a down block, the end squeezes and the linebacker scrapes. If they try to base the end, the linebacker screams into the gap and the end is outside in the D gap with the corner in the wide D gap.

The flat player is a run player first. Whoever is assigned flat coverage is a run player first. We want him to play the run first and recover to the flat. How many teams will try to move the ball down the field throwing to the flat repeatedly? It is too hard of a throw, and most do not have the patience to do it. With high school quarterbacks, it is too much of a risk to dink the ball down the field throwing to the flat. With the high school hash marks, your quarterback has to be good to get the ball outside the numbers into the wide field. We tell our flat players they play *run, run, run*, and get to the flat when they need to get there. If the offense wants to throw the ball into the flat, we come after the quarterback and make him throw the ball over the flat defender.

This past year, Fort Thomas Highland's defensive tackles were amazing. We scrimmage them every year. They play the tackle in a 5 technique on the outside shoulder of the offensive tackle and control the B gap. It looks like a simple play to turn out on the tackle, lead up on the outside linebacker, and have a great play. We have been blessed in that we have some big offensive tackles. Their defensive tackle pushed our tackle down inside, played over his face, and made the play. They closed on the out block and the lead blocker never got to the linebacker.

We do not have those types of tackles all the time. That is why I like to stack in the 4 technique. We get in a 5 technique, but it is generally in a long-yardage situation. We give the tackle a *jet* call that is a pass-rush mode. They get wider outside in an angled stance and come as hard as they can in a pass rush. If the offense runs the ball, they may get eight or nine yards, but they still have to punt.

In our base defense, our tackles play a 4 technique (Diagram 15-10). The linebacker reads the guard. I cannot change his rules completely. Because of the size of our school, we are a one-platoon football team. I play seven or eight players both ways. That is a minimum number because some years it is more than that. We do not have that much time during the week to work on our defensive scheme, because our players are involved on both sides of the ball. We have maybe two-and-a-half hours, tops, in any given week to get ready for our next opponent. We do not change reads for any given opponent. If the guard blocks down or up, the outside linebacker fires into the B gap. We do not worry about the offensive tackle reaching the defensive tackle, because the Mike linebacker's alignment is deeper than the other two linebackers are. He plays over the top to the outside and can fit outside the tackle.

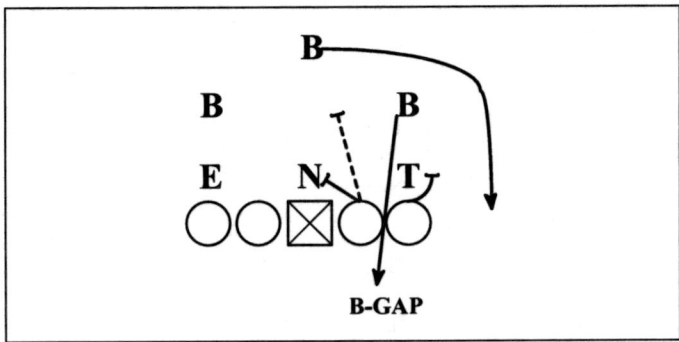

Diagram 15-10. 4-technique stack

The Mike linebacker's alignment is what we call an *inverted wishbone* look. The outside linebackers are in front of the Mike linebacker as far as his depth. I have not talked any pass coverage yet, but I am going to do that next.

If you are thinking about doing something like this, you need to start thinking early about how to get out of the eight-man front into the six-man front. Everyone runs the spread offense, and you have to defend it. I showed you how we do it. However, you may have another way that fits your personnel better. Our way is the way we do it—it is not necessarily the only way.

If you go back 15 years, particularly in single-A football, you saw maybe two teams in the spread. When Hal Mumme came to the University of Kentucky as head football coach, the entire state went to the spread offense and it has not changed since. High school coaches follow what is going on at the state level, which is probably a good thing. When Hal Mumme came through the state, everyone went to the spread and they never looked back.

If you go to the 3-3 defense and someone comes out in the tight-end set, you have to adjust (Diagram 15-11). One of the ways we adjust is to align the dog (who is a defensive end) on the tight end. The defensive tackle to that side aligns in a 4 technique head-up on the tackle. The reads are the same. If the tight end blocks down on the defensive tackle, the defensive end closes the C gap, and the outside linebacker scrapes into the D gap.

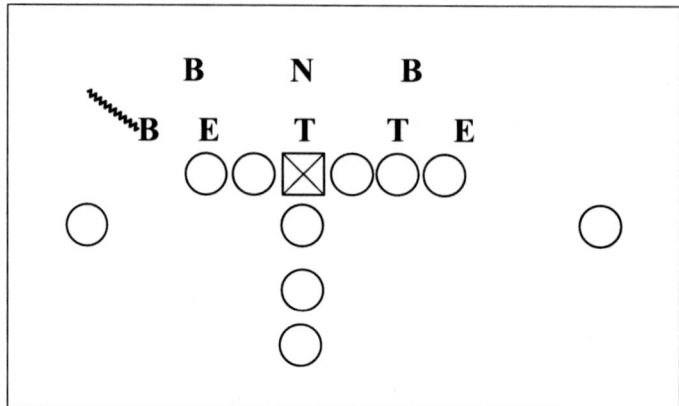

Diagram 15-11. Adjustment to tight end

The defensive ends in this defense have to be *special*. We have two outside linebackers and two defensive ends in four positions. In those four positions, you must find two players who are special players. If you look at the 5-3 defense, the Mike linebacker can be an average player. All the pressure is on the perimeter. That is especially true now because teams are not going to run in the A gap, B gap, and C gap as their only offense. They will stretch you laterally and vertically.

When we play 3-3 defense, we play many coverages in man defense. We bring six defenders all the time to rush the quarterback. We play the free safety as a linebacker quite a bit. He is a downhill player.

I want to look at the coverage from the 3-3 defense. When we go to our 3-3 defense, we call it nickel. The reason we call it *nickel* is that we have substituted two defensive backs into the defense. One of our nickel backs is an outside-linebacker type, and the other one is our fourth defensive back. The reason we play those types of players is the rotating coverages we play.

We do not like to take the safety out of the middle (Diagram 15-12). We use rotation coverage to get the nickel back into the deep outside third. We do not let the defensive end run this type of coverage, but when we substitute the fourth defensive back, we feel comfortable letting him run the third. This coverage is a rotation right.

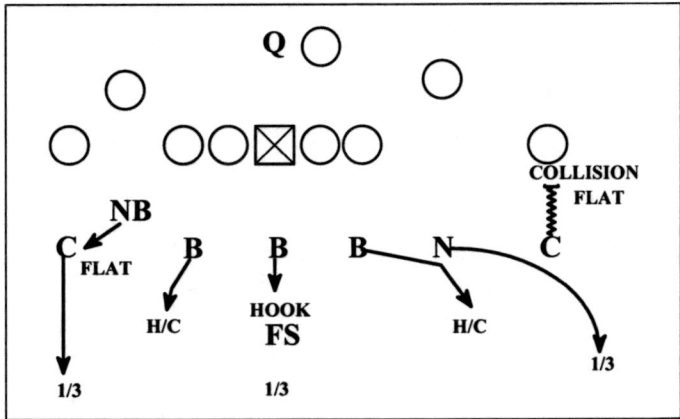

Diagram 15-12. Cover 3 with rotation

The right corner collisions the wide receiver coming off the line and settles into the flat coverage. The nickel back, who looks like he is playing the flat, retreats into the deep third, and everyone else plays the same.

You can do that a hundred ways, but that requires you to teach all the different techniques to all the players. We are not going to do that. We let the defensive back, who knows how to cover the third, make the adjustment. Remember the rule about the flat player. The flat defender plays the run first. That, now, is the corner. He reads the offensive tackle block for his key. He collisions the receiver and gets his eyes to the inside.

I tell our third players they should be making tackles on the run four to seven yards down the field. If they are making tackles at the line of scrimmage, we will get beat deep on a pass. Mom will be cheering when he makes the big play. However, she will not take any credit when he gets beat deep. When a player has third responsibility, he has to be late on run support.

If we want to rotate the coverage to the left, the fourth defensive back moves to the left side and runs into the outside third. We never let the linebacker type play a deep third. In their stance, the flat player will have a parallel stance. The third player opens to his third in his stance. He disguises his foot movement to keep from tipping his coverage.

We can go to a *dime* package from this scheme (Diagram 15-13). When we go to the dime package, the fourth defensive back in the game is now a half player. We have a 3-2 look on the inside, and the outside linebacker moves out to the hook-to-curl area. Both corners roll down into flat coverage. The outside linebackers are the hook-to-curl players, and the inside linebackers cover the middle hooks or come on a blitz. The safety and the fourth defensive back run the hash marks.

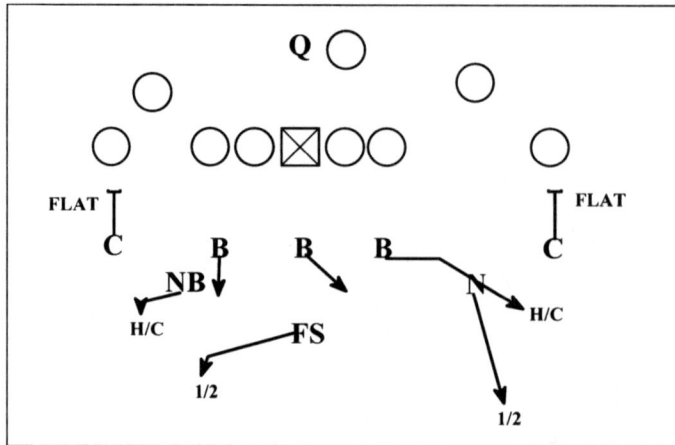

Diagram 15-13. Dime coverage

In this coverage, we can never call rotation coverage or dime coverage with the defensive end to the side that has to rotate into a deep zone. We have to be smart enough to keep the defensive end in a hook-to-curl area or a flat zone. He probably could learn how to do it, but when will we find time to teach him.

From our dime coverage we run two under (Diagram 15-14). The thing we have to do in this coverage is learn how to play man coverage. We play two types of man coverage. We play *outside-over-the-top* or *inside underneath*. We have more trouble teaching inside underneath than we do outside-over-the-top. That type of man coverage is the inside-trail position for the defender. The players understand over-the-top coverage because that is what they play in backyard football. You never play man under with a safety over the top in the backyard.

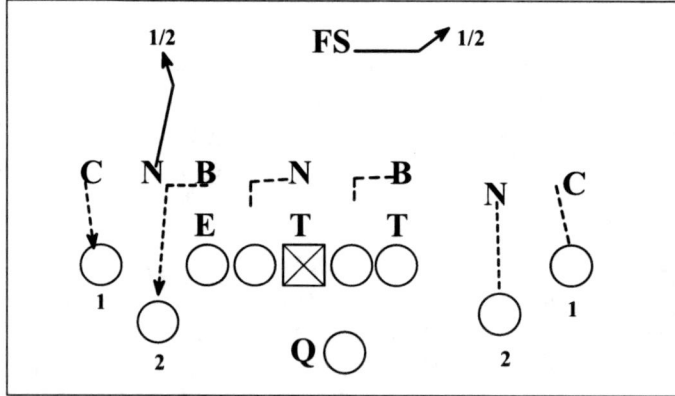

Diagram 15-14. Man two under dime

The corners' rule is press technique on the #1 receivers to their side. They collide with the receiver, force him outside, and get into trail man coverage under the receiver. The nickel backs play the #2 receivers to their side or the #3 receiver away. They play the same type of press technique as the corner. If the offense is a balanced formation, the corner takes the first receiver and the nickel takes the second receiver.

If the formation is a trips set, the backside end or linebacker has no second receiver to his side (Diagram 15-15). He comes over and takes the #3 receiver to the trips side. We always want to keep the end or linebacker on the #3 receiver. If the fourth defensive back has an away #3 receiver, he comes over, takes the #2 receiver, and puts the linebacker on the #3 receiver. We want our defensive end on the worst receiver. We do that by the scouting report. We played one team that played a trips formation all the time but had only thrown to the third receiver five times the entire season. We want our linebacker/defensive end type of player to cover that receiver.

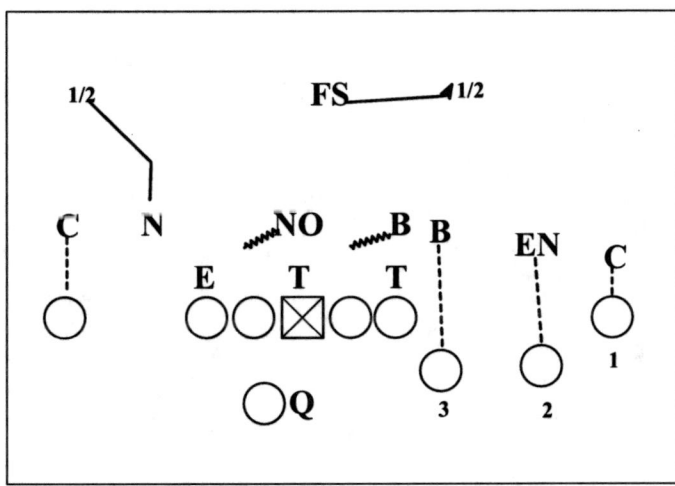

Diagram 15-15. Trips formation

We like to play press coverage because you can play zone out of the press technique (Diagram 15-16). We bring our defenders down into press coverage, which looks like man coverage. When they snap the ball, the defender collides with the receiver and drops into his zone. As soon as the quarterback starts the cadence, the nickel and linebacker covering the #2 receivers peek in at the tackle to see what he is doing. When they get their hands on the receiver, they look at the tackle to see what he is doing. If he pops up in pass protection, the defender goes to his zone responsibility. If the tackle shows a run-blocking mode, the defender gets into his run support responsibility.

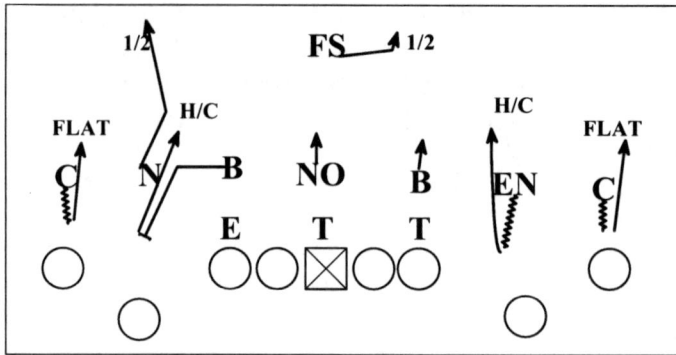

Diagram 15-16. Press cover 2

We can play cover 3 out of the press alignment (Diagram 15-17). The only thing you must have is proper footwork. The trick is the corner in press alignment bailing out into his third coverage.

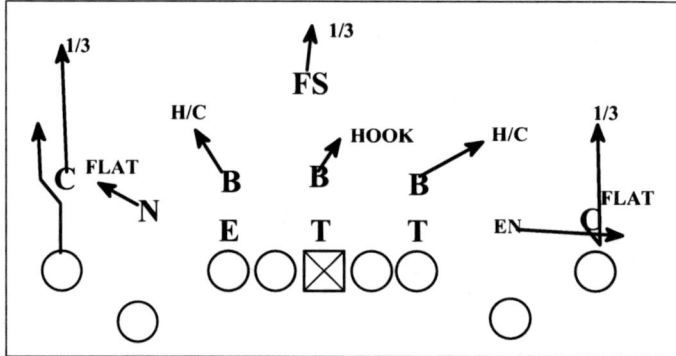

Diagram 15-17. Press cover 3

I have one last thing I will talk about. We call it spy 0. The corners have the #1 receivers to their side in man-to-man coverage. The nickel backs have the #2 receivers to their side or the #3 receiver away. They are in man coverage, but there is no help deep. They must play over-the-top man coverage because there is no help deep. They stay on top of the receiver and keep him in front of them. The safety lines up seven to eight yards deep and spies a particular back or the quarterback. This is a game plan type of coverage. We can account for the running quarterback or a back trying to take advantage of a mismatch with a defender. We can also blitz the safety out of this coverage.

Coaches, I will stick around as long as you want to talk. I hope that I was helpful to you. I appreciate your attendance and your patience with me. I will answer any questions you have. Thank you very much.

16

The 3-5 Nickel Nose Defense

Eric Redmond, Jon Van-Washenova, and Mark Hull
Carleton Airport High School, Michigan
2005

Today, I would like to discuss our "nickel nose defense" or our 3-5 look, so named because we had to come up with a different name for it because of some of our coverage packages. Perhaps, the easiest thing to call the defense is "3-5," and that is what we ended up doing.

The 3-5 nickel nose defense is not our base defense. Our base defense since 1990 has been an even 4-3 front (Diagram 16-1). In 1998, we needed an adjustment that

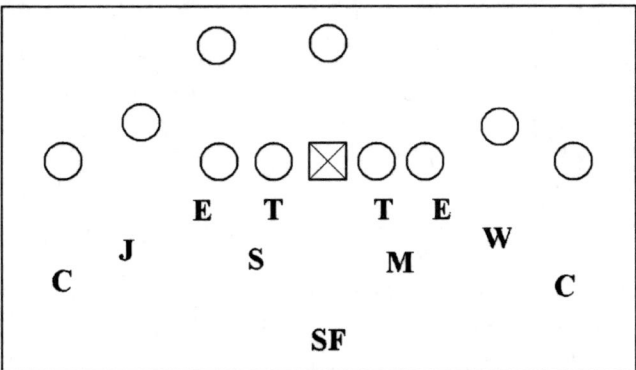

Diagram 16-1. 4-3 base defense

could address some of the things that the offenses were starting to run. Northwestern began to have success with the spread offense and the running offense that went with it. Their formation in our terminology was a shotgun 22 formation, which was a double-twin set with one back in the backfield.

In our adjusted defensive scheme, we took our Will linebacker and moved him out into coverage on the weakside slot back. Although we do not play a lot of man coverage, we took one of our better athletes out of the box. We had put him in a situation in which he was uncomfortable. We started looking at some other things. What we came up with was the 3-5 look.

From this adjustment, we try to keep six defenders in the box. Depending on what the offense does, we sometimes get eight in the box. My philosophy defensively is to be aggressive. We want to blitz and go after people. We want to confuse the offensive line's blocking assignments. With the 3-5 look, we can attack from different spots and angles. We did not want to change our basic coverage, which was zone, and the 3-5 let us do that.

We went from the 4-3 front, which had limited stunt possibilities to the 3-5, which has numerous stunt possibilities. We did not throw out everything that we had always done. In fact, we still do many of the same things. Against some of the teams on our schedule, we run nothing but a 3-5 defense.

We installed the 3-5 defense in 1998 and have tweaked it every year since then. Our defensive line plays gap control. While they are athletic, they are not the smartest people in the world. My linebacker coach is a special education teacher, and I accused him of recruiting players from his classes.

We do not have a big team. However, most of our defensive players run a 4.6-to-4.85 40-yard dash. Most of our players on the defense wear receiver's and back's numbers. When we are at full strength, we may have one player on the defense with a 50's, 60's, or 70's number. The rest of the defensive players are good athletes who can run.

We want people on the field who can play. We want them in positions, alignments, and situations where they can be successful. The linebackers are stacked behind the down linemen and are shielded somewhat from the offensive blockers.

In a game, if we were playing the 4-3, as well as the 3-5, we have to substitute to get to the 3-5 that we run. We replace a defensive tackle with a defensive back. Which player is chosen as a replacement depends on what type of athlete we have available that year. It does not depend on what the other team does. We put our next best pass defender on the field. Last year, that player was our back-up strong safety. Whatever player is in that position is referred to as the "X-player." The X stands for the eXtra player.

The linebackers line up behind the defensive linemen in a stack and are pinched according to the gap they are covering. Diagram 16-2 illustrates our base alignment in

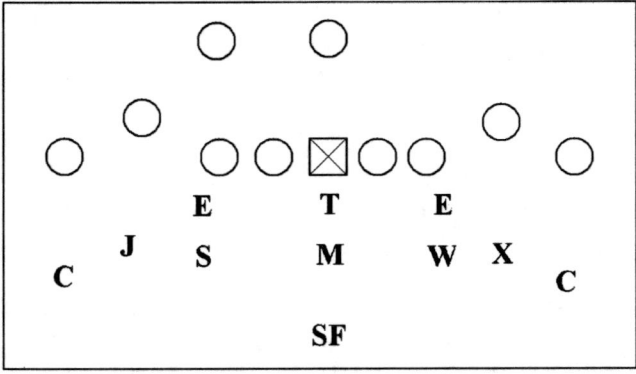

Diagram 16-2. Nickel nose (3-5)

the nickel nose defense, if we have no stunt called. In this alignment, the nose tackle is responsible for the strongside A gap. Both ends are C-gap players. It is that simple for them. On every play, the linebackers remind the ends of their gap responsibility.

The nose tackle aligns in a three-point stance, head-up on the center. He uses a smash technique or angle to either A gap, but in the base alignment, he angles into the strongside A gap. The smash technique is a straight-up charge on the center. He smashes the center and drives him back into the backfield.

If the offense is using a tight end, the defensive ends align on the outside eye of the offensive tackle in a three-point stance. If there is no tight end to his side, he aligns foot-to-foot on the offensive tackle. He plays as a C-gap player in his normal alignment. When he plays as the C-gap defender, he has to contain all passes. When we have trouble in the coverage game, it is generally because the defensive end has not contained the quarterback.

The strong linebacker (the SLB) aligns to the tight-end side or the strong side of the set. He stacks behind the defensive end. All of the linebackers place their hands on the down linemen's hips at the beginning of their stances. At this point, the linebacker pinches the down lineman on the hip in the direction he is to go. That disguises the direction because the offense cannot see the signal. The down lineman reads his normal keys and attacks the ball. He keys and plays the running back out of the backfield.

The middle linebacker (the MLB) stacks behind the nose tackle at a depth of one yard off the nose tackle's heels. He reads his normal keys and attacks the ball. The weakside linebacker (the WLB) aligns opposite the SLB and plays exactly like the strongside linebacker in his normal defense.

The corner in our zone coverage aligns on the number-1 receiver, six-to-seven yards off the line of scrimmage with inside leverage. If there is no wide receiver to his side, he aligns outside the tight receiver at a depth of four-to-five yards. In man-to-man coverage, he has the number-1 receiver.

The Jet is our strong safety. In zone coverage, he goes to the number-2 or number-3 receiver's side, depending on our scouting report. If he has a tight end, he aligns one yard outside and one yard back outside the tight end's shoulder. In man coverage, he has the number-2 receiver to his side.

The X-player aligns opposite the Jet and has the same basic rules, except he has the number-2 receiver if he comes to his side. If called for, he could go to the Jet side in a particular coverage. In man coverage, he has the number-3 receiver in a trips formation.

In zone coverage, the free safety (the SF) balances the formation, 10-to-12 yards deep in cover 3. In man coverage, he tries to remain free and reads the quarterback's eyes or picks up a man on certain stunts.

At this point, I would like to ask one of our assistant coaches, John Van-Washenova, to cover the play of the linebackers in our 3-5 defense and to discuss with you the stunts that we use.

Coach John Van-Washenova

The reason we went to the 3-5 defense was because of the spread offenses we were facing. The 3-5 gave us another secondary player on the field and allowed us to better adjust to the spread offense.

The most common stunt the linebackers and down linemen run is the "pinch" stunt (Diagram 16-3). In a pinch stunt, the linebacker "pinches" the down lineman on his hip. If he pinches him on the outside hip, the linemen go in that direction, and the linebackers blitz the other gap. We either run the stunt in situations dictated by our scouting report or when the players call their own stunts. The middle stunt is called the "slingshot," while the outside stunts are referred to as "mix it up."

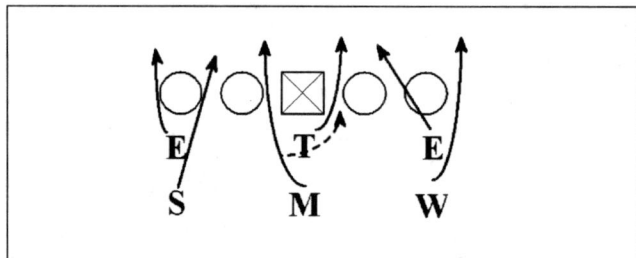

Diagram 16-3. Pinch stunts

At times, I call the stunts from the sidelines. That approach helps the players if they cannot figure out what is happening offensively. The slingshot steps the linebacker into one of the A gaps. The nose tackle angles into the same A gap, and the linebacker comes off his butt in that same gap. Of course, the MLB can also run a "mix-it-up" stunt and go to the opposite side of the nose tackle.

In a particular situation, we could smash the nose tackle and blitz the MLB and a safety into the A gaps. That puts three defenders in two gaps. We could use this defense as our goal-line defense. We are not looking to make a stop for a two-yard gain. We want to pressure the offense into a mistake or make a tackle for a loss. We come after the quarterback with penetration. When he sees the pressure coming, he may pull out early and fumble.

The next stunt we use is the "Sam stunt" (Diagram 16-4). This stunt involves both the Sam and the middle linebackers. The Sam stunt is a good combination stunt. The nose tackle goes to the weakside A gap. The SLB stunts first through the strongside A gap. The MLB follows the Sam linebacker into the strongside B gap. This stunt can do some substantial damage to the offensive line's blocking. Both the defensive ends are to the outside in the C gaps, while the Will linebacker stays at home in his B gap. In this stunt, all the gaps are covered and we can get good penetration.

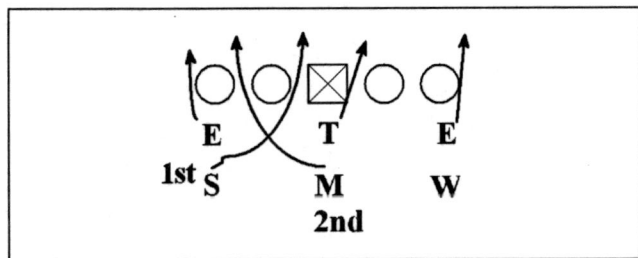

Diagram 16-4. Sam stunt

The "Wam stunt" is the same stunt, only to the opposite side (Diagram 16-5). In this stunt, both the middle and Will linebackers blitz. The nose tackle goes to the strongside A gap, while the middle and Will linebackers go to the weakside A and B gaps. The Will linebacker goes first into the A gap, and the middle linebacker comes off his butt into the B gap.

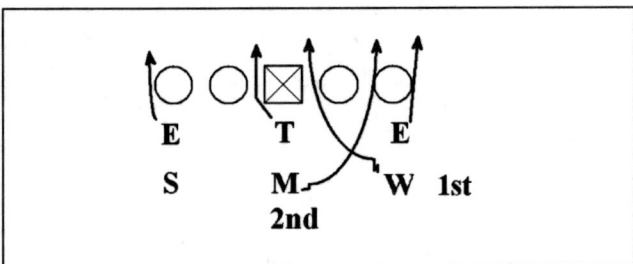

Diagram 16-5. Wam stunt

We have great success against teams that run the speed option. We see this play all the time from the spread offense. If the guard pulls, we probably will knock him over. The biggest thing on these stunts is the containment of the play. If you do not contain the play, all the pursuit is inside and deep. As we flush the quarterback, he reverses his field all the time. If the backside end does not contain, we have problems. If there is any play-action, such as the waggle pass, the quarterback flushes quickly. Accordingly, if you contain, you get a sack.

The next thing we do involves the Jet and X-player. The Jet or X makes a flash call to the outside linebacker to his side. If we run a "Jet stunt" (Diagram 16-6), the outside linebacker pinches his end into the B gap, because the Jet comes from the outside into the C gap. The strong linebacker takes the Jet's responsibility to the outside. The Jet becomes the contain player on the outside and keeps his outside arm free. The SLB checks the C gap for the running play and retreats to the flat on a pass.

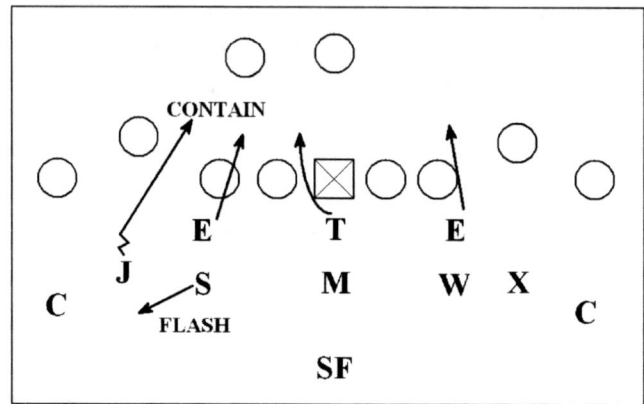

Diagram 16-6. Jet stunt

If we want to run the stunt to the other side, we run an "X stunt." Everything is the same in this stunt, except that the side reverses.

Another basic stunt we often run is the "Jet or X and LB opposite stunt" (Diagram 16-7). In this stunt, we run the "X-stunt" to the backside of the formation and a "mix-it-up" stunt with the SLB to the wide field. On this stunt, the backside defensive end has B-gap control because the X-player comes outside of him. The Will linebacker has pass responsibility. On the "mix-it-up" stunt to the strongside, we probably would send the defensive end inside and the Sam linebacker outside to contain into the wide field. However, we want him to mix up his stunt to keep the tackle guessing.

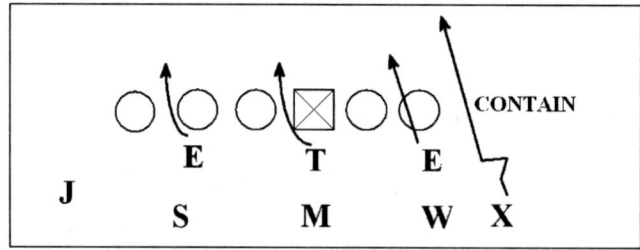

Diagram 16-7. X-stunt LB opposite

If we want containment to the wide side of the field, the best stunt we can run is "Jet stunt-LB opposite" (Diagram 16-8). This stunt brings the Jet to contain into the wide field and the Will linebacker to contain on the backside. Both defensive ends are B-gap players with no contain responsibility.

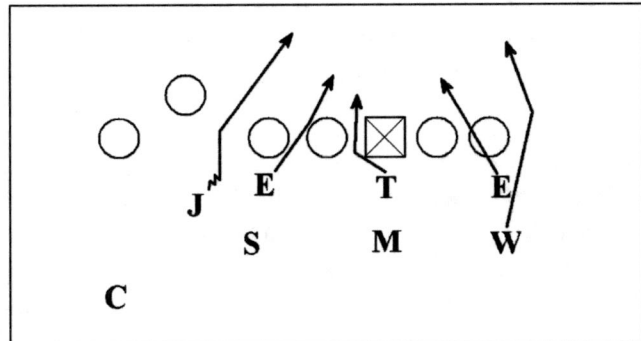

Diagram 16-8. Jet stunt-LB opposite

Because our secondary coverage in the 3-5 can get a bit complicated, I would like to ask our secondary coach, Mark Hull, to cover that aspect of our defense.

Coach Mark Hull/Secondary Coach

With regard to our secondary coverage in the 3-5, the first thing we have to do is to place the personnel correctly in the secondary. The free safety needs to be a smart player. He plays the middle third and the middle free in our coverages. When he is playing 12 to 14 yards deep, he does not have to be that quick. The Jet is more of a linebacker type and aligns to the strongside. Our X-player this past year was our backup at the Jet position. If they line up on the wrong side, it does not matter.

It would be nice to have fast, physical corners, but we do not always get what we want. If we definitely have a better cover corner, we play strong and weak corners. What we do depends on the ability of the corners and skills of the opponents we play.

Coach Redmond has reviewed our alignment rules. However, if the corner is into the wide side of the field and the formation is into the short side, he needs to adjust. The offense puts the formation into the short side for some reason. Accordingly, the corner's alignment into the wide side should be wider than normal. We adjust the alignment of the corner to the speed of the wide receivers. If they have an extremely fast wide receiver, we may back up.

The corners have the number-1 receivers in man coverage. The Jet goes to the number-2 or number-3 receiver's side most of the time. The change in that rule comes from the scouting report. If we play this defense in a goal-line situation, both the Jet and X-players are on the line of scrimmage and tighter to the tight end.

The reason we align the Jet a yard back and a yard outside the tight end is because of the stunts we run. We do not expect him to have great run support for that alignment. In man coverage, he has the number-2 receiver.

The X-player goes to the other side and has the same basic rules as the Jet. If he comes out and there is no number-2 receiver and no tight end, he can go to the strongside. We could position both the Jet and X-players to the same side. In man coverage, the X-player has the number-2 receiver to his side or the number-3 receiver in the trips set.

One set we face is a two-tight end set, with a flanker to the defensive right. In this set, the back in the backfield is positioned to the strongside of the formation (Diagram 16-9). The Jet declares right, and the X-player goes left. The Sam linebacker is right and the Will linebacker is left. If we play cover 2, we predetermine the rotation. We do not read the flow. Since the strongside of the formation is right, we roll the coverage to the right, with the right corner rolling down to the strong-flat area. The free safety takes the half-coverage to the right, while the left corner has the half-coverage to the backside.

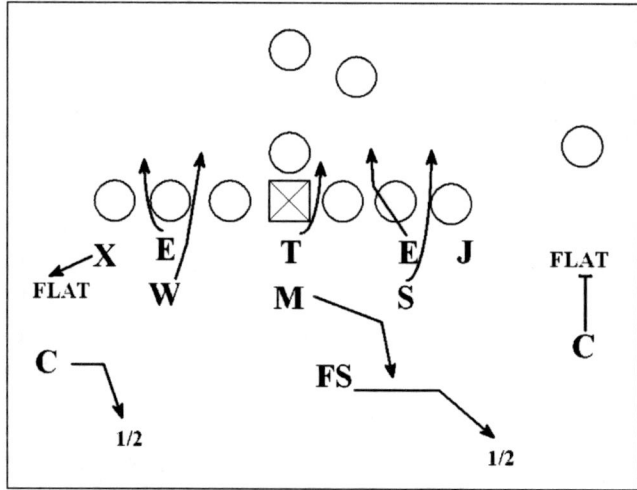

Diagram 16-9. Cover 2

Diagram 16-9 illustrates a "mix-it-up" stunt to the left and right with the Sam and Will linebackers. The nose tackle has the strong A gap as his normal responsibility. The X-player has the backside flat, and the middle linebacker balances the coverage into the middle of the field. We do not like to play a two-deep coverage, but we will play it with one wideout to one side.

If we played cover 3 from a set, the corners go to the outside third, and the free safety is in the middle third. The Jet and X-player are the flat players. If we go to maximum coverage, we have five under zones. We can play man-free coverage by matching up everyone.

The next set we face is a wing set left and split end right with the back set in the strong halfback set (Diagram 16-10). In this situation, the line stunt we often employ is the "angle weak-S stunt." In this stunt, the ends and nose tackle angle to the right side of the defense. The Sam linebacker blitzes the C gap to his side. The secondary coverage is cover 45, which is a half-coverage rolled to the left with the X-player in the backside flat. The Jet is outside the wing and expecting a run his way. The linebacker coverage tries to balance up if one of the linebackers is blitzing.

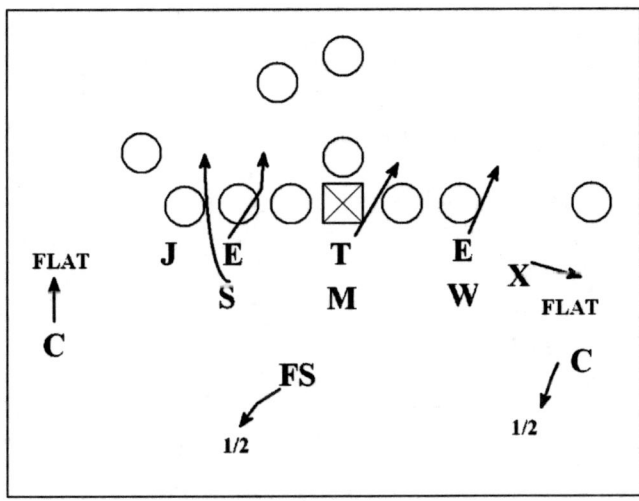

Diagram 16-10. Cover 45 angle wk-S

Since the Sam linebacker is blitzing in this stunt, the middle and the Will linebackers try to balance the coverage with Sam gone. The middle linebacker drops to the strongside, and the Will linebacker drops to the middle.

Against a pro set, we do not play any cover 2. Because a pro set has double-width receivers, we play cover 3 or man-free coverage. Diagram 16-11 illustrates cover 3 Wam. In this coverage, we are in cover 3 in the secondary. The corners and safety have the deep thirds. The Jet and X-player have the flats, and the Sam linebacker takes the middle of the field underneath. We send Will and the middle linebackers on a weakside stunt.

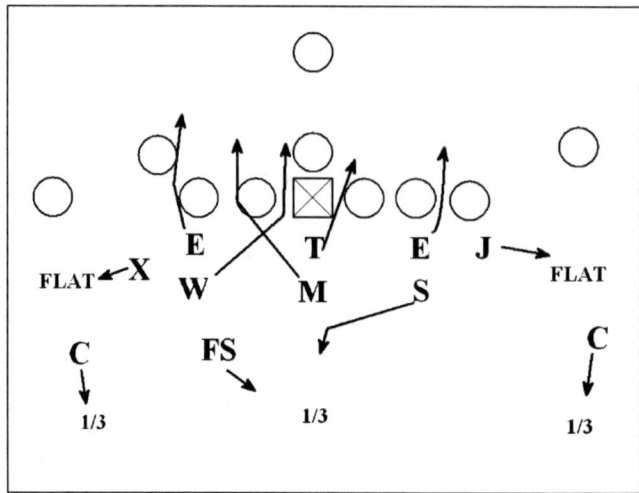

Diagram 16-11. Cover 3 Wam

The next offensive set we occasionally have to defend is a shotgun set with a double-slot look. Diagram 16-12 illustrates cover 1. In this coverage, the stunt we employ is a Will stunt weak and a free-safety blitz. The free safety sneaks up and has a choice of his blitz path. He is the smart one in the secondary and chooses which gap he wants. A good choice would be the strongside B gap or the weakside A gap. His blitz path might be away from the blocking back or away from the slide protection as dictated by our scouting report.

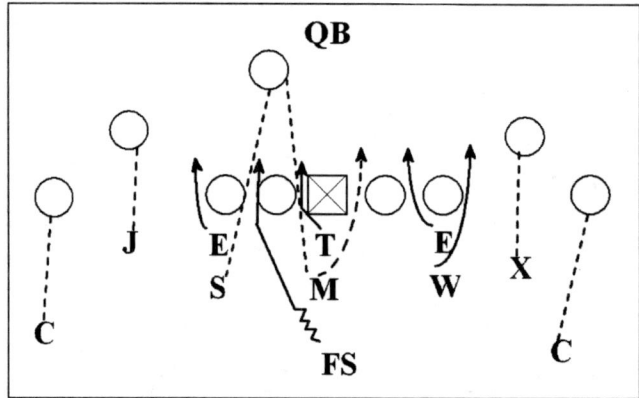

Diagram 16-12. Cover 1 SF/W

The important factor when blitzing people is the containment of the quarterback. If you do not contain the quarterback, he can run away from the blitz and can complete the pass.

If the offense sets the formation to the short side of the field, we feel comfortable running a Jet from the outside (Diagram 16-13). This set is a 21 set from the shotgun.

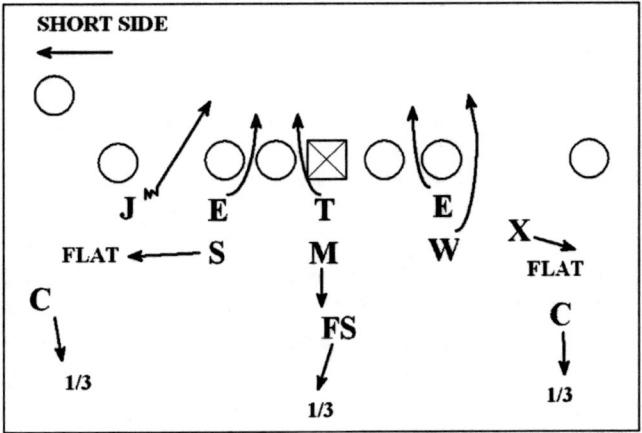

Diagram 16-13. Jet-LB opposite

The 21 set has two wide receivers to the left and one wide receiver to the right. There are two blocking backs in the backfield.

In this situation, we call cover 3 Jet-LB opposite. The Jet blitzes off the edge. The defensive end slants into the B gap. The Sam linebacker comes out to cover for the Jet. The opposite linebacker (the Will linebacker) runs a "mix-it-up" stunt, and the X-player goes to the flat. The middle linebacker balances the coverage underneath. We play three-deep behind this stunt.

If the X-player is aligned into the short side, he runs the stunt. However, if either of the players thinks he has too far to go, he can call off the stunt.

Against the twins' set left and a strong halfback to the twins, we can run cover 2 or 3 (Diagram 16-14). With the tight end to the right, we roll the left corner to the strong

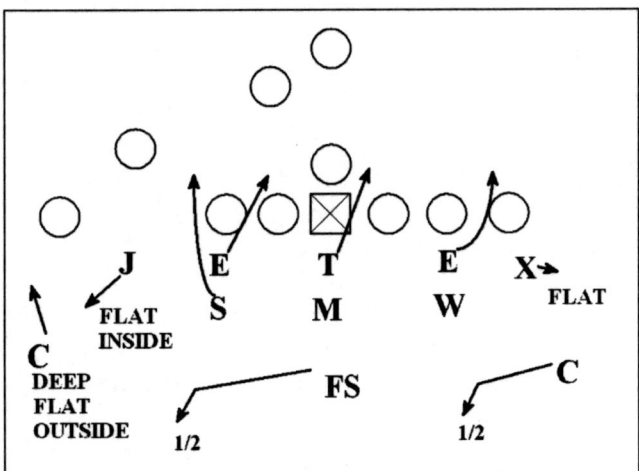

Diagram 16-14. Cover 2 angle-wk-S

flat. Since we have two receivers threatening the flat, we keep the Jet in flat coverage also. The free safety takes the left half of the field, while the right corner rolls into the right half of the field. The line stunt is "angle wk-S."

In this coverage, the rolled-up corner plays a deeper flat than the Jet. With this type of formation, you get combination patterns from the receivers. They are more or less playing inside-outside flat coverages.

If we are in cover 3 against this formation and the quarterback pitches the ball to the running back, we overlap the coverage. When the corner sees the ball on the sweep, he comes up. The free safety rolls over the top of the corner as a half player, in case the play is a halfback pass. We went from cover 3 to cover 2 when the quarterback pitched the ball. The free safety alerts the corner to go up and support, as he goes over the top. That gives us combination coverage. If we think they want to run the ball to the tight end, we play cover 2 predetermined that way. If the offense comes to the tight end, we roll into cover 2. If the offense goes the other way or drops straight back, we play cover 3.

Against the quad set, we bring our X-player to the same side as the Jet (Diagram 16-15). We play cover 3 behind the formation. Because the X-player has no number-2 receiver and no tight end, he goes to the strongside in coverage. The X and Jet play an inside-outside flat zone, with the corner playing the third.

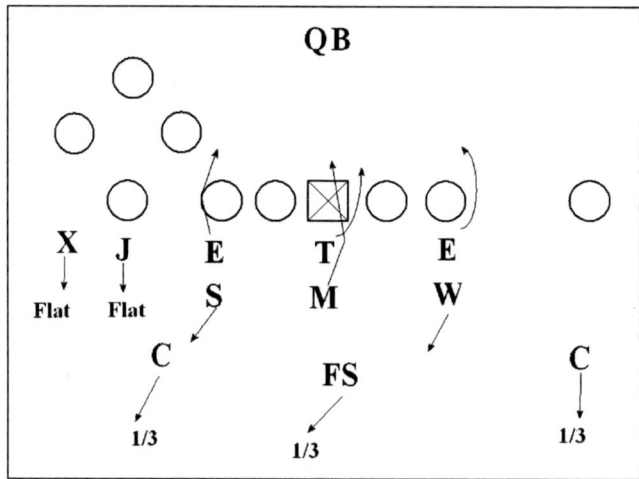

Diagram 16-15. Cover 3 X and Jet together-M

The stunt run inside is a "slingshot." The middle linebacker runs a slingshot with the nose tackle. The defensive ends go out and have containment. The Sam and Will linebackers drop to coverage. The right corner has no help and must play tighter on the wide receiver. His coverage is almost man coverage.

Another formation we have to defend against is a pro/twins set. Against this set, we play cover 3 and flash the Jet from the tight-end side (Diagram 16-16). To the backside,

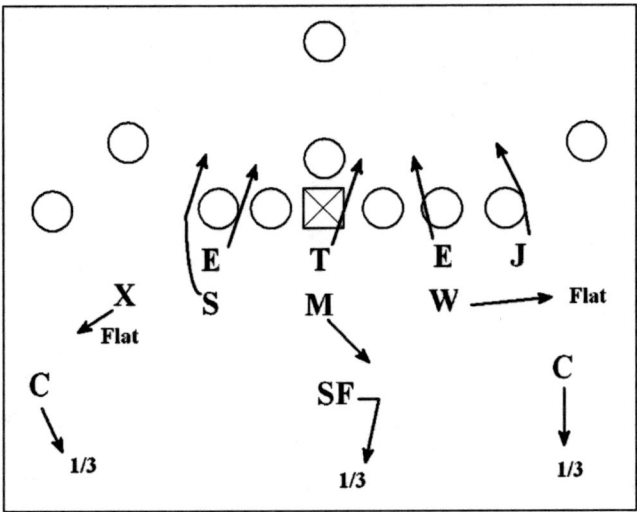

Diagram 16-16. Cover 3 Jet-LB opposite

we run a linebacker opposite. The Will linebacker on the flash call from the Jet takes his pass responsibility. The end goes into the B gap, and the Jet comes off the edge and has containment. The linebacker opposite is the Sam linebacker, who runs a "mix-it-up" stunt.

With a bunch set to the left, we could bring the X-player over on this set (Diagram 16-17). There is no number-2 receiver or tight end to the X-player's side. He can flop to the other side in this coverage, but he does not have to go over. If he does, the backside corner plays tighter. The line stunt is "angle wk-Sam." The Sam and middle linebackers run this stunt.

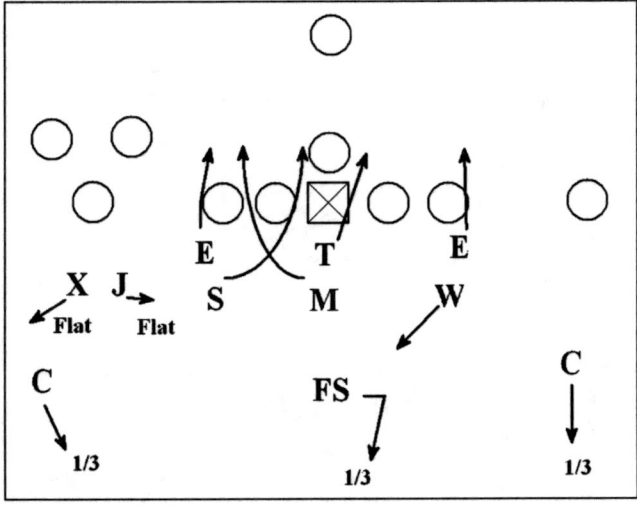

Diagram 16-17. Angle wk-Sam

The toughest set for us to cover is a two-tight end trips set (Diagram 16-18). The first adjustment we may make against this set is to align in a 5-2 defensive look. To do that, we put the Jet on the two outside receivers. We move the Sam linebacker up to the outside. The middle and Will linebackers slide over the guards.

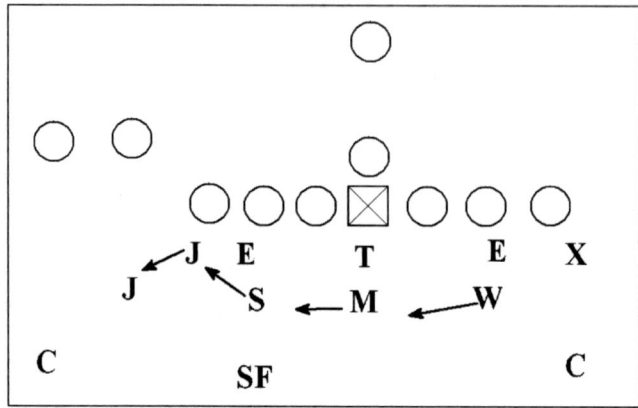

Diagram 16-18. Adjustments to tight trips

We can flip flop the X-player to the strongside flat. The weakside corner moves up and plays man cover on the tight end and provides run support if he blocks. The strong corner and free safety drop into half-coverage.

The third adjustment we can make in this situation is to play man-free coverage, with the weak corner as the free player deep. The strong corner and free safety take the two wide receivers. The Jet and X-player take the tight ends, and the weak corner is free in the middle.

The other problem set we sometimes encounter is the bunch trip set, with the tight end on the other side (Diagram 16-19). We could play it with cover 3 or cover 1.

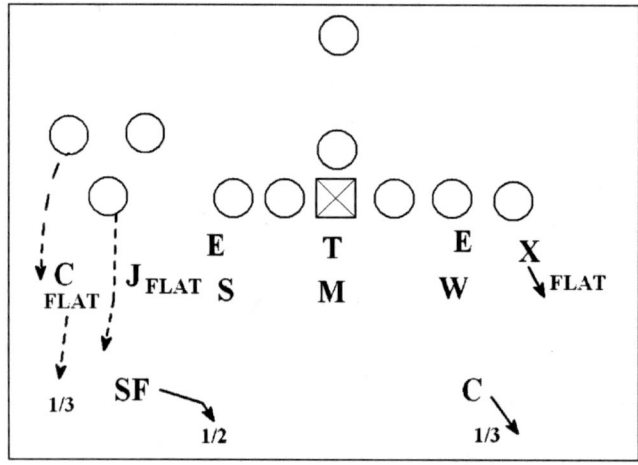

Diagram 16-19. Combination coverage

However, we felt we could play a combination cover on this set and be sound. We play the corner and Jet in flat coverage against the bunch set. The free safety plays the half-field over them.

The key is the strongside corner's read. He keys the bunch. If two of the receivers run deep, the corner goes to his deep third. If two of the receivers stay short, he stays in the outside flat. It may seem complicated, but our players pick it up without any problem.

I am almost out of time, but I would like to share two drills with you before I stop. The first drill is a deep-third drill against a wideout (Diagram 16-20). In this drill, the wide receiver starts up the field and breaks into a fade route. The defensive back shuffle-tilts his shoulders to the ball and runs deep to cut off the receiver. We do not want the corner face-to-face with the receiver. He cuts the receiver off with his butt. He has his back to the receiver and faces the quarterback. This is a simple drill, which we all have done at one time or another.

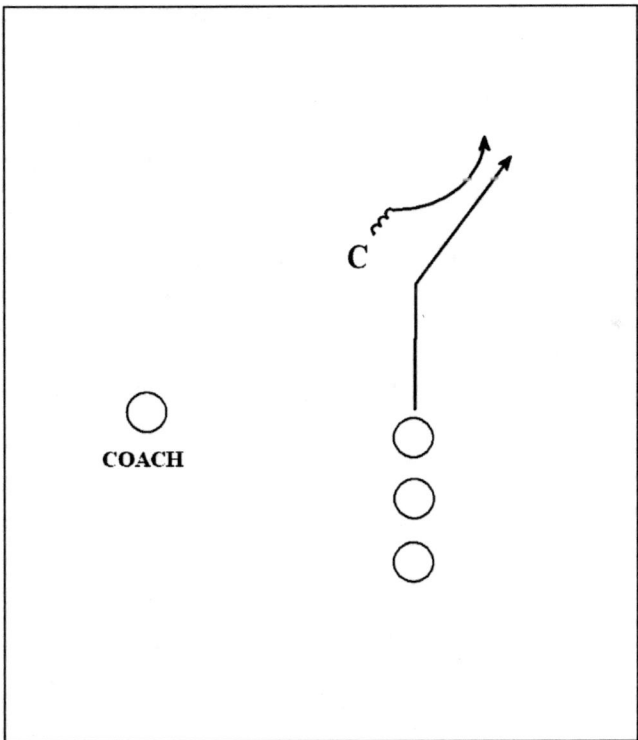

Diagram 16-20. Deep-third drill

The second drill we run is similar to the deep-third drill, except we employ the Jet, free safety, and corner in the drill, which we call the combination drill. In this drill, the coach does two different things (Diagram 16-21). He either drops straight back or sprints out. If he drops straight back, the Jet has the tight end going to the flat. The corner has the wide receiver running the fade, and the free safety drops into the middle third.

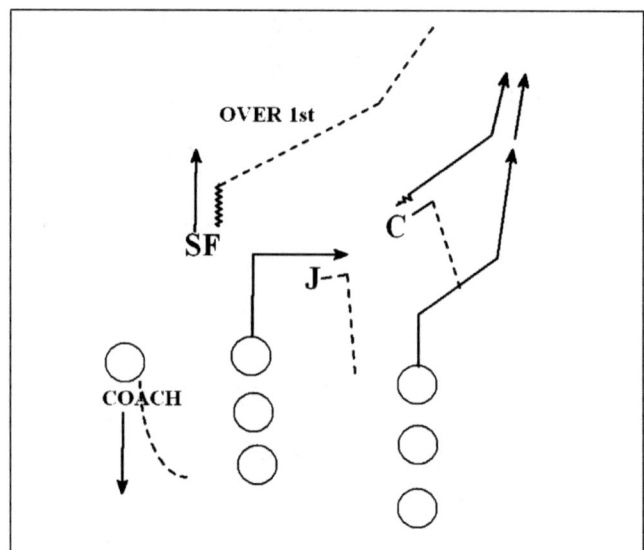

Diagram 16-21. Combination drill

However, if the coach sprints out with the ball, we play a cover 2 roll. The Jet comes for containment on the quarterback. The corners roll to the flat, and the safety goes over the top into the half-field. As the corner rolls to the flat, he wants to collision the wide receiver as he comes up.

The key to the coverage is the safety. He has to get over before he gets depth. If he takes the wrong angle to the half, he leaves a huge dead spot in the zone. He has to break almost lateral to close the dead spot and then get depth.

Thank you, we appreciate the opportunity to speak at this clinic. It has been an honor.

17

The 30 Defense: Alignment and Stunts

Ricky Ross
Calhoun High School, Georgia
2012

Thank you very much. I want to talk about some essentials of the core of who we are. These are things we feel are essential to our defense.

Essentials: Core

- Stop the run
- Eliminate big plays
- Turnovers
- Pursuit/run to the ball
- Control the passing game
- Play with passion
- Players who are tough mentally/physically
- Play within the team concept
- Simple
- Pressure—create it or feel it

The first thing we want to do is to stop the run. That is our #1 goal.

We must eliminate big plays. If there is one thing you must do in defense, it is to stop the big play. If we can force the offense to run 12 plays without scoring, we feel the defense will make mistakes. We are going to do everything we can to eliminate the big plays.

We have been good on defense. This year, we won a championship because we forced four turnovers in the championship game. In that game, everything was similar in the stats. They may have had more yardage than we had, but we caused four turnovers, and that was the difference in the game. That makes a big difference.

We feel that we must be good at pursuit and running to the ball. We must control the passing game. I am not sure if you can stop the passing game. You may not be able to stop it, but you must be able to control the passing game. When a receiver catches a pass, we make him pay for it. You control the passing game by not letting them go over the top of the secondary. This is my philosophy.

Play with passion. We want our players pumped. We work on our players to get them to play with passion. This is part of being tough both mentally and physically.

We must play within the team concept. I think our coaching staff does a good job letting the players know what the team can accomplish. They convey team concepts to their groups. They must know the team goals and what is necessary to play within the team goals.

We want to keep things simple. Believe it or not, we are simple.

We want the team we are playing to feel the pressure by playing against us. If they do not feel pressure, it is going to be a tough game for us.

Responsibilities as Coaches

- Take athletes where they can't take themselves
- Establish trust (love your players; the game is hard)
- Be great teachers
- Be sure players know what is expected
- Hold players to the standard every day (consistency)
- Play defense—not defenses
- Not what we do—it is how we do it
- Put players in positions to be successful
- Ask them to do what they can do
- Production chart/grade as a staff

As a staff, we want to take the players where they can't take themselves. We want to establish trust. At the end of the day, I want my players to know that Coach Ross loves them. We tell them the game is hard, and we work them hard. The bottom line is, we love them. Some of our players may not have great home situations, and we want to do what we can to instill that feeling of love. It is a big thing if the players know we love them. I think the players will play harder for you if they know you love them.

We have a reputation as being good teachers. As a result, we want to be sure our players know what is expected of them. Hold the players to the standards every day. Our kids know that I am going to talk about having a great day. I do this every day. We ask nothing more and nothing less. Every day, we are going to hold them responsible for the same thing.

I have been in a classroom where you could get by with almost any behavior, and the next day, the teacher was completely different. You can't turn it on and off every other day. I can't coach and teach that way. It is frustration. If you do not know what is expected, it is difficult. You never know when it is important. It is the same issue when I am a coach. My kids need to know every day what is expected. Nothing less! Nothing more!

We believe in playing defense and not defenses. We play with what we teach. We want to make it simple. It is who we are.

It is not what we do but how we do it. It is how we go about doing things. I am not the smartest coach in the world by any means, but I know what I know.

We want to place our players in positions where they can be successful. We ask them to do what they can do. Again, that comes down to love. It is not good to put a player in a position where he must cover the deep one half in the secondary if he does not have the tools to play the deep one half. We should not play him there. If he can't play against the power play, we must find a place where he can play. The job of the coaches is to place players in positions where they can be successful.

A few years ago, I went to some different schools to talk football with other coaches. One of the points I took from those visits was how other coaches grade their players from the films. As a result of that study, we do not give our kids a grade from the film anymore. Coaches may give a play a grade of 85 percent on a game. What is 85 percent? Did the player do something good?

What we do now is to produce a production chart. It covers a lot of information. It is who we are physically. The production chart has on it everything about us. It includes loafs, tackles, pass breakups, and missed tackles.

We have several areas that cover techniques. We list positive techniques and poor techniques. Everything on the chart has a point value. Our kids can check on what they did on each play. On Monday, when they come in, they can see the production chart to see how they did in the game on Friday night. The players can look at the chart and see the scores they received. They can see what they scored for each game. They can look on the chart and figure out why they scored a certain number of points.

As a coach, I can look at the chart and see why we gave up so many yards in a game. If we have 12 missed tackles, I know we have a problem. I can tell exactly how we played.

The best part of the production chart is that the coaching staff goes over the film together. It was the best thing we ever did as a staff. By doing it this way, we were all on the same page concerning the players and how we played and coached the game.

We all know exactly what we are looking for as a staff. We know what was good or bad about each play. It helped us, and it was a good tool for the coaches and the players.

What We Do

- Reps/recognition/communication
- Fundamentals/base (especially late)
- Practice fast = play fast
- Tackle/pursuit/turnovers daily
- Prevent the killing play
- Know the weakness
- It's about us being great (holding a standard)
- Pride in something/who are we (physical)

It is important in the late part of the season to stress fundamentals and to review your base defense. I keep a notebook on how we practice each week. I keep this to review each year. We have been very fortunate over the last few years in that we have been good and we had good players. The thing I write in the notebook is this: "Continue to stress fundamentals, especially late in the year."

We stress the fundamentals. How fast are we coming off the ball? What is the pad level? Do we recognize the plays? I never wrote in the notebook that we were unbelievable. I write about the fundamentals and the basic things we need to continue to stress to be a good football team.

If we practice fast, we can play fast. We run the spread offense. There are a lot of minuses to running the spread offense. One negative aspect is how it forces the defense to play a lot of plays.

One thing about our kids is the fact that they never panic. You can go as fast as you want. Our kids are going to get lined up and play fast. They are never going to panic. That is the best thing we do. They understand how to practice fast, and they understand how to play fast because that is all they ever hear.

We do not huddle on defense. Our young kids do not know how to huddle. We do not focus on the huddle. We focus on what is happening. They are focused on the personnel in the game or the personnel that is coming into the game. I want then focusing on their alignment and assignment.

We practice tackling, pursuit, and forcing turnovers daily. Those are things you must have. Turnovers are basic as far as I am concerned. They are the difference maker in the game. You can talk to all the experts in football, and they will tell you defense is tackling, pursuit to the football, and forcing turnovers. Those are the things you need to practice.

It is important for our players to know their weaknesses in our defense. If you are playing man coverage, you need to know where your help is coming from. You need to know if you have help on a play or not. These are points the players need to know. They must know the plays that hurt us the most. They need to know what plays we cannot allow to happen.

It is about us being good and holding the kids to our standard. I talk to the kids about this consistently: "It is about us." I do not really care about who we play. When we get to week #12, we need to be "week #12 ready." How do we do that? You do that by taking care of week #4. For week #5, you get better. For week #6, you must get better again. You get the idea. Everyone has problems, and that includes us. But we believe "It is about us!"

We must take pride in something that we stress each week. We are who we are. Our kids think they are unbelievable physically. It is because we talk about it constantly. We make them believe they are the most physical team and that they are going to smother our opponents. They will hit you, and they will never let up.

I tell the players all week to let me know when the other team has quit. They believe that at some point in the game, they are going to make the other team quit. They can look in the opponent's eyes and let them know they are the best team. On Friday night, before we go out to start the game and to start the second half, I ask the players to let me know when the opponents are ready to quit. This is what we talk about during the week.

If you tell a person something long enough, after a while, he begins to believe that what you are telling him is true. It is the same way with our kids in football. We try to instill confidence in our players by talking positive with them at all times.

Philosophy

- Be great at base defense
- Take away what they do best (finals: 2 for 10 on third downs)
- Practice faster than the game (70 reps)
- Turnovers—we always talk about turnovers
- Missed tackles—what will you do about them (tackle big red)
- Loafs—what will you do about them (pursuit drills)

We make sure we are great in our base defense first. When we are playing fast, everything else becomes unbelievable. If everything is going crazy, our kids know where we are going. They know we are going right to base.

In the state finals, our kids had to understand that we had to be good on first down and we had to get them into third down and long situations. If the turnovers were not the difference, there were some other factors that had to be a part of the picture. We knew that if the offense gained six yards on first down and ended up with third-and-two to go for the first down, it would win most of those situations. We were able to hold the offense to two first downs in 10 of the third-down situations. That was a big factor in the game. That was taking away what they do best.

We run about 70 reps per game. We want to practice fast. I want the game to slow down for our kids. On Monday, our kids feel great. On Tuesday, you can see improvements on what we talked about. On Wednesday, it is not that hard to see what we have worked on. It is about reps, communication, and the different by-products. The bottom line is this: if you can't line up and play fast, you are in trouble to begin with. It goes back to recognition and reps. "See it and go. See it and go." For us, we want to rep, rep, rep.

I want to talk about turnovers. What you talk about is what you get. As a result, we are going to talk about turnovers all of the time.

What are you going to do about missed tackles? To me, missed tackles are a big deal. I have four brothers that coach. I visit with them, and I hear about people that talk about missed tackles. One of my brothers made the comment: "I think a lot of people miss tackles because they are out of position." I started looking at what he said. I found this is true a lot of the times.

I coach the outside linebackers. I look at the number of tackles they miss. I can compare them with other players on the team. I know we are going to have a certain number of missed tackles each game. In getting back to the standards we hold for the team, missed tackles is not all on the players.

If we had a lot of missed tackles in a game, it may because I did something wrong. It may be because our kids were not really playing fast. It may be that they were not lined up where they should have been lined up. It could have been because they were not taking good fundamental steps. It may be a problem with their reads or their fits. It may refer back to me rather than on the kids. This is something with missed tackles that you can look at.

We talk with the players about a loaf on a play. We ask them, "What are you going to do about a loaf?" We keep a chart of loafs. We will not accept loafs. This is my philosophy on this issue. Instead of talking about what you do not want, talk about great pursuit. Talk about how great the team runs to the football. Talk about how many hats we had on a particular play. When you get what you want and against a running back who is running the rail, let him know how good he is. We want to remind them of the good plays they make. I think you will get more of what you want from the players by doing this.

Next, I want to talk on our game goal chart. These are the things we want to achieve each game.

Game Goal Chart

- Win
- Shutout (doughnuts)
- Handle sudden change
- Score or set up a score
- No big plays (20-yard pass/15-yard run)
- Three-and-out every three of five possessions
- Two or more turnovers
- 150 yards rushing
- 125 yards passing
- No 10-play drives

These are similar to what most teams have as team goals. We want to win. If we get a shutout, the kids get donuts. We all know it is difficult to get a shutout these days with the offenses we face. It is the best thing we can do, and at the same time, it is a frustrating thing for us. When we get ahead by a big score, we are going to play all of our players. It is difficult to get a shutout.

We talk about handling a sudden change. When we get a turnover, you hear it from our kids and everyone on the sideline. They know this is the most important time. Right now! We have to be able to handle the situation. This is a difference maker.

Score or set up a score is big. We want to score on defense. I think we do a good job on this aspect of the game. If we do not score, we want to put our offense in a great position to score.

We say no big plays. A big play to us is a pass completion over 20 yards and a run over 15 yards.

We want to play each possession. We want to be three-and-out three of five possessions. We want two or more turnovers per game. For the last two years, we have averaged 1.9 and 2.5 turnovers per game, respectively. I consider this good because we have at least six or seven games a year that our kids only have to play for one half. We may be playing our younger kids for the second half. The teams we are playing are not playing their younger kids, and it makes it difficult to accomplish our goals each game.

We want to limit the opponents to fewer than 150 yards rushing and 125 yards passing. We do not want any 10-play drives by our opponents. We want to get off the field as soon as possible. We have a great offense. That is one thing that really helps us.

We have great offensive players, so we want to get the ball into their hands as many times as we can. They are tough, and they know how to score. So, we want to get off the grass and give the ball to the offense.

Here are some statistics from our 2011 season. I know stats are a lot of numbers, so I will just point out a few items for you.

2011 Statistics for 15 Games

Regular Season:

- Rush yards 1,481; averaged 98
- Pass yards 1,548; averaged 103
- Turnovers: 37; averaged 2.5

Playoffs:

- First-round rushing 61; averaged 1.5
- First-round passing 233; averaged 6.8
- Second-round rushing 13; averaged .5
- Second-round passing 436; averaged 9.2
- Third-round rushing 84; averaged 2.2
- Third-round passing 144; averaged 6.0
- Fourth-round rushing 142; averaged 4.1
- Fourth-round passing 91; averaged 5.0

Championship Game:

- Rushing 212; averaged 6.6
- Passing 139; averaged 6.3

We averaged giving up 98 yards a game rushing. We gave up 103 passing yards per game. We averaged 2.5 turnovers. Those numbers could be a lot better if we played the starters more. I am not hung up on those numbers. I will be willing to take the pass average of 160 yards if our second- and third-string safeties get to play in the game. Those numbers can be skewed a lot.

We talk about stopping the run. That is the first thing you have to do. In the first round, we gave up 61 yards. You can see the other games and what we did against the run. I think that is what you have to do. Then, you have to control the pass. I know we live in a pass-happy world, but still, you must stop the run.

You could look at our 2010 stats and see there was not much of a change. There is one difference in the championship game. We gave up more yardage in the game this year than we did last year, but we still won the game. What was the difference? Two things were the difference. We got four turnovers this year, and we got them in third-down situations. It goes back to knowing who you are playing and knowing what they like to do on offense.

I want to take a minute to talk about personnel and coaching assignments. First, I want to tell you I am in a great situation. I want to tell you about Calhoun High School. We have great fans, and I work for a great man. He has a lot of trust in me. He lets me coach.

The way we divide the players up for practice and coaching groups is with four coaches. We think it is best to have four coaches on defense.

Personnel and Coaching

- Defensive line
- Stacks—three inside linebackers
- Spurs and safety players
- Corners

The person who is going to call this defense better coach the spurs and safety players. The most important thing the coach does is working with that group. The coach who makes the calls must have them in mind every time he makes a call.

Three-Man Pressures

- Base
- Loop
- Stack
- Right/left
- Strong/weak
- Mug
- Tiger base

We can play our base defense with three down linemen and eight defenders. We drop eight defenders a lot. When we bring the fourth man on the pass rush, it changes things. So, we do play three-man pressure defense.

I will show these calls in our film. I will only have time to give you the basic points on each. In the time that I have been allotted, I can't cover a lot of the things we do from each defensive look.

First is the base alignment (Diagram 17-1). We are in a 3-3 stack alignment. I can guarantee you, we are going to bring three-man pressures. We play a 5 read techniques

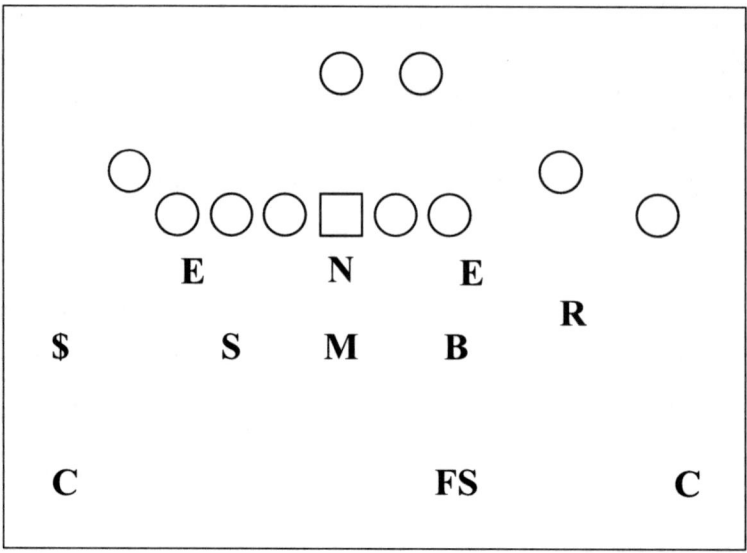

Diagram 17-1. Three-man pressure

with our ends and a 0 technique with the nose man. We play the five backs in normal coverage. It is as basic as we can get.

If we call loop, we want the ends to come out to where they can take a piece of the tight end (Diagram 17-2). We are still playing a 0 technique with the nose man. Against a power set with two tight ends, we draw it up tight where we bring the linebackers up tight. This is what we play against a power running football team. We want to get a hit on the tight end, create lanes, and run the linebackers through.

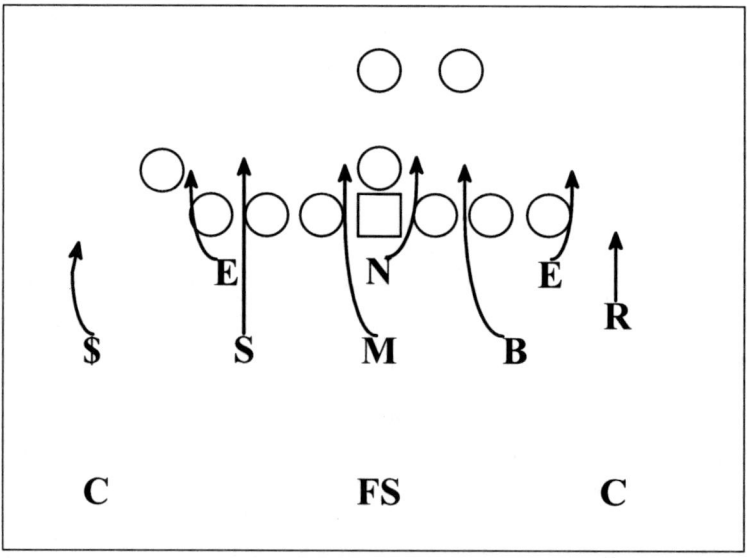

Diagram 17-2. Loop

When we call stack, we know we are going to play a 5 read with our end. We want to take a piece of the tight end and read inside (Diagram 17-3). We are a cover 3 football team. This does not mean we do not do other things, but against a spread team, we are a cover 3 team. We want to keep the linebackers protected as much as possible. We want to give the linebackers good lanes and good alleys to run through. We want good fits and good reads. We are going to be going downhill. We are in cover 3.

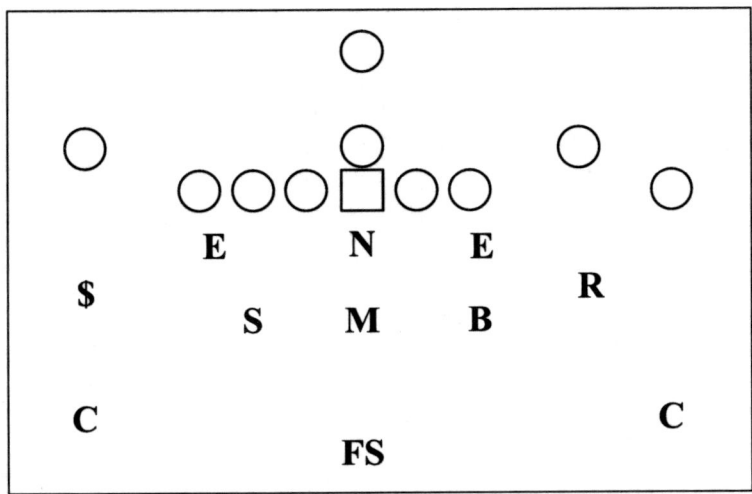

Diagram 17-3. Stack

Next, we go to our directional calls of right or left. First, we look at the front route. The noseguard is to the strength because we felt they had a tendency to go to the strength (Diagram 17-4). The ends play to the strength. Our linebackers are mixing it up and faking the blitz before the snap. Again, it depends on the scouting report in determining which direction we are going with the linebackers.

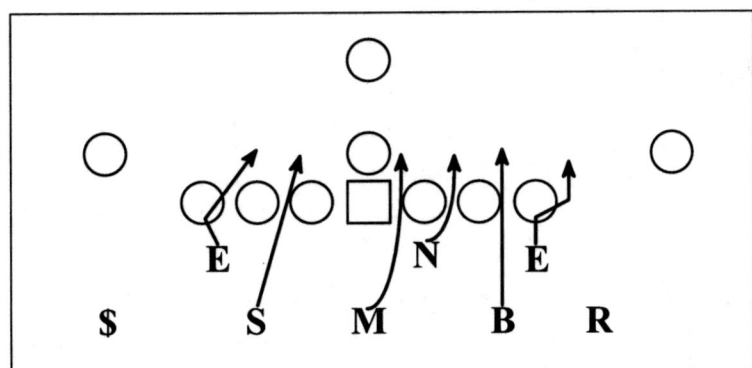

Diagram 17-4. Right call

The next call is strong or weak. For us, if we call weak, we can give a Liz call, which means the line is going to our right. It is similar to right/left. We are playing toward their strength (Diagram 17-5). We want to move the linemen up front and keep our linebackers protected. Against this set, we sent the tackles right and the nose left. The linebackers play the alleys and close on the football.

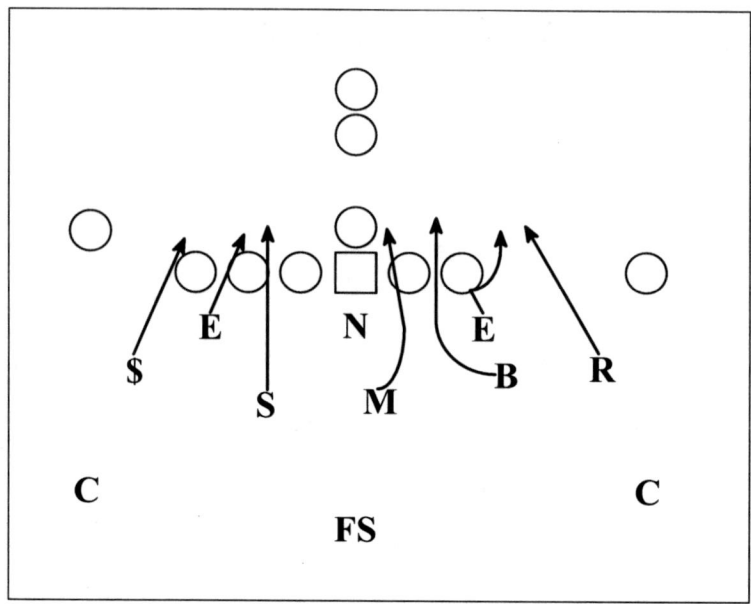

Diagram 17-5. Strong

We walk our linebackers up in the line a lot. If we call mug, we walk the linebacker up to almost a 7 technique, and he mugs the tight end and delays his release. He is not going to be a rusher. If it becomes a pass, we will get a late drop, but the tight end will be delayed in getting out on his pattern. The mug means the linebacker is going to anchor down the end. He gets his fit and holds up the end.

Next, I want to talk about Tiger base. Tiger means our kids get to have a little fun. They know their gap assignment. They can go anywhere they want as long as they can get to their gap. That is Tiger.

If we tie base to Tiger, we have Tiger base. That means we are going to play the same base defense that I showed you earlier. We are going to show you all of this craziness, but now, we are going to play base. We can show all kinds of pressure, but we can drop eight defenders. We are in cover 3, which is our base defense.

Our objective on defense is not to get into the coach's head. My objective is to get into the head of the quarterback. It does not matter what the coach knows. We are trying to confuse the quarterback.

Let me get into our four-man pressure package.

Four-Man Pressure

- Knob/snob
- Thunder/lightning
- Right bob/left bob
- X
- Slam/Bandit
- Stinger/Rover
- Seminole
- Cobra

These are a few of our stunts. We call our outside linebackers our stinger and Rover. We play Sam, Mike, and a Bandit as linebackers. Our corners are called spurs.

In our first look at our four-man pressure is our knob. That means wherever the strength of the offense is, we are going to bring the opposite side linebacker or the backside linebacker. We bring him in the B gap. He is the linebacker from the formations, and that means he is the Bandit through the B gap. It is a very basic blitz by the weakside linebacker. It is very simple.

The next call is our snob. Snob means we are going to bring the strongside linebacker through the strongside B gap.

The next stunt is our thunder. We slant to the wideside of the formation. We walk the Bandit up on the line, and we slant him down the line from the backside of the formation. We want the Bandit to have a tight fit. He comes down the line on his fit.

Next is our lightning stunt. Lightning means we are going to slant to the strength of the formation. These are basic stunts from our four-man game.

The next call is our right bob. We are telling our front we want them to go to the right side. We may face a team that likes to go to the field a lot or it likes to run the plays to the boundary a lot. This gives us a way to send our line regardless of the formation or the field position. This puts the call in my hands and not in the hands of the kids. It is a simple call for us.

We can go to the left if we call Left bob. The front down three guys go to our left. It is a good change-up for us.

On the X stunt, we bring the nose one way and the Mike linebacker the other way. Our Mike was a very good football player. Teams made a special effort to look for him on each play. A lot of times when we ran the X stunt, the nose man became free and made the play.

If we want to run a Sam blitz, it does not matter where the strength is; we still send the Sam linebacker. We bring Sam, and he is usually lined up on the tight end side. Sam is going through the B gap on the call. If we want to bring the field linebacker through the B gap, I can call Sam, and he comes hard.

If we want to bring the Bandit, we can call it from anywhere on the field. He is going to blitz the B gap on his side. He is usually on the boundary side of the formation. However, it does not matter about the strength or any other aspect.

For us, the Rover is our weakside outside linebacker. We bring him off the edge. If the end is split on that side, he goes inside the end and looks for the opposite jersey.

Next is our stinger. He is the strong outside linebacker. We can bring him from the field. He must understand when we bring him on a blitz, his help is on the outside.

On our cobra, we are going to bring our corner on the stunt. He must time the stunt where he can get a jump on the play. We are dropping seven defenders on the play. We are playing four under and three deep.

We can go to our five-man pressure and run several stunts.

Five-Man Pressure

- Miami
- Raider
- Trojan
- Bullets
- Sword/Rambo
- Storm
- Bomb/bomb switch
- Go/go switch
- Storm
- X/cobra

I will go through these very quickly. Miami means we are going to bring a stack backer from the strongside, which is our Sam backer. Also, we bring an outside spur, and we are going to bring them off the edge. They are on the same side. We know the help is behind them.

On raider, we are going to pinch the line and bring our stack linebackers up a little tighter. It is a short-yardage defense for us. They want to squeeze down and bring more defenders than what the offense can handle.

We do not want to tag a million things on defense. If we call Trojan, the players know we are going to send the line and the backers. It is similar to the raider call. The secondary knows we are in certain coverages on different calls. We are playing man free in Trojan. We are going for the quarterback.

Bullets means we are going to bring both stack linebackers. We are going to bring them through the B gap.

If we call sword, it means we are going to bring the Sam and stinger linebackers. We are going to cover all of the gaps. We play cover 3 with this stunt.

On Rambo, we are going to bring the pressure from the weakside or from the boundary. The linebackers are both on the backside, and they come hard. We are applying five-man pressure on the stunt.

Storm is next. It has been good for us. It is a power-type call for us. We bring the outside backer off the edge. We squeeze tight and close it down against the power-type time.

On bomb switch, we bring the Mike and the Sam backers on a crossing stunt. We can call it two ways. We can play man free with it, and we can play three under and three deep. When we call the bomb switch, the Mike backer shoots the A gap and Sam shoots the B gap. The nose man goes the other direction.

We are going to hit the quarterback as many times as we can. We are not playing dirty. We do not want to let the quarterback go without being hit. We want to get in his head.

If we call go, it means we are going to bring the strongside and the Mike backer. We have backers in both the strong A and B gaps.

Our six-man pressures consist of five stunts.

Six-Man Pressure

- Monster
- Raider X
- Zoo
- Tiger
- Rebel strong drop

Monster is a man package. We bring the strongside stack and the spur and the weakside spur. We are bringing three from each side of the ball. We are in a man-to-man package. We want to bring more than the offense can handle.

On raider X, we pinch the linemen and bring both outside backers. We put the nose in the weak A gap, and Mike is in the strong A gap. We run our man package on this call. It is a good short-yardage call for us.

If we call zoo, it means we are bringing all three linebackers. The nose is in the weak A gap, and the ends are in the C gaps. The Mike is in the strong A gap, and the two linebackers are in the B gaps.

I covered Tiger base. On Tiger, we are playing cover 0. The six guys up front know their gaps and responsibilities. They can go wherever they want. They can be creative, but they must know the job they have to do. We hope this alignment creates some chaos for the offense. Our kids enjoy this call.

On rebel strong drop, we line up with pressure on one side and get the checks that we want and get people running through the offense. We bring the corner off the edge from the backside. We zone-drop on the coverage. Again, we are bringing more than the offense can handle. We want to show one look and bring another look.

In the time I had to speak, I could not give you everything. Hopefully, what I covered will give you an idea of who we are! If you want to call me or visit with me, let me know. I appreciate your attention. Thank you very much.

18

Zone Concepts in the 3-3 Defense

Steve Specht
St. Xavier High School, Ohio
2008

I am an odd-front defensive coach. When I became the head coach, I struggled with trying to teach coverage drops to the players. I could not figure out how to teach them to drop to space. We put up the cones and taught them to drop to spots. We coached them well. They knew how to get to those spots even if the quarterback was in a full sprint the other way. As a result, we came up with a matching-zone concept. It is like a match-up zone in basketball.

Every scheme in football works. It is only a matter of what you believe in. You have to develop a defensive philosophy so your players know what you hang your hat on. They have to believe you have a system and a plan. They must know that in a crunch time we will run this system.

We are an odd front, but we are more of a read scheme now. In the past, we were more aggressive, but we have developed into more of a read scheme. We were always in a three-deep matching-zone concept until this year. Teams that we played began to catch up with what we were doing. We went to some different concepts of two-deep. We also ran some quarter coverage this year. We had 10 returning starters on defense, and four of them were three-year starters. We could do more with that personnel and we did a lot.

The defensive scheme boils down to how it fits your personnel. In 1999, we started running some odd-principled defenses. We started playing smaller defensive linemen.

What happened in our progression was that our big safeties became linebackers. The linebackers became defensive linemen, and the old defensive linemen became offensive guards.

I like the balanced front because it does not give the offense a bubble to check to. That is especially true of option teams. Against option teams, if we stay in an odd front, they do not have anything to check to. We can disguise our reduction and slant and angle on the snap. That gives us an advantage.

We run a multiple matching-zone concept. When we play three-deep, it gives us an additional man in the box. When we go to the two-deep scheme, we play a funnel-trail technique and a funnel-flat technique with our corners. The last thing we play is what we call alert and siren. Those adjustments are a combination coverage, depending on the formation.

I like the matching zone because it restricts our players from covering air. It gives us the ability to play seam and hole defenders. We went to the 3-3-5 defense because of the spread offense. We got more speed on the field. We got rid of the big outside linebackers who were a little stiff in their drops. We struggled with linebackers playing slot receivers. We needed to get more defensive backs on the field.

We can adjust to motion and formations quickly. We have one defender who makes all the adjustments. We call him the *adjuster*. He is the player who has to think. Outside of him, we only have two players who have to adjust to what the offense gives us. That enables our players to play faster. Once we hear the call, eight of our defenders are playing the call, no matter what happens before they snap the ball. We have three players who have to check somewhat.

Everything we accomplished is still available for us. We still have the balanced front, and we can disguise by reducing at the snap. It gives quarterbacks problems.

We have many options to disguise what we are doing. We have multiple options we call *falcon*, *sparrow*, and *ninja*. In our base alignment, the defensive ends are in a 4 technique on the offensive tackles, and the nose aligns in a 0 technique on the center (Diagram 18-1). The stacked linebackers are stacked behind them at three to four-and-a-half yards. The

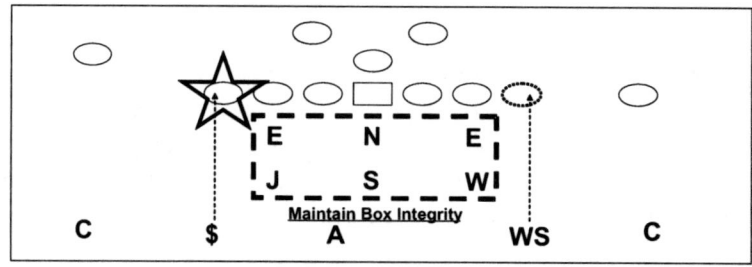

Diagram 18-1. Base defensive alignment

jet linebacker is the strongside linebacker. The Sam linebacker is the middle linebacker, and the Will is the weakside linebacker. We may cheat them closer against some option teams, and we have gotten deeper against some teams in passing situations.

We want to maintain the box integrity as much as we possibly can. We played 15 games this year, and 13 times we played some sort of spread offense. Those offensive coaches always look at the number of defenders in the box. We want to keep six in the box as many times as we can. The safeties play seven yards deep on the outside shade of the tight end or an imaginary tight end. If they are over a slot receiver, they stay at seven yards on their depth and move to an inside shade on the slot. The hash rule for the boundary hash is never go more than three yards inside the hash mark. That alignment can vary according to the game plan.

The corners align in an outside shade of the #1 receivers at four to seven yards deep. They have a six-yard sideline rule. They are never closer than six yards from the sideline.

The key to the defense was the player we called the *adjuster.* He was a three-year starter, and next year he is going to Stanford. He was a great player, and we could do many things with him. This position is designed for the most complete football player on our team. He may not be the *best* player, but he is the most *complete* player because we do so much with him.

The two biggest keys to what we do defensively are our jet backer and the adjuster. The jet backer is the strongside linebacker. The adjuster will normally align at seven yards over the strongside guard. However, that alignment will vary according to game plan. If we need to get someone over the tight end, we can adjust down and cover him. However, it has been better for us to keep defenders back at seven yards.

We found we played the run better because the tight end had to block someone in space. He blocked down on the defensive tackle, the linebacker, or someone in space. It was difficult to block our safety in space. In the scheme, if the tight end blocks down on the tackle, that makes our adjustments easier.

If we get a double set and teams start to spread us, we do not adjust too much. The safeties widen but still maintain their inside shade of the slot receivers. The box remains intact and the bonus player is still in the middle of the field over the guard.

If the offense gives us a 3 x 1 set, we adjust somewhat (Diagram 18-2). The strong safety plays on the inside shoulder of the #2 receiver in the set. The strong linebacker moves out into a position, splitting the distance between the #3 receiver and the offensive tackle. The adjuster moves to an inside shade on the #3 receiver. The bonus player is the weakside safety because he has no one in the set to match. We always match defenders. That is the basic alignment in our five-across look.

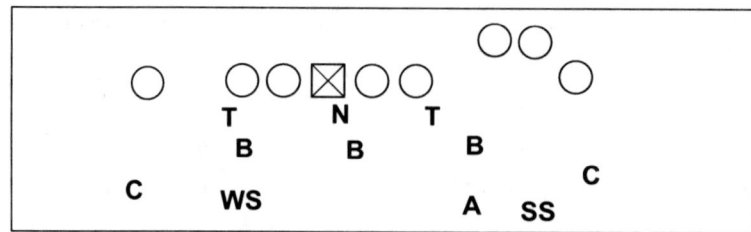

Diagram 18-2. Base alignment vs. trips

We have four fronts that we play with some regularity. We have *spread, falcon, bluff,* and *ninja* fronts. In the spread front, we walk our outside linebacker up on the line of scrimmage (Diagram 18-3). The secondary does not move on this adjustment.

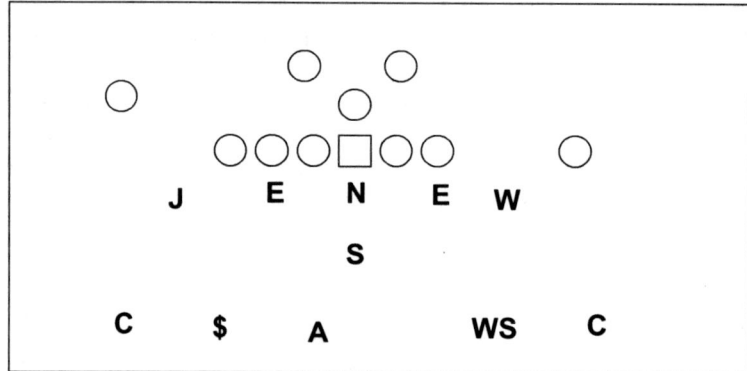

Diagram 18-3. Spread front

The falcon and ninja fronts are almost the same. On the falcon front, the strong safety walks down into the box on the tight end. In all of these adjustments, the defender doing the adjusting is 3 x 3 on the tight end or ghost tight end. In the ninja front, the weak safety walks down into the box. If we run the bluff front, both the strong and weak safeties are down in the box (Diagram 18-4). In the diagram, the bluff front

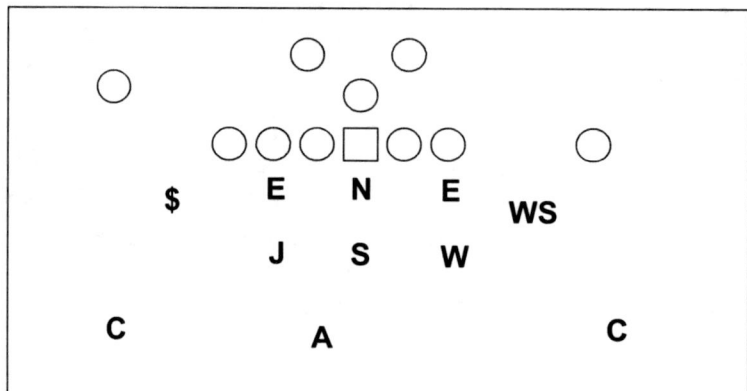

Diagram 18-4. Bluff

is shown. The position played by the safeties in the falcon and ninja are the same as the bluff front, except that in each front only one of the safeties is down in the box. The problem with the falcon, bluff, and ninja is that we have a two-deep look in the defense instead of a closed look.

We can combine the fronts by adding a tag to them. If we want to play the spread front, both outside linebackers give to the line of scrimmage (Diagram 18-5). If we add a bluff tag to the call, that brings both safeties down in the box at 3 x 3 outside the tight end and ghost. This gives the defense a 5-3 look. We can call spread and add a falcon or ninja call and get a different look. We are getting into multiple looks and using tags to move the players. That is the concept of the defense.

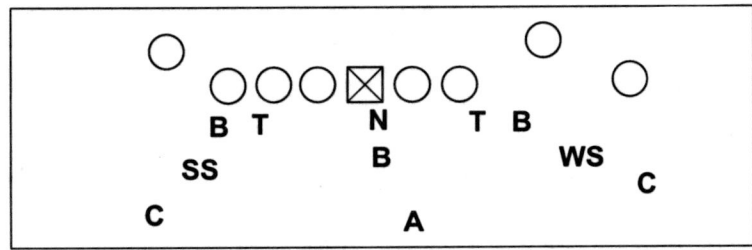

Diagram 18-5. Spread tag bluff

At the beginning of every year, we want to decide how many techniques we can teach our players. You can see we have many things going on within the defense. With 10 starters returning this year, we did most of the things in these fronts. Our adjuster played six different techniques. Normally, we do not put that much on one player. If we get more than two techniques, I start to get nervous. We have to sit down in the off-season and decide. Whatever we teach, we have to get good at it. In the secondary, we teach our *storm* and *fire* concepts most of the time.

The first matching-zone concept is the fire-and-storm concept. These are two separate coverages that allow us to play tighter outside man leverage on the wide receivers while playing match-up zone underneath. It enables us to get additional pressure on the quarterback without putting the secondary defenders on an island. You can play this coverage and not give up the pick routes to the offense. If you play teams that run rub and pick plays, this works well against that scheme. This enables us to run a five-man fire-zone package.

High school quarterbacks do not like to throw to receivers who they feel are covered. They want to throw to spots in the defense. They like zone-drop teams. We were able to play tighter coverage while maintaining our philosophy in the coverage. It also enables us to adapt to virtually any coverage scheme. We can change our deep-coverage scheme while the underneath scheme stays the same.

To run this coverage, you must have two corners who can effectively match up with two speed receivers. At the beginning of the year, every skilled player in our program is a corner. We find the two best players to play corner and build from there. We must have safeties and outside linebackers who can run with slot receivers for 15 yards. That is asking a lot from those players.

It is imperative for us to disrupt and reroute all inside receivers. The underneath defenders have to understand progression reads. We mix and match our underneath defenders with tags. *Fire zones* are five-man pattern blitzes. A four-man pattern blitz with a spy is *fire-zone coverage*. Any four-man pattern blitzes are *storm coverage*.

On fire-zone coverage, we have rules and responsibilities (Diagram 18-6). The corners play outside leverage on the #1 receiver. He plays him all over the field, and we hope we can effectively erase those receivers and play 9-on-9 with the rest of the defense.

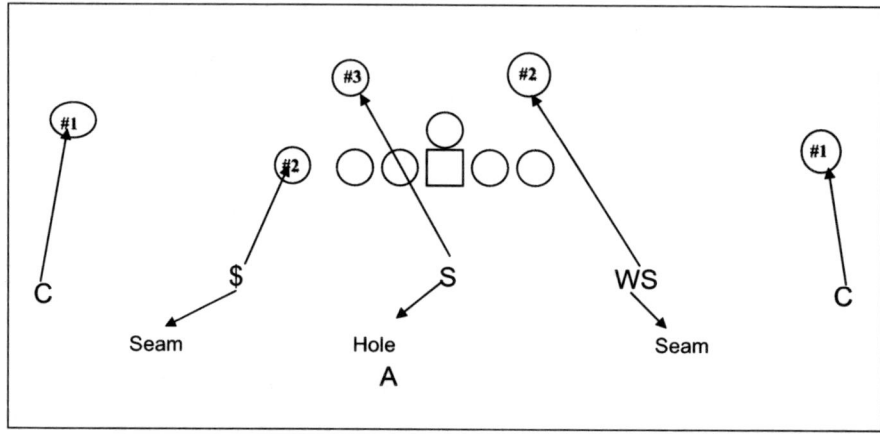

Diagram 18-6. Fire-zone coverage

We number the receivers because our seam defenders have to understand how they are going to match up in this zone. The seam defenders are generally an outside linebacker or a safety. Since this is fire-zone coverage, the seam players are the safeties.

Rules for Seam Defenders

- Read #2 to #3 route progression.
- If no immediate threat, get under #1.
- #2 vertical–collision outside in.
- Know where help is (safety inside).
- Carry to 16 yards unless #3 threatens the flat, then play flat man. Read quarterback outside-in and release late. Give up shallow.
- If #2 tries to fight to corner, maintain outside leverage and take away the corner route.
- #2 cross–carry the cross and deliver to hole.
- Look up #3 out of backfield.
- If no #3, think crossing route coming back (dig).

The progression for the seam player is the #2 receiver to the #3 receiver. That is generally a slot receiver or a back in the backfield. If he is on a single-receiver side, the #2 receiver is in the backfield. There is no immediate threat to the defender. In that situation, he plays underneath the wide receiver to that side. The corner has him man-to-man, and he helps him on inside moves.

If the #2 receiver runs to the flat, he takes him. If the receiver runs a wheel pattern, he runs with him. He has that man on any pattern he runs.

In the pattern, if the #2 receiver runs a vertical route, the defender collisions him from an outside-in leverage. He has help to the inside and wants to force the receiver that way. We want to squeeze everyone to the middle.

The defender carries the #2 receiver for 16 yards unless there is a threat to the flat. If the #3 receiver runs to the flat, he becomes the #2 receiver. The seam defender reacts back to the flat and arrives late. We give up all shallow routes.

The route that concerns us is the *smash* concept. If the safety feels the receiver is trying to get to the corner, he fights him and runs with him to the corner, trying to maintain his outside leverage. He tries to wall the receiver off the corner route.

If #2 runs a cross to the inside, we have to work in tandem with the hole defender. He calls, "Cross, cross," and squeezes the receiver and delivers him to the hole defender. He works outside and helps on the dig route or crossing route coming from the other side.

Rules for the Hole Defender

- Read #3 to #2 route progression.
- Always step with #3, sink 10 to 12 yards.
- #3 flat–deliver to seam and look up #2 on quick cross.
- Carry the cross and deliver to seam.
- #3 vertical–collision and sink to 15 yards.
- Keep eyes back on quarterback, expecting underneath threat.

The hole defender reads opposite the seam defender. He reads from the #3 receiver to the #2 receiver. That generally is the back in the backfield and the slot receiver. However, it can be the third receiver in a trips formation to that side. If the #3 receiver goes flat, he knows there is an outside receiver coming inside. He delivers the flat route to the seam defender and looks up the #2 receiver coming back inside. If a receiver vacates a zone, there will be a receiver coming back into the zone.

The second read is a vertical by the #3 receiver. We do not see this pattern much from the backfield. We see this pattern from a 3 x 1 set. He collisions the receiver and sinks to 15 yards. We tell him to sink to 15 yards, but he will never get there. For a high school player, if we can get him to 10 yards, we are happy. He sinks with the vertical and waits for someone to come back underneath. The two-seam players and the hold player work as a synchronized unit in the underneath coverage.

Storm coverage is the same premise and has been good for us (Diagram 18-7). It is a nice change-up. The five-zone coverage has only one hole defender in the middle. It is a five-man pressure scheme. Two defenders are involved in a blitz or spy technique, and that leaves only one defender in the low hole. In storm coverage, we bring four-man pressure, and we have two hole players in the middle. The seam defender reads the same as they did in the fire zone. The difference is on the crossing route. The seam defender passes the cross off. However, instead of reacting back outside, he drops back and sits on the dig route.

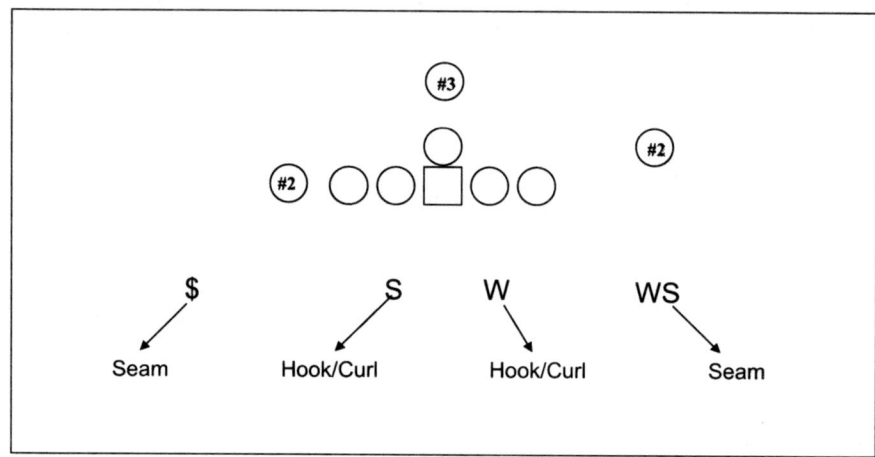

Diagram 18-7. Storm coverage

Since there are two linebackers in the middle, they can jump the #3 receiver going to the flat. With two linebackers, there is always someone to take the cross pattern. If the #3 receiver blocks, the linebacker should expect a check release by the back. His depth should not be as deep as normal.

This is an adjustment to a simple stunt in a 3 x 1 set. The stunt is a strong-edge stunt (Diagram 18-8). It is a four-man pressure scheme. The jet linebacker drops down and comes off the edge to the #3-receiver side. We want to match and collision every receiver in that formation. To match every receiver in this set, we have to *sling* the coverage. We have no trouble matching the #1 and #2 receivers. The corner and strong safety can match them. I do not like the Sam linebacker in the middle having to match on the tight end, and worse, a slot receiver. That is a mismatch.

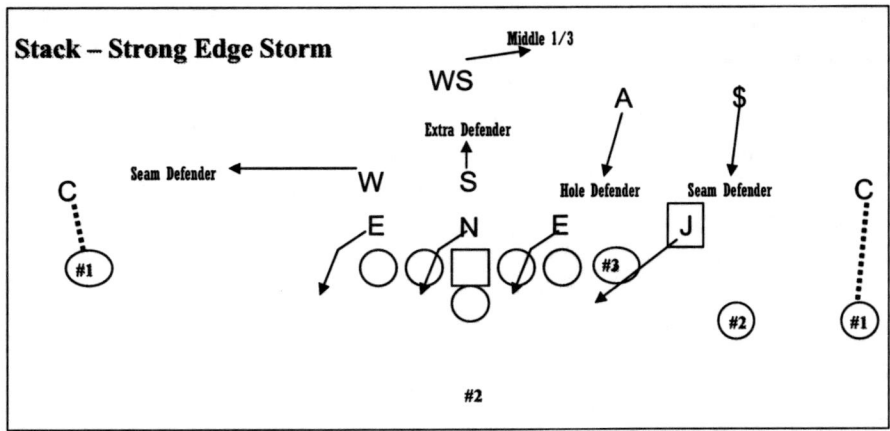

Diagram 18-8. Adjustment to 3 x 1

Sling Rules

- Strong safety rolls to seam defender.
- Adjuster automatically rolls into low hole.
- Weak safety rolls to deep middle.
- Will linebacker plays backside seam.

We sling the coverage and bring the adjuster down into the box, and he takes the coverage on the #3 receiver.

Coverage Scheme

- The weak safety slides to the trips side and plays the middle third.
- The strong safety slides to the trips side and plays the seam #2 to #3.
- The Will linebacker to the single side looks up #1 and gets under slant or plays #2 to #3 in seam.
- The Sam linebacker is an extra defender and can spy quarterback or deep drop.
- The adjuster replaces stunt to trips and plays hole.
- The corners play loose man on #1.

The Will linebacker and the corner to the backside bracket the wide receiver. The adjuster drops down in the box and does the adjusting to take the position of the jet linebacker who is on the edge stunt. Any sling adjustment tells the adjuster he is the hole defender. Every receiver is matched with a defender. We have a bonus defender (Sam) in the middle of the field.

We had to make a change in our 2 x 2 coverage to take away four verticals (Diagram 18-9). If we run the same edge stunt, the secondary plays what we call a *three match*. The strong safety replaces the jet linebacker and is the seam defender playing #2 to #3, which is no change for him. The weak safety is still the seam defender, and that is no change. However, he has to match any vertical from the #2 receiver—any other move by the #2 receiver, he plays normal. The Sam and Will linebackers play hook to curl and read #3 to #2.

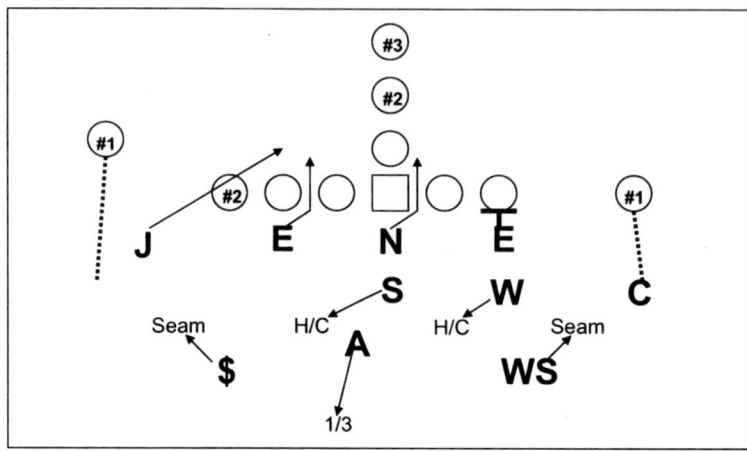

Diagram 18-9. 2 x 2 adjustments

The adjuster plays the middle third unless he gets a release by the #2 receiver to the side of the blitz. In this case, to the jet linebacker side he matches the vertical by the #2 receiver. That is our answer to four verticals in a three-deep look. Before we put in this adjustment, teams tried to exploit us with the four-vertical scheme. The corners are playing loose man coverage on the #1 receivers.

Three-Match Rules

- The weak safety matches any vertical from #2 (seam).
- The strong safety matches any vertical from #2 (middle third).
- Everyone else plays their normal responsibilities.

Our cover 2 concept is not that far away from what we do in our fire-and-storm coverage. Those coverages are good for our corners to press and take away the quick routes. If teams start using the three-step quick game, we can go to our cover-2 coverage. We are not going to have to teach everyone. We do not want to give the players too much to play. If you play too much, they will be thinking and not playing fast. You have to decide how much is enough.

Cover 2 can take away the short game, but it also can take away the intermediate routes (Diagram 18-10). In cover 2, nothing changes for the seam/hole defenders except

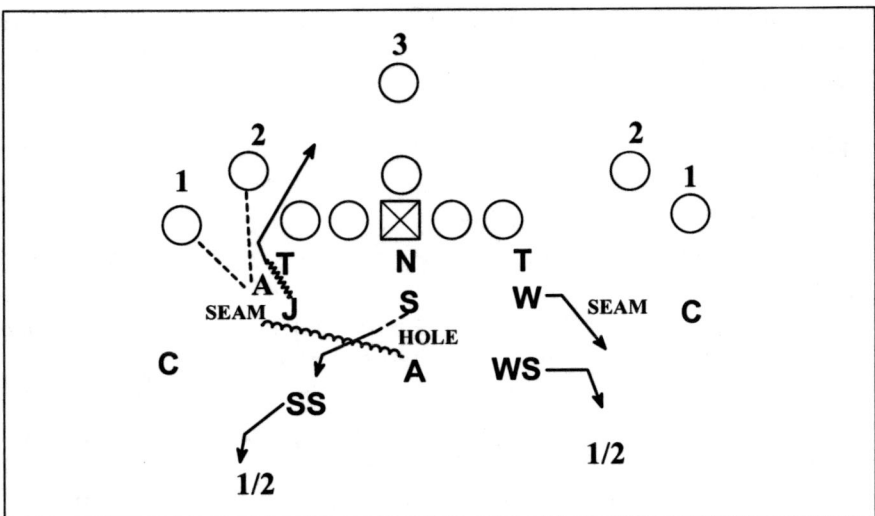

Diagram 18-10. Cover 2

that we teach funnel-trail and half-coverage techniques. The corner and safeties have to learn a new technique, but the underneath coverage is almost the same.

The key to the coverage is route disruption of the #1 receivers. We need athletic safeties who can run with the slots, play a good trail technique, and cover half the field. The variation we use for the corner is a bail technique—a cross-corner scheme—and we will play sparrow in this coverage.

The seam defenders play the same coverage they played in the fire coverage. The hole defenders have the same technique as the fire coverage, and nothing has changed. The safeties play deep halves of the field. We teach them to read from the #2 to #1 receiver. If #2 goes to the flat, they find out what #1 is doing. They will have help underneath their coverage.

The change-up is in the technique played by the corner. The corners funnel everything to their help in the middle of the field. They are going to play physical and collision the receivers. If they get the fade route, they open to the receiver and force him wide. Regardless of what happens, they assume a trail technique. If the receiver releases inside, the corner uses an offhand jam, gets up underneath him, and trails him on whatever route he runs. It is the same technique used in the fire-and-storm coverage, except it is from a press alignment. The corner knows he has help over the top from the safety and underneath from the three inside linebackers.

We do not worry about landmarks in our coverage. We worry about where the receiver is aligned.

Our *ice* coverage is a little different in our matching-zone philosophy. When we go into the football season, we always run the storm and fire concepts. This year, because we were so experienced, we went to a different type of zone match-up out of the cover 2. We try to stay ahead of the curve, and teams are beginning to catch up to what we are doing.

Ice coverage is a solid change up to our three-deep matching-zone concept (Diagram 18-11). This coverage enables us to get into a much tighter underneath matching zone with two safeties over the top to take away deeper routes. The match-ups change considerably, which gives the quarterback more to think about, yet remains relatively simple for the underneath coverage players. Unlike fire/storm, this coverage enables the underneath defenders to take away the quick game by pressing all receivers knowing they have help over the top. Because of the fact that we sacrifice run support in this coverage, we mostly run it in passing situations. However, we are able to better disguise our three-deep matching-zone concepts by giving the two-deep illusion and bringing our pressure packages off the look. Although we run this concept out of an odd stack, the matching-zone concept can be adapted to any defensive system.

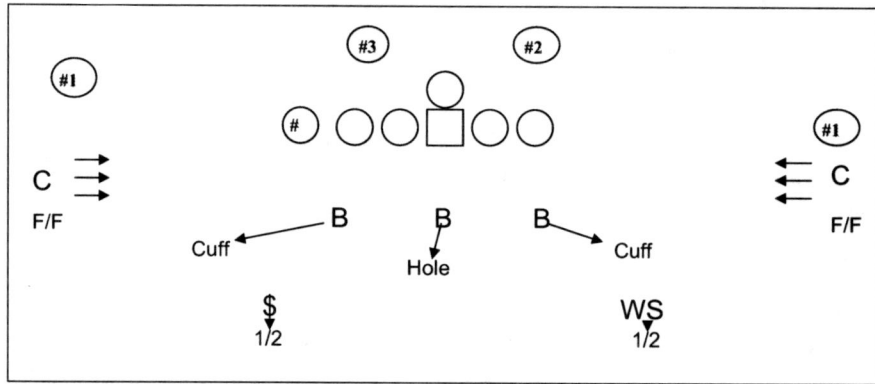

Diagram 18-11. Ice coverage

This gives us a way to play pass coverage and shut down the short passing game inside and outside.

Keys to Successful Coverage

- Great funnel on the #1 receivers
- Good collisions on all inside receivers—route disruption
- Quick, deep drops by both one-half defenders
- Deeper drop by the remaining hole defender when he is not threatened

Calls/Variations

- Three-man game with a spy
- Four-man games
- Sparrow/falcon

We number the receivers as we did in the other schemes. The funnel/corner plays the same funnel technique but does not trail the #1 receiver. They funnel the #1 receiver but play a flat defender after that. They read #1 to #2 receivers. If we get the flat-fade combination by the receiver, the corner carries #1 to the sideline for seven yards and comes off looking for the #2 receiver. He rallies back to the flat, late. We give up the shallow pass and force them to move it down the field a little at a time—if they have the patience to do it.

Funnel Flat Defenders

- Read #1 to #2 route progression.

Press Alignment

- Collision and route disrupt everything from #1 outside/in.
- If #1 releases wide, carry to the sideline for seven yards before opening to #2. Rally late to anything in the flat.
- If no flat threat, carry underneath #1.

The cuff defenders can be linebackers or safeties. Their progression read is from #2 to #1. If there is no immediate threat by the #2 receiver, they get underneath the #1 receiver. If #2 goes to the flat, they run and give the illusion they are going to be the seam defender. They invite the curl route by widening. They sink under the curl and play a robber technique on the curl. They can be a factor on the dig and skinny post inside.

Cuff Defenders

- Read #2 to #1 route progressions. If no immediate threat, think #1.
- #2 flat—widen and rob #1 (curl/dig post).
- #2 vertical—collision inside/out—squeeze the release of #1 and #2.
- Look for #1 coming back underneath.
- Know where help is (safety over the top).
- #2 crosses—widen and gain depth—deliver to the hole defender.
- Get underneath #1 and rob curl/dig/post (follow flat read).
- Rally up on shallow crossing routes.

If the #2 receiver goes vertical, the cuff defender collisions the receiver and squeezes him using inside-out leverage. The corner squeezes the #1 receiver outside-in. They funnel the receivers into the half safety. After the collision on the #2 receiver, they get their eyes back to the #1 receiver. If that receiver comes back underneath, the cuff defender works back up late on him. If #2 crosses, he widens and gains depth. They still have the hole defender in the middle to help them. They deliver the cross to the hole defender and read the quarterback's eyes. The hole defender and half safety do the same thing. Their technique does not change.

Hole Defender

- Read #3 to #2 route progression–follow normal hole rules.

Half (1/2) Safeties

- Follow cover 2 rules for half coverage.

This defense worked well for us this year but we had an experienced group that could play the coverage. We had a couple of combination coverages we ran. We ran alert and siren.

Alert is coverage that is dependent on the offensive formation. This coverage enables us to get into the matching-zone coverage. They defend what the offense likes to do out of 2 x 2 sets and a 3 x 1 set. We have used this concept primarily against spread offenses that like to isolate the #1 receiver backside while running concept routes to the #3-receiver side. Our matching-zone principles apply to this coverage. The coverage is dictated by the offensive set (Diagram 18-12).

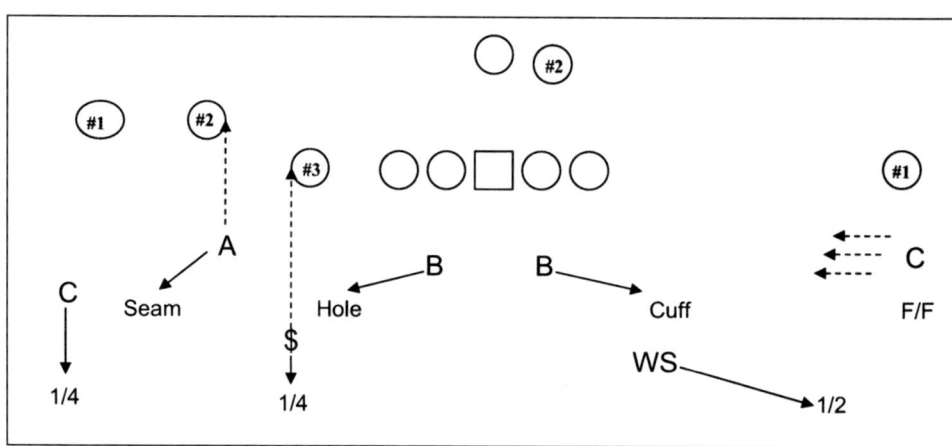

Diagram 18-12. Alert

Versus 2 x 2 balanced sets, we check to our cover-2 matching zone (Zorro) while a 3 x 1 set will jump to our cover-4 matching zone (thunder). The premise behind the coverage is to outman the offensive formation by at least one defender. We are able to double-team the isolated receiver with a bump-and-run corner, with safety help over the top and backer help underneath while maintaining a 4 to 3 ratio with the receiver set.

Keys to Successful Coverage

- Formation recognition and quick check to make sure everyone is on the same page
- Physical play on the isolated receiver by the cornerback
- Route disruption

- Quick progression reads by the seam and hole defenders
- Disguise scheme and mix and match safeties

Calls/Variations

- Field/strong stunts
- Key stunts

We want the corner to press or bail and give the illusion we are in cover 2. He plays quarter coverage.

Corner

- Play quarter coverage out of press/bail alignment (read #2 to #1).
- Vertical release by #1—lock on—outside/in.
- Quick cross by #1—sink and look for #2 on a vertical seam or skinny post.
- Hitch by #1—think corner by #2—rally up to #1.

The adjuster comes down in a falcon alignment and is a seam defender. He reads #2 to #3 defender and rallies to any kind of smash concept.

Adjuster

- Shift to an inside shade of #2.

Seam (4) Defender

- Read #2 to #3. Think smash concept off vertical release. Get underneath #1. (This is the only change from normal seam coverage.)

The strong safety shades the outside of the #3 receiver. That is the mismatch in this coverage because we have a linebacker on the slot receiver. We want the strong safety to help him on a vertical by the #3 receiver.

Strong Safety

- Outside shade of #3—quarter coverage (read #3 to #2).
- Vertical release from #3—lock on—outside/in.
- Shallow cross or flat from #3—sink and look up vertical (to skinny post) from #2.

The jet or Sam linebacker will be the hole defender and play his normal progression.

Jet/Sam Backer

- Hole defender (read #3 to #2). Normal hole progression reads.

The isolated receiver to the backside is the object of this coverage. We want to press him with the corner.

Corner

- Pressed coverage—cover 2 technique (funnel flat)—trail technique to the isolated receiver.

Backer

- Seam defender (get underneath #1).
- Flat release from running back—release to corner and rob #1 (curl/dig/post).
- Cross away/block away—look up #3 coming back from the concept side.
- Vertical collision inside/out and restrict passing lane for weak safety.

In this coverage, we have mixed and matched our fire and storm concepts with the ice concepts. We are playing the cuff backside and the seam and hole defenders to the strongside.

If we play the alert in a 2 x 2 set, the corners play their ice coverage (Diagram 18-13). The adjuster comes down in a falcon position and plays a cuff defender. The backside linebacker plays a cuff defender with normal progression read.

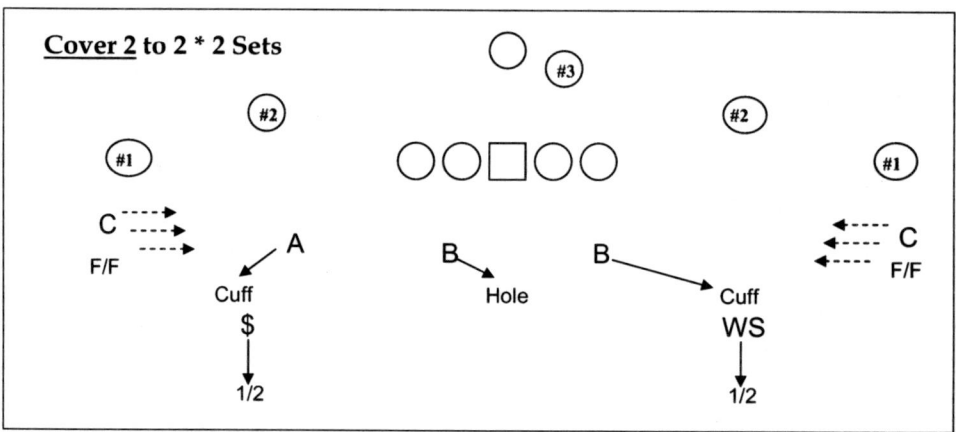

Diagram 18-13. Alert vs. 2 x 2

Alert Coverage Rules and Responsibilities

Corners: Pressed coverage—cover 2 technique (funnel flat). Normal progression rules for cover 2 corner

Adjuster/Weakside Backer: Shift to an outside shade of #2—cuff defenders (read #2 to #3). Think curl by #1. Normal progression rules for cuff defender.

Strong Safety/Weak Safety: Half coverage (read #2 to #1). Normal progression rules for deep one-half defender.

Backer: Hole defender (read #3 to #2). Normal progression rules for deep one-half defender.

That is our combination coverage we use against these sets. We decide at the beginning of the year who is the default. This year it was our adjuster in the falcon position. He has graduated now, and we have to find out who that player is going to be. In other years, the adjuster was more of a pass defender than a box player. In that case, sparrow was our default formation because the weak safety could play in the box.

19

The Basic 3-5 Radar Defense

Scott Tinsley
Nitro High School, West Virginia
2006

Thank you. It is a pleasure for me to be here on behalf of Nitro High School and speak to you about our concept of defense. We do some things a little bit different at Nitro, and usually the first thing people ask me when watching our film is about how we came up with this defense.

They call it radar defense but when I think of radar defense, I think of people standing up, moving down the line, picking a gap, and going, and that is not really what we are. We are standing up, but we are not moving around.

We came up with it after we had scrimmaged a wing-T team one year, and they had thumped us pretty good. When we broke down the film and charted all the stats, we found that our down linemen did nothing. They were not helping us at all. At the same time, our linebackers were pretty much getting where they needed to be and making all the plays. We began to wonder what would happen if we just stood our linemen up like the linebackers.

Our problem was that we were not very big. As a school we are not very big and our players are not very big. We only had 33 kids dressed for the AAA state championship game this year and we played with two kids who were less than 150 pounds at defensive tackles.

Anyway, when our defensive linemen would engage with offensive linemen, they would get knocked backwards, and if they finally did get off of the block, the ball was gone. We thought we were asking our kids to do something they could not do, so we tried standing them up.

The following week we stayed in our 4-4 look, but with our 2 techniques standing up, and we had a lot more success. Our opponent that week was another wing-T team and we shut them down pretty good. I believe that they went on to become the AA state runners-up that year. We thought that maybe we were onto something.

After that week, we went to a 3-5 look rather than a 4-4, but we kept our two tackles and our nose man standing up, with five linebackers standing behind them (Diagram 19-1). That is how we stumbled into this thing.

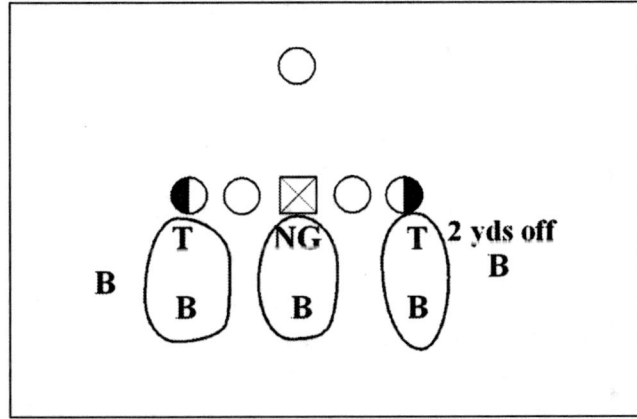

Diagram 19-1. Basic 3-5 look

Every offensive line coach spends time teaching the drive block and driving the sled, but against us that is useless. Our defensive linemen who are standing up are two yards off of the ball, and we are not there when the drive blocker gets there to block on us. We are gone and we are someplace else, so we believe that our scheme takes away the drive block from the offensive linemen.

Also, offensive linemen in high school cannot cut any defender not aligning within one yard of the line of scrimmage, so our scheme has eliminated the cut block and the drive block. Now that takes away a big part of any blocking scheme, so that gives us two big advantages from the start.

Strength coaches will not want to hear this, but I have been at Nitro High School for 10 years and we have had some success, and we have never had a weight room. I wish we did, and now that we have been to our second state championship game, they are building us one this year. Hopefully, now we will get stronger.

I do not know how many of you go into games realizing that you are just not as strong as the other team. I read in the paper all the time where coaches say that they got whipped up front, or that they just could not match up with their opponent up front. Well, this is a way of offsetting a bigger team's strength by using speed rather than strength.

The other advantage that we think we have in running this defense is that we have eliminated the guessing game. It was mentioned that we have had some success on offense by going no huddle. No huddle gives us a chance to line up, see what you are in defensively, and eliminate the guessing game. Well, the same goes with our defense.

If you call a slant, an angle, or a blitz, you may have some tendencies on the other team but you are still guessing. Well, this defense has allowed us to not ever have to call any of those things. We feel like we are slanting, angling, or blitzing right into the play on every snap, and I will show you more of what I am talking about. We do not ever have to call that kind of stuff so we do not have to guess with an offensive coordinator any more. Our kids are making their reads and we think we are slanting, angling, or blitzing into the play every time.

There is another advantage we think it gives us. If you put this defense in, people are only going to be able to practice against it for one week. They go out Monday and show it to their kids, they practice against it Tuesday and Wednesday, and they have some kind of pregame walk-through on Thursday. They really only get to block it for two days.

Their offensive linemen are going to be confused at the beginning of the game. We see it in almost every game that they are not sure where the defenders are, or where they are going. I think that any time you make a team practice against something they are not used to seeing, then that is an advantage. It gets their kids out of the comfort zone.

If you saw a team all standing up two yards off the ball and the next level of linebackers five yards off the ball, it may come to your mind offensively that you would just run sneaks and wedges, get your three or four yards, and then do it again. Well, that is not a normal game plan. Not very many people regularly do that.

What we have found out is that almost every coach who goes against us for the first time alters his game plan. He gets his kids trying to do something that they have not been doing the other 10 weeks of the season. We have played teams that have never been in two tights and a full-house backfield before, and in the very first series, here they come. They seem to think that pounding it right at us is the answer. It is yet another advantage for us that we have caused the opponent to alter his game plan.

I do not want to talk about how we read and get there and that kind of thing yet, but we have found that because we are so small and weak, when we were up there in our four-point stances and teams ran right at us, we went backwards every time we engaged. We were going to lose the line of scrimmage and the best thing we could do was maybe try to make a pile.

Now with the quick reads we give our guys, at least we are headed toward the ball on the snap with a full head of steam. That is better than lining up, catching, and getting driven backwards. We get a lot more stalemates this way than we did the other way. The stalemates may happen a yard off the ball rather than the line of scrimmage, but not many teams are satisfied with getting a yard. We are not saying we can stop you from getting one yard. What we are trying to do is keep you from getting three or four yards so you get behind the chains. Then you are playing into our game.

I will say that while we had two tackles who weighed less than 150 pounds, we did have a 300-pound nose. He was two yards off the ball standing up, but he was a force in the middle. That was another advantage we had.

The other thing that this defense allows you to do is get many, many multiple looks, and it is easy for the kids. Because everyone is standing up and reading, we can move linebackers up to the two-yard level rather than the five-yard level and they are just playing like a linebacker. We do not have to substitute linemen to go from a three-man front to a five-man front because all of our guys are playing like linebackers.

We have gone into many games with two linemen and played a 2-6 look. That is also confusing to the offense. We could also go with three linemen who are playing two 5 techniques and a 9 technique, and no nose in there. It would seem that you would have to run quarterback sneak in there but I will show you film in a minute where, when they do, there are a whole lot of people hitting it real hard. Then again, most people just are not patient enough, I guess, to run quarterback sneak on every play.

It is easy to adjust our scheme to formations. We have five linebackers, so any time we see trips or doubles or anything like that, we do not have to do a whole lot of adjusting to the formations. We have enough skill guys out there that we can spread out with you.

It is also very easy to disguise things. With that many people at the second level, it is easy to roll into other coverages or to bring pressure if we want to, but we do not bring pressure a lot. I say we do not bring pressure, but our game plan in that week may be for our outside backer to have a quick read that automatically brings him off the edge against certain formations. Or perhaps, if he gets a certain look, his automatic read is to come off the backside edge. So, we do bring pressure, but it is all off of the read rather than a huddle call that we are going to send someone. It is coming whenever their read tells them to come.

Now that you know a little bit about how we stumbled into it and what we think the advantages are, we can go a little bit on how we do it.

Every week we come up with a quick read for each lineman and for each linebacker. I will take wing-T teams for example. I want to be careful how I say that no one can do something, but for the last several years no one has been able to stay in the wing-T against us and have success. This defense takes away all the wing-T stuff. They cannot deal with it because of the quick reads it gives our kids.

We may read the guards or we may read the guard that the motion is going to. Some teams read the tackle that the motion is going to cause they will pull the tackle and tight end for that little inside handoff play, but whatever the read is that you come up with that week you have eight guys on that read. When they run the buck sweep and those guards are pulling out there, we got eight guys flying over there to the ball. We will have more people there than they do. It is fun to watch.

Then, when they think we are overpursuing and they try to run the little inside handoff coming back the other way, all eight of our guys are running over there. It has been very successful against the wing-T and I guess the reason is, if you remember when I first started talking, that we stumbled into this because a wing-T team had ripped us up pretty good, and then we stopped a wing-T team the following week.

In the beginning then, it was all based on stopping the wing-T but as we have found, it holds up against all of the offenses that we have faced. I will say that you have to totally buy into this and believe in it or it is not going to work. If you just half way go at it, you will really look silly standing all those guys up. It will either make you or get you fired.

Our kids really believe in this and I know it is not an easy sell. We have had several top coaches come to our office and look at film. Most of them are really impressed by it, but not all come away really sold on it.

If we play a splitback team, we kind of split it in half and offset our nose to either the strongside or weakside, and our Mike backer will be the other way. The nose will have one back and the Mike will have the other one. Everyone else reads his near back. That has really helped us against veer teams.

We play a team that has traditionally been very strong running the veer and since we went to this defense it has really helped us. They have had to go to more of a spread game against us than the veer because it is too easy for us to run and take all of their options away. We have people getting there for the dive, on the quarterback, and on the pitch, and the option game is really easy to defend with all these guys standing up running towards the option.

This defense is really hard on the spread offense and that is funny because we run the spread most of the time. In West Virginia's spread game, they run the tailback one way and the quarterback the other in a fashion that all of you are familiar with. Well, I think that this defense is really hard on that. We would give half of the field to this back and half the field to the other back. Even if they run back in to you, where they take the jab and go this way, our read would take us right into that and we should have them outnumbered on either side of the ball.

Of course, if they want to throw, they are throwing into eight deep. We are dropping eight, so it is hard to throw the ball against eight.

Now you may wonder if we can get any pressure on the quarterback with only three guys up there. All of our defensive linemen use a running-start bull rush. We are two yards off of the ball, so when we read pass we are coming. The offensive linemen are taught to set back, engage the rusher, and stop him. But with the natural separation between the blockers and our defensive linemen who are coming, it is easy for us to set the blocker up with an outside move and dip underneath. We get a full head of steam and we get a lot of pressure with just a three-man rush.

Maybe one of the hardest things for us to defend is just the I formation because it does not give us as quick a read. We always have to decide whether it is the fullback or the tailback we want to read, or if it is a team that is still pulling the guards and taking us to the play that way.

There are some key things that we will take away from the I formation teams. If it is a toss sweep or anything on the perimeter, we have been able to handle it fairly well. If it is the tailback on isolation plays, we have handled that real well. It is the play we call the double dive, that hurts us a little bit where they fake it to the fullback and hand it to the tailback. Usually our first read against I teams is the fullback because he usually takes us to the ball, so double dive gets us out of our lanes a little bit. We got hurt a bit in the championship game with that play.

We have about 50 plays on film here and it should take about 10 minutes to take a look at them. Then Coach Mike Scott will tell you about some technique stuff we use. If at any time you see something you want to ask a question about, feel free to ask a question about it. I will try to go through it with you and tell you what you are getting ready to see.

Okay, if there are no more questions on the film, our defensive coordinator, Mike Scott, is going to talk about our techniques.

Mike Scott, Defensive Coordinator

How are you all doing today? At our place, the number-one rule is that we are not going to get outworked as coaches. Coach Tinsley is the chemist and I am his lab assistant. It might be three in the morning until we decide after watching film what we have to do. Coach finally says what he wants done and he tells us to coach it up.

Up front, we want these three guys to eat up these five offensive linemen. That is the basic premise (Diagram 19-2). We give them the fullback, and then everybody is reading the fullback. They can do it because they are standing up and they are two yards off of the ball. Whichever angle he takes, it is the job of the tackle on that side to meet him. We do not talk about 2 techniques or 5 techniques; we say to go tackle the fullback. The playside guard wants to block a linebacker but he has to do something to slow the nose down. If he tries to check backer first, the noseguard is already flying over to tackle the fullback.

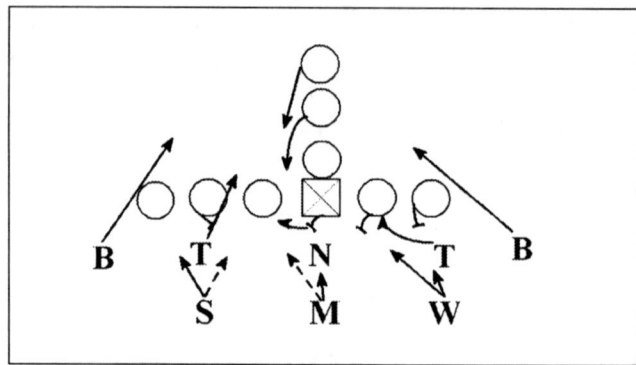

Diagram 19-2. 3-5 versus ISO

Now when the fullback is your read and you are the backside tackle, you have to go across two faces, but that is easy to do because you are not up on the line. You must make sure you rip across the guard's face so you are taking up two guys.

The center is trying to stop the nose from getting over there, so all five offensive linemen are "eaten up" by our three defensive linemen.

My outside backers are taught to run through. We do not get into a lot of detailed technique about outside arm free, or maintain leverage. We tell them that if anybody comes right at them, whether the fullback or the tailback, they are to run right through his face.

If they are running inside here and it gets all clogged up, the back will bounce and my outside backer will nail him. If they come outside with a lead block, we will run right through his face (Diagram 19-3). Do not worry about outside contain or any of that stuff. All I want him to do is run through him. Most of the time when that collision happens the tailback will cut back inside where we want him to anyway. If we taught too many detailed contain technique responsibilities, our guys would want to bubble out, and that would just widen the lane.

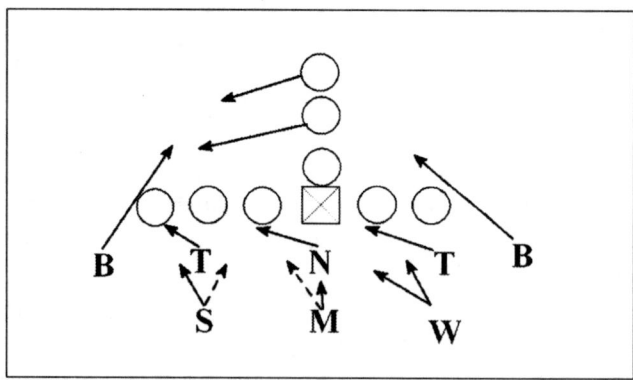

Diagram 19-3. 3-5 versus sweep

The key for the outside backers is to run through, and the defensive linemen are each expected to take up two blockers. If they can all do that, then my three inside backers are sitting here untouched and all the offensive linemen are taken up.

They are taught to "hit it from where they are at." If they get in a hurry, I will make them take a read step. I will put them in a closed stance and tell them to read the fullback. As soon as the fullback moves, I want our linebacker to take a read step and then "hit it from where you are at." Do not bubble, and do not try to run out here and do any of that because all of that is taken care of by those outside backers. Hit it from where you are at, and do not go anywhere until you know where your tackle went.

If the ball is at you, and your tackle has crashed down inside, it does no good for you to crash down in there, too. You should come right off that tackle's butt instead, so you can make the play untouched when the back tries to bounce.

Now each lineman and linebacker makes a team. We call the linebackers Sam, Mike, and Will, and we tell them not to go anywhere until they know what their buddy did. If the play starts way outside to Sam's side, our tackle is taught to tackle the fullback whether he has the ball or not, so he is coming outside fighting the offensive tackle and tight end.

Well, I do not need Sam to fly outside anymore because we already have the outside backer out there, so Sam will immediately step right inside off his tackle's butt. The guard cannot really step out to help on Sam because our nose is now ripping across two faces. No one can get to the backers.

The tackle occupies the offensive tackle and tight end. The nose occupies the guard and center, which is easy because he is two yards off of the ball, and Sam has an open door.

You might think counter and other kinds of misdirection would hurt us with all these guys getting these quick reads (Diagram 19-4). Well, the fullback goes one way

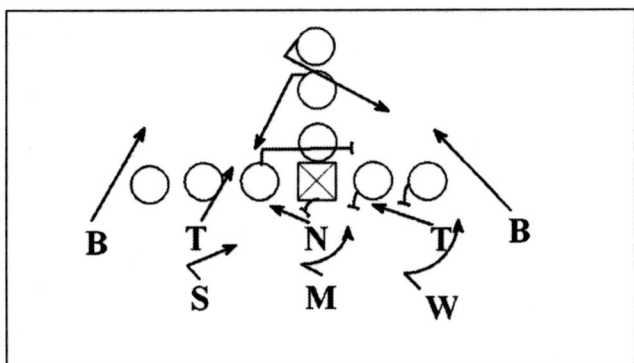

Diagram 19-4. 3-5 versus counter

on counter and the tailback is coming back, so if everybody is flowing that way we are in trouble. The thing is, everybody is going to the same place regardless, if that makes any sense. If we get counter, our linemen are all reading the fullback. One tackle is probably crashing because the fullback is coming right at him, while the other two are coming hard and fighting across two faces each.

Now to run that counter, they have to pull either the backside guard or backside tackle, which leaves our crashing tackle wide open and they are not going to get anything. Regardless of all that, it is still the front three helping our linebackers make plays.

The backers go through doors. We call them front door or back door. We try to keep it simple for them. If the play starts at Sam he has to know where his tackle is, but once it goes back the other way he goes through his same door regardless of what type of play it is.

Once his flow is gone he does not fit to his tackle. These other two also do not fit when flow is gone. Everybody scrapes back door at the same angle, and there is no place for the offense to cut back. The linebackers are going at the same angles to the same places regardless of what the play is.

I can stand there in practice and watch all five backers and the three linemen all at once in flow and I can see one person that is out of place because he is looking at something he is not supposed to look at. When we started this system, we had to tell our kids over and over again that they had to believe it. They had to trust their reads.

We have been described as an uncommon defense with a new look, featuring the utilization of speed when size is not available. All you really need is a bunch of kids who want to get to the football.

Our time is up here, men. If you are interested in hearing more, we are going down to the Allegheny Room, and we can spend some more time with you. Thank you for your attention.

20

Running the 3-5-3 Defense: Why and How

Tony Truilizio
Riverside High School, New York
2010

I want to start with a couple of random thoughts. In one hour, I am going to tell you about the defense in the simplest terms. The most important thing in the 3-5-3 defense is the *noseguard*. The second point is the outside safeties, which we call *spurs*. The third important thing you must have is one good cover *corner*. If you have two corners, you are in good shape. If you do not get anything else from my lecture today, please understand those three things.

I am not trying to sell the 3-5-3 defense, but as soon as I go through the history of our team, it will be an option for you to consider. My defensive run coordinator, Steve Pangallo, introduced this defense to me three years ago. He previously coached at a Buffalo Jesuit high school. They ran the 4-4 defense but were tinkering with the 3-5-3 defense. His head coach at the time did not want to add it as part of their package. They were to play Canisius High School, which was a powerhouse, in the state playoffs. They played them earlier in the season and lost 40-0. They installed the 3-5-3 in one week and took Canisius to overtime before losing.

He came to Riverside High School and brought the defense with him. We went to Georgia Military College to refine what we did. Everything we do comes from GMC. Coaches Bert Williams and Rob Manchester were instrumental in helping us with the defense. At that time, I was a 4-3 team with a cover-2 secondary. Our record over the last three years has been 26-6. Most of the six losses came in the first year when we were installing the defense. Since we have installed the defense, we have been in the state finals two of the three years. In the three years, we have had 17 defensive shutouts. Fourteen of those shutouts are on the record as shutouts. In three of the games, I gave up a safety, a special teams touchdown, and a fumble returned for a touchdown. So unofficially, the defense gave up no scores. In those three years, we were 7-4, 10-1, and 9-1.

Rationale Behind the 3-5-3

- Personnel.
- You only need a few defensive linemen. You tend to get linebacker/strong safety type of players.
- Speed kills—we want faster players to fit into the linebacker/strong safety type.
- Fewer coverages to learn.
- You remain balanced on both sides of the ball, so if an offense motions to an unbalanced formation, fewer players have to realign.
- You are showing an eight-man front, yet you are still strong against the pass. The emergence of the spread offense causes defenses to remove a linebacker from the box to cover a receiver. This causes a loss of gap integrity.

There are several reasons why we run this defense. The first reason is our players are smart. We have a lot of speed and true student-athletes. The key word in that statement is *athletes*. I was looking for a defense to stop the power running game. We needed something to stop the isolation, counter trey, and other power football plays.

When you play this defense, you need fewer defensive linemen. Riverside is a 2A school but we have a small enrollment. Our enrollment could be Class A football. We get between 60 to 70 players out for our varsity and junior varsity teams. The juniors and seniors are on the varsity, and, after that, I divide the team in half. The sophomores and freshmen make up the JV team. If we have a stud in one of the lower classes, we bring him up to the varsity team.

When we chose the defensive players, we took the fastest 11 athletes and put them on defense. However, I did pick my quarterback first before we did that. Working with a smaller group meant you got more reps in your practices. We are an urban high school and we have a lot of speed. However, you do not need speed to run this defense.

This defense helps you remain balanced on both sides of the ball. If you face teams that motion for a single-receiver side to a double-receiver side, you do not have to worry about adjustments. If the offense uses a trips set, it is no problem to adjust to that set.

We are showing an eight-man front, which helps us in our running game defense. At the same time, we are able to play great pass defense from this defense.

Advantages of Playing the 3-5-3

- Not many coaches know how to block or game plan for 3-5-3.
- It is a very flexible defense. Nickel and dime alignments can be made without disrupting the scheme, and with the right personnel, there is no need for subs.
- The defense is an eight-man front, yet five of the players are speed players (linebackers) and they can defense the pass.
- You can use smaller, faster players.
- Offenses do not know where the pressure is coming from.
- It confuses the offensive line.
- Great adjustment to two-minute offense (personnel does not need to be changed).

Another advantage of playing this defense is that teams do not see the defense very often. That presents a problem for game planning against the defense. In this defense, you can disguise the blitz very well. You can blitz from any number of places in this defense.

It is flexible in the secondary. You can play a nickel or dime in the secondary with no difficulty at all. It presents an eight-man front for the offense. Our speed players are the linebacker positions. It is a great defense versus a spread team. This is a balanced defense, which lets us get the extra defender on the triple option.

Offensive teams are beginning to concentrate on the two-minute offense. This defense will help you play in those situations. We do not have to worry about substituting personnel in and out of the game. We can play the situations without changing personnel. The calls are easy to communicate. That is important when you play a no-huddle team. The offense may play the no-huddle the whole game or go into it in the two-minute drill. We do not have trouble adjusting because of communication.

Teams that we play have five offensive linemen who must turn around and play defense for them. Most of the times, those players are playing a 3 technique or 1 technique and not one of the defensive ends. You get a lot of punishment playing that way. In this defense, we have one position where we play an offensive lineman and that is the noseguard position.

Disadvantages of Playing the 3-5-3

- Teams lining up and trying to smash your three defensive linemen
- The tight end is not covered
- Sometimes moving out of a cover 3 or man
- Not always giving a multiple look up front

With every defense, there are disadvantages. It is not good against two-tight end power running teams. The tight ends are not covered in this defense. We found this out with the option game. They come inside on the linebacker and get outside on the option. Another problem we had with the tight end was down the middle of the field with the single high safety.

In this defense, you give the same look to the offensive line each time you align. They have to combination block on the middle and outside stacks to block the defense.

Keys to Success

- You have to *believe* in the defense, and then convince your players it is sound. Stats and records help.
- Pressure—the use of many different pressures is the biggest key in this defense.
- Surge—the noseguard is the #1 key. He needs to force a double-team.
- Offensive coaches use valuable time practicing many different blitzes and stunts.

If you decide to run this defense, you have to believe in what you are doing. It gets frustrating sometimes. In the first year we ran the defense, we started out with a 1-3 record. I had to convince myself as the head coach that this was the right defense. If I give you one thing for the day, it is to do your homework and stay with the defense. You have to believe.

This defense is a pressure defense. It puts pressure on the quarterback. If the quarterback is not ready for the one- and three-step reads, he will take a beating. The noseguard has to force teams to double-team him. The first year we played with a short, stocky noseguard that was quick. This year, that player was injured and we played a backup tackle in that position. He was 6'2" and 300 pounds, but he had the same kind of success as the quick player. He took the double-team but also made plays for us.

The center has a problem, particularly if he is a shotgun center. He has to worry about snapping the ball and stepping up for leverage. The 300-pound player is not going to bull rush the center. He is going one side or the other to make the center move his feet and get to a gap. This defense is a place-and-replace defense.

When we pick our personnel to play this defense, we start with the noseguard. He needs to be a wrestler-type player. He plays in a 0 technique on the center (Diagram 20-1). The defensive ends are agile and fast. They align in a 5i technique on the offensive tackles. That is what people might call a head-up alignment on the offensive tackle. I call them basketball-type players. In a school like ours, Buffalo has a reputation for good basketball players. They were in the 6'3", 190-pound class. We had some other players that were the 6'0", 205-pound types of athletes. We played with quick players in that position.

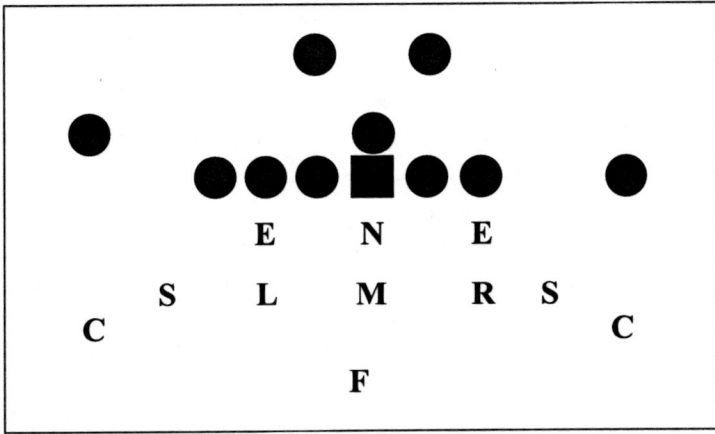

Diagram 20-1. Base defense

The Mike linebacker is the prototypical middle linebacker. He stacks behind the noseguard. All he is worried about is stopping the run and has to know how to blitz. He is going somewhere on every play.

The outside safeties or spurs are the best athletes we have on the team and they are the smartest defensive players. They align outside the tight end or uncovered tackle. Their alignment will vary based on situations and the scouting report.

The Lou linebacker plays on the strongside of the defense and the Rob linebacker plays to the weakside. They align in a stack position behind the defensive ends in a 40 technique. The only difference is the Lou is *stronger* and the Rob is *quicker*. These linebackers are the "betweeners" of the Mike linebacker.

The Mike linebacker is going to stop the run. The Lou linebacker has to stop the run, but he also has to get into the coverage. He has to cover the tight end or the #3 receiver coming out of the backfield.

The Rob is the speedster. He is a good player and he's smart. He has to cover the boundary plays in this defense. He is involved with more pass coverage and plays similar to the outside safeties.

The field spur is the best linebacker type. He is like a strong safety. What we did with our spurs was to match them up to the outside linebacker types. If we had a strong linebacker at the outside linebacker position, we wanted a strong pass coverage spur to that side. He could get into the flats and play strong coverage. To the other side, the spur was more of a blitzing linebacker type. He was on the side with the pass coverage outside linebacker.

Our corners are cover-1 defenders. They must be able to play man coverage. The free safety aligns in the middle and calls the defensive adjustment on the coverage. He is the free player in the middle and has to play the alleys to either side of the ball. He is our defensive quarterback.

We align in the base front at the beginning of each play. From the base front, we make our adjustments to what the offense does. We play some of the 4-3 rules from this front. However, you do not want to change the front from a 4-3 to a 3-5 look or go from the 3-5 to a 4-3 look. You will not be successful if you do that. We stay in the 3-5 and adjust the personnel in that scheme. We are not playing a 4-3 although it looks like it. All we are doing is moving the down linemen to different techniques and covering with the safeties or linebackers walking down in the front.

In the solid front, we move the defensive line away from the tight end (Diagram 20-2). We move the defensive end to the strongside down into a 3 technique on the guard. The noseguard moves to a weakside shade on the center. The designated spur walks to the line of scrimmage and aligns in what we call a 7 technique, which is on the outside shoulder of the tight end. The weakside defensive end aligns in a 5 technique on the outside shoulder of the offensive tackle.

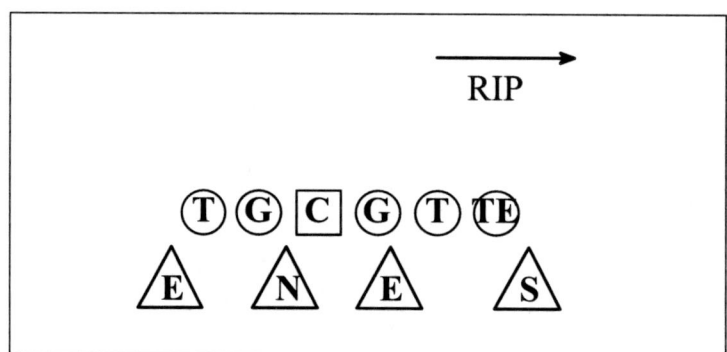

Diagram 20-2. Solid front

When the linebackers or spurs come to the line, they align in a two-point stance on the outside shade of the tight end or tackle. They play with the foot to the ball up in their stance. They must be up and ready to shoot the hands from their chest on the tight end.

When you play a defense that plays a 3 technique and a 1 technique, the offense has certain ways to attack that alignment. They want to trap the 3 technique and double-team the 1 technique. That is what we prepare for in this adjustment.

In the under front, we move the front toward the tight end (Diagram 20-3). The defensive end to the tight end will move to the outside shoulder of the tackle in a 5 technique. The noseguard moves to a strongside shade on the center, and the backside end moves into a 3 technique on the guard. In this front, we walk up the outside linebacker to the line of scrimmage and he plays a 6 technique on the ghost

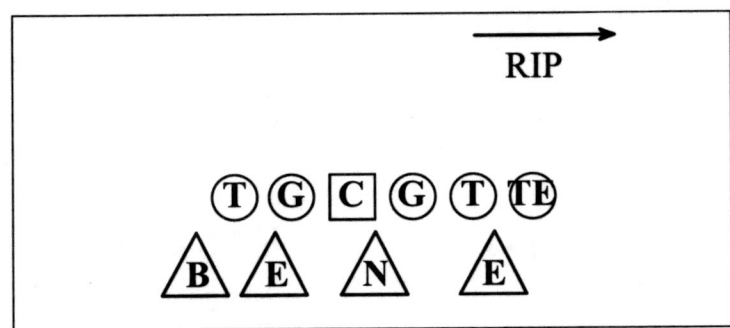

Diagram 20-3. Under front

tight end. In this situation, we call the linebacker a *Bat*, which means a backer. You can call these positions anything you like.

We play a tuff front against double tight end teams (Diagram 20-4). We put the defensive ends in 3 techniques on the outside shoulders of the guards and walk both Lou and Rob linebackers head-up the tight ends. Teams think they can go to the double tight ends and take advantage of the 3-5. If the offense wants to play power football, we adjust our fronts and play.

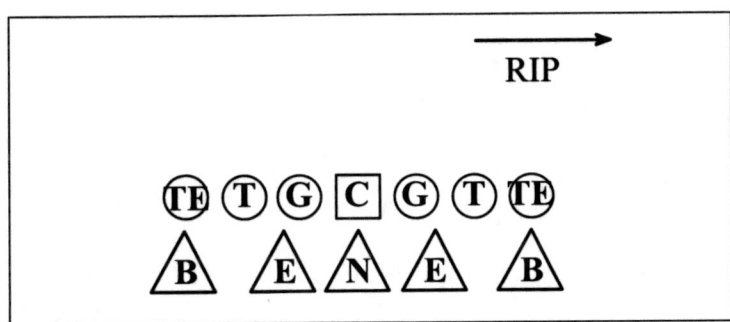

Diagram 20-4. Tuff front

We want to pound the center and slant the defense. This defense is a gap-responsible defense and we cannot two-gap in our scheme.

We can adjust and look like a 4-4 type of defense with a *heads* call. On this adjustment, we bring the linebacker to the tight end side into a 6 technique head-up the tight end. The strong end and noseguard move into 2 techniques head-up the guards. The backside defensive end moves into a 7i technique, which is a wide 5 technique on the offensive tackle. This is a great way to tinker with the offensive linemen with your alignments and it is good in a passing situation. You can run line twists with the 2 techniques and get the linebackers involved with a blitz game.

The eyes adjustment moves the end into a 4 technique on the inside shoulder of the offensive tackles, and the wide adjustment moves them to the outside shoulders of the offensive tackles. The wide is good against the pass because the ends are charging upfield with linebacker help underneath. That allows them to contain or box on the pass.

The next thing I want to cover is the line movement calls. The jacks call is an outside C-gap charge by the defensive ends. If they have a blitz coming to the B gap on their inside, this is the movement they use.

The slant and whip are three-man movement calls by the defensive ends and noseguard. On the slant, they go to the strongside call. If we call whip, they slant away from the strongside.

If we call strong, we get the three-man movement (Diagram 20-5). The defensive ends perform the jacks movement. They both have an outside C-gap charge. The noseguard slants into the weakside A gap. The Mike linebacker is responsible for the strong A gap on this movement. If we call weak, the noseguard goes to the strongside. The difference between strong and weak is the direction of the noseguard.

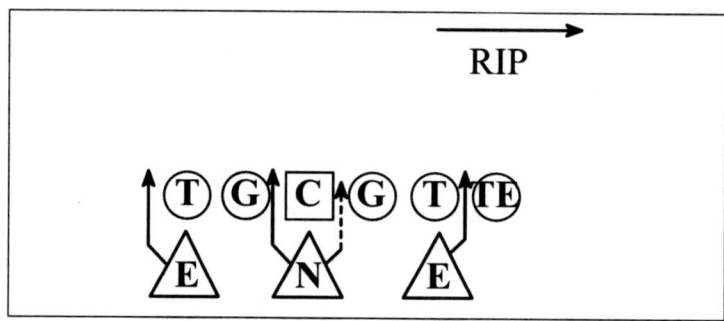

Diagram 20-5. Strong and weak

The *big stick* is one of our favorite movements (Diagram 20-6). The defensive end slants from his head-up position on the offensive tackle into the A gap and secures the gap. He cannot take a lateral step. He must attack at an angle that is gaining ground. He is attacking the A gap on any type of block except the down block of the guard. If he gets a down block from the guard, he squeezes off the guard's rear and looks for trap or some other inside block coming to him.

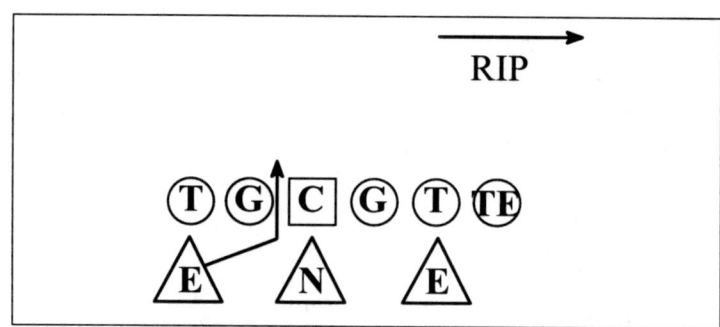

Diagram 20-6. Big stick

We ran this from the weakside most of the time. We used it against teams that ran the counter trey or power O to the strongside. If they pulled the guard, tackle, or both, the big stick was in the middle of their scheme. If it was a power O, the defensive end ripped across the tackle's face and chased the guard into the hole. The center has to block the nose, and there is no one left to block back on the slant.

The pinch helps against the power game and on the goal line. The defensive ends slant into the B gaps, and the noseguard slants into the strongside A gap. If we play a dive option team, this is a good movement to use. The defensive ends come down into the B gap and take the dive back. Those are our defensive line movements.

When the noseguard or defensive end is an A-gap or B-gap defender, they are to spill all plays outside. When the defensive end slants inside, he spills everything outside. If the guard pulls away from him, he chases the hip of the guard. He gets in his hip pocket and follows. If there is a double-team block, we want to fight the one-man surface and split the double-team.

On zone plays, we want to get vertical in our gap responsibility and penetrate. If the ball flows away, we want to be active in our cutback gaps. The noseguard wants to beat the center's block. However, if linemen reach him, he plays the backside of the center and the Mike linebacker plays the frontside A gap. On flow away from the defensive end, he gets vertical in the B gap and looks inside for a puller or cutback zone runner.

If the offensive guard drive blocks on the defensive end, he attacks the guard with his hands and eyes. He keeps outside leverage and collapses the gap back to the inside.

The line movement or stunt will determine the gap responsibility of the outside linebackers. If the Rob or Lou has a B-gap responsibility, he keys the guard and reacts off his action. If he has a C-gap responsibility, he reads the tackle.

Linda/Rita B-Gap Responsibility

Flow to:
- Down = Shoot B
- Out = Collapse B
- Pull in = Attack the down
- Pull out = Attack the downhill (call made?)
- High hat = Drop

Flow away:
- Lateral shuffle for cutback or counter

Linda/Rita C-Gap Responsibility

Flow to:
- Down = Shoot C
- Out = Collapse C
- Pull in = Shuffle contain
- Pull out = Attack the down
- High hat = Drop

Flow away:
- Shuffle eyes go to quarterback
- Play quarterback, cutback, counter

When we went to Georgia Military to learn this defense, this is what they taught us. It is what we teach our players. It is simple. The aiming point is the most important thing when you are teaching the slants. It is vital that the athlete works vertical on his second step. That helps him from getting washed inside by a down block. Working vertical helps to get the pads square and puts us in a great football position.

Anytime we go on a 45-degree angle, we always use a big rip move. We never try to swim as a move. Having great pad level is essential and using the big rip will help with those efforts. During practice, I try to use big rips and other hand motions in every drill we do. The goal is to use hand violence on every play. *If they cannot touch you, they cannot stop you!*

When we run the 45-degree vertical, the aiming point is the hip of the adjacent lineman. If the defensive end slants into the B gap, he aims for the offensive guard's hip. He steps with his inside foot at a 45-degree angle, squares his shoulders, and rips with his outside arm through the B gap.

The linebackers in the 3-5 defenses are stacked behind the nose and defensive ends. They align with their heels at five yards from the line of scrimmage. You must teach alignment, reads, blitz techniques, block destruction, tackling, and converge. When we work on tackling, we work on 1-on-1 tackling with an emphasis on open field tackling. We work the six interior defenders together. The spurs and corners work together in numerous drills. The spurs are in the open field more than anyone is. They have to combat the jet sweep all the time. The spurs have to get out in space and make the open field tackle or force the ball back to the inside.

Blitz Calls

Left side:
- Linda = Will (ILB)
- Leopard = LOLB (spur)
- Lion = Both LOLB and Will backer

Right side:
- Rita = Sam (ILB)
- Rhino = ROLB (spur)
- Ram = Both ROLB and Sam Backer

When we call our stunts, we can send the blitz from the left, right, or both sides. We can send two defenders from one side and one from the other. The number of blitzes you can run from this defense is more than anyone would ever want to run. Linda is an outside linebacker blitz from the left side. Leopard is a spur blitz from the left. If we want to send the left spur and outside linebacker, we call Lion.

If we want to blitz the outside linebacker and the Mike linebacker, we call Linda/Mike (Diagram 20-7). It is a simple blitz. The outside linebacker blows the B gap, and the Mike linebacker blows the A gap. The defensive end to that side knows he runs a jacks movement into the C gap. The noseguard knows the Mike linebacker is going into the A gap to the strongside and he has to slant into the opposite A gap.

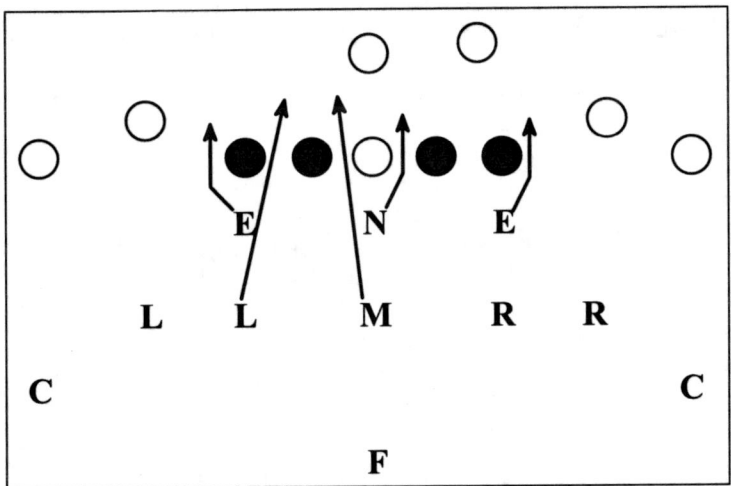

Diagram 20-7. Linda/Mike

If we want to reverse the stunts of the outside linebacker and the Mike linebacker, we call Linda/Mike X (Diagram 20-8). The outside linebacker goes first and blitzes the A gap. The Mike linebacker comes off his butt into the B gap. Everyone else in the stunt does the same thing.

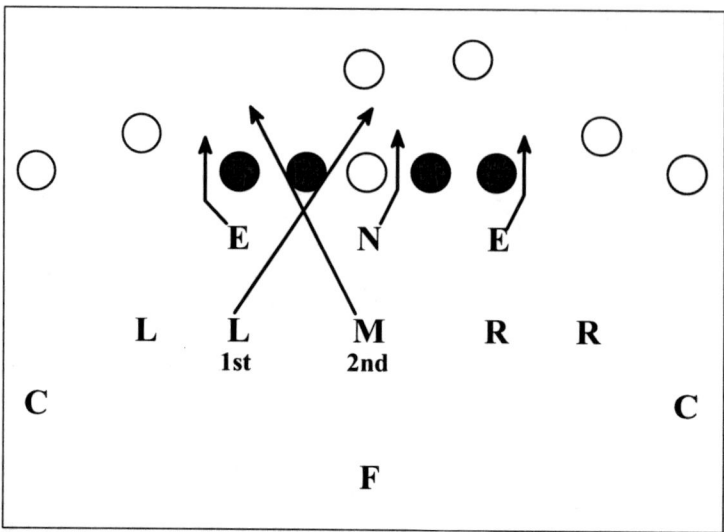

Diagram 20-8. Linda/Mike X

We can run a three-man game. If we call big stick Linda/Mike, the stunt starts with the defensive end (Diagram 20-9). On the big stick, the defensive end slants into the A gap. The Mike linebacker blitzes the B gap and the outside linebacker takes the C gap.

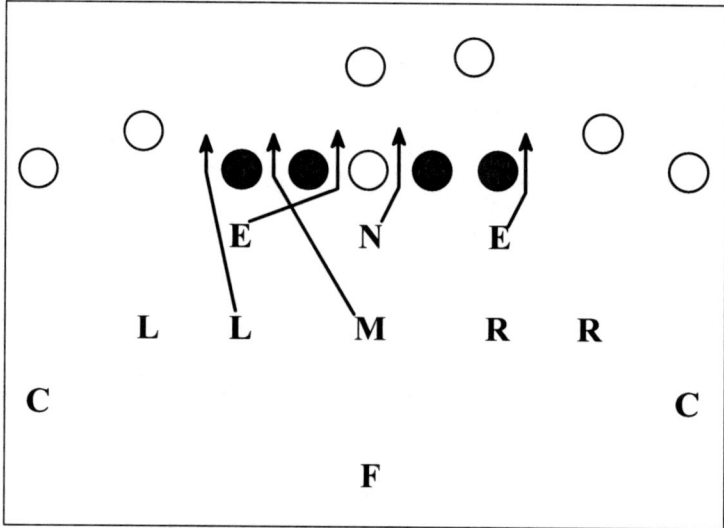

Diagram 20-9. Big stick Linda/Mike

If we want to send the spur, we use the term Leopard. On this stunt, I will use a multiple call. The call is Leopard Mike slant (Diagram 20-10). On this call, the defense runs a slant call to the tight end side. The stunt sends the Mike linebacker into the weakside A gap. The Leopard brings the left spur to the outside off the edge. We could run each component of the stunt by itself or put them all together.

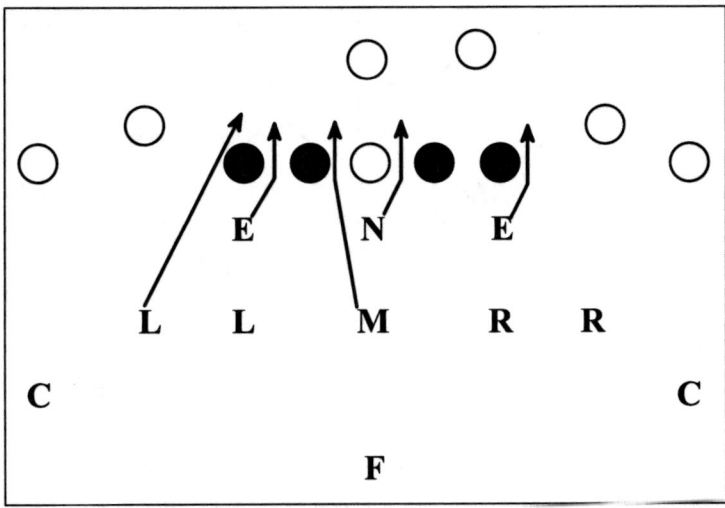

Diagram 20-10. Leopard Mike slant

If we want to involve the outside linebacker to that side, we use the term Lion. Lion is a term that sends the outside linebacker and the spur. If we run the big stick Lion, it is the same stunt as I showed you before except the Mike linebacker is not involved (Diagram 20-11). On the big stick Lion, the outside linebacker blitzes the B gap and the spur comes outside in the C gap. The line movement is the same as before. The defensive end runs the big stick, and the noseguard slants into opposite the A gap.

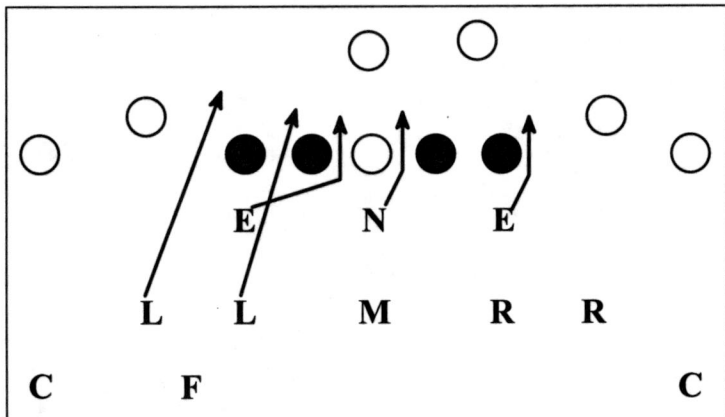

Diagram 20-11. Big stick Lion

As you can see, with these three people, the blitz package is as big as you want to teach. If we want to involve the free safety in those blitz schemes, we have the same capabilities. Anytime you want to switch the gaps in a blitz, you simply call *X*.

The alignment of the spurs is 3x3 yards outside the tight end. To the openside of the formation, the spur aligns at 4x4 yards outside the offensive tackle.

Sometimes, we tinker with their alignment and align them at five yards. We have all the linebackers and the spurs aligned at the same depth. If we play a twin set, the spur to the tight end side aligns in a 2x2-yard alignment on the tight end. The spur to the twin side aligns 1x4 yards deep to the inside of the slot receiver in the set.

We teach our corners to deny any inside releases by the wide receivers. We never want to get beat inside. We use the outside hand and foot to attack receivers. The corner accelerates to the receiver the more he widens. We want to put body between the quarterback and receiver. If the receiver's feet chop down, the corner slows and keeps his inside leverage.

If the receiver runs vertical, we want to attack his inside earhole and keep inside leverage. We want to close on the receiver and not let him slip to the inside. We want to knock him off course and use a trail technique. We play the receiver's eyes and hands in our coverage.

We use quarters coverage as part of our secondary scheme as a change-up coverage, but our primary coverage is man. If you have questions, I will be around.

21

The Simplicity of the 3-5 Defense

Jason Vandermaas
Carman-Ainsworth High School, Michigan
2008

I want to give you a quick overview of some of the things we do at Carman-Ainsworth, and then I am going to let my defensive coordinator, David Johnson, come up and talk about the details of the 3-5 defense.

I have been a head coach for six years. The last five years, I was at Croswell-Lexington, and this past year, I got the job at Carman-Ainsworth. I was hired late in the year, so we had a tough time installing everything. We struggled to a 2-7 record, but it was not because of our defense, which actually played very, very well. We do have some work to do on offense.

We had success with our 3-5 defense this past year and the year before at Croswell-Lexington where we originated our scheme. Our defensive coordinator over there was Rick Patterson who is here today, and he will answer some of your questions. Rick really instituted the defense. We had five shutouts with it that year, and our kids had a lot of fun playing it.

If you ask any kid why he plays football in high school, he will say he plays because it is fun. The majority of players want to have fun, and I think that is what you should base your program on. Certainly, having fun can mean winning football games.

When I first started coaching, I tried to coach like somebody else. I tried to copy what I saw other coaches doing, thinking that must be the right way to do things. But I have come to realize that is not the way to go about it. I think that you have to stay true to your beliefs and coach your personality. When you coach like someone else, your kids will read through that.

As part of my basic philosophy, I believe that you have to find out what your kids do well. We only have a small amount of time to really work with them, so why not take advantage of what they do well?

Also, everyone knows that KISS means to *Keep It Simple, Stupid*, but I think you have to find a happy medium in that. You cannot keep things too simple, but you can also lose games by outthinking yourself.

Especially in the things we are trying to do, fundamentals are extremely important. Every day you need to work on fundamentals and be willing to sacrifice a win or two at the freshman level, if necessary, to become fundamentally sound. The coaches at that level cannot focus on winning to the extent that time is not spent on blocking drills and tackling drills. You can win a freshman game at our school by running a reverse because we have some speed, but that is not going to necessarily give you success when those kids get to the varsity level. We have to remember that the whole goal of the program is for success on Friday nights, and if you can get everybody to buy into that, you will be successful much sooner.

In the off-season, we will have staff meetings periodically, but I try to have a seniors meeting at least once a month. That meeting is just with me and the seniors, and it is kind of an open forum. I buy them breakfast, and they come in and I can find out what they are thinking. We bounce ideas off each other and think about ways we can improve the program.

In the off-season, we will lift Monday through Thursday. We do a lot of Olympic lifts and multipoint lifts. We do not focus on a lot of the old traditional lifts that people have done in the past.

It is important to get the kids started young. A lot of young kids, especially freshman, are intimidated about coming into the weight room, particularly when the seniors are lifting a lot more than they can lift. We might have a different lifting session for those kids this summer so they can get more acquainted. We might bring some older kids in and let them get more comfortable so we can get them in earlier.

During the summer, we will run a team camp. We will bring three or four teams in and really get a lot done in two or three days. By the way, we still have one opening for this summer if any of you are interested.

Fundraising is a necessary evil that every coach has to work on, especially in today's climate of insufficient school funds. I have had a number of different things that have worked, and each coach has to find out what will work best in his school community.

There are a number of programs out there, including cards, mailings, and other such things that we have had success with, but it is something that everybody needs to do, and you just have to find out what works for you.

At Croswell-Lexington, college coaches were not exactly knocking down the door at such a small farming community, so I did not have to deal with recruiting issues there. Carman-Ainsworth, however, is a little bit different. Because of the expectations and some of the things that come up, I have to have a plan for dealing with recruiting and with college recruiters.

Every kid wants a personal highlight film now, so we try to put that together for them. We now have a spring meeting with incoming freshmen and all of our parents to discuss the recruiting process. All of that is necessary, but it takes a lot of time too, and we have to have a plan going into it.

Now, I want to get into today's topic. Our 3-5 defense has its origins at Croswell-Lexington. Three years ago, we were running a 50 defense and going from a 5-3 to a 5-2. We were having a lot of trouble stopping people, and we were involved in a lot of high-scoring games.

Going into 2006, we had a lot of linebacker, "tweener" type of kids. We did not have a lot of defensive linemen and we did not have a lot of size, but we did have a lot of athletes. We discussed our situation, talked about the 3-5 defense, and then tried it out at camp.

We really liked what was happening. The kids were having a lot of fun with it, and that was what was most important to me. They were encouraged by it, and it was a pretty easy learning process, so we became a 3-5 team.

We like the defense because it lets you take advantage of your athletes. It allows you to put your best players on the field. We already wanted to do that on offense, so it matched our philosophy there. It puts your best players in a place where they can be successful. They can be aggressive, and they do not need to think a lot.

It was simple to implement. We sat down and applied some of the things we knew and just plugged in our own terminology. We started it out as a gap-control system, and then we evolved from there to use a few different wrinkles.

Each year, we have to evaluate what worked well and what did not, and then change things up to better meet the athletes that we have. We always want to put the kids we have into the best position to be successful.

Now, I want to bring up our defensive coordinator, David Johnson, and let him discuss the details of our 3-5 defense. Also, when we finish, we will stick around and make ourselves available to answer any questions that you may have.

David Johnson, Defensive Coordinator

Thank you, Coach. I believe you have to have a passion for what you are doing. When we implemented the defense, it was something simple, the kids picked it up, they understood it, and they were excited about it. When they saw how simple it was, they felt they could really get into it—they could let their athleticism and abilities show and be successful in it. That is what we wanted the defense to do.

Our defensive philosophy is centered around constantly and consistently attacking the offense. We want to make sure that the offense cannot get a good read on what we are doing. Some people say that we live and die with the blitz, but it is not always a blitz.

We have our front three coming, and then there is always a fourth. We want to make sure we are getting pressure on the quarterback and on the running game, and with three guys coming every time, it is not going to happen. Three against five or three against six puts you at a disadvantage, so if we can line it up and have that fourth person coming, that is just a four-man front coming at you from different angles.

Of course, we are going to have two or three more guys coming from other positions on the field, and that would be a blitz. So when you hear *live and die with the blitz*, it is not always a blitz that is coming—it is just that fourth person.

It is a point of emphasis with our players that they have to be extremely aggressive. We are going to go a hundred miles an hour. If our guys know it is simple and they know what their responsibilities are, then they can be expected to do that without worrying about complicated responsibilities. This is an aggressive attack defense.

Players are to get to their responsibilities immediately, without being tied down by too much thinking. They come hard to their gap read, but after that first step, they just play ball. They take that first step, but once they see the play, they just react from there. It is all about the attitude and confidence with which they play.

In our 3-5 concept, we want to eliminate reading and reacting. We could line up in a head-up position and think two gaps, but we do not want to play two gaps. As Coach Vandermaas pointed out, it is a one-gap responsibility, so each player is responsible for just one gap, and they have to trust each other and play as a team. In the film, you will see that even when a player makes a bad read and goes to the wrong gap, the player behind him sees it and covers it up.

This defense is going to set the tempo for the game. Many of our opponents will script their offensive plays to start the game. After seeing us on film, they get an idea of what they are going to see, but starting with our first play, we are going to come out and put real pressure on them. In our 3-5 set, we will have someone coming from somewhere that they do not know about, so then we feel that we have evened the field.

The offense knows exactly what they want to do. The receivers, running backs, and linemen know exactly where they have to go to block. The defense really is reacting.

If we sit and have to think about it, rather than simply react, that can be the difference between a one-, two-, or three-yard gain. On the other hand, when we know which gap we are attacking, and we know the player behind us will cover for us, then we can set the tempo, make a play, cause a pile, or create some kind of advantage for our defense.

We want to make sure the offense is adjusting to us. When the offense first sees a 3-5 front, they may think they can run all over it because they see only three down linemen, but once the ball is snapped and we get our guys moving, the offense may get a little confused. They do not know who is backing off and who is coming, so now, they have to go through the first series, make sure the headphones are working with the coaches upstairs, and ask a lot of questions. We want to be able to force the offense to adjust to our defense.

We know that mistakes will be made, but we sell our kids on the belief that we will be okay as long as we are playing hard. As long as we play hard, we have the capacity to cover for each other and still make plays.

We will not harp on and scream at players who make mistakes because that tends to intimidate them, and it destroys their confidence. We try to eliminate all the pressure and just let them play and have fun with it.

Now, this is a flexible defense, and it can easily be converted into different sets. It is essentially a 50 front in which you take the ends and step them back, put them in space, and give them the opportunity to make plays. By moving people around just a little, we can easily give a 4-4 look, a 4-3 look, or a 3-4 look as well.

In selecting personnel, we want to put emphasis on speed over size. Size is great, but the kids we get here are a little quicker, a little faster, and not so big, so we want a defense that will allow us to make speed one of our strengths.

We took a running back who stood 5'4" and put him at one of our dog positions, which is like a strong safety in most defenses. He was an aggressive hitter, he was fast, and he was smart, so the move worked to our advantage.

We had a very strong linebacker who put on a little weight, and we ended up moving him to defensive tackle. He became an outstanding player for us. These are just two examples of our being able to utilize the "tweener" type of kids in our 3-5 package.

This defense gives us the ability to have multiple personnel groupings for various defensive packages. With us, we can match offensive personnel groupings, either by substitution or by moving individuals around within the grouping that is on the field, without making substitutions. That gives us an advantage in the game. Because of the versatility of our players, we can make adjustments by moving kids within the defense rather than bringing different players into the game, and thereby tipping our hand about what kind of defense we are going to be in.

Of course, we look for certain characteristics in players at each position. With our nose man, we want to have one of two types of players, and if you have them both, it is great because you can mix it up and wear a team down with them. We either want a big kid who is a two-gap player and will demand a double-team block, or we can play with that small, quick, wrestler type of player—a guy who understands he has to stay low and move because he is small. He will command the double-team block because he is able to shoot through the gap. The smaller nose man can disrupt an offense, while the bigger, stronger nose man is more of an anchor point type of guy.

Our tackles are what you might call "typical" defensive linemen. They are strong guys. They have to be able to recognize the run when it is directed at them and take on blocks. They have to be able to hold their gap versus the double-team block. Some people teach their tackles to sit down when they are double-teamed, but we do not teach that. You cannot make plays when you are on the ground, so we try to fight harder, push back out, and hold our gap. We can still make a play even if we do not make the tackle.

Our tackles must also recognize passing situations and be able to force the pocket if a pass develops, but they can still react to draw plays or runs if they develop instead. They might not always make the tackle, but they might still make the play.

We want to have a tackle on the weakside who is strong enough to win in a 1-on-1 situation, and we expect a lot of pressure from that position. The linebacker we moved to tackle is a good example of the type of player we need on the weakside.

Our Will linebacker normally lines up on the weakside, but we can change that up if we want him playing to the wideside. He needs to be a sure tackler. He must also be a strong kid who can take on a lead block, but fast enough to cover a #3 receiver in man coverage.

Our Mike linebacker is bigger and stronger, and he has to stop the middle. He has to meet things head on, and be able to attack the line of scrimmage. We did a lot of things with him—including a lot of blitz stuff—but his main responsibility is to come downhill from tackle to tackle and make plays.

His gap responsibility is determined by the defense called, but he never thinks to drop back in pass unless there is nobody in the backfield and he does not have a stunt called. He would step down and look for draw first, and then he would drop back in the middle, looking for any crosses. Mostly, he runs stunts with the tackles and the nose, and he is a run stopper.

The Sam linebacker definitely aligns to the strongside, and he is our best tackler. He is strong enough to step up in the hole and take on pulling guards. He is the one who will come clean because of what our line does in front of him. They should keep him clean so he can scrape and flow to the ball.

Our dog linebackers line up out in the flat at a depth of five yards. They are four yards off the line of scrimmage, unless you have a twins or trips set. At that point, we will put them maybe two yards inside of their receivers.

Their responsibility is run. They are that extra man for the run coming that way, but they also have to be able to recognize the pass. They are the strong safety/linebacker type of players. The guys who play the position for us are often the "tweeners" who really want to play, are sure tacklers, and are able to recognize quickly whether it is run or pass. The size of the player is not a limiting factor at this position.

In the secondary, we coach our cornerbacks to play both sides. We want each guy to be a complete corner, which means being able to cover the pass, support the run, and tackle. It also helps if he can catch the football.

In zone coverage, our corners line up with the outside foot up so they can see the zone, but if it is man-to-man, we teach inside foot up, because now we are focused on the man. For corners, it is pass first and run second, and they must have enough discipline to stay focused during the whole game.

Our linebackers stunt a lot and have a lot of fun while all the cornerbacks do is cover, so they might tend to get a little bored back there. They have to stay focused and disciplined enough to play man when it is man and zone when it is zone.

The free safety is probably going to be the smartest kid in our secondary. He is a good tackler and a kid who can recognize a play as it is developing. He is back 10 to 12 yards, and he is reading the quarterback. He is to the strength in certain defenses, and if we have a two roll where it is two over weak, he will line up on the weakside, but he is always able to read the quarterback.

He should be the second wave of defense right behind our linebackers. On sweeps, he should fill the alley immediately and get into position to help the picket fence and help control the gaps. He has to be a good tackler.

Our base coverage is cover 3. Our corners and safety are deep, our dogs are in the flat, and our backers are underneath in the windows.

In cover 2, we implement our 3-4 look up front. Both dogs become the rolled-up corners, the safety takes one side, and one of the backers that stepped out is a safety on the other. So now, you have your 3-4 cover 2 look.

Our 3-5 cover 2 over is what we call the roll. We will line up in a 3-5 for the quarterback to get his pre-snap read, and then we will roll the safety over to one side. The corner on that side will now sit and take the flat, and the safety will roll over top of him.

The backside corner takes the backside half, and the dog up on the line becomes the flat player. We have three down linemen, three linebackers, two dogs, and the corners and safety rolled to one side. That is our 3-5 cover 2 over.

The one thing we want to do is give you the same look on each play. That is part of our masking of the defense—part of our surprise. Part of our aggression is giving you the same look so you do not know what to expect from your pre-snap read. When the ball is snapped, that is when everything happens. Complete confusion gives us an opportunity to level the playing field.

Our cover 2 spy is what some people call the *robber*. Both corners will drop and cover halves, the safety steps down, spies any digs or runs, and takes away any mid-level route. Both dogs then become our flat players. That is cover 2 spy.

Cover 1 is man-to-man. Against twins, the dog covers #2, the corner covers #1, and the safety is free. Against trips, the dog covers #2, the corner covers #1, and the safety can roll over on #3, or the Will linebacker can cover #3 so the safety can still be free. That is our choice, but we really prefer to cover #3 with Will and keep our safety in the middle.

Cover 0 is pure man, and our kids love it. Everybody has a man, and those who do not are able to blitz. Against a pro set, the corners cover the wides, the safety covers the tight end, and everybody else can blitz. The only thing is, if a back flares out to your side when you are coming, you have to pick him up. Our kids want to run cover 0 every time.

Now, I want to draw up a couple of sets against different formations so you can understand some of the things I was talking about. We will start by looking at what we call twins (Diagram 21-1). The backers are five yards off, and they are almost in a stack. I labeled them all as backers and not as Sam and Will because we have not dictated where the strength is. Normally, if we are looking at it like this, our strength would be to the left side because a lot of teams we play have right-handed quarterbacks.

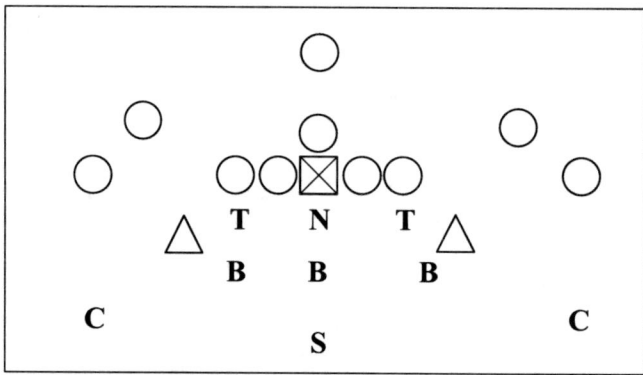

Diagram 21-1. 3-5 defense vs. twins

The corners are at seven yards deep in an outside shade if this is cover 3. Our dogs are normally at five and four off the last man on the line of scrimmage, but because we have twins out here, we will put them at five and one or five and two on the inside, looking for the quick slant. The quick slant normally comes from the split end with the slot running on out.

The quarterback will read the dog, and the minute he drops off, he will hit the slant in the seam and he is gone. So, when we say look for the quick slant, we mean to look for the #1 receiver. The inside slant will be picked up by the backer. This is our base defense versus the twins formation.

If we are going to line it up versus trips, the safety will shade that way (Diagram 21-2). The bigger threat is the three receivers to one side. On the backside, this corner is still an outside shade in our cover 3, but he will be able to squeeze this a little bit more because the safety is helping over here.

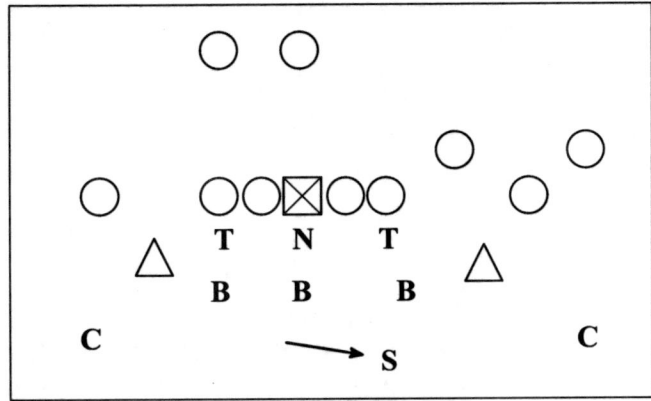

Diagram 21-2. 3-5 defense vs. trips

Also, this Sam backer will be able to help underneath. It is his responsibility to get out there and recognize the quick slant. The strong corner is in an outside shade, and the dog is on the inside of the #2 receiver.

Now, this will set up the offense to say we can *run the quick bubble screen.* Our backer is always looking at #3, so when he flares, he is ready to go right now. The safety helps over top, and we still have four versus three.

That backer to the trips side is always going to help with the quick slant from here to here and with any runs going that way. This is our help, but we can send the Sam backer and cover with Mike. We are not going to give away anything. When you step out to see us, everything looks the same. We can also get in an *over* look, especially if the ball is on the hash, because we really do not like cover 3 against trips in that situation.

I want to draw up a stunt or two before I finish. We run a pinch, a slant, an angle, and a pinch out. When they hear that, the linemen know automatically where they are going, and the backers know what gap they have. This is a gap-controlled offense, so in our base defense, he will go outside, and the nose can go to strength or he can go opposite (Diagram 21-3). We were set on going to strength every time, but then Coach noticed that when we called this, the nose would go to strength every time. That is a tendency he picked up on, so now you can switch it up, and we did. We went with

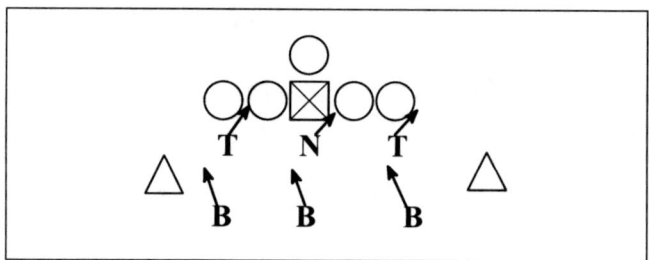

Diagram 21-3. 3-5 defense base stunts

base opposite, so then the nose would go opposite. Our dogs have outside, and you can see our gap responsibility.

If we go to a pinch defense, these guys will pinch to the inside, and then the backers will go to the outside. If strength is to the right, our nose goes to the right, and the middle backer goes to the left.

On the slant and angle stunts, we slant everybody one way, and the backers are responsible for the opposite gaps. It is a gap-control defense.

We ended up running gaps with double dogs and cover 1. The defensive linemen are stepping down for their gaps, and the inside linebackers are stepping back for pass. We can call slant double-dog cover 1 or slant weak-dog Sam fire, and every gap is still accounted for. As I said before, it is a gap-control defense. Now, I want to show you some film.

That about does it. We will be around to answer any questions. Thank you.

22

The 3-5-3 Stack Defense

Dave Walker
Martinsburg High School, West Virginia
2012

I have coached for 24 years as a head coach. I am fortunate to have a great coaching staff. I have coaches that have been with me for a number of years, and some of my coaches played for me. Having people like that on your staff makes it more enjoyable.

When I got the call to speak, they gave me the topic of defense. I am the offensive coordinator, and although I am in on the game planning, the defensive staff runs the game on game nights. I had to go back and do some studying to get ready for this lecture.

Not everything we do on defense is original by any means. We have borrowed and stolen ideas and accumulated this information for many years. It is what we have done over the years, and it has taken us a long way. We went to the odd stack about six years ago. We can slide the front and look like an even four-man front. When Rich Rodriguez was at West Virginia University, he helped us and influenced what we did.

In West Virginia, there are not many large schools. There are about a dozen large schools with good athletes. Martinsburg is one of those schools. I have been at Martinsburg for 15 years, and we have had three Division I players. I know some teams have that many every year. We have a fourth player that just committed to Marshall University for next year.

This past year, we did not have many linemen, but we had a number of skilled players. We took some of the size off the field and replaced it with speed. The last couple of years, we have been very fortunate and have won 28 straight games. We averaged 40 points a game on offensive. However, on defense is where we have excelled. In the last two years, we gave up 7.7 points a game in 2010 and 7.3 points a game in 2011.

We play with three down linemen (Diagram 22-1). We have two defensive ends and a noseguard down. The inside linebackers are Sam, Mike, and Will. The outside safeties are the Bandit and Spur. We have two corners and a free safety. It is no different from anyone else, but it is a communication factor for us.

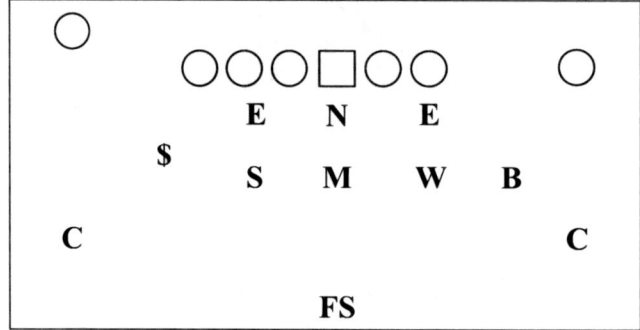

Diagram 22-1. Base front

We give our strength call as left and right. The Spur and the Sam linebacker go to the side of the strength. The Bandit and the Will linebacker are the boundary side defenders. The Mike linebacker is the middle linebacker. The free safety makes the coverage calls. In our terminology, we play the cutback with our defensive ends on a chase technique. The outside force players are the Spur and Bandit.

We adjust the front to the offenses we play against (Diagram 22-2). If we play a team that runs a wing-T offense, we may play an additional down lineman or reduce the front. We do not live and die in the odd look if we need some help on the run. We will not sit back and take it on the chin. If we reduce the front, we slide the down three to the strength of the offense and walk the linebacker up to that side. We end up with the boundary side end in a 3 technique. The nose slides to a 1 technique on the strongside guard and the defensive end to the strength moves to a 7 technique on the inside shoulder of the tight end.

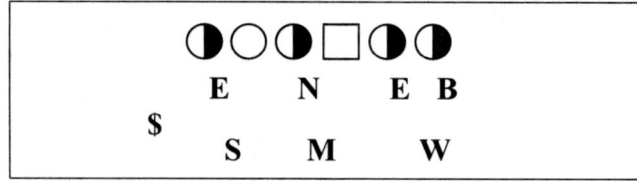

Diagram 22-2. Reduced front

The Bandit steps down to the line of scrimmage and plays on the outside shoulder of the boundary offensive tackle. The Mike linebacker has a triangle read on the guards and the back. Those reads vary depending on who we are playing and what type of scheme they run.

If we play a pro-I team with a tight end, we make an adjustment. The Spur walks down on the line of scrimmage, and the defense begin to look like the old 5-3 defense. The Spur and Bandit are athletic types of players. They run and play in space. They are not like the old defensive ends in the 5-3 defense. However, they are force players, are physical, and can tackle.

The defensive front depends on the type of offense we play. If they are a tight end running team, we will reduce or slide the front to the tight end. We have the ability to blitz off any of the fronts. We play this defense against teams that play the spread, and we like to play it in long-yardage situations. When we align in the 3-3, we like to bring heat at the quarterback. This is not our first-down defense. We will be in some kind of even front look.

We work our pursuit drills all season long. We work them especially early in the season and during two-a-day practices. We work them throughout the year, and I think it is important that the team learn proper angles in pursuing the football. It is about teaching, but we do our pursuit drills as part of our conditioning. On defensive days in our two-a-day workouts, we end practice with these drills. Instead of running 40s, we do the pursuit drills. Everyone has his own way of teaching pursuit.

If the offense sprints out with the football, our linebackers have a definite reaction (Diagram 22-3). If they sprint toward the Sam linebacker, he is the force defender on that play. The Mike linebacker runs for the strongside curls area, and the Will linebacker plays back through the middle hook area of the field. The Spur drops into the flat area. That is the standard zone for us. If we have some other type of scheme, that could change.

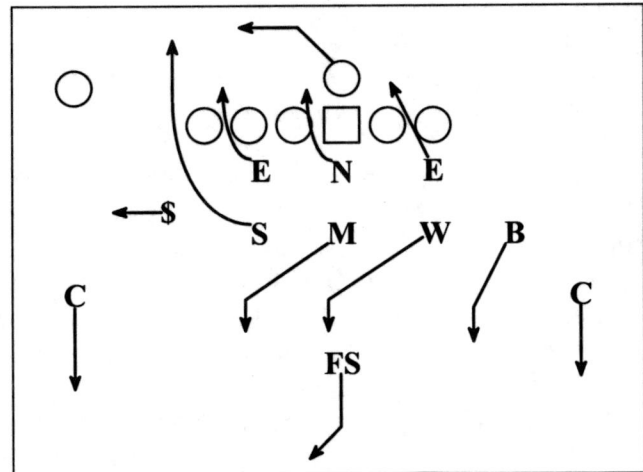

Diagram 22-3. Sprint reaction

If the offense sprints into the boundary, the responsibility of the linebackers reverses. The Will linebacker is the force linebacker, the Mike linebacker goes to the curl, and the Sam linebacker goes to the middle hook area.

The reads we teach our linebackers depend on the teams we play. The first 10 years, out of the 10 games we played during the season, eight of them were wing-T teams. We teach the Sam and Will linebackers to read the guards to the near back. If the guard doubles down on the noseguard, the linebackers are downhill immediately.

That could change in the next week if we play a different style of offense. If we play a one-back zone team, we would not play that read. Our defensive players play the zone scheme well because that is the scheme run on offense.

The Mike linebacker has to see the triangle read. He reads the guards, the center, and the backs. The coaching point we have for him is he has to get downhill immediate. He cannot take any false steps in his technique.

The Mike linebacker has to make the nose right. He plays from A gap strong to A gap weak. If the noseguard draws the double-team, the Mike linebacker plays over the top of that block.

Against the zone play, the Mike linebacker is the cutback player. Our Mike linebacker makes many plays versus the zone teams. The thing that gives him trouble is the misdirection or false reads. We tell him he is going to make mistakes but make them at full speed. He wants to go hard every play and blow something up.

If the center blocks back and the guard blocks down, the Mike has to play the opposite A gap. He knows the guard is coming around or there is going to be a down block coming from the outside.

The Bandit and Spur are force and alley players. If the Spur is the force player, the Bandit is running the alley. We do not hold him on the backside with flow away from him. They want to play with outside leverage. They are the force players and have to force the ball back to the inside. They play the slot receivers in a twin or double slot formation. They want to jam the slot receivers and knock them off their routes. We want them to disrupt routes and hold up receivers.

The corners flip-flop from side to side. That will vary from year to year. We did not do that as much this year because we had two corners who were equal in talent. If we have a corner who is more of a cover player, we put him on the weakside of the defense. However, if we play a team with a major receiver, we take the cover corner and mirror that receiver. Ten years ago, we had a corner who was 5-7. He could not cover anyone, but he was tough and could tackle. He was the starting strongside corner. When it got to third-and-long, we took him out of the game. We want the strong tackling corners on the strongside of the formation. When we play the wing-T and pro-I teams, he will be in a better position to tackle. The corners have some outside contain responsibility, especially in the option game.

The weakside corner is our cover corner. He is probably our best athlete. The free safety plays toward the passing strength of the formation and is the alley runner. He aligns at 8 to 10 yards off the line of scrimmage depending on the coverage. Last season, we had a free safety who was involved. He played Bandit the year before that. The Bandit and free safety are the same types of players. We can play two-high safeties using them.

Against a 2x1 formation, we will play cover 3 (Diagram 22-4). Everybody in America plays cover 3. The corners are outside third players, and the free safety plays the middle third. The Sam and Will linebackers are hook-to-curl players. The Bandit and Spur play the flat areas. The Mike linebacker can rush, drop, or spy on the quarterback. That depends on the scouting report.

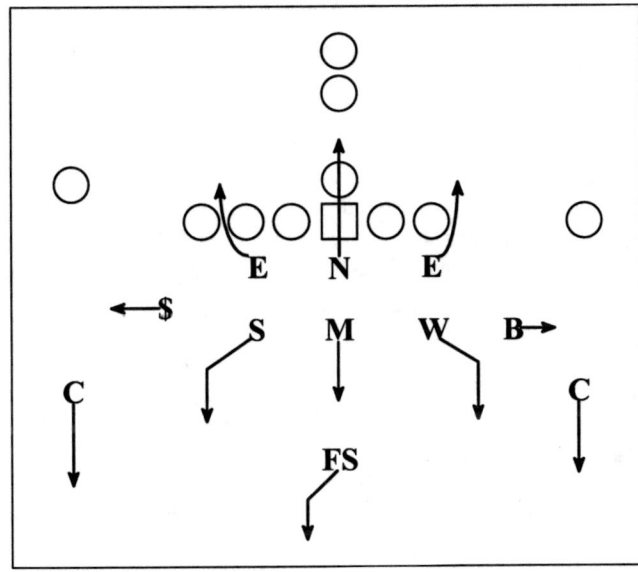

Diagram 22-4. Cover 3

The coverage we play more than anything is cover 1. If we feel like we have better athletes, we lock up with the other team's receivers. We try to deny the ball from getting to the receiver and try to bring pressure on the quarterback.

We do play cover 2. When we play cover 2, the Bandit plays off the top of the corner to his side. The corner rolls up and forces the receiver to the inside of the field. The Bandit drops to the third behind the corner and plays the deep field.

Against 3x1, we like to play quarter, quarter, and half (Diagram 22-5). The strong corner and free safety play quarters of the field to the trips side. The boundary corner plays the backside half of the field. The type of receivers the opponents has will determine what we do with the receivers. We can walk the Spur out on the #1 receiver. We can bump our linebacker over a half man to the trips side. The Sam linebacker plays inside the #2 receiver to the trips side, and the Mike linebacker plays underneath the #3 receiver from his alignment in the strong A gap.

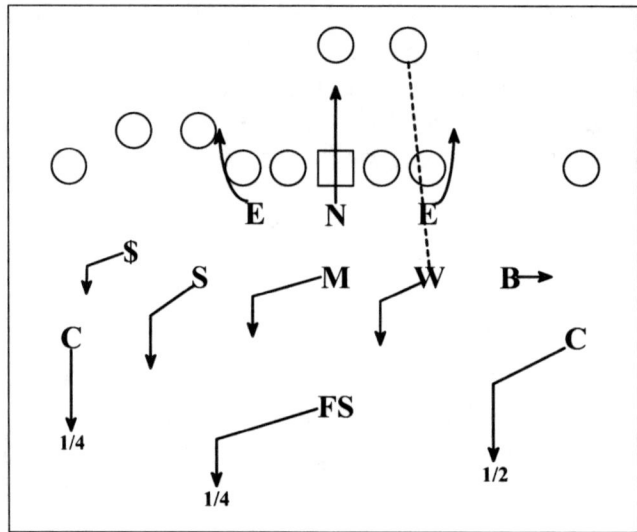

Diagram 22-5. Quarter-quarter-half

We are playing zone coverage with the Spur in the flat area. The Sam linebacker drops to the strong curl area, and the Mike linebacker plays the middle hook, favoring the trips side. The Will linebacker plays the #2 receiver to the boundary side. The Bandit is underneath the #1 receiver to the boundary side.

We can play combination coverage against the 3x1 formation. We call it "121" (Diagram 22-6). We lock the corners in man coverage on the #1 receivers to both sides. To the trips side, we play cover 2 on the #2 and #3 receivers. The Sam linebacker and Spur play underneath coverage, with the free safety over the top. The Mike, Will, and Bandit linebackers can be involved with some kind of pressure package.

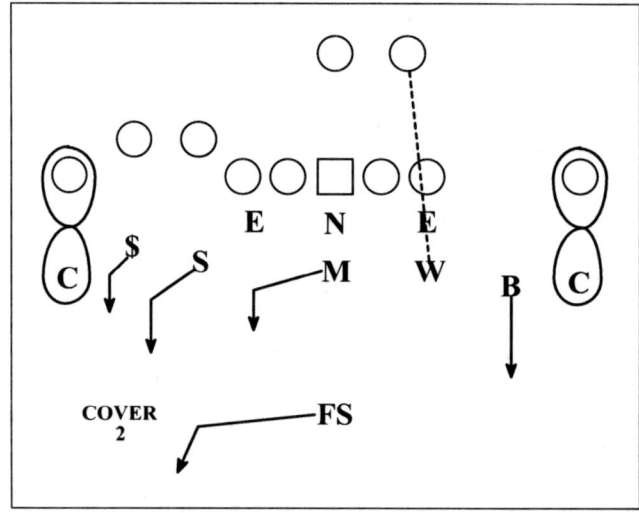

Diagram 22-6. 121

The opposite coverage against the trips set is 2II. On this coverage, we play cover 2 on the two outside receivers in the trips set and man-to-man on the inside receiver. The corner to the single receiver side is man-to-man on the single receiver.

We do not play these coverages many times. I would rather bring heat than play man coverage. An old coach told me years ago that you put pressure on the good passers. The bad passers, you let them throw. The coverage is like the rest of our defense. The reads and the coverage we play depend on the opponents.

In this defense, we use line movement. We start with line slants (Diagram 22-7). We can slant the line right and left. We can also slant the line strong and weak. The thing about the movement is that when they slant, they have to get where they are supposed to go. If the noseguard slants into the A gap, he has to get penetration through the gap. He has to hold the gap and not get washed out of the gap.

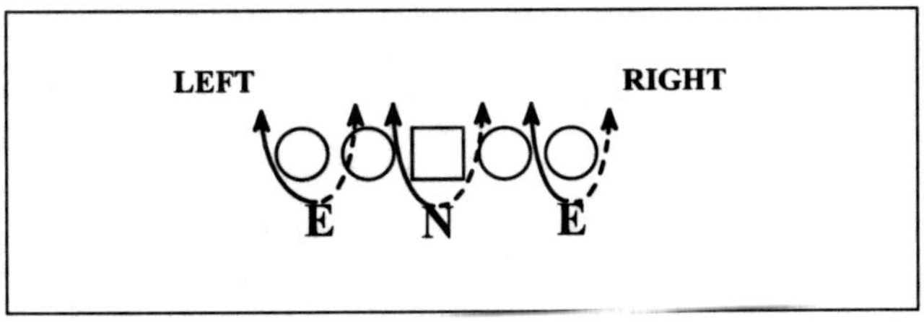

Diagram 22-7. Slants

We can fire all the linebackers. We generally fire one at a time, but we have the capability to bring all of them at once. If we fire the Mike linebacker into the A gap, the noseguard knows he has to slant into the weakside A gap. If the Sam linebacker fires into the B gap, the defensive end has to slant outside into the C gap. You must maintain gap sound when you fire linebackers.

I hope you went to see Jerry Glanville speak last night. I love listening to his stories. He talked about a shin technique. I was 23 years old when I first started coaching. I did not know what I was doing. I knew you had to work hard and yell a lot. I did that. We would play teams that were a lot better than we were.

When I was playing and someone cut me, it made me mad. That is how we played people better than us. I ran the shin technique and just tried to create piles. I had a bunch of country boys who were not very good, but we submarined all those players. The back stopped and reset his feet. I was amazed at a coach in the NFL teaching the same things we teach in high school.

I think that sometimes people try to make this game more complicated than it is. We can show slides and schemes and talk a good game. However, if you cannot block and tackle, it does not matter what your scheme is. You have to practice and play with fundamentals. If you do not have a player who knows how to run block or a player who knows how to tackle, it does not matter what the scheme is.

We run an orbit stunt (Diagram 22-8). It involves the defensive ends and the Bandit and Spur. This is a gap exchange stunt. The defense end squeezes the offensive tackle in his normal technique. In this stunt, he fires outside. The defensive end charges through the outside shoulder of the offensive tackle and works for containment. The Spur cheats his alignment and comes under the defensive end into the C gap. He becomes the C gap defender, and the defensive end becomes the D gap defender.

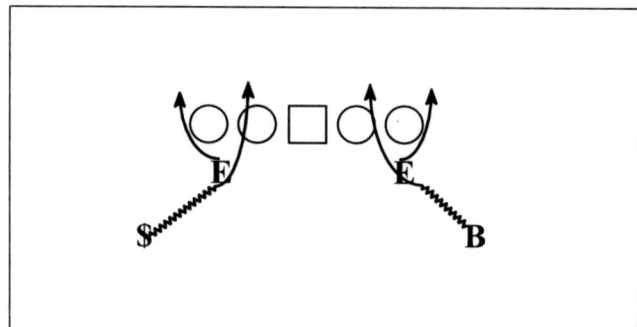

Diagram 22-8. Orbit

We can run the same stunt with the defensive end taking the inside into the B gap, with the Spur coming off the offensive tackle's butt into the C gap off the edge (Diagram 22-9). The Sam linebacker is over the top of both stunts. We can run these stunts from both sides at the same time or individually.

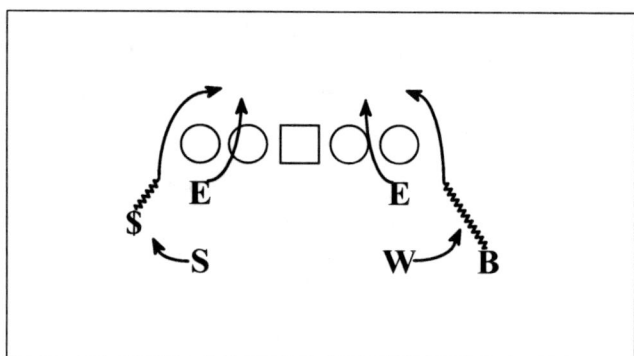

Diagram 22-9. C gap

We have two-linebacker stunts we run. We call this stunt the "wave" (Diagram 22-10). We like to run this blitz to the backside of the 3x1 formation. We like to run it away from the set back. We bring the defensive end in an outside charge on the offensive tackle. The Will linebacker cheats to the line and blitzes off the edge. The Mike linebacker blitzes through the B gap.

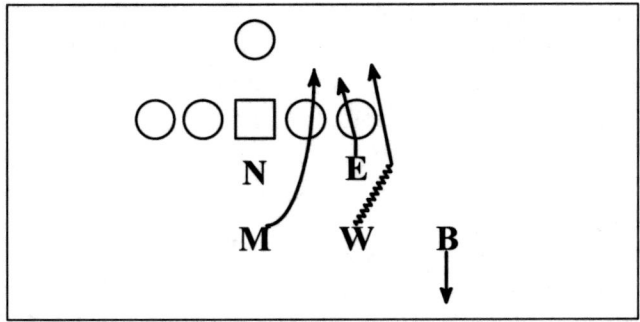

Diagram 22-10. Wave

The next two-linebacker blitz is the razor (Diagram 22-11). We run the Bandit and defensive end on an X-stunt. The defensive end goes out, and the Bandit comes under his movement into the B gap. The Mike linebacker blitzes the weakside A gap and the noseguard runs through the strongside A gap.

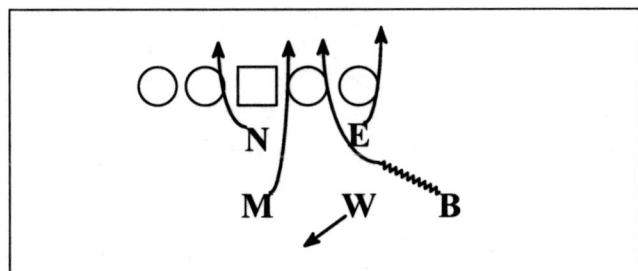

Diagram 22-11. Razor

The razor is a good blitz against the quarterback belly play. You can run multiple blitzes from this defensive scheme.

The last blitz I want to show you is what we call "fireworks" (Diagram 22-12). On this stunt, we pinch both defensive ends into the B gaps. The Sam and Will linebackers fire the C gaps. The Mike linebacker and noseguard run fire in the A gaps.

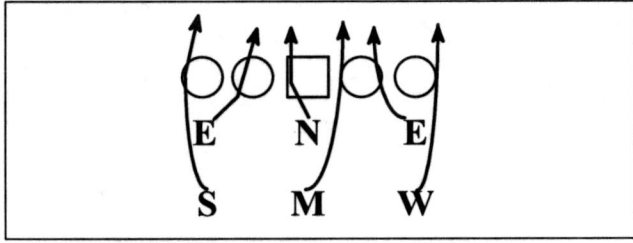

Diagram 22-12. Fireworks

When I first started coaching, I ran the 5-2 defense. We ran eagle and double eagle. My first year of coaching, I went to Myrtle Beach and heard Jerry Claiborne speak. He coached at the University of Kentucky and the University of Maryland and was a wide-tackle-six coach. I still believe in situational defense. We went from the 6-2 to a four-man front, and finally, we ended up in the 3-3 defense. I think it started out as a fad. West Virginia was running it, and it seemed to suit what we were doing. We had many athletes and not very many linemen.

The defense has changed for us, and we are better at running it. We made a commitment to it. I was afraid it would not stop the run, but we are able to play the run just as well. It is much better against the pass and is the answer to what the spread offense is trying to do.

Offensive football has changed. The spread is the thing that everyone seems to be running. This defense fits that style of offense because we can adjust to those sets so easily. Motion does not affect us much because we are balanced.

This next year, we do not have many linebackers coming back, but we do have a potful of linemen. Your offenses and defenses in high school football have to adapt to the players you have. You cannot recruit and must take what you have to play. You cannot force players into situations they cannot be successful in. If you have great a quarterback, you are going to throw the ball. If you have a great running back, you are going to run the ball.

In 2001, the first time we played for the state championship, we played the wide-tackle-six. We had six good defensive linemen, and we hid the linebackers. At our school, we have a bunch of players who play hard. We do not have big-time players.

It does not matter whether you are an even front or an odd front. If your players believe in what you are doing, it all works. You philosophy does not change, but you have to make it fit the players you have. If you believe in what you are doing, you can be successful. It takes take very little talent to be successful.

The bottom line is this: In football, it is not the X's and O's that win games; it is the Jimmys and Joes. The kids play the game, but you have to get them in the right positions so they can make plays. I am very fortunate to have good coaches who work together to make it all happen. Thank you very much.

About the Editor

Earl Browning is a native of Logan, West Virginia. He currently serves as president of Telecoach, Inc.—an organization that conducts the Nike Coach of the Year Clinics (www.nikecoyfootball.com) and produces the annual *Coach of the Year Clinics Football Manuals and Clinic Notes*. A 1958 graduate of Marshall University, he earned his M.Ed. and Rank I education certification from the University of Louisville. From 1958 to 1975, he coached football at various Louisville-area high schools. Among the honors he has been accorded are his appointments to the National Football Foundation and to the College Hall of Fame Advisory Committee on moving the museum to South Bend, Indiana. He was named to the Greater Louisville Football Coaches Association Hall of Legends in 1998. From 1992 to 2010, he served as a radio and television color analyst for Kentucky high school football games, including the Kentucky High School Athletic Association State Championship games.